*Every* **Family's**
*Guide to* **Computers**

# Every *Family's*
## Guide *to* Computers

WINSTON STEWARD

Ziff-Davis Press
Emeryville, California

| | |
|---|---|
| Copy Editor | Margo R. Hill |
| Technical Reviewer | Mark Hall |
| Project Coordinator | Barbara Dahl |
| Cover Design | Regan Honda |
| Cover Illustration | Dave Feasey |
| Book Design | Winston Steward |
| Word Processing | Howard Blechman |
| Design Adaptation and Page Layout | Bruce Lundquist |
| Indexer | Valerie Robbins |

Ziff-Davis Press books are produced on a Macintosh computer system with the following applications: FrameMaker®, Microsoft® Word, QuarkXPress®, Adobe Illustrator®, Adobe Photoshop®, Adobe Streamline™, MacLink®Plus, Aldus® FreeHand™, Collage Plus™.

If you have comments or questions or would like to receive a free catalog, call or write:
Ziff-Davis Press
5903 Christie Avenue
Emeryville, CA 94608
1-800-688-0448

ISBN 1-56276-333-4

Manufactured in the United States of America
10 9 8 7 6 5 4 3 2 1

## Dedication

To Trevor and Larisa and Barbara, and
to a handful of friends I really miss.
"Now, my friend, we're out of time."

# CONTENTS AT A GLANCE

# TABLE OF CONTENTS

## About the Author

Winston Steward has developed his computer skills through hands-on experience. He and his family taught themselves how to install a CD-ROM drive, additional RAM, and video and sound cards. They have also set up an entire software-based school curriculum on their home computers. Steward and his family live in the Los Angeles area.

# Chapter 1

## FLOPPY DISKS AREN'T FLOPPY!

### AND OTHER STUNNING REVELATIONS

No, floppy disks aren't floppy. In fact, they're quite stiff. Don't laugh.

When my kids and I purchased our first computer game, the manual directed us to "load Floppy Disk 1 in Drive A." We tore the box apart, looking for something bendable and floppy to insert into our computer. Finally, my then six-year-old son pointed out that these hard, square things buried at the bottom of the box were just about the right dimensions to fit into the slot in the front, which we surmised must be the mysterious Drive A. It turns out that the phrase "floppy disk" dates back to computer antiquatum, when the disks you loaded into your computer were indeed bendable, and, yes, you could flop them around a bit if you chose. The terminology sticks, just as, in this day of CDs, show-offy musicians will still brag, "Yeah, I'm makin' a record."

## THE BEAST ARRIVES

Computers entered my life the day I walked in on my children and their friends watching "Gilligan's Island." Everybody sat like lizards on a rock, in suspended animation, while the words and semi-jokes wafted by. Without effort, they had memorized the same portions of the show's dialogue that I had absorbed, in a similar state of catatonia…20 years ago. They were going to grow up inheriting the same TV-bred legacy of passivity that my generation had, unless I acted fast.

Books and museums seemed the ideal answer. We began reading aloud more, and bought more books. On our living room shelves a healthy new library grew, slightly edging out the mountainous rows of videocassettes that had always taken up half a wall. Amidst squeals of protest, we hit the museums, staked out "science workshops" and art classes, and just about any other half-day trip away from home that smelled like ('scuse me, let me catch my breath) a "learning opportunity." These measures helped break up the sitcom parade, but still, more often than I liked, our house was bathed in that familiar, mesmerizing cathode glow. Television still ruled. However, I had been looking into computers, and it seemed as though some of the new software coming out struck a good balance between entertainment and genuine learning. So we bought one.

## OK, NOW WHAT?

Not surprisingly, our personal computer was the single most expensive purchase our household made during the early 1990s. I set out to understand a little about how the thing worked, and decided that everybody in the family should at least learn the basics about computers and get some genuine use out of this thing. I suppose we bought a computer because we realized the future was upon us, and computers, whirring and chattering away, would undoubtedly be a big part of it. Heaven knows we wouldn't want our children growing up attached to something as primitive as pen and paper! But for a while, the big machine sat there, underutilized, smelling of unfulfilled promise. Our computer came with a bunch of games that the kids mastered quickly and got bored with. Other than that, it functioned as kind of a glorified typewriter. I knew it was capable of more. But what? How?

I didn't know where to turn.

We started to look at some of the wild and extravagant software that, I supposed, normal people were putting on their computers, programs that, if the label on the box was to be taken seriously, could walk, talk, sing and dance, and take you to outer space and back. Perhaps software like this could become a suitable alternative to TV and violent video games, as well as a self-directed educational tool.

As software titles began piling up on our computer, I thought it would be great if my children, then ages 7 and 10, could have quick access to their favorite programs. Computer time would be much more fun and spontaneous if they were not dependent on me to set up every little thing for them. As much as possible, I wanted it to be *their toy*, without having to worry about "breaking the computer" and making dad really mad. How much work would it take to make sure everyone knew their way around this machine? I wasn't sure. But I possessed no desire to live and breathe for computers, or learn all there is to know about my PC's features and gadgets. I cared only to get things up and running and not worry about it further.

I was hoping it wouldn't be much work.

## THE RELUCTANT DEVOTEE

In order to go beyond the most simple and elementary uses for our computer, I had to pick lots of brains, ask endless questions, and carefully jot down number sequences that I'm sure made sense to somebody, but not to me. Every time I tried something new, I got terribly lost. I could either go on using our computer at about 5 percent of its real capacity, or get some help.

The books for PCs that I could find around town were either technical beyond belief and reason, or began with phrases like, "Please keep your computer area neat and clean." But really, most of them were directed towards those ultra-serious computer users, guys who love discovering everything a computer can do, especially marveling at those uses that seemed entirely impractical. I couldn't find a book made for people who wanted a two-sentence answer to everything and then be done with it.

Perhaps such a book did not exist...yet.

# EXILED IN TECHNOVILLE
### Close only counts in horseshoes and hand grenades.
#### –Anonymous

Setting up software to run smoothly on our computer was not as easy as the colorful boxes made it sound. Plus, the whole science of it went against my grain as a free-wheeling person who never pays much attention to detail. Mastering a PC was a challenge for me because, when typing a command into a computer, you get no points for *almost* getting it right. There is no passing grade for approximating the instructions. If you type the command wrong, you are left with a blank screen, a frozen monitor, and a computer that has no idea what you are trying to do. You must type it exactly right, down to the final space and semicolon. And thus, my early computing days were accompanied by some serious lip biting, when strange and unfriendly messages appeared on my screen.

The kids would saunter up, "Broken again, Dad?"

"Well, I wouldn't say it's *broken*."

"But we can't use it right now, correct?"

"Um...yes."

"Can't use it until you fix it, correct?"

"Yes, I suppose"

"Sounds like it's 'broken' to me."

I was not a fast learner. It almost seemed as though there was this subculture of people who spoke "computer-ese" as their native tongue. I was not so gifted, and acquired a habit of asking my computer friends to slow down and repeat themselves. I spent too many long-distance hours talking to technical support people who would patiently explain to me what must have seemed obvious to them. I envied all that insider knowledge, and wondered if someone was laughing at me as I pulled my hair out, staring at that screen, which, quite often, was covered with inexplicable, frustrating gibberish.

## HAPPILY EVER AFTER

But after a few months of trial and tribulation, we're quite happy with things, and I have more than a few stories to tell you. Indeed, this book is made up of the 500 things I wished someone had explained to me when I first bought my computer. It took some work, but now my kids can get up out of bed, wipe their eyes and wander downstairs, press a few keys, and access any one of dozens of programs designed to creatively teach a myriad of subjects. I must admit, we're rather enjoying ourselves.

What I hope to accomplish with this book is to let you know about all the cool and fun family-oriented and children's software that's available for your IBM-compatible computer. We'll talk a little bit about how to set the software up, and how to fix some of the common problems that arise between machines and the programs that are supposed to run on them. In order to feel comfortable getting around on your computer, you'll need to know a little bit about files and directories and learn some nonintimidating facts about your computer's main components. You'll need to know what upgrades might be worth investing in, and which ones are a total waste of time. You'll need to learn how to make a "boot disk," and when to use it.

You do not need to become an expert, or be forever dependant on the good graces of people who live and breathe computers. There are some things that can go wrong on your computer that, at first, can appear downright baffling, but in reality, you and your kids can take care of the problems yourselves. And if you do need to call up those technical support people, being familiar with this book will help you get to the point quicker, without getting bogged down in an expensive and frustrating long-distance phone call. I'll show you how to keep your computer running fast and glitch-free, even after you load on some of that new and bizarre software that promises you the moon (as long as your system can really handle it). You'll also get acquainted with some simple tricks that can make using your computer more fun and spontaneous, and less of a chore. In short, lucky for your pocketbook, you will learn from *my* experience. You don't have to be Marco Polo. This has all been done before.

## OVERCHOICE

Let me say that your most difficult job as a new computer owner will be to keep clearly in mind what you and your family want to accomplish with this machine. It is the nature of the computing beast to provide you with option after option, choice after choice, until you forget what you originally wanted. There are a zillion cool things you can do with your computer, and computers are designed to provide you with an ever-expanding tree of options. Your computer can be programmed to pay your bills, remind you of your anniversary, coo like Betty Grable, and growl like Jack Nicholson. But what's important to *you*? Computer books and literature will dazzle you with all that your machine can do. But we only have a limited amount of time to spend learning a few computer skills, and a limited amount of money to spend on programs. Hopefully, this book will help you keep your head on your shoulders.

For me, the real purpose of owning a PC is to forget that it exists, to jump in and use the software, enjoying the games with your family and friends, and appreciating the access to so much interesting information. The sudden incursion of some stupid hardware conflict or software incompatibility when you are having fun is like when the film breaks in the middle of a movie. You want your money back.

The three things I want from my computer are

- **Speed**  Why should our kids have to have to sit and watch this hour-glass spin 'round and 'round while we wait for a program to load? We like the computer to provide spontaneous access to information, to satisfy the lightning-paced curiosity of young children. A clunky computer or program undermines this.

- **Flexible accessibility**  Computers are fun because you can leap from here to there, to move from one program to another without big hassles. If someone in our family is working on a newsletter, and wants to add a little picture of a dog holding a newspaper, for example, he or she should not have to spend 45 minutes just accomplishing this one simple task.

- **Freedom from technical hassles**  Software conflicts, screen freeze-ups, boot disk problems, well, a little bit of that is okay. In fact, it's good for the kids to learn how to put a machine through its paces. But if there are too many problems, kids get frustrated and scurry back to the TV, where there are no problems, only mind-numbing catatonia.

## TIPS FOR TURNING COMPUTER TIME INTO QUALITY FAMILY TIME

**Don't habitually use the computer as a baby-sitter**  Don't say, "Why don't you go play on the computer?" to get rid of the kids for a while. They will end up resenting this mechanical baby-sitter as deeply as the biological version.

**Let *them* use the mouse**  It's their toy, not yours. During family computer time, put them in front of the keyboard and computer screen and mousepad. Place yourself to the side. They need to be in charge of what's going on up on the screen, exploring and figuring things out for themselves. Your job is to sit to the side of the computer and encourage them.

**Go slowly**   Pay careful attention to how your child is absorbing what's up on the screen. Don't overexplain, but when you show your child how to play a new game, be thorough and systematic. It might take more than one sitting for them to get the whole point. Also be attuned to your child's interest level. Is he or she getting bored? Some kids jump in right away like a duck to water, clicking and dragging the mouse as if it was some sort of third hand. Others can't seem to grasp that their actions with the mouse influence what happens on the screen. I have seen many parents of young children invest lots of time and money into computer training for a child who just does not enjoy using a mouse. Remember, for most kids, hand and finger dexterity develop slowly between the ages of 6 and 8 (although you'd never know it from watching those younger Nintendo fiends). For the moment, computers just might not be your child's cup of tea. Try again in a year or so.

**Don't burn out**   You will need to spend a few hours doing the purely technical work of setting up your system so your kids can access it freely and safely. On your part, there will be frustration and trial and error. If you spend too much concentrated time in front of the screen solving these problems, you'll get a headache and feel dizzy, and when your kids come and ask if you want to *play* with them on the computer, you may use foul language.

**No food near the computer**   At our house, there is no eating and drinking near the computer. Nothing will ruin the party faster than overturned Hawaiian Punch oozing into your components, or greasy fingers gumming up the keyboard.

**Too much of a good thing**   Eye strain is also a consideration. A computer screen emits far less radiation than a TV (almost any computer monitor purchased since 1993 will conform to EPA low-radiation emission standards—check to see if yours does). But kids sit closer to a computer monitor than they do to a TV. A young person may safely curl up in a corner and read for hours at a time. (Remember when they used to do that?) Not so for computer usage. Moderation is the rule.

**Only an adult should turn off the computer**   Our kids know that only a grown-up may turn off the computer. Frequent powering down is bad for your hard drive, and turning off the computer from within a program can damage your files. Our computer is on all day, and an adult turns it off at night. Sometimes rebooting is necessary, so make sure the kids understand the process of rebooting, and that doing a soft reboot (pressing the Alt+Ctrl+Delete keys simultaneously) is easier on the components than pressing Reset on the computer's front panel.

**Have fun yourself**   Buy programs that both you and your children enjoy. Don't feel bashful about having fun with a computer game that says "Ages 6 to 10" on the box. This is your chance to initiate a mutually enjoyable, interactive family activity, which is a rare bird in the mid-1990s. If you act condescendingly and uninterested in the cartoony, elementary learning programs they enjoy, they might decide you're right, and rent a Sharon Stone movie. Allow yourself a little childish pleasure.

Conversely, it's fine to purchase a game or learning program that's a bit over their heads, and take the time to learn it thoroughly yourself (admit it, you probably don't even remember how to balance a chemical equation!—see Sierra On-Line's **Island of Doctor Brain**) before

---

### Here's a Conversation You Never Want to Have

*Mum or Dad: Remember, you can press Control+T*

Child: (Nothing. Concentrating.)

*Mum or Dad: You didn't do that quite right.*

Child: I know. I'll fix it later.

*Mum or Dad: When you double-click that way, it comes out crooked.*

Child: It's all right.

*Mum or Dad: You keep using that same color over and over.*

Child: But I like it like that.

*Mum or Dad: But there's all these other things you can try out with this program.*

Child: Later.

*Mum or Dad: Click on the upper left over there to save your work.*

Child: I know. (Silent.)

The screen freezes.

Child: My picture doesn't work anymore.

*Mum or Dad: If you had done it the way I said, this wouldn't have happened.*

---

demonstrating the game to them. *The key word is **demonstrate.*** Take advantage of the graphic component to these games, and after your initial introduction, just let them have at it. Kids will surprise you by how quickly they latch on to programs that originally seemed too advanced for them. Purchase something that you enjoy, and share that enthusiasm with your children.

**Spend time learning the program before handing it over to the kids**   Once you've learned the "ins and outs" of a piece of software, you can use the program to steer your children towards the areas where educational growth is needed. You can see to it that the software is really utilized in an intentional and effective manner, rather than being fooled with briefly and then quickly set aside. One of my children will talk in endless detail about Ancient Greece and Rome, but can't differentiate between short vowel sounds to save his life. So, I have him play **Word Munchers,** a game by MECC that emphasizes phonics. If you know your child needs work in higher multiplication, but can get by in basic division, then, working with one of the math programs available, you can set the game so that it reviews more multiplication skills, rather than advancing to division. Also, by working with a program yourself, you can troubleshoot and catch any glitches in the software, saving your children the frustration.

## INCORPORATING COMPUTER TIME WITH REAL-WORLD LESSONS

Much of the new computer software takes the form of "interactive role-play adventures." Playing these games is like being dropped into a full-length movie in which your child becomes the main character. These interactive games are a new way for kids to learn about faraway places, unusual people, objects, and concepts. Games like this can open the door to some real learning. If you are embarking on a role-playing adventure set in the middle ages, use this opportunity to inspire your kids to imagine the world as it was in the pre-scientific age, when all phenomenon was ascribed to magic. Sierra On-Line's **Lost Secret of the Rain Forest** is about a young boy's journey down the Amazon River. But rather than zip through the story and quit, you might pull out a good map, find Brazil, and talk about products that come from the rain forest, for example, and the difficulties in enforcing laws that protect Earth's resources. The game itself should merely be a launching pad for your child's curiosity.

The amount of research that goes into developing a good role-playing adventure is comparable to writing a script for an hour-long PBS documentary. The people that develop good educational software have a fair idea of what they are trying to accomplish academically. They are not merely Nintendo programmers with a guilty conscience. They've developed resources that you can use to pique your child's interest in many subjects that he or she might not come across in school textbooks. *Take the time to pause the game and get the kids to go look up a fact or two.* They'll appreciate your interest in something that they find entertaining, and feel that the new information must be valuable because you directed them to it.

## PICTURES BEFORE WORDS

Computers help teach concepts pictorially, with simulations and animations, and can impart ideas that just don't come across easily with words alone. My seven-year-old boy asked how a virus was different than a bacteria. First I tried to explain, pointing out that a bacteria attacked and overcame the body's cells, while a virus entered the cells and reproduced in them. A blank stare. He was probably wishing he hadn't asked.

We pulled out a program that featured a brief slide show on the topic. Pictures were the key here. What we needed was a short, colorful animation that could be paused or repeated as needed. With multimedia tools like these, concepts that are usually considered "over kids' heads" become comprehendable.

# AND NOW FOR THE WARNINGS

Computer games are an addictively private activity, and without much effort, you could end up with an increasingly antisocial beastie on your hands who never wants to leave the game room except to take phone calls from cute girls. You must make the effort to direct the computer learning into good conversations and fun family times that can be shared with others. People are difficult, machines do whatever you say. Don't underestimate the allure of such an insight, when it occurs to your kid that he or she can have a perfectly good time without putting up with loud-mouth friends who always hit your arm too hard and don't fight fair. When your child needs a productive way to relax during a long, rainy afternoon, computer learning programs beat the pants off television, but even the best software should supplement, not replace, books and Legos, crayons and real (not virtual) humans.

## WATCH THE ONLINE TIME

Also, if you own a modem, keep an eye on the kid's online activity. Not only do the hours add up (see Chapter 8), but **networks like the Internet are totally unregulated.** There are many "adult situations" afoot on the open wire. On the Internet and other bulletin boards, people are relatively free to download and share pornography. In one instance, on one of the Big Three online services, an 8-year-old girl was logging on and off various "chat lines" hoping to find someone her age to talk to. (For kids and adults online, this practice is fairly common.) She stumbled upon an open line called "TV Talk." In this case, TV stood for transvestite. One of the participants realized the error and sent her a personal message gently coaxing her to go listen in on something else.

There have been times that young people have been coaxed into something un-pleasant after believing that they had just found a nice online friend. In reality, most of the "chatting" that goes on across the online services would do no harm, but, as is true for any other kind of "meeting" with a stranger, a little parental screening isn't bad.

## INHERITING UNCLE JED'S OLD COMPUTER: YOU CAN'T CHANGE THE BASIC ANIMAL

From the outset, I need to caution you about spending scads of money upgrading an older computer, as tempting as the proposition might be. I've tried this many times myself: Install a new "add-on" to an older computer, hoping to make it work well with today's software. I've spent money on a plow horse, hoping to turn it into a racer. Sorry. No go.

Consider the two following scenarios:

- Mom brought her old 286 home from work. Her office upgraded to 486s, so now we can keep this one. Turn it on. It looks brand new. It hums and purrs convincingly and boots up without a problem. Neat.

- Seven years ago, a college-bound nephew bought a great computer (paid $3,000 for it) and used it only to do term papers. He's giving it to us! What could be better?

**Even expensive systems that are a few years old will either not work with today's graphics-intensive, memory-hogging, CPU-hungry software, or will run it very, very, very slowly.**

More bad news: Upgrading the old computer, buying a bigger hard drive for it, more RAM, and a new video card, probably will not make the essential difference. For starters, you can't run Windows 3.1 very well on a 286 computer, no matter how much you tinker with it. After installing a sound card and a brand new CD-ROM player with all the trimmings, you *still* have not changed the basic animal.

## WHAT DO YOU NEED?

If you are intrigued by the newer software, and all its fascinating capabilities, you pretty much need at least a 486 DX computer with 33MHz clock speed, if not a 486 DX-2/66. You'll need at least 4 megs of RAM and, if you plan to spend much time in Microsoft Windows, you'll wish you had 8 megs. You'll want a double-speed CD-ROM player, which most 486 computers come with. You'll want a 16-bit stereo sound card, and a SVGA card with at least 1 meg of RAM, not to be confused with the RAM included with the computer itself. And, oh, yeah. Your old computer would make a very nice donation to a nonprofit organization that needs a computer as a database tool to store important phone numbers and addresses. Just because an old computer cannot run well with the newest programs does not mean it should be junked. But if you donate it, don't try to deduct very much from your taxes. The IRS reads the trade journals, too.

## DID YOUR COMPUTER COME WITH PRELOADED SOFTWARE BUT NOT WITH THE ORIGINAL DISKS?

The ad for the computer you bought showed a picture of your new toy-to-be surrounded by at least a dozen software boxes, but when you brought the computer home, all that was in the package was the computer. Where's the software? Many computers come with dozens of programs loaded on at the factory, but that doesn't mean that they are sending you the disks for the programs. Many computers come preloaded with MS-DOS, Windows, and other useful utilities, and they count on you to *back up* those important programs yourself, on your own floppy disks. Most come with a *Disk Imaging* utility that will back up all the preloaded software automatically. The program will simply prompt you for disk after disk, perhaps 20 to 30 floppies, and you do this until all the preloaded software is backed up on your floppy disks. After doing this, if your hard drive were to crash and you lost your data, you could go find the "backup disks" you created and reload the software from scratch. (No big deal. It happens all the time.) If your computer came with preloaded software, no disks, and no helpful "self-backup" utility like what I've just described, then the company expects you to have the brains to back it up yourself. Please see Chapter 7 of this book for directions on how to use Microsoft DOS's and Windows's backup programs. *Please make sure you have all the files in your MS-DOS directory backed up on floppy disks, and stored in a safe place.*

## DON'T LET THE COMPUTER REPLACE PEN AND PAPER IN YOUR HOME

I personally have read and thought a lot about whether or not heavy use of computers as an educational tool discourages the development of writing skills. On one hand, it is true that children can think creatively and put ideas together at a very early age, usually much earlier than they possess the verbal or written skills to express what they've learned. But as we all know, being "bright" doesn't mean that a youngster will necessarily shine under examination. Most schoolwork is set up for the convenience of the recordkeepers, those who must monitor Johnny's progress (is he ahead or behind in his studies?). So Johnny must be good at expressing what he has learned, and able to express himself on demand, either verbally or on paper…or be considered a dummy.

An attractive, graphically oriented computer program can provide a way for kids to enjoy tooling around with what they know. With the right computer programs, kids can enjoy exploring many subjects, long before they've acquired complex skills of written and verbal self-expression.

On the other hand, too much "computer learning" can create children who "sort of know" things. My experience has been that, in order for a child to transform an idea or a concept into a fully grasped "learning tool," he must understand it thoroughly enough to commit it to paper in his own words. When a child learns new ideas, thinks about them, then puts them into his own words on paper, those ideas are now *his* tools, and he may now apply them in new and different ways, and not merely regurgitate them as they were first learned. Learning to write things down is an important part of learning. A computer cannot help much with this process. It takes pencil and paper, shaping the letters, picking up the paper you've written on and being proud of what you are holding in your fingers. Creative computer programs help a young person grasp new ideas and understand bits of physics and geometry and other far-reaching concepts. But writing teaches a child to mix something they are learning today with yesterday's lessons, and *cumulative learning* becomes possible. Computer programs provide such an alluring graphic environment for learning that it's easy for a young person to become overly dependent, for example, on a frisky little robot on the screen to bring to mind the correct math or spelling answers.

So lessons taught on the computer should supplement, not replace, a child's normal penmanship progress.

# Chapter 2

## NECESSARY BABBLE
### A Brief Primer of Computer Talk

Not much operating skill or expertise is required for you and your family to have a ripping good time with your computer. However, in order to get the most out of today's software, you will need to know how to copy, delete, and move files around your computer. It's helpful to know how to work with files and directories, and how to interpret those intimidating "error" messages that will pop up on your screen from time to time. Let's get started by talking about DOS.

> **If your computer automatically puts you in Windows when you turn it on, you can get to DOS by pressing the Alt and F4 keys at the same time.**

## WHAT IS DOS?

DOS is your computer's operating system. Almost all IBM-compatible computers "run on DOS." Having a universal operating system common to all PCs provides lots of benefits. The software that works on my computer will work on yours. There is a common language of "commands" that users of DOS-based computers can take for granted. If I type "edit" on my computer, a blue screen will pop up, the familiar menu bar will be present along the top, allowing me to cut and paste, save, and print the file I am editing. (This edit feature is part of DOS versions 4.0 and later.) The same is true for your computer. DOS is our computers' language in common.

### NOT JUST ONE DOS

There are several versions of DOS. Microsoft, the company that sells DOS, updates it from time to time, providing new features. If you type

> **What do you mean, "At the DOS prompt"?**

When your computer is idle, and you are not running a program, then the screen is blank (black screen), except for three short references:

- One capital letter which tells you what drive you are on. Unless your computer has two hard drives, this letter will always be C:\.

- Following C:\ will be the name of the directory you are logged on to, perhaps C:\DOS or C:\WINDOWS.

- Next you will see a blinking cursor. The blinking cursor tells you that the computer is awaiting your command.

`ver`

at the DOS prompt, the screen will tell you what version of DOS you are running.

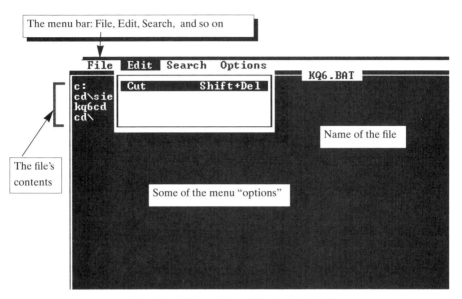

The menu bar: File, Edit, Search, and so on

Name of the file

The file's contents

Some of the menu "options"

**The big, blue friendly DOS "edit" screen**

If your computer was purchased in the last three years, you are probably running DOS 5 or 6. DOS 5 is very adequate, stable, and presents no problems or operating conflicts.

DOS 6 comes with several important new features, and DOS 6.2 corrects some of the problems (known as "bugs" in computer jargon) that arose with DOS 6.0. DOS 6.22 is the most recent upgrade. If you are using a version lower than DOS 6.22, you may *upgrade* to 6.22 at little expense. The upgrade is worth it. **Since newer upgrades are always becoming available, your software dealer will tell you which version is truly the most current.** Please see the section "DOS Upgrades" at the end of this chapter for a discussion on why you should upgrade from DOS 5 to DOS 6.22. Upgrading to a new version of DOS is very easy. After buying the new software, simply insert the upgrade disk into your A: drive, type the word **setup** and press Enter, and follow the on-screen instructions (you'll need a blank floppy disk handy). **No special computer knowledge is required to upgrade to a new DOS version.**

# WHAT IS A HARD DRIVE?

A hard drive stores your data. It has the distinction of being one of the few moving parts on your computer. It is a round disk that circulates upon demand. When data is needed for one of your programs, it must rotate and allow access to the files you need. Since your hard drive is a mechanical device, you need to maintain it regularly. Mostly, this consists of running a regular "disk maintenance" program on your computer. In Chapters 5 and 10 of this book we talk about some simple tasks you need to perform regularly to keep your hard drive running well.

During your computer's working day, files are removed from your hard drive and put back again. They are not always put back in perfect order (see Chapter 7).

Your hard drive is a disk that rotates around. Since it is a moving part, it can wear out and must be maintained.

## WHAT IS A CD-ROM DRIVE?

If you really splurged when you bought your computer, you have perhaps a 540MB hard drive. Most people have 170 to 420MB hard drives. A CD-ROM is a single disk that can contain up to 680MB of data. Just like CDs that you buy at the store, CD-ROMs are removable, and you change programs by changing CD-ROM disks. The fascinating thing is that each CD-ROM disk can hold **2 to 3 times the amount of data that exists on your entire hard drive**. By definition, you cannot save data to CD-ROM disks (ROM stands for Read Only Memory). Still, CD-ROMs give your computer access to unbelievable amounts of information. CD-ROM drives cost around $200, and most brands can be installed by the user, although most home computer systems selling for $1,000 or more include a CD-ROM drive. **Possessing no mechanical aptitude whatsoever, I managed to install my CD-ROM drive and have it up and running in two hours.**

One CD-ROM disk holds more data than your entire hard drive. This is why CD-ROM programs have more features than disk-based programs.

The standard CD-ROM drive (in fact, the only one you want anything to do with) is a **double-speed CD-ROM drive.** Single-speed drives are as valuable as week-old bread. At the time of this writing, quadruple-speed CD-ROM drives are still above $400, and do not, by any means, work twice as fast as a double-speed CD-ROM drive. As their prices fall, quadruple-speed CD-ROM drives would be a worthwhile investment.

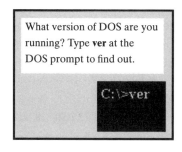

What version of DOS are you running? Type **ver** at the DOS prompt to find out.

`C:\>ver`

## THINK *OF* THE *POSSIBILITIES!*

The arrival of CD-ROM technology presented software designers with extraordinary capabilities. Just three years ago, owning a 170MB hard drive was extravagant. But when CD-ROM technology became widely available, software writers suddenly had the ability to stretch out a **single program** onto a 680MB CD disk. The effect was like donating a symphony orchestra to every piano player in the United States.

CD-ROM disks look the same as those you buy at record stores, and yet you can fit all of Shakespeare's known writings on a single disk. Not surprisingly then, the first CD-ROM products simply exploited the huge data-storage capabilities: They were encyclopedias, archives, entire libraries, and collections of important works, all stuffed on one CD disk.

Software programmers have always been anxious to shed the limitations of floppy-disk-based programs. Prior to CD-ROMs, programmers had to devise cumbersome and time-consuming tricks just to squeeze the smallest voice overdub or "real-time movie sequence" into their programs. Suddenly, with CD-ROMs, software creators could include myriads of video clips and hours of animation and voice-over without worrying about program size. It became possible to write and direct an entire "interactive movie," recording and filming as many "plot branches" and "multiple endgame" ideas as the imagination can muster. If you purchase a CD-ROM adventure game, the characters will audibly talk (if you have a sound card installed—see Chapter 5). In fact, famous actors (oh, boy) are sometimes employed to "perform" characters in CD-ROM games. Actors and actresses who appear as characters in CD-ROM adventure games are sometimes confused by the process. They say, "I thought we just filmed the ending!! Why are we doing it again?" But segments of the story must be filmed over and over again with slight variations, permitting you, the game player, to explore and roam the terrain. Since computer adventure games are *interactive*, the story has to allow for many different outcomes based on the choices that the players make.

CD-ROM educational programs make liberal use of movie clips, but yes, the mini-film of the Wright brothers' first successful flight looks just as grainy and tattered on a $3,000 computer as it did in your history class umpteen years ago. A company known as Mindscape, for one example, offers the CD-ROM-based **Twentieth Century Almanac,** dividing the century into various categories, complete with video clips and speeches from Teddy Roosevelt's day to the present. Microsoft's **Encarta** is a total multimedia encyclopedia, with slideshows and educational videos on just about every subject imaginable. Based on the Funk 'n Wagnall's

*Encyclopedia,* there are 26,000 article entries, with 90 minutes of video and 8 hours of audio. It costs around $80. (Compare that to the hundreds you would pay for a new hardbound encyclopedia.) One major benefit to owning a multimedia encyclopedia on CD-ROM is that the yearly upgrades are available for around $50, whereas purchasing a new book-bound encyclopedia year after year is not really an option.

For a full review of hundreds of available educational programs on the market today, see Chapter 15 of this book.

## CHEER UP! YOU'VE GOT A FAN

If your computer is a 486 or better, you most likely have a fan under there. Yup, jes' like a car, computers can overheat, and your fan is there to cool it down. I take pains to point out the existence of this fan because 1) a fan is a moving part, and therefore can break, and 2) if it does break, and your components get hot, the effects are devastating. Listen for that little hum. (Actually, that little hum can create obnoxious vibrations. If your computer workstation is on very level ground and is made out of a substantial grade of metal or wood, the fan's vibrating should not become too fierce.) If the fan stops, and you don't notice it for a while, you've got a baked computer. A computer's fan must be high-quality and sturdy.

> Do you own a 486? Then your computer, just like your car, probably has a fan to stop it from overheating.

## WHAT IS A FLOPPY DRIVE?

**Your floppy drive and your A: drive are the same thing.** The floppy drive holds data and spins around just like your hard drive, but on a much smaller scale, obviously. There are three kinds of floppy drives:

- $5^1/4$", the big thin disks that are actually bendable
- $3^1/2$" high density
- $3^1/2$" double density

I want to point out the difference between $3^1/2$" high-density disks and $3^1/2$" double-density disks. High-density disks hold 1.44MB of data, which is twice as much as $3^1/2$" double-density disks, which hold only 720K of data. Confusion occurs because

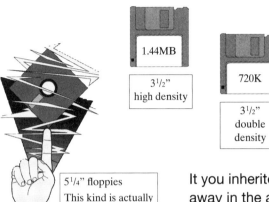

1.44MB

$3\frac{1}{2}$"
high density

720K

$3\frac{1}{2}$"
double
density

$5\frac{1}{4}$" floppies
This kind is actually
a bit floppy.

the disk types look identical. **Double-density drives, meaning those drives that are designed specifically for double-density disks, will not work with high-density (1.44MB) disks.** These days very little new software comes on double-density disks. If you have a newer computer, it most likely came with a high-density floppy drive. It you inherited the one that Uncle Milton had wasting away in the attic, you'd better double-check before you go buy a program at the software store.

## WHAT DOES RAM DO?

Extra RAM on your computer means your computer has to make fewer trips to your hard drive to retrieve data to run your programs. By far, the most time-consuming task your computer must perform is searching your hard drive for data. If the information you need can be temporarily stored in RAM, then your computer operations will move along more quickly. **More RAM, if configured correctly, means your game plays faster, and your kids won't yawn and wipe their eyes and forget what's going on while your computer tries to locate the files on your hard disk.** Also, lots of RAM is often necessary for Windows programs to run properly.

Extra RAM allows your computer to keep more information on the "front burner," and have access to it quickly.

For more discussion of what RAM does for your computer, please see Chapters 3 and 4.

DOS 6.2 or 6.22 brings lots of great features to your computer at no extra cost. See the section "DOS Upgrades" at the end of this chapter to learn more.

A Reminder

Lookit me!

## FILES AND DIRECTORIES: SEE HOW THEY RUN

Files are the most basic unit of computer information that you can manipulate yourself. Files hold a program's operating code. Files contain the database that you read from the computer screen. The pictures, beautiful animated sequences, and sound clips you enjoy on your computer are all files. The actual guts of the game, how the characters move or talk or progress from scene to scene, that information is stored in program files. If your child is playing a spelling game that tests his or her proficiency in various words, those words and test scores are stored in data files. When you move, erase, or copy information on your computer, you are doing it to files. When you "save a game," which causes the computer program to remember your exact position in the play, the number of points earned, etc., your computer makes a new file remembering that data for you.

Your computer has many "system files" (files which have a **.sys** at the end of the name). When you see a system file in one of your directories, such as **mouse.sys** or **himem.sys**, just tell yourself, "This file runs something." *A system file makes a computer device work.* It could be your mouse, your CD-ROM drive, or a sound card, but all system files (.sys) operate something.

Your computer also contains numerous "hidden files." For example, each time you create a directory, you have also created two hidden files, represented by the two sets of dots at the top of your directory listing. Some hidden files, like **IO.sys**, are central to your computer's basic operations, and, unless you aspire to become Joe Computer and take everything apart for yourself, hidden files are not to be messed with.

## WHAT ARE DIRECTORIES?
## CHANGING DIRECTORIES AND VIEWING FILES

Most of your files are stored in directories. Files are like pieces of paper, small and large, covered with instructions and information of all kinds. Directories are like the manila folders that we shove those thousands of pieces of paper into. Then we label the manila folder so we know what papers are stored inside it. And so it is with directories. On your computer, your directories are given names that will help you keep track of which files are stored inside them.

You can quickly view your files and directories by typing **dir** at the DOS prompt.

After you've typed **dir**, you'll notice dozens and dozens of entries scrolling by, finally coming to a stop. Here's what you'll see:

These dots before <DIR> are **hidden files**

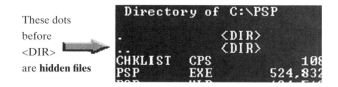

```
Directory of C:\PSP
                     <DIR>
                     <DIR>
CHKLIST   CPS              108
PSP       EXE          524,832
```

- ■ **Directories**   Directories will have <DIR> to the right of their names.
- ■ **Files**   To the right of a file name is the three-letter file extension, the file size (how many bytes it is), and the date showing the last time the file was manipulated.

Its size is 405 bytes

The file extension is .CPS

This file name is CHKLIST

This is a view inside the directory MOUSE. You are looking at a list of files. Using the entry "CHKLIST" as an example, moving from left to right, you can learn the filename (CHKLIST), the file extension (.CPS), how big the file is (405 bytes), and when the file was last manipulated (May 13, 1994, at 1:14 a.m.).

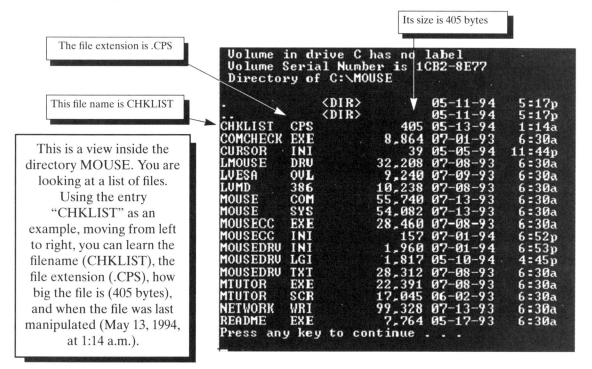

```
Volume in drive C has no label
Volume Serial Number is 1CB2-8E77
Directory of C:\MOUSE

.              <DIR>         05-11-94    5:17p
..             <DIR>         05-11-94    5:17p
CHKLIST   CPS           405  05-13-94    1:14a
COMCHECK  EXE         8,864  07-01-93    6:30a
CURSOR    INI            39  05-05-94   11:44p
LMOUSE    DRU        32,208  07-08-93    6:30a
LUESA     OVL         9,240  07-09-93    6:30a
LUMD      386        10,238  07-08-93    6:30a
MOUSE     COM        55,740  07-13-93    6:30a
MOUSE     SYS        54,082  07-13-93    6:30a
MOUSECC   EXE        28,460  07-08-93    6:30a
MOUSECC   INI           157  07-01-94    6:52p
MOUSEDRU  INI         1,960  07-01-94    6:53p
MOUSEDRU  LGI         1,817  05-10-94    4:45p
MOUSEDRU  TXT        28,312  07-08-93    6:30a
MTUTOR    EXE        22,391  07-08-93    6:30a
MTUTOR    SCR        17,045  06-02-93    6:30a
NETWORK   WRI        99,328  07-13-93    6:30a
README    EXE         7,764  05-17-93    6:30a
Press any key to continue . . .
```

Remember:

⇒ **From your root directory, you may not see too many files if most of them are placed inside subdirectories.**

⇒ **In order to find a particular file, you have to log on "inside" the correct directory.**

To change to another directory, simply type **cd\** followed by the name of the directory you want to be logged on to, for example **cd\windows**.

Typing **cd\** alone (followed by pressing **Enter,** of course) will land you at the very top of the chain. You'll be logged on to your "root directory."

There are 5 files that ought to remain in your root directory. They are called COMMAND.COM, AUTOEXEC.BAT, CONFIG.SYS, HIMEM.SYS, and EMM386.EXE.

## SHAKIN' THE TREE

One way for you to visualize how files and directories are organized on your computer is to type the word

```
tree
```

This command will draw for you a branching diagram, showing how "subdirectories" are actually stored inside "parent directories." With so many directories on your computer, you can see why searching for a particular file can make you feel like a dog digging up a yard searching for a misplaced bone, but fear not. In Chapters 3 and 4 of this book, we'll explore ways to quickly locate and manipulate important files on your computer.

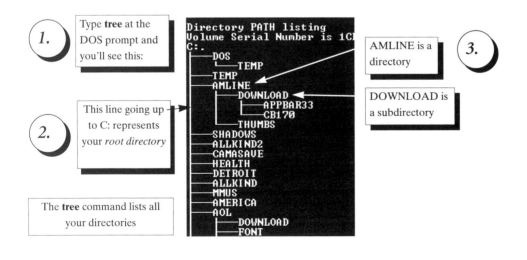

1. Type **tree** at the DOS prompt and you'll see this:

2. This line going up to C: represents your *root directory*

The **tree** command lists all your directories

```
Directory PATH listing
Volume Serial Number is 1C
C:.
├───DOS
│   └───TEMP
├───TEMP
├───AMLINE
│   ├───DOWNLOAD
│   │   ├───APPBAR33
│   │   └───CB170
│   └───THUMBS
├───SHADOWS
├───ALLKIND2
├───CAMASAVE
├───HEALTH
├───DETROIT
├───ALLKIND
├───MMUS
├───AMERICA
└───AOL
    ├───DOWNLOAD
    └───FONT
```

3. AMLINE is a directory

DOWNLOAD is a subdirectory

## GETTING USED TO SWITCHING BETWEEN DIRECTORIES

1. Let's log onto the DOS directory, and view all the files inside. To do this, type

    **cd\dos**

2. You are now inside your DOS directory. Type

    **dir**

Files are like instructions placed inside a folder

and

A DIRECTORY IS LIKE A FOLDER

You will see a long list of files scroll by, files that you did not see before. Those files were there all along, but can only be viewed if you are logged on to the DOS directory, which you are now. Any computer commands you type now would only affect the files inside the directory you are logged onto.

3. Let's return to your *root* directory. This is done by typing

    **cd\**

You are at the top of the chain, so to speak, and almost all the files on your computer are safely stored inside their corresponding subdirectory. Therefore, any command you type *will not* affect the files inside them.

4. Now, pick a directory associated with one of your family's favorite

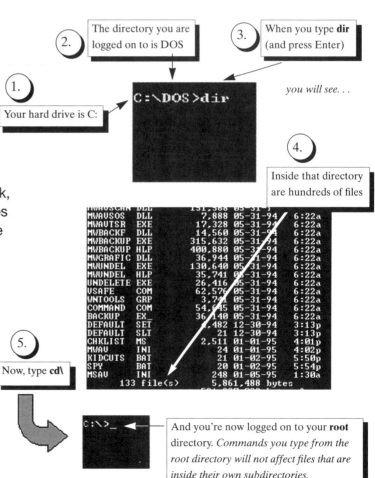

**1.** Your hard drive is C:

**2.** The directory you are logged on to is DOS

**3.** When you type **dir** (and press Enter)

*you will see. . .*

**4.** Inside that directory are hundreds of files

```
MWAUSCAN DLL    151,568 05-31-9
MWAUSOS  DLL      7,888 05-31-94   6:22a
MWAUTSR  EXE     17,328 05-31-94   6:22a
MWBACKF  DLL     14,560 05-31-94   6:22a
MWBACKUP EXE    315,632 05-31-94   6:22a
MWBACKUP HLP    400,880 05-31-94   6:22a
MWGRAFIC DLL     36,944 05-31-94   6:22a
MWUNDEL  EXE    130,640 05-31-94   6:22a
MWUNDEL  HLP     35,741 05-31-94   6:22a
UNDELETE EXE     26,416 05-31-94   6:22a
USAFE    COM     62,576 05-31-94   6:22a
WNTOOLS  GRP      3,72  05-31-94   6:22a
COMMAND  COM     54,645 05-31-94   6:22a
BACKUP   EX_     36,140 05-31-94   6:22a
DEFAULT  SET       ,482 12-30-94   3:13p
DEFAULT  SLT         21 12-30-94   3:13p
CHKLIST  MS       2,511 01-01-95   4:01p
MWAV     INI         24 01-01-95   4:02p
KIDCUTS  BAT         21 01-02-95   5:50p
SPY      BAT         20 01-02-95   5:54p
MSAV     INI        248 01-05-95   1:30a
        133 file(s)    5,861,488 bytes
```

**5.** Now, type **cd\**

C:\>_

And you're now logged on to your **root** directory. *Commands you type from the root directory will not affect files that are inside their own subdirectories.*

games or programs. Let's move inside of it. The command to change to a new directory is

**cd\**_directory_

(Don't really type the word "directory." Type the name of a directory that you see on your own computer screen.)

Please note that the figure at the end is a backward slash. Your command should look like **cd\**, not **cd/**. After having logged on to a new directory of your choice, now type **dir**. You'll see an entirely different list of files than you saw before. Those files were there all along, but were sitting inside their assigned directory. Let's move on.

## WHY YOU NEED TO LEARN BASIC FILE COMMANDS

You may enjoy your computer's programs for months and months and never have any reason to manipulate files on your own. Most family-oriented software does it all for you. When you install software, you are usually required only to type one command and answer a few questions about your computer. It's possible to always stay inside your programs, and not have to use DOS commands to copy, edit, move, or delete files.

But there are many basic computer procedures that involve copying, saving, altering, and moving files.

- You may want to move some finished projects out of your way, and place them in directories where they can be off by themselves, not getting in the way of your more current projects.

- For safety reasons, you may want to rename your computer's start-up files, so that if some dopey program comes along and alters them undesirably, you'll still be able to start your computer.

- Sooner or later (probably sooner), you'll have to learn to make a boot disk, which involves altering your computer's startup files.

Hey, Dad, what's
Del-star-dot-star
mean?

Your kids don't need to be familiar with delete commands. You ought to be the one removing files from your computer. Even a responsible young child can be tempted to experiment with commands like **del \*.\*** and **format c:**, which can wreak irreversible damage when used inappropriately.

(**del \*.\*** deletes all files in whatever directory you are logged on to, and **format c:** will remove the entire contents of your hard drive.)

■ Finally, you'll want to delete older programs from your computer, but keep on file the work you have accomplished with those programs. Information such as your "saved game" data and "number of levels completed" will be stored in file form. You will not want to undo your hard work just because you need to temporarily remove a program from your hard drive.

All the above chores are accomplished with simple, brief, unintimidating DOS commands, and are covered in this book.

"Check out these tricks, D.J."

## CREATING AND DELETING DIRECTORIES

First, to make sure that you're in the root directory, type

    **cd\**

At the DOS prompt, type

    **md boombox**

and you've made a directory called **boombox**. (Don't forget the space after **md**.) Now, switch to the new boombox directory (cd\boombox). Once inside boombox, you can make another directory called **hitsongs**; just type

    **md hitsongs**

If you are inside the boombox directory, and want to log on to the hitsongs directory, you *don't* have to type

    **cd\boombox\hitsongs**

From inside boombox, you only have to type

    **cd hitsongs**

(no backslash, *just the space*) and you're there!

Now, let's **delete** these directories so they won't confuse you later. First, make sure you're in the boombox directory, then type **rd hitsongs** (*rd* means remove directory) and press **Enter**.

To get rid of boombox, you must move into the root directory so type **cd\**. Now, enter the command **rd boombox**. Both subdirectories are now deleted.

## DOS UPGRADES

In DOS 6.0, Microsoft put features at your disposal that you would have had to buy several other programs to obtain. Trouble is, DOS 6.0 had lots of bugs. There were many problems with this new version of DOS that didn't get worked out before it was sent to the stores. The version you want to use is DOS 6.2 or DOS 6.22. DOS 6.2 was made available to 6.0 owners for a mere $10.

However, DOS 6.0 and 6.2 included a disk compression program that was ruled in court to be too similar to a popular disk compression program known as Stacker. After much legal wrangling, Microsoft decided to properly license the disk compression technology from the Stacker company. That is why you'll see various upgrades of DOS 6 floating about: DOS 6.1, 6.2, and 6.22. Your computer will be quite happy if you are running with DOS 6.2 or 6.22. DOS 6.0 is unstable and should be upgraded immediately. *Go to your software store and tell them you want 6.2 or 6.22.*

# Chapter 3

# THE ONLY TWO FILES ON YOUR COMPUTER THAT YOU NEED TO UNDERSTAND

Having a computer is like having a little brother. Loading a program is like teaching it something. Printing something out is like making it do homework. When the screen freezes, it's like a little brother having a temper tantrum. So you reboot it, which is like spanking it. But computers don't usually wake up in the middle of the night and cry. At least not yet.

WHAT HAPPENS WHEN YOU FIRST TURN ON YOUR COMPUTER

WHAT IS A BOOT DISK? (AND WHY YOU'LL SOMETIMES NEED ONE)

FREEING UP MORE CONVENTIONAL MEMORY

WHAT ARE THESE VARIOUS COMMANDS IN YOUR AUTOEXEC.BAT FILE?

SETTING UP AND CHANGING YOUR SMARTDRIVE CACHE

## WHAT HAPPENS WHEN YOU FIRST TURN ON YOUR COMPUTER

When your computer turns on, it seeks two startup files that direct your computer to load the DOS operating system and to load a memory manager and your various start-up programs and device drivers…all in a specific order. These two files, which MUST be in your root directory, are known as **autoexec.bat** and **config.sys.** Think of them as two hunting dogs sent to "fetch" the things you need to get your computing day started. They'll go find your mouse driver and your CD-ROM driver and extensions, and they will detect how big your hard drive is and what kind of video display card you have. They also load "memory resident" programs like SmartDrive.

Additionally, when MS-DOS starts, two other "sister files," known as HIMEM.SYS, and EMM386.EXE are loaded. These two files direct your computer to make use of RAM and upper memory blocks. Without HIMEM.SYS and EMM386.EXE, your computer will take you for a bumpy ride indeed. Never alter the *location* of these four files. But we we'll work with **autoexec.bat** and **config.sys** in this chapter. Your autoexec.bat and your config.sys files, together with your COMMAND.COM file, establish your computer's configuration. The diagrams at the end of this chapter will make this topic easier to understand.

## WHAT IS A BOOT DISK? (AND WHY YOU'LL SOMETIMES NEED ONE)

There are times when your computer's automatic configuration will not suit your needs. To run certain programs, you will have to remove some lines from these two files and get rid of a few device drivers and special equipment that your computer loads on automatically. A piece of software with special needs will require that you make some alterations before you can run the program. Some need lots of memory. Some programs might not like your memory manager. Some older programs,

Before you copy your alternate config.sys and autoexec.bat files onto a floppy disk, it must be formatted as a system disk. You might remember that to format a floppy disk, you simply type

format a:

and follow the on-screen instructions. To format a disk as a bootable system disk, simply type

format a: /s

and follow the on-screen instructions. Now it will be "bootable."

especially those from Europe, are not compatible with SmartDrive, which is a standard disk cache program. Rather than undo these important startup files on your computer, **you can make new versions of your autoexec.bat and config.sys files.** Your computer cannot have two autoexec.bat or two config.sys files on it at the same time. Nope, unfortunately, you can't just switch back and forth. These alternate versions of your startup files **need to be put on a floppy disk**. Once those two files are on a floppy disk, put that disk in drive A: and reboot your computer. Your computer, by the way, will always look for startup files *in drive A: first*…and that's what a boot disk is, an alternate set of

**Any changes you make in your autoexec.bat and config.sys files won't be in effect until you restart (reboot) your computer.**

startup files that you can reboot your computer with. If your computer sees a boot disk in drive A:, it will **ignore the regular autoexec.bat and config.sys which is on drive C:,** and get going according to the set of directions on your boot disk. A special boot disk can make your system compatible with that particularly fussy piece of software.

**Complete boot disk instructions can be found  at the end of Chapter 10.**

When you turn me on or reboot me, I first check in my A: drive to see if there is a "boot disk" for me to start from. If not, then I'll use the regular startup files on C:\.

After you have "booted up" using the floppy disk, you may remove it, if you wish. The way your computer runs will reflect the configuration changes you effected by starting up with that disk.

# FREEING UP MORE CONVENTIONAL MEMORY

## PRODUCTS YOU CAN BUY THAT WILL GIVE YOU MORE LOWER MEMORY

Making a boot disk is only one way to free up more memory for those big, resource-hungry programs that we all like so much these days. But there is another way around the 640K barrier that makes it hard to run these programs. There exists this under-utilized region of **upper memory,** and with clever programming, you may coax your computer to use it. This "upper memory area" is normally set aside by the DOS operating system to serve purposes that are not that important anymore, such as using a black-and-white or four-color monitor or accommodating various kinds of keyboards that really aren't used these days. Of course, the only people daring enough to seriously tinker with putting these startup files in upper memory were experts, guys who spent every waking moment fine-tuning their machines with obsessive enthusiasm. Allocating upper memory is a shell game using complicated "addresses" and "pages" and region indicators. I have neither the time or the patience for such trial-and-error experimenting. What we normal people can do is buy a product that wades through that complicated monkey business for us. You see, your autoexec.bat and config.sys files are a series of precise orders: "First load the video driver. Now recognize and acknowledge the hard drives. Now load the mouse driver." What "magically" restores more lower memory to your computer is the clever way that these automatic "memory managers" can find "upper memory areas" to stuff your device drivers in, such as your mouse, your CD-ROM, disk cache programs, and so on.

Automatic memory managers you can buy at the store, such as QEMM and 386MAX, will give you extra memory for your programs. Please note that an "automatic memory manager" is not the same as your HIMEM.SYS and EMM386.EXE files. These two files referenced in your **config.sys** are memory managers that tell your computer to make upper memory and RAM available for your programs, but they do not change your startup files to give you more lower memory, which is what QEMM, MEMMAKER, 386MAX, and NETROOM all do. All these clever programs are worthwhile and sometimes necessary, but the results are far from perfect. Some of your favorite programs might also make use of this unused upper memory area, and when they try to access it, if they find your memory manager already using the area, your program could freeze up. Also, not all programs are compatible with the way these memory managers provide extra memory. **You may find that, even though you're running a program like QEMM on your computer, you still have to resort to a boot disk occasionally.** Windows programs are especially fussy about usage of upper memory blocks. I have found that I cannot always run Windows with my memory manager on my computer, and must have a "clean" boot disk on hand, one without an automatic memory manager on it, in order to work reliably in Windows. Happily, Windows can run with as little as 500K free lower memory, so the marriage does work.

## DOS 6.0 COMES WITH ITS OWN AUTOMATIC MEMORY MANAGER

Users of DOS versions 6.0 and higher will be happy to learn that their operating system comes with an adequate memory manager, called Memmaker. Not surprisingly, in order to activate it, all you must do is type **memmaker** at the DOS prompt, and the program will guide you along the way. Memmaker is not as imaginative and clever about how it places your programs. After running it, you might find yourself a few K short. When you use Memmaker, you'll find that the program keeps asking you to watch your screen carefully for error messages. Indeed, Memmaker depends greatly on you, the user, to halt the process if things go wrong. (In Chapter 7, we'll discuss renaming your startup files to keep them safe.) Although Memmaker comes with an Undo option, there's always the problem of "What happens if my computer 'hangs in loading' before I can select 'Undo'?" This does happen, so keep that boot disk handy. **QEMM** is considered by many people, including myself, to be the best memory manager. Also, the software industry as a whole is very familiar with QEMM, and most companies strive to write software that will work with it. I've found QEMM to be very thorough in selecting the best configuration for my system.

Please see the diagram describing your computer's memory at the end of this chapter. A picture helps to clarify things.

# WHAT ARE THESE VARIOUS COMMANDS IN YOUR AUTOEXEC.BAT FILE?

## "PROMPT=$P$G" AND WHY YOU WANT IT IN YOUR AUTOEXEC.BAT FILE

Did you notice the line **prompt=$p$g** (or something similar) in your autoexec.bat file? Having the command line **prompt=$p$g** in your autoexec.bat file tells your prompt to always reflect your current directory location. Your "prompt" may look like this: **C:\**. By now you've noticed that when you type CD\DOS, your computer screen probably shows this: **C:\DOS**. If you did not have the command prompt=$p$g in your autoexec.bat file, then when you logged on to a directory, perhaps **CD\MECC**, your prompt would still read **C:\** on your computer screen. It would not show that you had logged on to the **MECC** directory. Your computer screen wouldn't have this on it: **C:\MECC**. Even though you were indeed logged on to the **MECC** directory, your prompt would not reflect that fact. This can lead to much confusion. So just be aware that **prompt=$p$g** ought to be in your autoexec.bat file.

## WHAT'S "ECHO OFF" AND WHY IS IT IN MY STARTUP FILES?

ECHO OFF means "Don't type the contents of this file on the screen." Your auto-exec.bat is a batch file, and including the "echo off" command in any batch file means that when that batch file runs, you will not see the words of that file typed on the screen. I never use "echo off," because if I made a mistake when I created a batch file, I want to be able to see what I wrote, and hopefully, recognize my mistake when I see it typed on the screen. Putting the command **cs** (clear screen) in a batch file has the same effect as ECHO OFF. Putting **cs** at the beginning of a batch file means: "When this file is run, keep the screen clear of the words that I'm typing."

## SETTING UP AND CHANGING YOUR SMARTDRIVE CACHE

To understand SmartDrive and "disk cache software," we need to briefly discuss the difference between retrieving information from your hard drive and accessing data from RAM. First of all, **your hard drive is a physical, moving part**. Data is physically stored on this big metal circle, and it will spin 'round and 'round mechanically in search of the data you requested. However, **RAM is an electronic microchip**. There are no mechanical, moving parts involved. Searching for data stored "in RAM" is a lightning-speed process. Obviously, a program that can predict what you are going to ask for next, and then, keep that information available in RAM will save you lots of time. SmartDrive is such a program. SmartDrive can speed up your computer's performance greatly, and can be installed simply by typing **smartdrv** at the DOS prompt. In fact, SmartDrive might already be running on your computer. Check your **autoexec.bat** file, and look for the line that says C:\DOS\SMARTDRV. (Something similar might be in your **config.sys** instead.) SmartDrive takes advantage of the fact that a large portion of your computing day is actually spent doing repeated tasks, such as saving and opening files, editing documents, or "walking from room to room" in a computer game. SmartDrive will "remember" those tasks you have recently performed and keep that information available to you as a temporary RAM file. Getting data back from RAM is much faster than having to search your hard drive for that same information over and over again. **All "disk cache" programs, big or small, cheap or expensive, are applying this same concept: "Let's take advantage of the fact that reaching back into RAM for information is much faster than searching a hard drive."** The difference between the various disk cache software packages on the market is how clever they are in predicting what you might do next. But SmartDrive is fine. SmartDrive is included with your DOS and Windows disks, and thus, it costs you no extra money. Why not use it?

## LOW MEMORY MESSAGES:
## SMARTDRIVE IS GREAT,
## BUT IT USES RAM—DON'T LET IT USE TOO MUCH

There is a line in your **autoexec.bat** file (or it may be in **config.sys**) that permits you to allocate how much RAM you want SmartDrive to use for its disk cache activities. Remember that many other programs on your computer also use RAM, so you should not allocate too much memory to SmartDrive, or some programs, especially Windows-based programs, will report "low memory" error messages. The top diagram on the next page shows a typical SmartDrive configuration. Note that the SmartDrive command should appear after the **himem.sys** and **emm386.exe** commands. Please remember that any extra spaces or forward-slashes where there should be back-slashes will make the commands not work.

The first number after the command **smartdrv.sys** tells the computer that *while in DOS* you want to allocate 2,048K of RAM for SmartDrive.

Knowing that Windows sessions require much more available RAM than DOS programs do, you may include this second number, as shown in the diagram, which allocates only 512K bytes of RAM for SmartDrive while running Windows. So remember: For SmartDrive, the first number is how much RAM is allocated for SmartDrive while in DOS, the second number is for Windows. So, to review, knowing how to edit your SmartDrive line can help get rid of those pesky "low memory" warnings. If a program reports that it needs more memory to run, simply open your **autoexec.bat** file (or your **config.sys** file), locate the line that includes your Smart-Drive command, and **reduce** the number of bytes used by SmartDrive. Remember, the *more* RAM you set aside, or allocate for SmartDrive, the *less* you have available for other programs to use. SmartDrive does not run your programs. It merely helps them run a little perkier. Understanding this concept will help you fine-tune Smart-Drive to your needs. Please see the following two diagrams and your DOS manual for more detailed information on editing your SmartDrive command line.

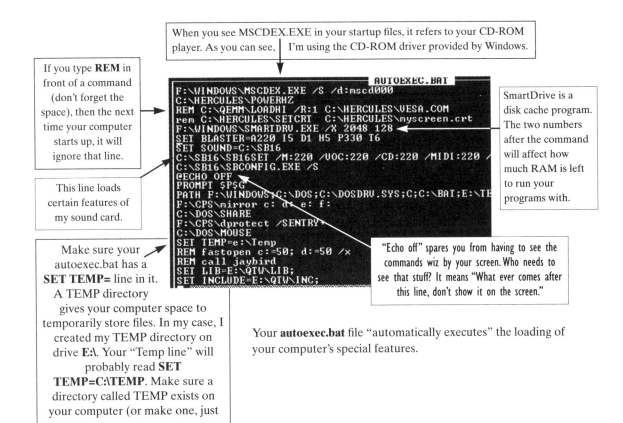

When you see MSCDEX.EXE in your startup files, it refers to your CD-ROM player. As you can see, I'm using the CD-ROM driver provided by Windows.

If you type **REM** in front of a command (don't forget the space), then the next time your computer starts up, it will ignore that line.

SmartDrive is a disk cache program. The two numbers after the command will affect how much RAM is left to run your programs with.

This line loads certain features of my sound card.

"Echo off" spares you from having to see the commands wiz by your screen. Who needs to see that stuff? It means "What ever comes after this line, don't show it on the screen."

Make sure your autoexec.bat has a **SET TEMP=** line in it. A TEMP directory gives your computer space to temporarily store files. In my case, I created my TEMP directory on drive **E:\**. Your "Temp line" will probably read **SET TEMP=C:\TEMP**. Make sure a directory called TEMP exists on your computer (or make one, just

Your **autoexec.bat** file "automatically executes" the loading of your computer's special features.

```
                                          AUTOEXEC.BAT
F:\WINDOWS\MSCDEX.EXE /S /d:mscd000
C:\HERCULES\POWERHZ
REM C:\QEMM\LOADHI /R:1 C:\HERCULES\VESA.COM
rem C:\HERCULES\SETCRT  C:\HERCULES\myscreen.crt
F:\WINDOWS\SMARTDRV.EXE /X 2048 128
SET BLASTER=A220 I5 D1 H5 P330 T6
SET SOUND=C:\SB16
C:\SB16\SB16SET /M:220 /VOC:220 /CD:220 /MIDI:220 /
C:\SB16\SBCONFIG.EXE /S
@ECHO OFF
PROMPT $P$G
PATH F:\WINDOWS;C:\DOS;C:\DOSDRV.SYS;C;C:\BAT;E:\TE
F:\CPS\mirror c: d: e: f:
C:\DOS\SHARE
F:\CPS\dprotect /SENTRY
C:\DOS\MOUSE
SET TEMP=e:\Temp
REM fastopen c:=50; d:=50 /x
REM call jaybird
SET LIB=E:\QTW\LIB;
SET INCLUDE=E:\QTW\INC;
```

These two files are very important to running Windows and configuring RAM so that your computer can use it.

All those numbers in my CDPLAY line affect how my CD-ROM player loads and functions. The "X" at the end of the line tells my computer to load the CD-ROM player in "upper memory," which is an absolute must if I want any lower memory left for my programs.

```
     File   Edit   Search   Options
                                     CONFIG.SYS
DEVICE=A:\himem.sys
DEVICE=A:\EMM386.EXE RAM on
BUFFERS=30,0
FILES=50
dos=high,UMB
LASTDRIVE=M
FCBS=1,0
device=C:\DOS\SETVER.EXE
device=C:\DOSDRV.SYS C: D: E: F:
device=C:\CDPLAY\SB563.SYS /D:MSCD000 /P:230 /M:48 /X
stacks=9,256
break=on
dos=HigH
SHELL=C:\DOS\COMMAND.COM C:\DOS\ /p
rem device=sndbk12.sys 1 5
device=F:\WINDOWS\IFSHLP.SYS
```

Your **config.sys** file loads devices in an exact order. Sometimes the order itself makes a difference to your computer

MEMORY ISSUES

1. Conventional memory
2. Upper memory
3. The RAM chips that you buy that everybody seems to want more of.

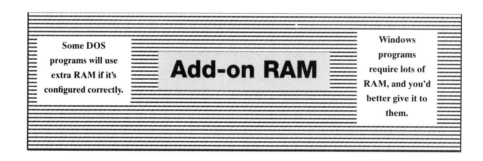

Some DOS programs will use extra RAM if it's configured correctly.

**Add-on RAM**

Windows programs require lots of RAM, and you'd better give it to them.

Memory managers move devices and drivers out of "conventional memory" (lower memory) and find room for them in unused "upper memory blocks."

Windows also uses upper memory blocks, and therefore, Windows programs will often behave badly if you use a memory manager.

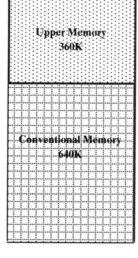

Upper Memory
360K

Conventional Memory
640K

**Many DOS programs need 570K or more of conventional memory or they won't work at all.**

**Windows programs work just fine with very little conventional memory. It's RAM that they care about.**

DOS Memory Usage

Windows Memory Usage

# SmartDrive

If you have 4MB of RAM or less, Your SmartDrive allocation should probably be 1,024 256. The first number allocates memory for DOS, the second number allocates memory for Windows.

SmartDrive will improve the performance of many programs, both DOS- and Windows-based. But let's say your computer has 4MB of RAM. You've bought a program that wants 4MB of RAM. Fair enough, you say. BUT you've allocated 2,048K (2MB) to SmartDrive. That leaves only 2MB left, so your new program won't start.

How much memory for SmartDrive for DOS programs?

How much memory for SmartDrive for Windows programs?

```
File                              tions          AUTOEXEC.BAT
SET PCTOOLS=f:\cps\data
F:\WINDOWS\MSCDEX.EXE /0   :mscd0
C:\HERCULES\POWERHZ
F:\WINDOWS\SMARTDRV.EXE /X 2048 128
SET BLASTER=A220 I5 D1 H5 P330 T6
SET SOUND=C:\SB16
C:\SB16\SB16SET /M:220 /UOC:220 /CD:220 /MIDI:22
C:\SB16\SBCONFIG.EXE /S
```

# Chapter 4

# WHAT DOES WINDOWS DO?

The software industry treats each new version of Microsoft Windows either as a messianic event or as some unfulfilled promise. But what does Windows do? Why does the computer industry make such a fuss over it? The five-sentence answer is this:

- Windows allows you copy information of all kinds—video clips, music, pictures, and text—and share that information with any other Windows-based program.

- Windows allows you to start any program with the click of a mouse, rather than by typing a long string of letters and numbers, as in DOS.

- Windows can display very high quality graphic images, and can take full advantage of a video card's capability of transmitting up to 16 million colors to your screen.

**Russian icon**

Control Panel

**Windows icon**

- Even if you are using one of the low-cost desktop publishers, the Windows printing environment still allows you to create a good looking document.

- Windows provides a standardized programming environment, making it possible for a person who knows very little computer programming to come up with some nifty (and even profitable) programs for all to use and enjoy.

> To learn how to install Windows programs, see the diagrams at the end of this chapter.

**There you have it. If you simply must know more, read on.**

# THE BRIGHT SIDE

Windows gives IBM-compatible computers a taste of that wonderful "graphic interface environment" that Macintosh users have always taken for granted. No elongated and cryptic commands to type. No computer syntax to remember. Windows turns your computer work area into groups of pictures of small labeled boxes. Just point and click on one of the boxes, called "icons," and it will open into a window containing your favorite computer programs, all organized in categories that make sense to you. You may design or re-design your program groupings to your heart's content. They exist for you and are designed by you, and can be made to look very cute.

In Windows, you are freed from hunting and pecking through directories and files. Your workspace is arranged as a "desktop," where you arrange the appearance of your program groups, and decide which programs you want the groups to contain.

**A Windows icon can represent a program or a document (or file) within a program.** Windows is fun and convenient because you may have many programs open at once, and share information between them. For example, a picture designed in the Windows **Paint** program can be exported and used to spice up a paper you wrote in Windows **Write**. **You may keep both Paint and Write open at the same time**, and the changes and editing you do in one program will be visible in the other program as well. Pretty nifty, huh?

This means you can share information between an encyclopedia article, for example, and a term paper. Rather than formally exiting the encyclopedia program, then opening the program that contains your term paper, you can have them both open at once, and zip back and forth between them with the click of a mouse. If you are working on a project in need of a drawing or picture, you can keep your project open while you browse through libraries of clip art or photos to import into your other program. For example suppose you are playing a computer game about Mars, and want to quickly jump out of the game and get some useful information about Mars. You don't have to stop your fun by closing the game down, opening your source of information, then finally opening the game program again. In Windows, simply

1. "Minimize" your game window, which turns it into a tiny box on your screen, but does not close the game.

2. Now open the information source, find what you'd like to know, then either minimize or close your information source.

3. Next, click on your minimized game icon, and you're back in the game again.

Also, the information you glean from one program can be permanently stored or utilized by other Windows programs. For example, a video clip, such as a slice of a political documentary, can be copied from your source and "pasted" into your own multimedia slide show. Music, sounds of all types, artwork, and written text can be passed back and forth freely from program to program. Most often, the working

Every Windows-based program has a "minus sign" (–) in the upper-left corner. Clicking on it gives you the option of leaving that program without closing it. You may **minimize** the current program (see the diagram next to me) or select **Switch To**, which lets you move on to any other *open* Windows program on your system. Remember that the program you left behind is NOT closed. Double-clicking on a minimized program, such as the ones to my right, will instantly restore the program to the way it was before you left to go do something else.

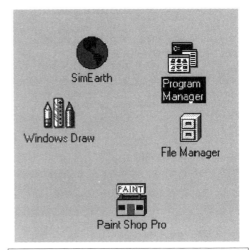

The five programs pictured here are open but **minimized**. *The amount of available RAM limits how many programs you can keep open at one time.*

environment you set up for Windows on your computer will be available to ALL of your Windows programs. The best desktop publishing software runs through Windows, and takes advantage of your Windows system's printing capabilities. Documents printed in a Windows environment can look magazine publishable. Multimedia encyclopedia and learning programs will all take advantage of your Windows video driver, which has more capabilities than its DOS counterpart. And your sound card can perform more tricks through Windows than are generally available in DOS.

## IF, AND YET, BUT, AND HOWEVER

All this flexibility and information sharing comes at a price. You see, although Windows makes your computer LOOK like a million bucks, Windows is a shell on top of DOS. This means that Windows "plugs in" on top of DOS, attempting to behave as though IT (Windows) is in charge of your computer. But in reality DOS is still your computer's operating system, and Windows is an *attractive widget* sitting where you can see it. The shell, Windows, tries and tries to work with DOS, but the glitches and hang-ups you encounter still leave you with the feeling that you are building a

It's Bernard. Long time no see. You can move any **program icon**, like *DOS Prompt*, for example, to any other group. It need not stay in the group it came with. Move and arrange! Move and *rearrange*! What could be more fun?

house of cards on the deck of a moving ship. Windows programs can produce near-magical results. The graphics are beautiful. Your printed work will look ten times better than just about anything you could do in a DOS-based program. But after having your session abruptly ended by some technical error, you get the feeling that the programmers are too smart by half, and have tried to provide you with many features that the system can barely support.

And because Windows sits on top of DOS, you will notice that **programs in Windows run slower than DOS programs, simply because anything you do in Windows has to be recognizable to both Windows and DOS**. In a Windows computing session, every action you take must jump through two hoops, instead of one. Windows programs tend to "freeze up" and incur "general protection errors," especially when you attempt to do anything the least bit fancy, like keeping two or three graphic files open at once. Windows can take you and your computer to some very interesting places, but it may be a bumpy ride.

**While working in any program in Windows, the rule is to save your work often.** One never knows when your computer screen will suddenly read, "General protection error. Please close all programs, exit Windows, and try again."

Windows programs are often very elaborate and multifeatured, providing you with so many tools for so many jobs that you may find yourself in over your head.

# WHAT'S DIFFERENT ABOUT WINDOWS 3.1?

Microsoft **Windows 3.1** was introduced to the public with a fresh promise that DOS programs could now run easily in Windows, eliminating the need to "go out to DOS" at all. If this promise proved true, then your whole computing day would be a pleasant series of mouse clicks. No more typing commands. At hearing this, all the PC users who wished they had Macintosh computers sighed like rescued maidens in distress. Windows 3.1 did bring us new tools for allocating enough **startup memory** to each individual DOS program. Before Windows 3.1, all DOS programs had to make do with the same allotment of memory. Please read the chapter on Program Information Files (PIFs) in your Windows 3.1 handbook for a description of how to run DOS programs in Windows.

### TWO FACTS O' LIFE I'VE FOUND TRUE

- Any DOS program that uses your sound card at all, that plays music or talks, will not run well in Windows. The program might work for a while, but sooner or later, it will freeze up and make you reboot your computer.

- DOS programs that run in Windows will go slower. That's because Windows is still open in the background, hogging the lion's share of your computer's resources, while you've taken a trip out to DOS to run one of your DOS programs. Since most educational software uses some sort of speech or music component (and since we hate slow programs), my family has pretty much given up running DOS programs in Windows. We at Winslow Manor still have to eat our broccoli and type our DOS commands.

## IMPROVE WINDOWS'S PERFORMANCE: KEEPING YOUR DRIVERS CURRENT

The most advanced and revolutionary Windows software in the world is only going to be as good as the hardware and other software it has to work with: Your printer, your video card, and your sound card dictate an awful lot of what reaches your eyes and ears through your computer. Even the newest and coolest programs must make peace with the drivers that run your Windows system. It's up to you to "update the drivers" on your computer. (A "driver" is a program that tells your computer how to use something, like a mouse or printer.)

Happily, the companies that manufacture sound cards, printers, and video cards are usually willing to update their software and send it to you. They are hoping that if their products run reliably on your computer, you might not rush out and buy "The Other" brand. So once you go out of your way to buy one of these peripherals, you will most often receive the updated drivers free in the mail, or be invited to download them free via modem. Keeping your drivers current is not a bad idea. Let these guys tinker and get out the program bugs. That's what they're paid for. But when it comes time to update the video, printer, and sound card drivers that already exist on your Windows system, there are a few steps to remember.

### TO UPDATE YOUR VIDEO CARD DRIVER

1. Stay in DOS, but enter the Windows directory by typing **cd\windows**.

2. Type the word **setup**.

To install a new video driver *while in DOS*, log on to your Windows directory and type the word **setup**. Select **Options**, and choose **Change System Settings**.

New video drivers are installed from Windows Setup.

Click on **Display**, scroll down to the bottom, and select **(Other display. Requires disk from OEM)**.

| Windows Setup |
| --- |
| **Options   Help** |

| | |
| --- | --- |
| Display: | Hercules Dynamite - 640x480 256 col. |
| Keyboard: | Enhanced 101 or 102 key US and Non US |
| Mouse: | Microsoft, or IBM PS/2 |
| Network: | No Network Installed |

Insert the disk with the updated driver in drive A:, *or* type in the correct path, perhaps **C:\drivers**.

The Windows Control Panel. Boy, does fun stuff sure happen here!

Unlike your printer and video display drivers, changing your sound card drivers requires removing the old ones first. Get help if you're not sure how to do this.

To change your Windows sound card driver, open the Main group, click on Control Panel, and select Drivers.

| Control Panel |
| --- |
| **Settings   Help** |

Color   Fonts   Ports   Mouse   Desktop   K

Printers   International   Date/Time   Sound Mapper   MIDI Mapper   E

Drivers   Fax   Sound

Installs, removes, and configures drivers

From the **Control Panel,** you can
1) **Alter your swap file**
2) **Remove or add fonts**
3) **Change printers**
4) **Add or remove video and sound drivers**
5) **Change the way Windows runs, looks, and sounds on your computer**

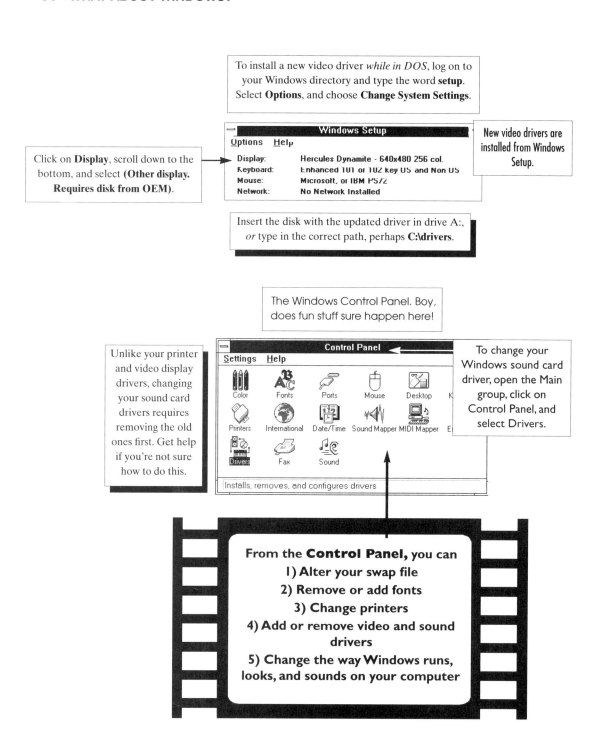

3. Select the section **Video Display Driver**. Scroll down, down, down, through your options until you reach one that says **Updated driver disk required from manufacturer**. Select this option.

4. You will be prompted to place the updated video driver disk in **drive A**. Do so. Don't go get a cup of coffee yet because you might be prompted to insert one or two of your original Windows disks as well. (If you downloaded the new video driver from your modem, simply direct "Windows setup" to the right location on your hard disk to find the new files.) Please keep in mind that the drivers will still have the same names. The only thing different you will notice after you close the operation is that your computer zips along a little faster, and perhaps with a bit more stability. Some games you buy will demand specifically that you have the most recent and updated video driver on your system, and some particularly mammoth productions go so far as to send newer drivers along with the program, knowing that if the video driver runs more smoothly, their product looks better on your screen.

## TO UPDATE YOUR PRINTER DRIVER

1. From the **Main** group, select **Control Panel.** Once inside Control Panel, select **Printers**.

2. Look for the option **Add**. Select it, and again, scroll down until your reach the selection **Updated disk required from manufacturer**.

3. Click on **Updated disk required from manufacturer**. You will be prompted to provide the new driver disk in drive A. Do so, press **Enter** after you insert the disk, and very quickly, you'll be done.

Again, you might not notice much difference, but newer
printer drivers can affect the overall quality and speed of output.
It's worth spending a few minutes to make sure you're running
with the newest and bluest.

## TO UPDATE YOUR SOUND CARD DRIVERS

**Sound cards** are often the most temperamental Windows component, forever freezing your computer or cheerfully throwing you out to DOS just because another device was already using some upper memory block that your sound card hoped to claim for its very own. Boom. You're out. General Protection Error. Reboot that computer. You can minimize this frustration by making sure you are running with the latest drivers provided by your sound card's manufacturer. Get 'em off of the bulletin board, or wait for the overworked office staff to get around to mailing the disk to you. Here's what you do:

■ Open the Control Panel like you did with the printer, but now select the icon labeled **Drivers**.

You'll see a box of unfamiliar names that you may scroll through and wonder if you should even be touching any of these. You're right to be cautious. Most of this stuff you'll never need to fondle directly, but the nasty trick with loading updated sound card drivers on your system is that **the old ones have to be taken off first**. I'm not going to tell you which ones to take off because subtle differences in wording can lead to removing the wrong drivers and to long, fitful evenings loading and reloading and holding your breath waiting for some reassuring noise to come out of your speakers. **Read the README file that came with the drivers.** It will spell out which drivers to remove and which to add. If you are at all confused about which drivers to remove first, don't do anything yet. Get on the phone with someone who'll talk you through it.

**That's it for updating your three main Windows drivers.**

I made the mistake of looking bored, so now I have to tell you about important programs in your Main group. There's **File Manager**, where you can view, copy, and move all your files in "tree" form. There's your **Control Panel**, which is where you can change the settings of your drivers, desktop, and so on. Don't forget **Print Manager**, which helps you sequence and arrange your printed documents. Your **DOS Prompt** is here, which lets you open and use a DOS program without exiting Windows. I'd tell you more, but Blockbuster has a sale on

# UNDERSTANDING YOUR TEMP FILE AND YOUR SWAP FILE

When you set up Windows to run on your computer, Windows will also set up for itself locations to store temporary data of all kinds. For example, when you edit a painting or a document, Windows actually sets aside room for both the edited and the unedited version of your artwork. When you print a term paper, Windows must have available a temporary space to store large amounts of data needed for your final output. Much of what Windows does while you work in your programs is pass information back and forth between these temporary storage areas, showing you what you have indicated you wish to see at the moment, and keeping the rest in the background, should you change your capricious little mind and revert your project to the way it looked before. What you need to remember is that Windows needs room. Boy, does Windows need room!

## YOUR TEMP FILE

At the DOS prompt, type

```
cd\temp
```

and you will be in an empty directory. You probably do not remember making a directory called temp. If you can't find the temp directory, type

```
cd\dos\temp
```

Whoever configured your computer might have set up your temp directory as a subdirectory of DOS. It doesn't matters where it is, but many programs—especially Windows programs—need a designated area to conduct this background shadow play of managing your files. Windows will use your **temp file** the way that you would use the back part of your desk, tossing an unneeded piece of paper in the background, until you decide you're ready to look at it. When you install a program, the setup files are temporarily stored in your temp directory until they can be fully expanded into their new home on your hard drive. Your temp file is important to you, and there are three things you need to know about it.

- You define your temp directory in your **autoexec.bat** file. If you type the line

  ```
  temp=c:\temp
  ```

  in your **autoexec.bat** file, you have told your computer to conduct all its "temp" work there. Both your DOS and your Windows programs will now know to use **c:\temp** as part of their operating environment.

- **Put your temp directory on your fastest available drive.** If you have two hard drives, and one of them is larger than the other, be assured that the larger drive is also faster, and you should edit your autoexec.bat file to place your temp directory on that larger, faster drive.

- Set your temp directory on the drive that is the least cluttered and the least fragmented. Many Windows programs require *contiguous* disk space in the temp file in order to function well. Contiguous means that your temp directory area must hang together as **one big chunk of hard drive space,** and not be spread out all over your hard drive. When you type **dir** in any directory, all the files scroll by neatly as one unit, but the files found in one directory are not necessarily grouped together on your hard drive. The only way to ensure contiguous space for your temp file is to run your defrag program regularly (see Chapter 9) and resist the temptation to load lots of new games or programs on the the same drive as your temp directory, if you have the option. **Make sure the drive that contains your temp directory is not filled to the brim.** If you use Windows frequently, try to keep your hard drive 20% free. Windows likes room to breath.

## YOUR WINDOWS SWAP FILE

One of the chief new features of Windows 3.1 is the ability to make Windows believe that you have more RAM than you really do. This sleight of hand has many great benefits. It's quite a nuisance to have to work around "Out of Memory" messages all the time. Some Windows programs would just not be usable if we were still limited by the amount of actual RAM we had on our systems.

Enter the Windows *swap file.* The benefit of a swap file is also known as running Windows in **Enhanced Mode**, as opposed to Standard Mode. It is also referred to as Windows Virtual Memory. Here's how it works.

♦ When you set up Windows 3.1 on your computer, it grabs up to one-half of your available hard disk space and sets it aside as its Windows **temporary swap file.** Windows does this without telling you. A temporary swap file means that, when Windows is running on your computer, this hard drive space is used as if it were RAM. If you have 4MB of RAM, and an 8MB temporary swap file, Windows will behave as if you had 12MB of RAM at your disposal. Since this swap file is temporary, the disk space will be returned to you when you exit Windows.

♦ Temporary swap files are not the best thing. Windows will run more reliably with a **permanent swap file**. When you first set up Windows on your computer, it will seek out a chunk of hard drive space that is **not fragmented**, but all clumped together without breaks. If such space is available, Windows might just go ahead and dub this space as its permanent swap file. Windows will run faster and more reliably with a permanent swap file. Since Windows is taking that space away from you permanently, you will get a message on your screen asking your kind and honorable permission to do so. Here are the issues involved:

⇒ A permanent swap file will run faster and create less problems for your Windows sessions than a temporary swap file will because Windows always knows where the permanent swap files is; a temporary one must be recon-structed every time you open Windows. You may always change the size of your swap file. To make sure your swap file is permanent,

1. From **Control Panel**, select **Enhanced**.
2. Once inside the Enhanced dialog box, select **Virtual Memory**.
3. From inside Virtual Memory, select **Change Settings**.
4. Move down to **New Swapfile Settings**.
5. Under **Type**, select **Permanent**.
6. The size ought to be twice as much RAM as you have on your com-puter. If you have 4MB of RAM, select an 8MB swap file.
7. Your Windows sessions will now run as if you have 12MB of RAM available.

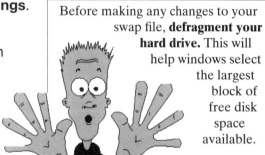

Before making any changes to your swap file, **defragment your hard drive.** This will help windows select the largest block of free disk space available.

♦ The other important issue is that **Windows almost always grabs too much space for its swap file**. Step right up and demand that it take less. Unless you are editing huge graphic files or insist on having several large documents open at once, the biggest swap file you'll ever really use is 6 to 10MB of hard drive space.

# WINDOWS WARNINGS

If your Windows sessions are plagued by freeze-ups, crashes,and other situations that cause you to have to reboot your computer and start over, there are two very common Windows trouble areas for you to investigate:

**First, find out if some device or program is eating up your free memory and system resources.**

∅ If your **screen driver is running at a resolution of higher than 256 colors** (8-bit), you could experience erratic Windows behavior. Higher screen resolu-tions are not needed except during those times you are doing precise editing of graphics.

∅ Is your screen covered with, say, **more than 30 icons visible at once**? Avoid plastering your screen with dozens of Windows icons. See if you can close some of those groups so Windows doesn't have to display so many objects at once.

∅ Do you have **more than 150 fonts on your system**? Too many fonts will make Windows operate slowly and deplete system resources.

∅ Do you have **colorful wallpaper running most of the time**? If Windows is going slow or behaving poorly, ditch the wallpaper. (Behind all your Windows icons and program groups is a panel, or wall, of light color. You can replace that simple color with photos, artwork, or special effects. These interesting backgrounds are called *wallpaper.* Check out **Desktop** in your **Control Panel** to see the wallpapers Windows provides.) Conducting your work-a-day computing tasks as well as displaying all those colors on your screen might be too big a job for Windows to carry out.

∅ Do you have **icons that talk or sing**? For example, every time you open a program, do you hear the Little Mermaid chewing out her father about something? Ditch it. Making Windows run out and access your sound card just to hear

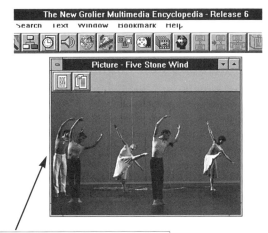

A picture gleaned from Grolier's **Encyclopedia** can be pasted into a paper you are writing. (*The source of your photos must be properly credited.*)

An essay, *The History of Ballet* (composed with Windows **Write**)

The Bolshoi Ballet, the principal BALLET company of Moscow, takes its name from the city's Bolshoi (or large) Theater, as distinct from its MALY (or small) THEATER, which has its own ballet company.

## WHAT IS "DRAG AND DROP"?

The joy of Macintosh computers is that you never have to type commands. If you want to print something, just click on a picture of the document you want to print, drag it to the little picture (icon) of a printer, then release the mouse to drop the document on the printer. Your printer begins humming, and all is well. Some Windows functions are "drag and drop," such as the ability to drag program item icons into groups, and within file manager, dragging files to the new directory of your choice. Most Desktop Program Manager replacement programs increase Windows's drag and drop capabilities.

little Ariel sing for a moment will interfere with the work you are really trying to do on your computer.

∅ Have you recently **allotted more RAM to SmartDrive**? While making some programs go faster, allotting extra RAM to SmartDrive makes less RAM available for your regular Windows programs. If Windows has not been acting quite right since you made that last change to your system, consider changing it back.

∅ Also, as mentioned elsewhere, **Desktop Managers** that make your life more convenient in some aspects, perhaps allowing you to start your programs with a single mouse click, or increasing your drag and drop capabilities…well, these wonderful programs use memory and system resources, making less available to the programs you are trying to work with.

∅ Have you loaded on a new program recently that set itself up as **"running in the background"**? Spell check and grammar check programs tend to do that. Don't let them. If a program gives you the option between "always on top" (which means the program will always be running when Windows is open), or "standard Windows behavior" (which means it won't be open until you open it), select "standard Windows behavior." It's better to configure your desktop to have quick access to any program you might want to open, rather than keeping even a small program open all the time.

∅ And finally, as previously mentioned, if your **hard drive is getting close to full**, Windows will protest in odd, unpredictable ways, or, most often, just move terribly, terribly slowly.

**The second major area of Windows trouble to investigate is device conflict.**

■ Your sound card and one of your new programs might be trying to grab the same "memory address" at the same time, and your screen will freeze, or you will get a general protection error message. Mouse drivers that let you configure the second and third mouse button for special uses are frequent offenders in this regard. Screen drivers are the worst. I have a very fast video adapter, but unless I run Windows in a very streamlined fashion it causes general protection errors. If I add any of the Windows doodads and extras that I've described elsewhere, my Windows session goes very poorly. In general, remember that Windows runs better with as few TSRs as possible.

Chapter 10 of this book thoroughly discusses
troubleshooting your computer.
This, my friend, is merely a warm-up.

# USING TASK MANAGER

## WHY IS THIS TAKING ALL DAY? TIPS FOR SPEEDY WINDOWS

### Spending Money on a Desktop Manager
### vs.
### Just Hitting Ctrl+Esc

There are a number of desktop managers on the market that make your Windows setup more convenient, letting you access all of your favorite programs with a single mouse click, letting you drag and drop files on a particular program so that that program opens with that file already running. Some of these make your Windows opening screen look more like a Mac, turning your screen into a neatly labeled display of folders. Some desktop managers will automatically update the "look" of your desktop every time you add a new file. You won't have to create an icon for that new drawing or document or spreadsheet; these programs will make one automatically, and place it where other similar documents are.

Trouble is, besides using up system resources, as I've previously mentioned, Desktop Managers are not universally compatible with all popular software. Some of your programs might not work right, and it will take hours of trial and error to track down the offending culprit. This is a real-life scenario. It happens all the time. Desktop Managers will probably work just fine for you if you use Windows for a small set of familiar programs. Desktop Managers help you whiz around Windows, and they help you see the logic of keeping several programs open for your editing ease.

But some of these tricks are available to Windows users without having to purchase an additional Desktop Manager.

- **Creative resizing** of groups and screen placement can give you visual access to almost all of your Windows programs with very little scrolling. By using the scroll bars, you can view almost all the Windows programs on your system with very little maneuvering.

- You need not buy an alternate Desktop Manager to whiz around between various Windows applications. At any time, you may press the keys **Ctrl+Esc**, calling up the Task Manager. **Task Manager permits you to open any new program without closing the program you are working on**, or without even minimizing the program you are working on. Task

'CAUSE I'M THE TASKMAN!

Manager can also get you back to any program you have running in the background and make it active, front and center, and full screen. Task Manager also allows you to select a small piece of a document, cut it or copy it to the Windows Clipboard, then press Ctrl+Esc, leaving that program for the time being, and use the material you've selected in any other Windows program. See the section below, "Search, Sweep, and Save," for more on how to navigate through Windows using Task Manager.

■ Put your DOS program icon in a familiar group of programs that you use often, and you can easily switch to a DOS program and back again. When you switch to DOS from Windows, read the directions on your screen to learn how you can run your DOS program in its own window alongside other Windows programs, easily working two or three operations at a time.

■ At any time, from Program Manager, you can select Tile Windows, and all of your open applications will be resized to fit together on your screen.

All of the above are all standard Windows features that you don't have to pay an additional penny for. And remember, when you've resized your program groups and positioned them to your exact liking, select **Options** from the Main group screen menu bar. From there, select **Save Settings on Exit,** and next time you open Windows, your setup will be just as you left it.

### TO BYPASS YOUR STARTUP GROUP, PRESS SHIFT

That's right. It's that simple. Many people create an elaborate startup group that automatically loads when Windows starts. It includes tools and programs they think they will find useful for all their Windows sessions: perhaps a clock, pictures of Christie Brinkley winking down on them while they work, a calculator in the corner of the screen, and so on. Sometimes, when you want to get to work quickly, loading all this bric-a-brac can be time consuming. Lots of startup doodads decreases memory available to run your main programs as well. You can bypass yesterday's creativity, and tell Windows not to load your startup group, simply by **pressing Shift as Windows loads**.

## SEARCH, SWEEP, AND SAVE

Here is a wonderful tip for utilizing and saving the information you glean from just about any Windows program. If you are reading text from a multimedia encyclopedia, Encarta or Grolier's for example, or browsing through some large, boring document that is bound to offer one or two promising paragraphs, Windows has a quick text saving program called Notepad. Notepad is a small, unobtrusive program that you can easily keep running in the background, bringing it forward long enough to drop off little bits of text that you find interesting enough to save and look at later. Using this resource is great for children. It teaches them to identify the important segments of information in a document, zeroing in on what they need in order to complete an assignment. **The trick is not to keep closing and opening your source documents over and over again, but merely switch back and forth, using Ctrl+Esc, cutting and pasting and saving what you need.** Here's how you do it.

1. After finding a swatch of text that you'd like to save, go to **Edit** on your menu bar, and cut or copy the text. The text is stored in the Windows Clipboard, which makes it available to other Windows programs just by selecting Paste when you are in the new program.

## Cut, Copy, and Paste

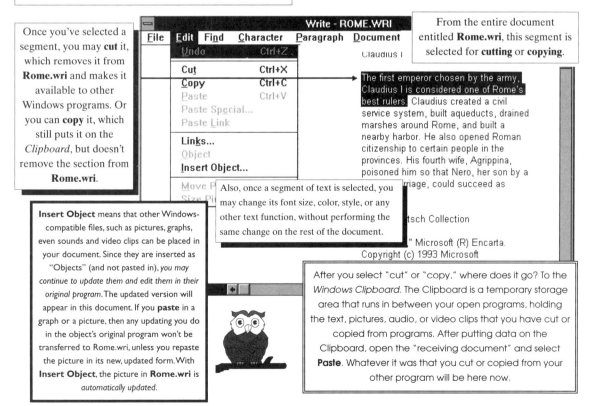

Once you've selected a segment, you may **cut** it, which removes it from **Rome.wri** and makes it available to other Windows programs. Or you can **copy** it, which still puts it on the *Clipboard*, but doesn't remove the section from **Rome.wri**.

From the entire document entitled **Rome.wri**, this segment is selected for **cutting** or **copying**.

The first emperor chosen by the army, Claudius I is considered one of Rome's best rulers. Claudius created a civil service system, built aqueducts, drained marshes around Rome, and built a nearby harbor. He also opened Roman citizenship to certain people in the provinces. His fourth wife, Agrippina, poisoned him so that Nero, her son by a marriage, could succeed as

Also, once a segment of text is selected, you may change its font size, color, style, or any other text function, without performing the same change on the rest of the document.

**Insert Object** means that other Windows-compatible files, such as pictures, graphs, even sounds and video clips can be placed in your document. Since they are inserted as "Objects" (and not pasted in), *you may continue to update them and edit them in their original program.* The updated version will appear in this document. If you **paste** in a graph or a picture, then any updating you do in the object's original program won't be transferred to Rome.wri, unless you repaste the picture in its new, updated form. With **Insert Object**, the picture in **Rome.wri** is *automatically updated.*

After you select "cut" or "copy," where does it go? To the *Windows Clipboard.* The Clipboard is a temporary storage area that runs in between your open programs, holding the text, pictures, audio, or video clips that you have cut or copied from programs. After putting data on the Clipboard, open the "receiving document" and select **Paste**. Whatever it was that you cut or copied from your other program will be here now.

2. Next, press Ctrl+Esc. This brings up Windows **Task Manager.** Task Manager allows you to open other windows programs **while you keep your current program running**. Go to **Program Manager**, and open **Notepad**. (You may use Write, or your favorite word processor or desktop publishing program, rather than Notepad.)

3. Pull down **Edit**, and then select **Paste**. The new information is copied to Notepad or your word processor for future reference. In the meantime, back to the source program for further research. Keep your new Notepad document open in case you find more information to use for your own work.

Remember to **occasionally save the destination document that you've been copying to**. If Windows freezes up while you are having fun cutting and pasting, any work you have not saved will be lost. It happens, believe me.

## DELETING WINDOWS PROGRAMS

### UNINSTALLER AND WINDELETE: YOU CAN'T GO HOME AGAIN

There exist at least two programs that will aid you in the thorny process of deleting Windows programs off of your hard drive. As explained earlier, when you install Windows programs, they often take the liberty of dropping their own versions of drivers and system files all throughout your Windows directory. **Just because you've erased the directory of the program does not mean that you've erased every trace of the program.** Programs like Uninstaller and Windelete aim to do that for you. Both of these programs search your Windows directory and subdirectories for orphaned files that look like they could have something to do with the program you've just eliminated. If this process sounds a bit risky, it is. You could easily end up deleting a file vitally important to your system. For this reason, Uninstaller lets you "test run" your system after you've deleted a file. If your computer acts funny, you can bring back the deleted file with a single mouse click. But even with a program like Uninstaller to help, removing Windows applications from your computer is a hit-or-miss process. If you've installed an "updated version" of a program, and wish to only delete the older version, Windelete and Uninstaller can't always distinguish between the new and old versions, and will remove files important to your updated product, not just the old one you wanted to nuke.

Another disappointment comes with the realization that Windows programs don't merely add files, they also update commonly used drivers and data files, making them more to their liking. Many programs drop their own versions of files like **mmplayer.ddl**, which is a file used by many multimedia programs. It's very common to have one program eliminate the old **mmplayer.dll**, replace it with its new "updated" driver, and all the sudden, some of your other programs that used the older version will start exhibiting bad behavior. Uninstaller cannot do a darned thing about this. It's up to you to snoop around, **compare the size and date of new and old versions of these commonly used files**, and follow the advice of Chapter 10 of this book, which is to save your old "ini" files before adding a new Windows program to your system.

## REG.DAT: "KILROY WAS HERE"

The bloat continues. There's a file in your Windows system directory called **reg.dat**. This file is like legalized graffiti for your computer. Every new Windows program you add leaves its mark there. A program uses this file to tell Windows what makes it tick and what it needs to run and work properly. This file, like the markings on a wall on the bad side of town, gets more confused and messy the more scribbling that is done in it. Bad behavior can result when **reg.dat** gets too big, and neither Uninstaller nor Windelete can restore this file to its earlier, more manageable state.

**The important message here is to avoid loading too many Windows programs on your system.** As more cool Windows software becomes available, people often fill up their hard drive with programs they never use. Stick with the most worthwhile software and avoid tinkering with the rest.

## YOU WANT TO EXIT WINDOWS?

Sometimes the fastest way "out" is to use the keyboard:

1. **Press Alt+F4**. This closes all active programs and after hitting it once or twice, you'll see the message "This will end your Windows session." Click on **OK** to exit.

2. If Alt+F4 doesn't work, press **Ctrl+Esc**. This switches you to Windows **Task Manager**. From the list of open programs, select **Program Manager**. This returns you to the Windows main screen, from which you should be able to use Alt+F4 to exit Windows.

Using a semicolon (;), you can leave yourself a note.

You can also use the semicolon to disable lines that you suspect might be causing you problems.

**Notepad - SYSTEM.YE2**

File    Edit    Search    Help

```
;this one works great before wordstar july 12, 1994 has two good groups
[boot]
mouse.drv=mouse.drv
drivers=mmsystem.dll mmmixe
;;drivers=mmsystem.dll
386grabber=v7vga.3gr
oemfonts.fon=vgaoem.fon
fixedfon.fon=vgafix.fon
fonts.fon=vgasys.fon
display.drv=vga4aht.drv
shell=progman.exe
network.drv=
```

In your **system.ini** file, putting a semicolon before a line causes Windows to ignore that line. I put a note to myself that "this system.ini" worked *before* I added WordStar. That information could prove to be helpful. To use this file, I would only have to rename it **system.ini**.

# WINDOWS DIAGNOSTIC SOFTWARE

I'M A DOCTOR, JIM, NOT A MIRACLE WORKER.
—*Dr. McCoy, "Star Trek"*

These three programs I describe (and yes, there are others) will tell you how well Windows is running on your computer. They will "examine" your system, and make some suggestions, perhaps directing you to add a line or two to your system.ini file or your config.sys file. Central Point's **PC Tools** will even make the recommended change for you, and then undo the change if Windows acts funny after the change was made. Lanmark's **Winprobe** provides a little widget called "Optimize Memory." Click on a button, and some of the RAM that was not properly returned to you when you exited a particular Windows program will now be yours again. Norton's **Diagnostics** is the best, the king of diagnostic software, and will be reviewed in Chapter 9 more thoroughly.

Let me, however, save you a little money. Most of the advice you are going to coax out of these programs will look something like this:

1. Use a permanent swap file rather than a temporary one.

2. Defragment your hard drive frequently.

3. Open your **system.ini** file to the line that reads DMA=16. Change that number to 64 or higher.

4. If you are sure you do not use extended memory with your programs, add the line "noems" to the emm.386.exe line of your config.sys file. Do not do this unless you are 100 percent sure you will not need extended memory.

5. In your **config.sys** file, there is a line that reads buffers=30 (as low as 10, as high as 40). Reduce this number to 15 (buffers=15) if you are sure that none of your programs need the higher buffers. If you are not sure of this, then leave the line alone.

6. In your **config.sys** file, there's a line that reads stacks=(some number). Make that line read stacks=9,256

Unfortunately, many of the problems that drive people to buy Windows diagnostic software are intermittent. The problem doesn't happen all the time. The diagnostic software **cannot detect it as an existing problem at this exact moment**, and thus, the new diagnostic software you spent $40 or $50 for will not report the problem at all. The errors that will drive you to mayhem and murder are the type that happen only when various programs are running, device conflicts or memory address errors that are not predictable. Perhaps every once in a while, without warning, your sound card or video card will complain and cheerfully end your session just like that. Out to DOS. The black screen treatment. Diagnostic software cannot predict: "I see a sound card on DMA=1 that will sometimes argue with your video driver while Aldus PhotoStyler is running." This is hard and frustrating territory and no piece of software is going to figure it out for you. Sorry.

## CAVALRY TRUMPETS, PLEASE

However, at the time of this writing, future versions of Windows are in the works, and are said to greatly reduce device conflict and the occurrence of general protections errors while Windows is running. Hope springs eternal. The following diagrams will enlighten where words have failed. Enjoy.

# Memory and System Resources

1) From the main Windows screen, click on **Help** on the menu bar.
2) From the bottom of the list of options, select **About Program Manger**.
3) The two lines at the bottom of the text box list your available *memory* and *system resources.*

---

**About Program Manager**

Program Manager

[ OK ]

MICROSOFT. WINDOWS.

Microsoft Windows for Workgroups
Version 3.11
Copyright © 1985-1993 Microsoft Corporation

---

This product is licensed to:
**Larisa And Trevor Steward**
**Computer Learning Center**
**Product Number:**          02326-100-0 8257

---

**Memory:**                      22,163 KB Free
**System Resources:**      73% Free

---

If you are using Windows 3.1 or higher, this number will be greater than just your available RAM. Windows 3.1 in *Enhanced Mode* will set aside some of your computer's empty disk space and treat it as if it were RAM. This is called a **swap file**, and you may alter it by selecting **Main**, then **Control Panel**, and then **386 enhanced**.

During the course of your Windows session, *system resources* are used. Unlike memory, you don't get them all back when you close a program. **Letting this number fall below 50% can cause Windows to behave badly.** The higher this number is when you begin your Windows session, the smoother your session will run.

If you are going to be using Windows for any work that is the least bit complex, graphics-intensive, with lots of audio, or projects that require keeping many programs open while you edit documents elsewhere, then AVOID Windows doodads like screensavers, wallpaper that changes images every so often, talking icons, and fancy desktop managers. All these devices eat into your system resources. Icons that belch like Fred Flintstone or reason like Spock when you click on them are accessing your sound card. If they do this at the same time that your computer is trying to do something like back up a document, then your computer could freeze up, and you could lose any work not yet saved.

Here's a list of things that will reduce your available system resources:
1) Programs that replace your Windows desktop and make it into something more convenient
2) Too many fonts
3) Too many icons
4) Video modes above 256 colors
5) Screen savers

# Hey, I installed my new multimedia encyclopedia, and when I run the program, I can't hear any sound.
## *What happened?*

As I install myself on your computer, I find that the files

**msacm.drv**

and

**msadpcm.acm**

are already on your system. So I won't install my versions of those files.

If you find that your program has no sound, that's probably because I did not install MY VERSION of those files.

To force me to install my version of those two crucial files, you will have to

1) Log on to the **c:\windows\system** directory.

2) Type **del msacm.drv**, then type **del msadpcm.acm**.

3) Now reinstall my program from scratch. ➡

Windows-based multimedia programs all need certain multimedia drivers to be on your system, or they won't work. Most of these programs come packed with the necessary drivers on the CD-ROM itself.

Problems arise when a program decides not to update the drivers already on your system because they have the same name as the CD-ROM's drivers. However, your drivers could be older, newer, or otherwise incompatible with the new program.

**This time,** I won't see other versions of those two files, and I'll go ahead and install my versions from my CD-ROM. If my versions of those files are newer, they will probably work with your other programs as well, and you need not worry about these drivers any longer.

WELL, THEN, WHAT'S A MOTHER TO DO?

When you install a new Windows multimedia program and the program doesn't run,

1) *Log on to the CD itself,* and look for files that end with the file extension **.dll, .drv,** or **.acm**.

2) Note the sizes and dates of those files.

3) Now log on to to your windows\system directory, and see if files by those names are already there.

(Yes, windows\system is a huge directory. Use the file-searching techniques we discussed in Chapter 7, or you'll go blind before the day is done.)

If you find that those files already are in your windows\system directory, and that they have different dates and sizes than the corresponding files found on your new CD-ROM program, then perhaps your new multimedia program did not install its version of those files because files of the same name were already there. Just delete those files (saving them in a different directory first) and re-install the whole program from the CD.

**You come home from the store with a new Windows program. How do you install it on your computer?**

## FILE
Select **File** from Program Manager.

## RUN
From File, select **Run.**

## BROWSE
Log onto **drive A:,** or if the new software is a CD-ROM product, **log on to your CD-ROM drive**. You're looking for an .exe file called **setup.exe**. To find this file, click on **Browse**.

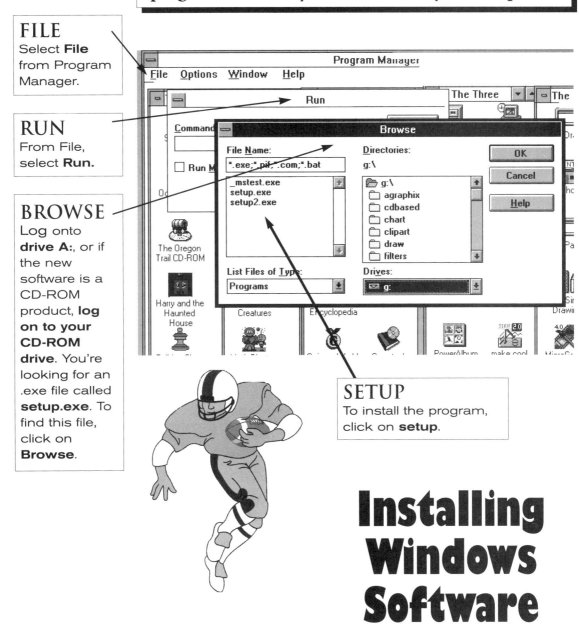

## SETUP
To install the program, click on **setup**.

# Installing Windows Software

# Chapter 5

# READ THE BOX FIRST!

## Will Your System Support
## the Software You Want To Buy?

**HOW TO FIGURE OUT YOUR
COMPUTER'S VITAL STATISTICS**

**MEMORY ISSUES**

**MEMORY CACHE**

**MISCELLANEOUS "BEFORE YOU
BUY" CONSIDERATIONS**

## ...BEFORE YOU BUY THAT PROGRAM...

■ Any program that uses lots of digital photographs, "movie" segments, video clips, "digitalized actors," or long segments of digitalized speech is going to require a faster computer to run well. If you buy one of these programs and your computer is slower than a 486/33, you will probably be spending lots of time waiting for video data to load, and waiting for your computer to process the digitalized speech. This can be frustrating.

■ Slower computers, such as 386/33, will reproduce "audio soundtrack" music just fine, and will not keep you waiting too long. But these slower systems get overtaxed when they are asked to load several kinds of data at once, such as is likely to occur in an adventure game, where "digitialized actors" walk across the screen and speak, all while music is playing. These complex actions can cause long pauses in the game play.

■ Multimedia encyclopedias will run slow on a 386/33 computer, even one with a double-speed CD-ROM, but not slow to the point of being unusable. If you look up "Taj Mahal" for example, you might have to wait 20 seconds, rather than five. This might not sound like such a major frustration, but if you are planning to zip around the encyclopedia, comparing information on various entries, you'll probably notice yourself and your kids getting a bit antsy.

■ Programs that are largely cartoon-based will run fine on slower computers. Just about anything by The Learning Company, MECC, Broderbund, Davidson, and some of Sierra On-Line's eductional titles will do well on older computers. Taken together, these companies put out some of the best learning software available, but think twice about buying that high-tech photo-realistic stuff.

■ Just about any popular Windows educational title for children will run very slowly on a 386 computer—slow enough to prompt a young chiled to begin wondering what TV show she's missing right about now.

■ When browsing the shelves looking for software you might want to buy, don't let the box artwork immediately turn you off. Many software companies operate under the premise that 14- through 17-year-old boys are the only substantial buyers of computer games. With that in mind, the box will emphasize arcade violence and bodacious babes, when, in reality, the product itself has something to do with teaching trigonometry. Read the label carefully. There might be a good learning game buried in there somewhere.

*Any piece of software you might want to buy will have the product's hardware requirements written on it. This information will answer the question: "WILL IT WORK FOR ME?"*

*IT'S NOT ENOUGH TO BUY THE PROGRAM. YOU HAVE TO INSTALL IT WHEN YOU GET HOME.*

## HOW TO FIGURE OUT YOUR COMPUTER'S VITAL STATISTICS

**The software box says. . .**

#### ♦ Requires MS-DOS 5.0 or better. Do I have that?

If you purchased your computer any time since 1989, you almost certainly are running with DOS 5.0 or better. Your computer's documentation also has that information. But why not go to the source? Sitting at your computer, type the word **ver** at the DOS prompt (press Enter, of course), and your computer will report what version of DOS you are running.

#### ♦ 3.5" high-density disks? Why does that matter?

Older computers came with the capacity to only use "double-density disks." Double-density disks can only hold 720K of data, whereas high-density disks can hold 1.44MB. If your computer was manufactured since 1992, you probably don't have to worry about this. All newer computers have high-density drives, which can use both high-density and double-density disks. Check your computer's documentation if you are not sure about the kind of floppy drive you have.

#### ♦ What do you mean "VGA" or "SVGA"?

VGA stands for Video Graphics Array. It represents your computer's ability to transmit high numbers of colors to your screen. Not so long ago, when air was clean and only eggheads had computers, many computers for sale on the market could display only black and white, or perhaps as many as four colors. But before too long, it became possible to buy a computer that could display 16 colors on your monitor, a veritable feast for the eyes. Software programmers no longer had to be content with second-rate artwork and barely recognizable stick-figures populating their computer games. Why, with 16 colors, you could take over the world!

That was then, this is now. Today, you probably couldn't buy a home computer system that displays less than 256 colors on your monitor. **Most of the best educational software will only run on systems that support 256 colors.** If you purchased your system new any time since 1992, your computer almost certainly supports 256 color displays, which will give you access to almost any program you wish to buy.

RUG RATS FROM MARS!

Requires 386/33hrz or better, VGA or better, SVGA required for hi-res mode, 100% Microsoft compatible mouse, 578K conventional memory, 4 megs of RAM, AdLib, Sound Blaster, or Pro Audio compatible sound card. CD-ROM version requires double-speed CD-ROM drive.

Your computer's color display is determined by your video card (and as I said, video cards that display 256 colors are standard on today's systems), but to be able to display 256 clear colors in Windows, and to be able to display 256 colors in high resolution, you'll need an SVGA card, and a monitor capable of displaying colors in the SVGA (Super Video Graphics Array) mode. Once again, if you purchased a new system any time since 1992, your computer probably has SVGA capabilities. Running in SVGA means that images on your screen will be less "grainy," more clear and distinct, especially in Windows, where color capabilities extend up to 65,000 or even 16 million colors. Unless you are doing fine artwork on your computer, or reproducing magazine-quality photographs along with written text, having 65,000-color or 16 million-color capability is of no concern to you. But many Windows programs require your computer to **run in SVGA mode with 256 colors**. Before purchasing a software title that "requires SVGA," check your computer's documentation to make sure that both your video card and your monitor have SVGA capabilities.

To transmit 256 colors or more, my screen has to be VGA or SVGA. Most software out today requires

Most computer software you're likely to buy these days will detect the type and quality of video card you have, and install the program so as to take advantage of your system's higher

## DOS CALLS IT "INSTALL," WINDOWS CALLS IT "SETUP"

When you buy a game and bring it home from the store, there's one general rule about how to get it going on your computer: DOS programs will ask for the first disk and require you to type the word **install**. Windows programs, on the other hand, require that you enter Windows before you install them. From Windows program manager screen, select **File**, then scroll down to **Run**. With the first disk inserted into drive A:, type in the command **a:\setup**, and Windows will begin loading your game.

To install a DOS game, insert the disk in drive A: and most commonly, you would simply type the word **install**. The install program will prompt you for each disk, and after the files are on your computer, *the install program will probably ask you questions about your sound card.* What kind do you have? How is it configured? Please see the section later in this chapter about sound card configuration.

capabilities. Unless you delve into the netherworld of using professional quality art programs in Windows, you will hopefully never have to monkey with your video driver. Occasionally though, a particular piece of DOS software will fail to recognize your video card. This problem is usually fixed by typing a couple of extra letters that will "force" both program and video card to behave nicely together. The exact wording you type will be explained in the manuals that come with the program. Also, you may find solace and help in time of need by reading Chapter 10 of this book, which contains extensive troubleshooting tips. Chapters 4 and 9 also discuss video drivers.

♦ **The box says I need an eight-bit video card. Do I have one?**

An 8-bit video card is any card that will produce 256 colors. See the above section about VGA and SVGA.

♦ **The box says it supports popular sound cards like AdLib, Sound Blaster & 100% compatible, Pro Audio Spectrum, Gravis Ultrasound. Which one of those do I have, if any?**

The software box will list the popular brands of sound cards that their product will run on. If your computer has a sound card, then the music, narration, and sound effects that came with the program will play through your computer, and out your speakers. If you do not have a sound card, then your computer will attempt to play the program's soundtrack as a series of blips and beeps.

Regardless of what kind of sound card you have, it helps to know that **almost all the sound cards on the market will "emulate" the most popular kinds of cards.** In other words, even if you don't have a Sound Blaster or an AdLib card, your sound card will more than likely run as if it were one of those two popular kinds of cards. For this reason, if you are not sure of the sound card you have, you can

1. Select Sound Blaster Pro from the list of possible sound card selections. If your game freezes up or does not produce sound,

2. Rerun the sound card selection process, and select Sound Blaster (not Sound Blaster Pro, just regular Sound Blaster). If that doesn't work,

3. Run the sound setup program again and select AdLib, and then Thunderboard. If that doesn't work,

4. Call the company that manufactured your sound card. If your computer came with a sound card, then call the company that manufactured your computer. Their technical support line can help you make the right selection. Also, for further help see the section near the end of this chapter entitled "Playing Cards."

## LOADING YOUR DOS SVGA DRIVER

Your **video card** is a circuit board inside your computer. You for sure have one: No video card means no images. Occasionally when installing DOS-based software, you'll be given the option to run the program "in SVGA mode" (sometimes called "high-resolution mode"). In this mode, on-screen colors look a bit sharper for those **DOS** programs that have high-resolution capabilities.

If your computer was manufactured in 1992 or later, you can probably install your SVGA driver (a "driver" is a small program that tells your computer how to use something, like a mouse or printer) by pressing a few keys on your computer. First, check your computer's documentation to find out the name of your video card. Then, at the DOS prompt, enter **vesa** (or the name of your video card file, it it's different). Does your monitor read **VESA program 1.2 is now loaded** or something similar? If so, your SVGA driver is loaded and will stay loaded until you reboot your computer.

If your monitor reads **bad command or file name** instead, you must search for the directory that contains your SVGA program. Using the skills outlined in Chapter 7, you'll need to look for the video card file. (Perhaps it's called vesa.exe or vvesa.exe. It may also be called vesa.com.) When you find the file, log on to its directory and enter the file name (minus the .exe or .com extension.

♦ **This CD-ROM game says I need CD-ROM Microsoft extensions version 2.0 or later. How can I be sure I have that?**

Remember quadriphonic sound? The music system that was destined to replace stereo? Music came at you from four distinct sound sources. Imagine the possibilities! Well, quadriphonic sound never took off because the big companies couldn't agree on a universal format to implement the new technology.

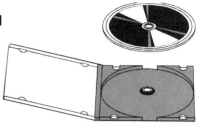

CD-ROM issues are covered more extensively in Chapters 2 and 9.

To prevent the same sort of incompatibility from crippling the CD-ROM industry, all home computer systems that run on MS-DOS will carry on nicely with all DOS-based CD-ROM software sold in the stores today. Please note that the phrase "CD-ROM extensions" does not refer to a cable or adapter that you need for your CD-ROM player. "CD-ROM extensions" are a set of files loaded through your **auto-exec.bat** file. If your CD-ROM player boots up, then they are there. If needed, the company that made your CD-ROM player can send you a disk containing the **newest drivers** for your machine, and are on hand to help you through any set-up problems. Also, see Chapters 10 through 12 of this book for discussions on updating and installing new drivers on your computer. Please remember that even though the files in question are called "Microsoft extensions," it is not the Microsoft company that will be of help to you. Rather, the company that made the CD-ROM player itself will answer your questions and walk you through the process, if need be. Setting up new drivers for a CD-ROM player is usually a snap. Still, though, always keep your CD-ROM player's technical support number handy, as well as the tech number of the company that made the computer itself.

So remember, if your CD-ROM player boots up correctly, you can rest assured that you have the necessary CD-ROM drivers and extensions to run a CD-ROM-based game made for DOS computers. For a smooth ride, you may have to "adjust the buffers" and tinker slightly with your config.sys and autoexec.bat files. This process is covered in Chapters 3, 7, and 9 of this book. Check your CD-ROM player's manual for instructions on how to allocate more buffers and place your CD-ROM player's drivers "in upper memory." Remember, though, that your family's enjoyment of the game will be hampered by an under-powered computer. For the most part, CD-ROM products will run aggravatingly slow on anything below a 486, with a few exceptions. Most selections by the Mindscape company run well on 386 computers.

Older CD-ROM titles by The Learning Company and MECC and some of Sierra On-Line's older CD-ROM games do okay on a 386 computer.

Bored with all this? Go on to Chapter 6 to learn how to start any program on your computer by typing a few keys.

♦ **"Must have a 100% Microsoft compatible mouse." Do I?**

Don't worry, you almost certainly do. Microsoft mouse drivers are standard on almost any computer you are likely to have purchased since the late 1980s. This message, "must have 100% Microsoft compatible mouse" is concerning the mouse driver, more than the physical mouse itself. **A "driver" is the software-based "language" that the computer uses to talk to your mouse, your printer, your CD-ROM player, or any computer "peripheral device."** Since Microsoft's very own computer operating system DOS is running on most home computers in the United States, you can rest assured that your computer is directed to detect a Microsoft compatible mouse on your system. If you purchase a program and have difficulties with your mouse, please read the following segment of this chapter.

## GENERAL RODENT CARE AND MOUSEY ISSUES

Your computer has very few moving parts, and your mouse is one of them. Day in, day out, that little silver ball rolls across that pad, its belly collecting dirt and oil. Mice do break, but if you notice your mouse "sticking," meaning that when you move it, the cursor on the screen does not move smoothly, the problem is more than likely your mouse pad. This is good news. A new mouse pad costs $2 to $5. A new mouse costs 10 times that much A common practice is to rub alcohol across the mouse ball surface to clean the dirt off. But the mouse ball comes in contact with electric parts, so any liquid, including alcohol, can cause damage. Few people rush right out to the computer store just to buy a mouse. They're usually content with the one that comes with the computer system they bought. The mouse will break down. The innards will get gummy and it'll be time to buy a new one. There are several brands of mice you may choose from. The Logitech corporation makes mice that come with features such as the ability to program special tasks just by clicking the middle or right mouse button. However, these special features require that you use a mouse driver other than Microsoft's. And

*After reading this chapter, you'll know how to pick out software that will run well on your computer.*

A *mouse driver* is the device "language" that your computer uses to talk to me. Call the company that made your mouse and see if they have an *updated driver* for it.

It's time for a funny story, but it wasn't funny at the time. One day, in a fit of careless maneuvering, Mr. Mouse went crashing to the floor. The mouse was in my capable hands at the time, so I couldn't even blame my kids for it. We picked it up off the ground, dusted it off, and got back to the game we were playing on the computer.

The cursor wouldn't move. It was frozen on the screen. We clicked the left mouse button, the right mouse button. We checked the connection, we tried everything. Finally, we rebooted the computer. And the screen reads: "Microsoft mouse not found. No mouse driver loaded." I was then sure that I broke the thing by dropping it. Stupid me. Go buy a new one. Then I looked closely on the right side of the mouse.

since software manufacturers set up their programs to run with 100% Microsoft compatible mice, your computer might act funny when you try to use these fancy features. But worry not, the mouse itself is perfectly capable of working with all your programs. *You might have to edit your computer's startup files to make your computer use the Microsoft mouse driver,* rather than the driver that loads on the fancy doodads. **If you find your mouse giving you problems, see the section "Mouse Setup" at the end of this chapter.**

## THE CHEAP RODENT OR THE EXPENSIVE ONE?

What exactly are you paying for when you buy a mouse? Generally speaking, if you pay a little bit more for a mouse, it will be more durable. The mouse you purchase largely depends on whether you are in the mood to spend $29 and be back in 6 months, or $59 and be back in a year. You may also buy a cordless mouse, which costs nearly $100. My family uses one, and we love it.

## IF YOUR LIFE IS ROSY AND NOTHING IS GOING WORNG…OR…WRONG, RATHER…

If you are not experiencing "Out of Memory" error messages when loading or running your programs, and if your sound card and mouse are not giving you problems, then you may, with much pride and gloating, skip the rest of this chapter and proceed to Chapter 4. However, problems with allocating memory are almost universal to computer users. You may, therefore, wish to at least glance at the next section.

## MEMORY ISSUES

**This section is a bit technical. But keep in mind that Chapters 5 and 10 contain more information about what to do if your computer ever gives you a "not enough memory to load program" message.**

### MEMORY AND HARD DRIVE AND RAM, OH MY!

These three terms, just like Dorothy's lions and tigers and bears, spark a good deal of fear and confusion along the road. Looking at the box of a computer program you are thinking of buying, it might say that you need at least 5MB of available hard drive. **Your hard drive stores your programs. It does not run your programs.** A large hard drive means that you can keep lots of software loaded on your computer without having to run back and find the floppy disks and load the game up from scratch. You may have a huge hard drive, but still not have enough "available memory" to run many programs.

Memory is another animal entirely. When the DOS operating system was first developed, a fateful decision was made to allow computer users a mere 640K of memory be available to run their computers with. **If your IBM-compatible computer cost you $400 or $4,000, you still only have 640K lower memory available.** There is no magic purchase or upgrade that will cleanly give us more lower memory than the DOS overlords deemed was necessary way back when. Now, back to that piece of software you're thinking of buying,

Aha!! A tiny button. A switch, really. And there, if you got out your magnifying glass, you could see the words "PC" on one side of the switch, and "MS" on the other side. The tiny, flea-sized switch was indeed bumped over the "PC" side. And when I took out a (very small) ballpoint pen and shoved the switch over the the "MS" side, and rebooted my computer, everything was fine.

What happened? Well, "PC" stands for Personal Computer, and this switch would make this mouse compatible with an older operating system, and "MS" stands for Microsoft. Not surprisingly, to make my mouse work with my computer, or just about any modern (MS-DOS-based) computer, that switch had to be pushed to the Microsoft side. And yes, when I dropped the mouse on the floor, the little switch got bumped into the wrong position. The odd thing is that the existence of this switch was not acknowledged in the manual that came with the mouse. The lack of reference is probably a result of the fact that just about everybody uses Microsoft DOS, so why should the mouse company have to mention anything else? Some things you just have to figure out for yourself. 🖱

search the label for "memory requirements." What does it say? "Must have 589K free lower memory available"? Perhaps as low as 560, or as high as 590? Ah, you say, but DOS has given us 640K, so keeping 580K available to run a program should be no problem, right? Wrong.

- ♦ Your mouse needs 14K to 17K memory in order to run.
- ♦ A CD-ROM player requires 30K to 40K.
- ♦ Disk compression software like Stacker requires 20K to 40K.
- ♦ Cache programs like Print Cache and SmartDrive want a chunk of memory for their own uses.
- ♦ Memory managers essential for running Windows, such as HIMEM.SYS and EMM386.EXE, require bits of your lower memory.
- ♦ And DOS itself requires a portion of conventional memory to run your computer's programs.

Now after these devices take their share of the action, your programs must make due with whatever is left. Often, you'll be left with a mere 540K. So, if you were to buy that piece of software and take it home to your computer, after loading it you would probably get a message that reads something like: "You need 32,875 bytes more available memory to run this program."

Well, somebody buys these big, new, memory-hungry programs. How are we supposed to use them?

## UPPER MEMORY

Every computer has at least one megabyte (one million bytes) of RAM. DOS only allows you to directly use 640K (640,000 bytes) of it, leaving 360K left over. This 360K from your "first meg" of RAM is called **upper memory**. The trick is to figure out how to put that extra 360K of memory to good use. That's what *automated memory managers* do.

## AUTOMATED MEMORY MANAGERS TO THE RESCUE!

Not surprisingly, an entire leg of the software industry is dedicated to getting around this 640K barrier. They are called "memory managers." These automated memory managers will search your computer's upper memory area, and run your computer's components "from up there," thus leaving you more lower memory available for your fun software. These memory managers are real miracle-workers and will get your new software up and running. The old "You need 22,987 more bytes…" message can become a thing of the past.

## TEMPERMENTAL MIRACLE WORKERS

But these programs, such as Memmaker, which is included free with DOS 6.0, QEMM from the Quarterdeck corporation, and Qualita's 386MAX, have their glitches and drawbacks. They are miracle workers, but they throw tantrums. Please see Chapter 5 for more information on memory managers.

> Software companies will usually send you the newest version of their games for little or no extra charge.

## SO ADDED-ON RAM DOES NOT GIVE ME MORE CONVENTIONAL MEMORY?

Nope. New computer owners are often disappointed to find that the 4 or 8MB of RAM that they spent extra for does not mean that you have more lower memory available than anybody else. Some of your programs still might not start without a memory manager, since lower memory is what actually runs most programs. Still, people buy RAM for a reason. Here's the basic breakdown: Four or more megabytes of RAM is **necessary** for most Microsoft Windows-based programs. (Windows can run just fine with very little lower memory, even 490K, because it directly makes use of your system's available RAM.) Also, most good DOS-based programs will make use of your RAM, and will run smoother and faster because of it. But if you have a CD-ROM drive, use disk compression, use SmartDrive, or imbibe in any of the host of available extra goodies for your computer, you will probably have to use some sort of "automated memory manager" to start some of your favorite (or soon-to-be-favorite) programs. Chapter 3 explains these issues more thoroughly.

## IF RAM WON'T RUN MY DOS PROGRAMS, THEN WHAT GOOD IS IT?

Have you ever been given the job of stuffing 100 envelopes with a form letter, or something equally repetitious and boring? I'll bet that the first few you stuffed were quite a chore, but once you "got the system down," the rest of the stuffing went very fast. You probably figured out the best place to lay the paper and envelopes to make your hand movements more efficient. After you got used to the movements, you picked up your speed, and before long, you were done.

Guess what? Your computer can do that to. It can remember all the tasks you most recently performed on your computer and do them much faster next time. The more RAM you have, the more pronounced this advantage will be. That's why one of the uses of RAM is to create a storage area to hold your last several procedures. It will

## WHAT DO YOU MEAN, "NOT ENOUGH FREE MEMORY"?

One day, I bought a program that my kids where very excited about. It looked fun and we were looking forward to playing it. I loaded it, started it up, and the screen was black, except for one cryptic message:

"You need 6,387 more bytes free to run this program. Please provide more available memory and try again. See your DOS manual for instructions on removing TSRs to free up memory."

That was it. End of story. The kids grunted and headed for the TV room and I was left with a load of questions. What now?

What baffled me is that my computer had "lots of RAM," and that's memory, right? Therefore, I should have tons and tons of memory to run my programs. But RAM is not conventional memory. And **no matter how much RAM you have**, programs need to detect a certain amount of conventional memory before they start. Those wild, new, spellbinding programs that sound and look like feature films often need 590K to run, and if you have Doublespace, a CD-ROM player, some DOS features like Smart-Drive, undelete, and antivirus online, you might find yourself knocked down to 537 bytes free. Unfortunately, RAM does not just tack itself on to conventional memory and provide more of it. 🖳

remember the last time you saved a document, or, if you're playing one of those elaborate role-play adventures, your computer will remember, as part of the game-play, the last time you "walked into a room" and "opened a dresser," for example. RAM stores the memory of these actions, and should you repeat them, the process will not take nearly as long.

## MEMORY CACHE

RAM does this memory trick by setting up a memory "cache." A cache is a designated amount of memory that you set aside to remember the procedures you just did. If you would like to see this process in action, and you are really bored one afternoon, try opening a large document in Windows. Now save it. Repeat that two or three times and you'll see that the more you repeat that procedure, the faster your computer completes it. For a full description of cache programs like SmartDrive, please see Chapter 3.

If you purchased a DOS program (especially a graphics-intensive program) that says it will make use of your extra RAM, the screen will also probably flash warnings that you had better have your RAM configured to their particular liking (a distinction between "extended memory" and "expanded memory") or your extra RAM will do that game no good whatsoever. Happily, this distinction between "expanded memory" and "extended memory" is no longer something that software buyers themselves have to be concerned with. Divvying up your available RAM and allocating some as "extended memory" and some as "expanded memory" has thankfully become less important over time. Most memory managers will take care of this arcane distinction for you, and you never have to think about it. You actually could monkey with your **autoexec.bat** file for hours, allocating perhaps 1044K as "extended memory" and the rest as "expanded memory," and afterwards, you'll be amazed at how little difference your tinkering actually made to your computer's speed and efficiency. Unless you are running older versions of some DOS word processing or data management software, you can safely let the memory managers divvy up expanded and extended memory for you.

```
There is insufficient conventional memory to run Alien
Legacy.  570K <583,680 bytes> is required. Remove
unnecessary TSR's until enough is free
```

If you see this message on your computer screen, all the RAM in the world won't fix it. If a program wants more *conventional memory*, you'll have to make changes in your computer's startup files in order to use it.

```
You need 31,400 more bytes of free memory available to
run this game.  If you have any resident software
loaded, please remove it and try again.
Script #; 0,IP; 0
```

"Resident software" means the same thing that "TSR" does in the example above. Memory managers like QEMM, Memmaker, and 386MAX can help solve this problem.

## MANY NEWER DOS PROGRAMS ALSO WANT 4MB OF RAM

Another reason why extra RAM is a good idea is that there are some extra-greedy DOS programs coming out that are hitting you up for that 4MB of RAM right

Games that will work well even on older computers include
THE OREGON TRAIL
READER RABBIT
SIM CITY
MATH BLASTERS
CARMEN SANDIEGO
  (early versions)
MECC, Sierra On-Line, Davidson, and Broderbund make special attempts to accommodate users of older computers.

Games that require a **fast** 386 or better (**usually better**):
OUTPOST
INCREDIBLE TOONS
MULTIMEDIA
  ENCYCLOPEDIAS
TURBO SCIENCE
SIM CITY 2000
QUEST FOR GLORY 4
CARMEN SAN DIEGO
  (deluxe versions)

If installing a game from a floppy disk doesn't work, type the command `loadfix install`, rather than just install. **Loadfix** is a DOS program that helps correct floppy disk errors. You need DOS 6 or higher to use this feature.

from the start. And they not only want 4MB of RAM, they want it configured **their way**. (Chapter 3 explains how to edit your computer's startup files to accommodate various programs.) There are not too many titles that demand this extravagance yet, but if the trend continues, 4MB of RAM could end up being standard to run even DOS programs. Greedy, greedy, greedy.

## THE PROGRAM SAYS "YOU NEED 4MB OF RAM TO RUN THIS PROGRAM." BUT I HAVE 4MB OF RAM!

Your computer might be configured to set aside 1 or 2MB of RAM "for SmartDrive." SmartDrive, as mentioned above, is a memory cache program designed to speed up your computer. What you have to do is tell your computer not to set aside so much of your RAM for this SmartDrive program. Once your computer knows not to spend so much of your RAM on SmartDrive, the next time you load that RAM-hungry program, more RAM will be available for it, and it should stop complaining.

To get you out of your current fix, at the DOS prompt, type

```
edit autoexec.bat
```

Find the line that refers to SmartDrive. It ought to say something like

```
C:\DOS\SMARTDRV.EXE 2048 1048
```

Without explaining much more at the moment, change your SmartDrive line to read

```
C:\DOS\SMARTDRV.EXE 512
```

If the line reads

```
C:\WINDOWS\SMARTDRV.EXE 512
```

that is perfectly okay. If your computer's "SmartDrive line" is in your **config.sys** and not your **autoexec.bat**,

Remember that if your floppy drive only supports double-density disks, and the software you are loading comes on *high-density disks*, you cannot load the program until you write to the company and get replacement disks that are compatible with your computer's floppy drive.

simply follow the above steps, but open your **config.sys** file instead. In your config.sys file, the line would read

```
C:\DEVICE=C:\DOS\SMARTDRV.SYS 512
```

or something very similar.

# MISCELLANEOUS "BEFORE YOU BUY" CONSIDERATIONS

## GOT A TANDY?

If you own a Tandy computer (a computer purchased from Radio Shack) please be aware that Tandy computers are not 100% IBM-compatible. Tandy was the first company to jump headlong into making computers for home and family use. They believed that they could make more money for themselves by making their computers slightly different from other IBM-compatibles, and thus force Tandy users to return to Radio Shack to upgrade their hardware.

> Some of us already knew that compression software like Stacker will misreport how much space you have left. Oh, the burdens of brilliance.

Some software designed for IBM-compatibles will not work on your Tandy, but back when Tandy controlled the lion's share of the home computing market, software manufacturers would always go out of their way to design special versions of their games for Tandy computers. Now that Tandy is no longer king, many software companies don't want to waste their time doing the extra programming to accommodate Radio Shack's computers. If you own a Tandy computer, make sure the software you buy specifically says IBM/Tandy on the label. If not, jot down the phone number of the software company and see if they sell a Tandy version of the software you want.

```
     7,444 08-14-93     2:00a
    84,672 01-14-93     4:16p
    21,766 08-14-93     2:00a
>)    909,781 bytes
    59,342,848 bytes free
```

## WHAT DO YOU MEAN, I DON'T HAVE ENOUGH DISK SPACE? MY COMPUTER SAYS I HAVE TWICE THAT MUCH!

Perhaps you've discovered that if you type **dir** at the DOS prompt, the number at the bottom of your screen tells you how much disk space you have left. Using that number, you can

> If you use disk compression software like Doublespace or Stacker, the "bytes free" report that you get when you type **dir** may *no longer be accurate*. A good rule of thumb is, **the lower you are on disk space, the less accurate the number is**. If you use Doublespace or Stacker, and the "bytes free" report shows that you are low on free space, then in reality, you are *very, very low on free space*.

gauge if you have enough disk space to store a program on your hard drive. But if you are using any disk compression program like Stacker or Doublespace, the reported "free disk space" number is no longer accurate. For a more complete discussion on disk compression software, see Chapter 9.

## WHAT DO YOU MEAN, I DON'T HAVE THE "LATEST VERSION"?

As soon as a software product hits the streets, complaints start coming in. Not every computer product will be instantly compatible with every single video driver on the market, sound card, or disk cache device. So software companies respond to these problems by releasing an "upgrade," in which the guys went back to work and rewrote part of the program to make it more compatible with what everybody's running at home on their computer. Software companies somewhat depend on your feedback to tell them where the bugs (problems) are, and what aspects of the program need to be smoothed out or made more efficient. Upgrades tend to be a little faster than the earlier version and less prone to problems, and some have additional features. If you own an earlier version of the same product, the upgrade is often free or offered to you at a nominal price.

## PLAYING CARDS:
## INSTALLING AND CONFIGURING A SOUND CARD
**(You only want to bother with this section if you have tried to set up a program that you know has sound, but it didn't work for you.)**

Your computer came equipped with several "add-on" slots: long, thin spaces located near the back of your computer, only visible if you remove your computer's case. There are plenty of extras, or "peripherals" you may buy for your computer, such as a faster video card, a CD-ROM player, sound card, hard drive control card, or scanner. The extras you can buy come with "cards," long green circuit boards that fit into your computer's slots. Fortunately, there is a standard size that all these add-on products' cards adhere to, meaning that they can plug into just about any IBM-compatible computer.

Chief among these extras is your sound card, and **if you purchased your computer system any time since 1992, your computer probably has one.** Your sound card determines whether the new game you bought will produce music to move the stars or obnoxious beeps. That new piece of software your purchased may indeed play back live musical clips from the Grateful Dead and the London Symphony, but you'll never hear it without a sound card. Sound cards, once

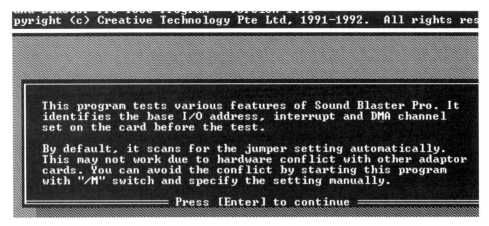

pyright (c) Creative Technology Pte Ltd, 1991-1992.   All rights res

This program tests various features of Sound Blaster Pro. It
identifies the base I/O address, interrupt and DMA channel
set on the card before the test.

By default, it scans for the jumper setting automatically.
This may not work due to hardware conflict with other adaptor
cards. You can avoid the conflict by starting this program
with "/M" switch and specify the setting manually.

Press [Enter] to continue

Hopefully, you will never have to alter your sound card's operating parameters. If your
program freezes whenever the music begins, however, you will at least have to change
its "Interrupt." This is an easy job, usually requiring a simple software adjustment. See
your sound card manual for details.

installed, produce music, speech, and sound effects through speakers, and just as
with tape and CD systems, the final sound quality largely depends on the dent the
speakers made in your personal spending account. Two decent speakers plugged
into the back of your computer through your sound card will set you up just fine. If
you purchased a Sound Blaster card, your card will be compatible with 99.9% of
all the sound-producing software made today. There are cards that sound better,
but they may not be compatible with all of your programs. As part of the setup
program that comes with the commercial software you buy at the store, you will
be prompted and guided through all the steps necessary to make your sound card
work with each program.

## CORRECTLY SETTING UP YOUR SOUND CARD

First of all, when installing a sound card, check your computer's manual to make
sure you have a "16-bit slot" available. Sound cards manufactured for 16-bit slots
work and sound better than sound cards designed for 8-bit slots. If your computer was manufactured since 1992, you almost certainly have a 16-bit slot for a
sound card.

Sound cards must be told how to work with with the other components of your
system, and be directed to the correct channels to "interrupt" other activity going
on with your computer. These interrupt numbers are clearly laid out and assigned
to each of your computer's main components. When you move your mouse, your

These three sets of numbers

**IRQ 5 (or 7)**

**DMA 1**

**HEX 220**

set the ground rules for how your sound card is going to work with your computer and not get in the way of your computer's other components, like your mouse and printer.

During your long, productive life as a software consumer, you will be asked about these numbers whenever you install software that runs from DOS on your computer. Just remember, if you have a CD-ROM player, then the settings

**IRQ 5**

**DMA 1**

**HEX 220**

will probably work for you.

If you don't have a CD-ROM player, you can use

**IRQ 7**

**DMA 1**

**HEX 220**

computer must allow for that action on your part not to interfere with other computer activity, such as your CD-ROM player sending information into a temporary file. When you print something, you are "using an interrupt," and printed information must be routed away from other component functions. Everybody gets their little interrupt number. Your sound card wants Interrupt 7, 5, or 10. Sound cards will grab channel 7 by default, and never tell you a word about it, but when your printer or CD-ROM player also makes a try for interrupt channel 7, your sound card could make your computer "freeze up." You may, without much trouble, set your sound card to Interrupt 5. The complaining should stop. These adjustments are easy, but they differ from card to card, so please refer to the manual that comes with your sound card.

Since 90% of the people who bought computers recently have Sound Blaster's sound cards, I'll talk a bit about what to do if your Sound Blaster card starts acting up. First, the symptom: If your computer "freezes," that is, the screen stays exactly the same and no matter what buttons you press, nothing changes, your sound card's interrupt setting is probably incorrect. If you also notice a musical note repeating endlessly, or a sound effect repeating forever and ever, then your sound card's setting has almost certainly gotten in harm's way.

Some programs come with a helpful "setup" or "reinstall" feature that, should your sound card begin to act temperamental, allows you to reconfigure your sound card settings without having to go find the floppy disks and start from scratch. The sound card configuration program will ask you three questions, and here is a basic rule of thumb: If you have a Sound Blaster card **and** a CD-ROM player, your sound card is probably set at Interrupt 5. So answer the three questions about your sound card's configuration as follows:

      **IRQ 5, DMA 1, and hex 220**

If you do not have a CD-ROM drive, then set up your sound card as follows:

      **IRQ 7, DMA 1, and hex 220**

To find out what your Sound Blaster card's configuration is, follow this procedure: If you have the Sound Blaster Pro card, at the DOS prompt, type

      **CD\SBPRO**

This gets you in to the directory where your sound card's files are located.

Once inside the SBPRO directory, type

      **sbtest**

and follow the on-screen instructions. After the program checks for its three operating parameters, it will tell you what you need to know about your sound card.

If you have the Sound Blaster 16 card, type

      **CD\SB16**

This gets you in to the directory where your sound card's files are located. Once inside the SB16 directory, type

      **sbconfig**

and follow the on-screen instructions.

Just as above with the Sound Blaster Pro, after three quick tests you'll be told what your card's configuration is.

---

### Hey, What's "Plug and Play"?

*Plug and Play* technology, not yet fully developed at the time of this writing, should make device setup much easier. When you install a printer or set up a CD-ROM player or sound card, for example, you won't have to be as concerned about possible device conflicts. Plug and Play will set proper DMA channels, interrupts, and port addresses.

## MOUSE SETUP

These are directions for you to add the appropriate mouse driver into your config.sys or autoexec.bat file. Directing your computer to use the most universal mouse driver (which is Microsoft's) will solve most mouse software problems.

Again, please note that just because you are having trouble using a "Microsoft compatible mouse driver" does not mean that the Microsoft Corporation can help you. It is the responsibility of the company that sold you the mouse to help you fix things.

1. First, let's make sure you have a Microsoft mouse driver on your computer. We need to quickly search your subdirectories and track down what mouse drivers you might be using. Then we'll tell your computer to start up with the Microsoft mouse system or driver, which will be found in your DOS or Windows subdirectory. So, at the DOS prompt, type

   **`dir mouse.* /s`**

   Please note that the slash in the above command is NOT the familiar "\" (backslash), which you use to change directories (as in CD\). In the above command, you are using a forward slash, which is a switch you use to modify DOS commands.

2. Your screen will list for you every kind of mouse driver on your computer. You most likely have mouse.sys in your DOS directory, and mouse.sys in your Windows directory. Given the choice, we'll direct the computer to use the driver (mouse.sys) in the Windows directory, since it's probably more up to date than your DOS version. The DOS mouse driver will work just fine, though.

3. Now we are going to edit your computer's startup files to tell your computer to run the mouse with the Microsoft mouse driver, rather than some other generic driver that might have been causing you problems. Type

   **`edit config.sys`**

   The DOS big, blue edit screen will appear, filled with the cryptic and arcane commands of your config.sys file.

4. Find the line that refers to your mouse. It will say

   **`devicehigh=mouse.sys`**

   or perhaps

   **`device=C:\DOS\mouse.com`**

or

```
devicehigh=C:\windows\mouse.sys
```

If there is no reference to a mouse in your config.sys file, then the command exists in your autoexec.bat file instead. In this case, the command line in your autoexec.bat file would read

```
mouse=C:\DOS\mouse.com
```

or something similar.

These are various kinds of ways and paths that your mouse might be set up to run on your computer. The **devicehigh** command is one way of loading your mouse into upper memory. For more information on upper memory, please see Chapter 3. For now, we want to find out which mouse driver your computer is currently using. To be sure that your computer system is indeed using a Microsoft compatible mouse driver, the line referring to your mouse (in either your autoexec.bat or config.sys file) should be directed to use the mouse driver found in the DOS directory, or the Windows directory. If the line in either your autoexec.bat or config.sys file reads something like this:

```
mouse=C:\mouse\mouse.com
```

or

```
device=C:\mouse\mouse.exe
```

your computer is starting up with some other company's mouse driver. It won't say "Logitech" or "Genius," but if your computer is loading a mouse driver from a directory other than DOS or WINDOWS, then you are using a driver that might claim to be "100% Microsoft compatible," but might not entirely be such. No, "'*tain't necessarily so*." When a new mouse is set up on your computer, at the end of the installation process, this other mouse company asked permission to "edit your autoexec.bat file" and make *their mouse driver* the driver for your system. Well, somebody said "Yes, go ahead." And now somebody's sorry. **Let's fix that, and make the Microsoft mouse driver the one used by your computer.** So edit your autoexec.bat file (or config.sys file) to direct the computer to use the driver found in DOS or Windows (which will be 100% Microsoft compatible, of course). The diagrams on the next two pages will be helpful.

**1.**

Log on to your DOS directory to see your mouse driver there.

**2.**

Once inside the DOS directory, type **dir mouse.*** to view all the files related your mouse's operation.

**3.**

MOUSE.COM is a safe and stable mouse driver for your computer to use.

**4.**

Is the "mouse line" in your autoexec.bat pointing to the mouse driver in your *DOS directory*? (See Chapter 6 for directions on how to edit this file.)

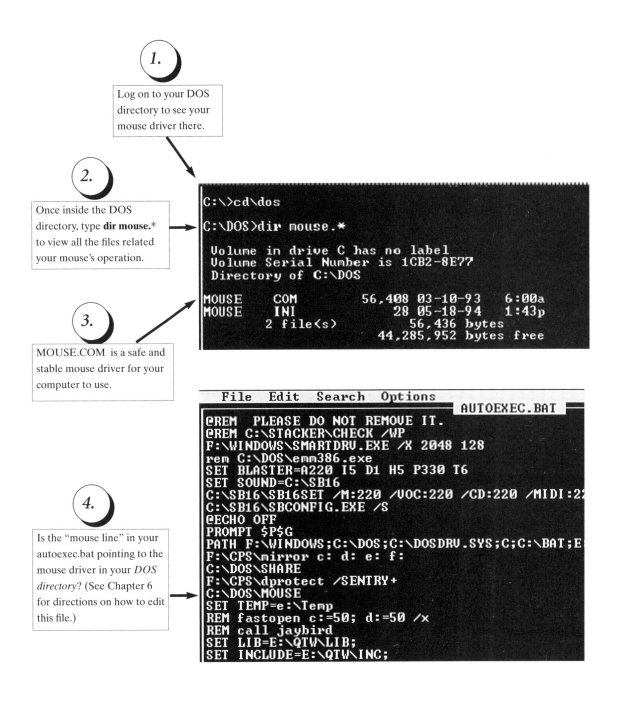

```
C:\>cd\dos

C:\DOS>dir mouse.*

 Volume in drive C has no label
 Volume Serial Number is 1CB2-8E77
 Directory of C:\DOS

MOUSE      COM        56,408 03-10-93    6:00a
MOUSE      INI            28 05-18-94    1:43p
        2 file(s)          56,436 bytes
                       44,285,952 bytes free
```

```
    File   Edit   Search   Options
                                       AUTOEXEC.BAT
@REM   PLEASE DO NOT REMOVE IT.
@REM  C:\STACKER\CHECK /WP
F:\WINDOWS\SMARTDRV.EXE /X 2048 128
rem C:\DOS\emm386.exe
SET BLASTER=A220 I5 D1 H5 P330 T6
SET SOUND=C:\SB16
C:\SB16\SB16SET /M:220 /VOC:220 /CD:220 /MIDI:22
C:\SB16\SBCONFIG.EXE /S
@ECHO OFF
PROMPT $P$G
PATH F:\WINDOWS;C:\DOS;C:\DOSDRV.SYS;C;C:\BAT;E
F:\CPS\mirror c: d: e: f:
C:\DOS\SHARE
F:\CPS\dprotect /SENTRY+
C:\DOS\MOUSE
SET TEMP=e:\Temp
REM fastopen c:=50; d:=50 /x
REM call jaybird
SET LIB=E:\QTW\LIB;
SET INCLUDE=E:\QTW\INC;
```

## BEFORE YOU BUY A NEW MOUSE, ASK YOURSELF...

Does your computer require a round (PS/2) port? ───────

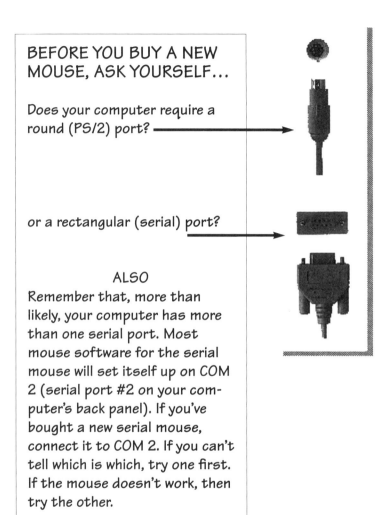

or a rectangular (serial) port? ───────

### ALSO

Remember that, more than likely, your computer has more than one serial port. Most mouse software for the serial mouse will set itself up on COM 2 (serial port #2 on your computer's back panel). If you've bought a new serial mouse, connect it to COM 2. If you can't tell which is which, try one first. If the mouse doesn't work, then try the other.

# *Chapter 6*

# CAN THE KIDS HANDLE IT ON THEIR OWN? YES!

# OPEN ANY OF YOUR PROGRAMS WITH A FEW KEYSTROKES

## HOW TO LAUNCH PROGRAMS

The way you launch a program on your computer is to type the name of the program's main "executable" file. For example, to launch the program Oregon Trail, you would log on to the appropriate directory, and type the word OREGON. An executable file most often has a **.exe** extension, and software makers will make the name of the executable file very easy to remember. On some programs, the name of the main executable file could end with a **.bat** or a **.com** extension, but whatever the file extension, **the name will always resemble the name of the program itself**. To launch the game Theme Park, not surprisingly, you must type the word THEME. To launch Broderbund's Print Shop Deluxe, you must type PSD. Happily, when you install a program, you'll be told how to start it, and what you are being told is the name of that "executable file," which ought to be a simple, memorable keyword. **You never have to type the file extension (.exe). You only have to type the file's name.**

Programs, or "executable files," have a
**.com**, **.exe**, or **.bat** file extension

Tree
Undelete
Xcopy
All three are programs
we will be looking at in
this book. Because they
have the file extension
**.com**, **.exe**, or **.bat**, we
know these files are
**executable** programs
of some sort.

```
SYS          ...    9,432  09-30-93   6:20a
TREE     COM        6,945  09-30-93   6:20a
UNDELETE EXE       26,416  09-30-93   6:20a
XCOPY    EXE       16,930  09-30-93   6:20a
DEFAULT  SET        4,211  09-01-94   5:59p
DEFAULT  SAV        5,833  08-13-94   1:47a
DEFAULT  CAT           66  09-01-94   5:59p
DK40509A FUL       11,264  05-09-94  11:18p
CK40509A FUL       17,408  05-09-94  10:58p
DOSSHELL INI       16,912  05-10-94  11:03a
CD40507A FUL       37,728  05-07-94   2:15a
DD40813A FUL        5,504  08-13-94   1:46a
TEMP      <DIR>            05-11-94   5:22p
MOUSE    INI           28  05-18-94   1:43p
QBASIC   INI          132  01-12-94   4:39a
MSBACKUP INI           43  09-01-94  11:49a
DEFAULT  BAK        4,211  09-01-94   5:59p
DEFAULT  SLT        5,472  09-01-94   5:59p
CC40901A FUL        8,064  09-01-94   5:59p
MSBACKUP TMP        4,998  09-01-94   5:59p
MSBACKUP RST          224  09-01-94   6:00p
       205 file(s)      6,805,955 bytes
```

Of course, the command line to launch the program only works *within the directory that contains the program's files.* For example, if you are logged on to the Sierra directory (C:\sierra), and you type PSD, hoping to launch Print Shop Deluxe, your computer will search the Sierra directory for the program that the command PSD starts, and, not finding it, the screen will read

```
bad command or file name
```

So first, you must log onto the Print Shop Deluxe directory, by typing **cd\psd**, and then type the simple command **psd**. Your computer will search the PSD directory, and finding the command, will start your program.

♦ Problems arise when you find yourself the proud owner of dozens of pieces of software, safely nested within their own directories. Now if you or your children should commit even the smallest typing error in trying to reach your programs, the screen will read "bad command or file name." Consider the following frustrating near-misses:

```
cd\sierra\turbots
bad command or file name
cd/sierra\turbosci
bad command or file name
cd\sierra\turboci
bad command or file name
cd\sierra\turbosci
```
(Finally, the program starts)

If you are logged onto the directory for "World Atlas," and you type **psd** to try to start Print Shop Deluxe, I won't be able to find **psd.exe** because it's in a different directory.  All you'll see on your screen is
**"bad command or file name."**

I kept typing that STUPID command over and over and nothing happened.

Please note that, if you are trying to type cd BACKSLASH (cd\) and you type cd FORWARDSLASH (cd/) you might as well be typing gibberish, as far as your computer is concerned. You'll get no "online help" encouraging you: "You almost got it. Just fix that one little typo."
**Nope, all you ever get is "bad command or file name."**
Except for this sullen, cryptic, ambiguous message, the screen remains dark. Your children think to themselves, "Enough of this frustration. Back to the video games."

You weren't logged on to the right directory.

# HOW EVEN YOUNG CHILDREN CAN SAFELY START THEIR OWN PROGRAMS

Of course I never have trouble remembering that cd\ is not the same as cd/, although I understand that *certain* people do.

Before I describe the ways in which your children may run rampant on your computer and thoroughly enjoy themselves, let's talk about protecting your own data and programs from little eyes and fingers. There's a great piece of software called KidDesk, which turns your computer screen into rows of little pictures that your child may click on in order to start his or her favorite programs. When your child exits the program, he or she returns to the KidDesk desktop, and **never has access to the computer's real main screen**. Only you, by use of a password, can turn off the clowns and happy faces and access the rest of your computer. KidDesk ensures that your children can never invade your private files, or alter the computer's configuration. You set up the pictures associated with each program by searching for each program's "executable file," or command line, and associating it with a KidDesk picture.

Nonetheless, we've noticed that many of our programs do not run through KidDesk. The way that KidDesk appropriates your screen and sound drivers makes it incompatible with some software. You see, KidDesk is a shell, which means it's an

Screen from Edmark's **KidDesk,** which turns the computer screen into a desktop so kids can manage their own programs. KidDesk is a full-color program.

```
Directory of C:\SHADPRES
                <DIR>        06-30-94   7:48p
                <DIR>        06-30-94   7:48p
JMFILTRL TXT        3,033 08-25-92  11:21a
ADVISORU TXT        4,522 10-02-92   8:26a
TEXT     FIL      920,777 11-11-91  10:26a
SCENINST TXT          181 08-28-92   5:37p
ADVICE0X TXT          365 10-02-92  10:25a
SNDSETUP EXE       60,705 09-09-92   4:21p
SHADOW   EXE    1,387,551 01-19-93   5:43p
MWDB4    MAT      172,166 11-29-91   2:19p
SYSTEM08 FNT        1,890 11-09-89   5:31p
EVENT    S0            0 09-14-92   4:22p
QUEUE    S0          744 09-14-92   4:22p
TROOPS   S0        1,500 09-14-92   4:22p
TROOPS   S1        1,500 09-14-92   4:22p
ASSET    S0       30,240 09-14-92   4:22p
COUNTRY  S0       33,936 09-14-92   4:22p
MISC     S0          409 10-30-92   5:14p
FALLFLAG S0          336 09-14-92   4:22p
Press any key to continue . . .
```

Files from the game **Shadow President.** The **.exe** file SHADOW.EXE starts the game. The **.exe** file SNDSETUP.EXE makes the game compatible with your sound card.

```
C:\TLC\SSA>dir

Volume in drive C has no label
Volume Serial Number is 1CB2-8E77
Directory of C:\TLC\SSA

                <DIR>        05-11-94   5:21p
                <DIR>        05-11-94   5:21p
SSA001   DAT      360,674 05-03-93  11:46a
SSA000   DAT      228,727 08-03-94   6:26p
SSAPROG  EXE       79,190 05-03-93  11:46a
CHKLIST  CPS           27 05-04-93  11:24p
CHKLIST  MS            27 01-04-94   3:44p
        7 file(s)       668,645 bytes
                     36,110,336 bytes free
```

Game files from The Learning Company's **Challenge of the Ancient Empires.** SSAPROG.EXE starts the game. The .DAT files hold the program data.

"operating environment" that sits on top of DOS (your computer's main operating system). Also, KidDesk is a TSR, which means it uses a teeny bit of your conventional memory, a commodity that is sometimes in short supply. KidDesk also creates and uses its own "swap file," which can cause your memory manager to act up and freeze your programs from time to time. My children love KidDesk, and we often use it when some of the neighborhood kids come over to play on our computer. But for regular, quick access to our programs, we had to think of something else.

## USING BATCH FILES TO LAUNCH PROGRAMS

There is a way that you can type a long and complicated command on your computer, give that ridiculously long command a title, and the next time you want to type that same command...all you have to do is type the title you gave it. What I've just described—typing something once, giving it a title, and saving it under the name of that title—is called **making a batch file**.

Batch files exist for the purpose of reducing your keystrokes. You create batch files because you do not want to have to type long sequences of keystrokes every time

> Our family uses batch files so that my kids can choose any of their programs from any directory or drive on their computer, and select it by typing any word or initials they have chosen to represent that program. This is a nice feature because you are saved from having to search through various directories and drives to find the game you want to play.

you do something on your computer. Over time, your computer becomes overgrown with software and programs; some you use all the time, and some gather dust (cyberdust, I suppose) but you lack the will to delete the old programs from your computer because they might get used again someday. So there they all are on your hard drive, taking up space. Each of these programs requires a long, typed sequence of keystrokes to start them up.

1. First, you log on to a particular directory, and next,
2. Type the command line itself.

Why should you clog your mind with all this arcane data just to start up a program? You don't have to. You can write a batch file, which contains the exact sequence of keystrokes to start up that particular program. Then you name the batch file something catchy and memorable, like the name of an old girlfriend or whatnot. Then in the future, you need only to type the name of the batch file, not the long sequence of keystrokes themselves. Here's an example.

To play the game **Word Attack Plus,** normally you must first log on to the directory where the game files are located, which is C:\WA3. So you would type

> **CD\WA3**

Next, you must type

> **WORD**

to start the game.

♦ Our family made a batch file named **ATTACK** that starts the program. Now, from any directory, typing the word **ATTACK** starts Word Attack Plus on our computer. Here is how you create such a batch file:

♦ **FIRST, CREATE A DIRECTORY TO STORE ALL YOUR BATCH FILES.** You do not want to litter your root directory (**C:\** with nothing after it is your root directory) with dozens of these small files. Your first step should be to make a directory you can store them all in. So, make sure you are logged on to your root directory, and not inside your DOS directory, for example. Does your computer screen read C:\ with nothing after it? Fine. So now, type

> **MD BATCH**

(**md** means make directory) and press **Enter**. You have just lcreated a directory called **BATCH**.

Type **md batch** and you've just created a directory called "batch."

Log on to the **BATCH** directory, like this:

> **CD\BATCH**

♦ **LET'S CREATE THE BATCH FILE.** Type

> **EDIT ATTACK.BAT**

You'll be greeted with the standard blue DOS "edit" screen. It will be blank, because you haven't typed any commands yet. Now type exactly the keystrokes you would use to start the program. In this case, type

> **C:\**
> **CD\WA3**
> **WORD**

(Please remember to press Enter after each of the above three lines.)

This "edit" command is available with DOS 4 and higher. If you purchased your computer since 1991, you can almost certainly use the edit command. See Chapter 2 for more information about DOS versions and upgrades.

♦ NEXT, SAVE YOUR FILE.

1. Move your mouse to the menu bar near the top of the screen that says File Edit.

2. Click your mouse on the word **File**. A scroll-down menu appears. With your finger still pressing the left mouse button, drag your mouse pointer down to the word **Exit**.

3. The screen will then ask you if you want to save your file. Select **Yes**.

```
Volume Serial Number is 1CB2-8E77
Directory of C:\BAT

.              <DIR>            05-11-94
..             <DIR>            05-11-94
NEWSWEEK BAT               31  05-04-94
CAMELOT  BAT               27  04-16-94
CHKLIST  CPS               81  06-10-94
MENU2    DOC           10,323  11-10-93
CONFIG   SYS              714  05-27-94
JAYBIRD  BAT               70  11-10-93
DAUGHTER BAT               53  10-28-93
QG3      BAT               34  06-24-94
AMAZON   BAT               35  09-05-94
KRONDOR  BAT               38  01-09-94
RAIN     BAT               35  06-30-94
SSA      BAT               34  01-03-94
VISTAPRO BAT               34  01-09-94
BIGMACH  BAT               34  01-20-94
TOONS    BAT               34  05-27-94
OREGON   BAT               34  06-27-94
SAMMAX   BAT               14  05-16-94
Press any key to continue . . .
```

This is a directory of "batch files" used to start programs. You, the user, create these files and name them whatever you want.

You have just created a batch file. You may repeat the above steps with any command that starts a program on your

IN FACT, YOU CAN CREATE BATCH FILES TO TAKE CARE OF OTHER CHORES LIKE COPY OR FIND FILES. IN CHAPTER 7 OF THIS BOOK, WE'LL COVER WORKING WITH FILES.

computer. Put all your batch files in the directory you just created, called BATCH. As explained next in this chapter, we are going to put the BATCH directory in your "startup path," so that you can type your batch file name from any directory on your computer, and your program will start.

HAVING A CONVENIENT LIST OF BATCH FILES GIVES KIDS ACCESS TO THEIR PROGRAMS. YOU CAN POST A LIST OF THOSE FILES NEXT TO YOUR COMPUTER, SO THAT IF A PARTICULAR PROGRAM SLIPS THEIR LITTLE MINDS, THEY CAN TYPE A WORD AND BE OFF. (USUALLY, THE GAMES THAT ARE MORE LIKE SCHOOL GET FORGOTTEN.)

When you make a batch file for a game, put that file in the directory with all the others you made. That way, when you type your batch command, I'll know where to look for it.

## THE PATH MOST TRAVELED

There's one more step to this process. Once you have written a veritable gaggle of batch files (a school of batch files? a pride of batch files?) and stored them in their own directory, called BATCH, you have one easy job left. Perhaps by now you have noticed that there are certain commands you can type from any directory on your computer, and they always work. For example, when you type **dir**, the files scroll along, down and down. Type **mem** from any directory, and you'll get a report on how many bytes of free memory are available. If you have Microsoft Windows installed on your computer, you can type **win** from any directory on your computer, and Windows will start. Why do certain commands work from everywhere?

♦ Our goal is to create that same level of convenience for the batch files you created…**to make them work from everywhere, not just from the BATCH directory you made**. The reason why DOS commands like **dir** are always available to you is because they are *in your computer's "startup path."* And we are going to put your BATCH directory in your startup path as well.

## WHAT IS YOUR PATH?

When you first boot up your computer, your computer searches its **autoexec.bat** file for the directories that hold the commands you use all the time. You can add a directory you created yourself to that list if you want to. Of course, your DOS directory will be in this path, which is why you can type **edit** or **dir** at any time, and they always work. *You don't have to be logged on to the DOS directory for those commands to work.* They work from anywhere. Also, your Windows directoryis part of this startup path arrangement, which is why you may type **win** from within any directory and be on your way. What other directories are in your path? Type the word

**set**

and read the list. The set command tells you about your computer's operating environment. It lists all the directories in your path.

---

**Where Do You Think You're Going?**
**The Two Uses of the Word "Path"**

■ This statement

    C:\DOGS\COLLIES\LASSIE.EXE

represents a "path." Software setup directions will often tell you: "Identify the complete path where your such-and-such game files are stored." You have to type the drive, directory, any subdirectory, file name, and file extension. If you make a mistake or leave something out, you will get the message

    invalid path specified

or

    path not found

■ If you look at your **autoexec.bat** file, you'll see a line that begins with "path." This line tells your computer **all the places it should look for a command** that you enter. Think of it like geography. This line,

    PATH=C:\CALIFORNIA; C:\COLORADO;
      C:\FLORIDA

in your autoexec.bat file tells your computer: "When I type a command, it might be in California, Colorado, or Florida, so please search all three if necessary."

Now, by editing the path line in your **autoexec.bat** file, you may add directories to it. Adding a directory to your path line means that whenever you type a computer command that's stored in that directory, your computer will find it, regardless of the directory you are logged on to at the moment. So, you may, without pain or much effort, add your BATCH directory to your **autoexec.bat** path line, and ensure that your computer will always and forever recognize the batch files that you have written for you and your children to use. Let's do it!

1. Type

   **edit autoexec.bat**

   Flash! The blue edit menu appears on the screen, and your computer's **autoexec.bat** file fills it.

2. Find the line near the bottom that says **Path=**.

3. Move your cursor to the very end of that Path= line, after DOS, Windows, and whatever else might be there.

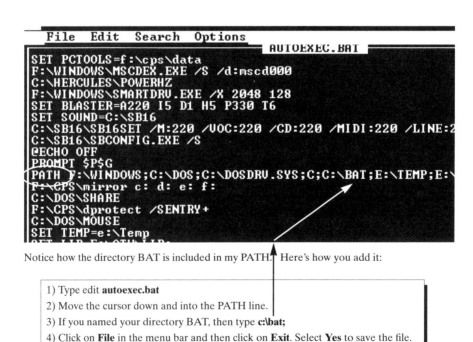

Notice how the directory BAT is included in my PATH. Here's how you add it:

1) Type edit **autoexec.bat**

2) Move the cursor down and into the PATH line.

3) If you named your directory BAT, then type **c:\bat;**

4) Click on **File** in the menu bar and then click on **Exit**. Select **Yes** to save the file.

4. Type

### ;C:\BATCH

(The semicolon is there to differentiate between the different directories in your path.)

So, perhaps your autoexec.bat path line used to look like this:

### PATH=C:\DOS;C:\WINDOWS

But now it looks like this:

### PATH=C:\DOS;C:\WINDOWS;C:\BATCH

> Remember that rule: "*In order for a command to work, you have to be in the correct directory*"? Now that your BATCH directory is in your path, you can break the rule. Any command you put in that BATCH directory, Oh, wise one, I will recognize and obey...*from anywhere!*

You have added your new directory, C:\BATCH, to the path line, and from now on, any time you type the name of one of the batch files that is in your BATCH directory, your computer will carry out that command and start the program you specified...oh, happy day...and you'll be on your way.

# USING A DOS COMMAND TO START A SPECIFIC PROGRAM IN WINDOWS

If you are in DOS, and want to start a specific program in Windows, you can create a batch file to do that for you. This saves you from having to type **win**, wait a while, then search for the icon that starts your program. Imagine you and your kids wanting to look up something in *Encarta,* for example, which is a Windows-based multimedia encyclopedia by Microsoft. You could, from DOS, type the word **Encarta**, run upstairs to get some ice cream, come back to the computer, and find Encarta waiting and ready to go. Here's how you do it:

1. From within your BATCH directory, type

   **edit encarta.bat**

   The big, blue edit screen will appear.

2. Type

   **win c:\encarta\encarta.exe**

3. Go up to **File** in the menu bar. Scroll down and click on **Exit.**

4. You'll be prompted to save the file. Select **Yes.**

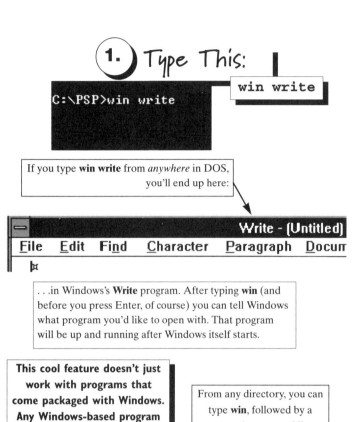

**1.) Type This:**

**win write**

`C:\PSP>win write`

If you type **win write** from *anywhere* in DOS, you'll end up here:

Write - [Untitled]

File   Edit   Find   Character   Paragraph   Docum

. . .in Windows's **Write** program. After typing **win** (and before you press Enter, of course) you can tell Windows what program you'd like to open with. That program will be up and running after Windows itself starts.

This cool feature doesn't just work with programs that come packaged with Windows. Any Windows-based program will open in this way.

From any directory, you can type **win**, followed by a program's command line, and the program will open.

`C:\SIERRA>win c:\pictpub\ppub40_`

If you type **dir**, you'll now see a file called **ENCARTA.BAT**, which you created. The next time you type the word

**ENCARTA**

Windows will start, and so will your multimedia encyclopedia. Please remember that, in the above example, **Encarta** is a CD-ROM product. You must, of course, have the CD-ROM in your CD-ROM drive for the en-cyclopedia to start up. Also, in composing the batch file **win c:\encarta\encarta.exe**, it is assumed you installed your **Encarta** files on drive C:\. If you installed them on some other drive, your batch file must direct your computer to look for them in the right place, perhaps D:\ENCARTA. Don't use C:\ just because I did so in the example above.

Please note that your batch file must include the name of the startup file itself, not just the directory. It must read

`win c:\encarta\encarta.exe`

not just

`win c:\encarta`

Let's make a batch file for Windows's very own **Write** program. We'll call the batch file **WRITER**. This way, when you enter the word **writer** from the DOS prompt, you can take a break for a minute or two, and when you come back, Write will be open and ready to go.

1. Log on to the directory that contains your other batch files, the one referenced in the path line of your autoexec.bat file. If you created a batch directory according to the instructions in this chapter, you would type **cd\batch**.

2. Type

   ```
   edit writer.bat
   ```

   DOS's big, blue edit screen appears.

3. Type

   ```
   win c:\windows\write.exe
   ```

4. Now click on **File** in the menu bar. Scroll down and select **Exit**. You'll be prompted to save. Select **Yes**.

Again, if you installed Windows on a drive other than C:\, your batch file will only work if you tell the computer to go to the correct drive and directory. For example: **win d:\windows\write.exe**.

## SIMPLE WAYS TO OPEN FILES IN WINDOWS

### OPENING TO AN EXACT DOCUMENT, PICTURE, OR SAVED GAME

Windows has a feature called Associate, which allows you to double-click on the name of a document or picture and open the file, ready to be edited, in the program of your choice. Let's say your desktop publishing program of choice is Page Plus, and you would like any document of any kind, be it **.wri**, **.txt**, or **.doc**, to open in Page Plus. Here's how to make that happen:

1. Go to **File Manager** (in the Main group)and click *once* on the name of the document. Do not double-click.

2. Go up to the menu bar. Select **File**. Move down to **Associate**.

3. You will see a list of programs that you may designate as THE program that documents of that extension will always open into, when double-clicked on.

4. Scroll down the list and select Page Plus. (Page Plus is included here only as an example. In reality, you can choose any single desktop publishing or word processing program from the list before you, as long as it supports the file that you want to open automatically.) You may select only one, since it would be impossible for a document to automatically open into two programs at once.

> The program you choose must truly be able to support the document. The **Associate** feature only *tells* the file to open into that program. Whether it really can or not is up to the program.

**From now on,** when you double-click in Windows File Manager on the name of any document with that file extension (**.txt**, **.wri**, **.doc**, or whatever file extension you chose to associate) that document will always open automatically into your specified program. This does not mean that documents with that file extension cannot open in other programs. It only means that when you select that document individually, the program you selected will be the designated default program.

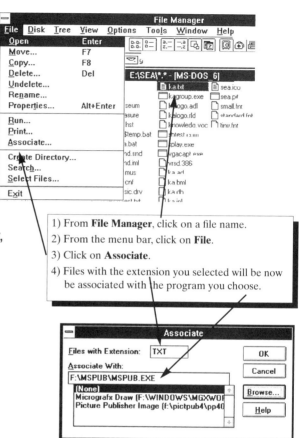

1) From **File Manager**, click on a file name.
2) From the menu bar, click on **File**.
3) Click on **Associate**.
4) Files with the extension you selected will be now be associated with the program you choose.

### Some DOS-to-Windows Examples

♦ Want to use the calculator? Type **win calc**.

♦ To check your calendar, type **win calendar**.

♦ Need to print something? Type **win printman**.

♦ If you and your kids are working on a newsletter in Microsoft Publisher, for example, if you know the exact saved filename of your project, you may type

    WIN C:\NEWLETT.PUB

Windows will open, and your newsletter project will open into Microsoft Publisher, while everyone takes a bathroom break.

**W**indows already knows the "associated program" of many kinds of files. For example, if you have WordPerfect for Windows installed on your computer, Windows understands that all documents with the **.WPD** file extension must be opened into the WordPerfect program.

## OPENING A FILE WITH A SIMPLE MOUSE CLICK
### (IF YOU HAVE NEVER USED MICROSOFT WINDOWS, YOU MIGHT WANT TO READ CHAPTER 4 OF THIS BOOK FIRST, THEN COME BACK HERE TO CHAPTER 6 AND LEARN THE FOLLOWING TIME-SAVING TRICK.)

♦ Pictures are worth a thousand words. At the end of this chapter are diagrams that illustrate the technique I'm about to describe. We are going to talk about turning your project (like a term paper or a school report) into an icon on your Windows Desktop. After doing this, you can click on it to start it up quickly.

I want to show you how to make any project of yours, perhaps a resume, a term paper, or anything, into a "Program Item." In Windows, you can open any Program Item with a mouse-click by assigning a convenient Windows icon to the item. Click on the icon, and the program starts. Normally a Program Item is a Windows program, such as Microsoft Money or Windows Recorder. But you can place your project, maybe a school report, on your Windows Desktop **as if it were a program**, and start it by clicking on its icon. In the case of this example, the Program Item is simply your project, your term paper, school newsletter, or any other long-term project you want quick access to. Once you create a desktop icon for your project, you can start it up with a mouse click. See the diagrams on the following two pages to learn how to assign an Windows icon to a Program Item.

**.bat outta hell**

Occasionally a batch file gets written incorrectly, and is given the task of looking up a directory that doesn't exist, or that no longer exists. But a batch file does not give up its task easily. It will loop on itself, and your screen will show your batch file scrolling downward, forever and ever. At first glance, it would appear that you could not stop the batch file scrolling without re-booting your computer. But you *can* stop this errant behavior by pressing **Ctrl+Break**. It's that easy. You'll be prompted with a question: **Terminate batch job?** Select **yes**, and go fix the file. Why did the batch file go crazy? Perhaps, long after you wrote the batch file, you moved the directory containing the program the batch file was looking for. Use the DOS editor (type **edit** [filename]) to make the changes. Test the batch file. If again you get the out-of-control scrolling, just press **Ctrl+Break**, and try again to fix the errant file.

**1.** Open a program group that you and your family use frequently. For this example, I'm using the group **Kid's Extra**.

**2.** Next, locate **File Manager**, usually in the Main group, and open it.

**3.** Press **Ctrl+Esc** to open **Task Manager**. Click on the word **Tile**. Now the program group you opened in step 1 and File Manager are "tiled" next to each other, similiar to the diagram below.

> # Turn a project into an icon you can click on to open instantly

**4.** In **File Manager** locate the file you want to turn into a self-opening icon on your desktop. Click on it **once**.

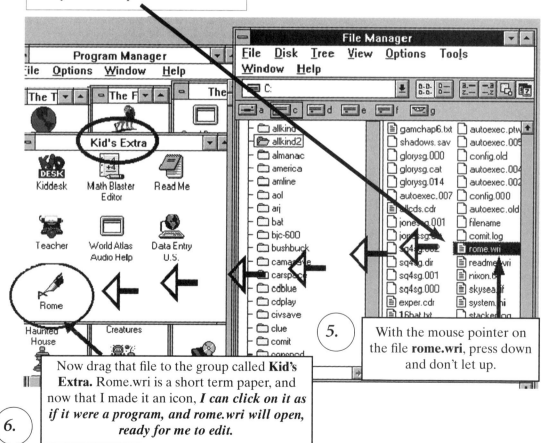

**5.** With the mouse pointer on the file **rome.wri**, press down and don't let up.

**6.** Now drag that file to the group called **Kid's Extra.** Rome.wri is a short term paper, and now that I made it an icon, *I can click on it as if it were a program, and rome.wri will open, ready for me to edit.*

# Chapter 7

# THE SCARY CHAPTER

## COPYING, SAVING, EDITING, AND DELETING FILES

## WORKING WITH FILES

First, we'll look at how to recognize certain types of files on your computer. You'll learn the difference between text and graphic files, for example, and how to group files together in directories that make sense to you, and can help make your time at the computer less frustrating. Also, you'll see how to spot which files are crucially important to the health of your computer's programs. This is important because some programs tamper with your startup files without telling you about it. In Windows, for example, you'll learn how to preserve "old" versions of your **win.ini** and **system.ini** files. Certain upgrades and programs could actually prevent Windows from starting on your computer. Having previous versions of your **win.ini** and **system.ini** file will help you out of that jam. Next, we'll learn how to group kinds of files together and load them off of your computer to save disk space. I'll show you how to locate files quickly, and even how to keep track of your computer's past activities. Finally, well take a look at how to undelete files, which means retrieving files you've erased from your computer, and now wish you hadn't.

# HOW TO RECOGNIZE IMPORTANT FILES

```
CGA.EXE
VGA.EXE
SBLAST.EXE
CIV.EXE
```

The diagram to the left shows various kinds of **.exe** files found in the directory of the MicroProse game **Civilization**. With a little background, one may guess that **VGA.EXE** and **CGA.EXE** have something to do with the screen driver used by the game. (Chapter 5 discusses what VGA and CGA mean.) The command **SBLAST.EXE** refers to the Sound Blaster driver necessary if you own a Sound Blaster card. None of these **.EXE** files will be of any concern to you. Software companies would rarely require you to monkey with any **.EXE** file other than the one to start up the game. In this game, the startup file is **CIV.EXE**, identifiable because the name of the file is similar to the name of the game, that is, **Civilization**. Log on to the directory of one of your other educational games. Type

**DOS** commands, like lazy teenagers, don't distinguish between uppercase and lowercase letters.

        **dir /p**

(**Dir /p** allows the screen to come to rest at the bottom of one screen full of file listings.)

Look to the right and notice the file extension. Files ending with **.com** are sometimes used to start the game. Sometimes a batch file is the startup command you would use, so take note of any files ending with **.bat**. But most often, a file with a **.exe** extension is used to start the program. Some programs come with a helpful "setup" or "reinstall" feature that, should you purchase a new sound card or printer, or should your sound card begin to act temperamental for some reason (it happens), you can reconfigure your game settings without having to go find the floppy disks and start from scratch. Should you lose the manual (everybody does) and not know the name of the "reinstall" program, type

      **dir \*.bat**

or

      **dir \*.exe**

and you should see some sort of "reinstall" program. (Don't forget to put a space *between* **dir** and **\***.) It is usually called **install.exe**, **setup.bat**, or **sbconfig.exe**. (Sound Blaster configuration, get it?) Knowing a little bit about which files in your programs are "executable" files can be helpful.

Pressing **Shift** and the **8 key** produces the DOS wildcard \*. When it is used in the command **dir \*.\*** it means "**list all files**." Typing **dir \*.pcx** means "find all files with the extension .pcx." This little time-saver can truly…er…make your heart sing.

## TIME-SAVING TRICKS FOR LOCATING FILES

At times you will need to access a particular file or directory, and won't be able to remember the exact name of it. If you simply type **dir**, you'll have to sit and watch all your directories and files scroll by at breakneck speed. When the scrolling comes to rest, you'll only be able to read the end of the list, whatever names fit on a single screen. Computers are mercilessly unhelpful unless you remember the exact name of the file you are looking for. Happily, there are a few DOS tricks at your disposal here. Instead of typing **dir**, type **dir /p**. This tells your computer to stop scrolling at the end of one "page" until you press a key. It will then scroll for one more page, stop, and wait for your directions to continue scrolling. This lets you view all the directories and files on your drive.

Another trick: If you are looking for a file, and remember that its name begins with "M," type

> **dir m***

and you will see a list of the files and directories on your drive that begin with "M." If you are looking for a file, remember that many of your files are inside directories.

When you list files by typing **dir**, there will be some between the file and its extension, as follows:

> RESOURCE 001
> RESOURCE CFG

a file
named
**kitchen**

of **every**
kind of file
extension

and search every
**subdirectory**,
will you?

**Show me**

It's a file you seek! A file named **kitchen**. You don't know the file extension? You don't know the directory? *I shall find it* by typing **dir kitchen.* /s**.

However, when you look for a file yourself, you identify it by putting a period between the name and extension, as follows:

> RESOURCE.001
> RESOURCE.CFG

If no file extension is included, your computer will report

> bad command or file name

## TRICKS THAT WILL HELP YOU SEARCH FOR A FILE

When searching for a file, even if you don't know the exact name, try to be as specific a possible. If you remember that the file extension of your missing file is **.pcx**, then use this *wildcard*, the asterisk (*), to help you narrow your search.

Switches like **dir /p** and **dir /s** use

**forward slashes**   /

*not*

**back slashes**   \

as in **cd\**

Imagine that you are composing your file search command as if it were a brief sentence. In that sentence, including the asterisk means "all" or "anything." Therefore, typing

**dir \*.pcx**

means

**"Show me all the files with the file extension .pcx."**

and typing

**dir \*.txt**

means

**"Show me all the files with the extension .txt."**

At your command, all the files in your current directory with that file extension will scroll down the screen.

There are letters, known as **switches,** that you can tag on to the end of the **dir** command that affect the way **dir** works. Here's how to assemble a switch:

**dir** (then a space) (then a forward slash) (then the letter identifying what switch you are using)

The switch **/s** (that's forward-slash s) adds this meaning to your command: **"And while you're at it, search ALL subdirectories, will you?"** That is a very powerful command. From your root directory (C:\), you can direct your computer to search for all .doc files, for example, in each individual directory.

The command to look for every single .doc file in every single subdirectory of where you are currently logged on to would look like this:

**dir \*.doc /s**

Imagining the above command as a sentence, it would read

"Show me (**dir**)
every (**\***)
.doc file you can find (**.doc**)
and search all subdirectories below this current directory (**/s**)."

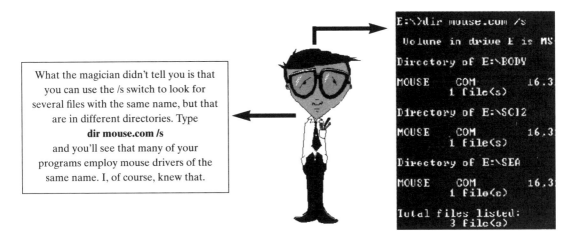

What the magician didn't tell you is that you can use the /s switch to look for several files with the same name, but that are in different directories. Type
**dir mouse.com /s**
and you'll see that many of your programs employ mouse drivers of the same name. I, of course, knew that.

Still too vague. Still can't find the dang file. Gotta get more specific. You just remembered that your file begins with "F." Use your wildcard, the asterisk, but **add the "F" to narrow down the search**. Here's your new, revised, more specific command:

```
dir f*.doc /s
```

Let's put it in a sentence form:

> "Show me (**dir**)
> every file that begins with the letter F (**F***)
> with the .doc file extension (**.doc**)
> and search all subdirectories as well (**/s**)."

Wildcards can help you on the other side of the file extension as well. If you know the name of the file, but not the file extension, you may type

```
dir trek.* /s
```

As a sentence, this command would mean

> "Show me (**dir**)...a file named trek (**trek**).
> Ah, but I can't remember if it was a **.tif** file or a **.tga** file, so you better make it EVERY (*****) file named trek...and look in every subdirectory (**/s**)."

If you suspect the list of qualifying files is more than a page long, type

```
dir trek.* /s /p
```

This means

> "Show me (**dir**)...a file named trek (**trek**).
> In fact, show me ALL the files named trek regardless of their file extension (**.***), and search every subdirectory (**/s**), and so I don't get dizzy, stop scrolling after each page (**/p**), will you?"

Ah, yes, you finally remember the full name of the file, but can't remember the directory. It could be ANY directory. It was late at night. Who knows what I was thinking? The file was called **taxes.txt**, not trek.pcx, and it was a text file (**.txt**) of course. Who could blame me for forgetting. You'll need to use the "search all subdirectories" (**/s**) command, but to make it search every directory on your hard drive, **you must be logged on to your root directory**, since, the **/s** command simply tells your computer to search for files **below the current directory**. So type **cd\**. This ensures that you are logged on to your root directory. Now type **dir taxes.txt /s** As a sentence, this command would read:

> "Show me (**dir**)
> the file taxes.txt (**taxes.txt**),
> and search every subdirectory to
> find it (**/s**)."

This time your search has been narrowed down to one specific file. Since you included the /s switch, *if the file is anywhere on that drive, that command will find it.*

**Using the wildcard "*" to find a file**

```
F:\BARBWRIT>dir *.wri

Volume in drive F has no labe
Directory of F:\BARBWRIT

RESUME    WRI      2,688  05-
QUAKE     WRI      1,152  05-
HTSCHOO   WRI      3,072  07-
FRONTPGE  WRI      5,888  01-
MISC321   WRI     10,880  04-
          5 file(s)         23,6
```

1. Let's see, I know I'm looking for a *"write"* file, so I'll type **dir *.wri**

2. and I'm sure it began with "r," so I'll type **dir r*.wri**

3. and here's my file **RESUME.WRI** →

```
F:\BARBWRIT>dir r*.wri

Volume in drive F has no l
Directory of F:\BARBWRIT

RESUME    WRI      2,688
          1 file(s)
                    75,82
```

## TWO MORE TIME-SAVING DIR TIPS

You can make your computer scroll your files five columns wide across the screen, which lets you peek at more files than scrolling downward would allow. It's called the **wide** switch. Type

```
dir /w
```

One last tip: Sometimes I forget which project I worked on most recently, and I need help locating it...what did I call it? I can't quite remember. To solve this, I can type

```
dir /od
```

Typing **dir /od** lists all files with the oldest first, so that the scrolling comes to rest with the **most recently updated or created file staring me in the face at the bottom of the screen**.

You can also combine dir options to your own liking: For example, the command

```
dir /od /p
```

tells your computer to list the oldest files first, scrolling only one page at a time. You may prefer

```
dir /w /p
```

which scrolls files five columns wide across your screen, pausing after each page.

The **"wide"** command (burp)

Type **dir /w** and your files will be spread several columns *wide* across your screen, which lets you view more of them at once.

Can't remember what you worked on last? Type **dir /od** and your most recently edited file will be at the bottom of your scrolling.

Remember...

## MODIFYING THE DIR COMMAND

### MAKING THE DIR COMMAND AUTOMATICALLY USE YOUR FAVORITE OPTION

If there is an option that you know you'd like to use every time, but would like to spare yourself typing this alphabet soup just to list your files, **you can tell your computer that every time you type dir, what you really mean is dir /w /p, for example**. Now, to make your favorite option into the one always used when you simply type **dir**, here's what you do:

1. Log on to your root directory (by entering **c:\**), and type **edit autoexec.bat**. (What we are doing is making this version of the dir command a permanent part of your startup files.)

2. Having typed **edit autoexec.bat**, your autoexec.bat file appears, open before you, filling the DOS big, blue edit screen.

3. With a mouse click, or by using the arrow keys on your computer, move the cursor near the end of the file.

4. Hit the Enter key to insert a blank line. This provides room for a new command to be added to your autoexec.bat file.

5. Now, type **set dircmd=/od/p**. (This is only an example. If the option you prefer is **dir /p /w**, then you would type **set dircmd=/p /w**.)

6. Using your mouse, click on **FILE** on the menu bar. Select **EXIT**. You will be prompted to **SAVE** the file before exiting. Do so.

Pick a favorite dir variation and put it in your autoexec.bat file, so you can use it every time. If you like the /p (page) and /od (oldest first) options, then put the line:
set dircmd=/od/p
near the bottom of your autoexec.bat file.

And now, starting from the next time you boot up your computer, when you type **dir**, the options you selected will be operative.
*Please note that any changes you make in your autoexec.bat file will not be effective until you reboot your computer.*

## COPYING FILES TO NEW DIRECTORIES

As you and your family work on more and more projects over time, you'll find it convenient to organize everybody's work in directories that make sense to each of you. Putting similar project files in their own directories helps you remember where everything is.

Let's round up all those old files of yours that have similar subject matter, and put them into one directory. First, make a directory called "projects." This is done by logging on to your root directory, and typing

```
md projects
```

You've just made a directory called PROJECTS. Let's find that old school banner you did with the Print Shop Deluxe program. Was it called banner, or ban-something? Type

```
dir ban*.pds /s
```

(**.pds** is the file extension for Print Shop Deluxe projects.) You find a file—perhaps called BANSCHOO for school banner. Of course.

Log on to the directory where the file is located. Now type

```
copy banschoo.pds c:\projects
```

You've just copied a file from its original directory to its new home in another directory.

Now it turns out that there are several old Print Shop Deluxe (.pds) projects that you would like to copy to your new directory PROJECTS. Why copy them one by one?

Use the **wildcard \*** to tell your computer to copy ALL the files with the .psd extension to the new directory you just made.

First, make sure you are logged on to the directory that contains your Print Shop Deluxe files. Now type

```
copy *.pds c:\projects
```

You've just told your computer to copy ALL the projects with the .pds file extension to a directory called PROJECTS.

We'll talk more about copying files later.

# RENAMING FILES

Some programs or upgrades you add to your computer will tamper with your system files. If the programs run in Windows, they'll also change your **system.ini** and your **win.ini** files. They mean no harm. They make these changes to set up a suitable *operating environment*. **But the changes they make affect your computer's entire operating environment, not just one program's.** If you put a program on your computer, especially a Windows program, and then find that Windows, or your computer in general, does not start up or run correctly, you will wish you had an old version of those four system files on hand, versions that ran just fine BEFORE this dopey program or upgrade messed things up.

You can protect yourself from these instances. **If you're about to load a program that you think will alter your system somewhat, you can**

1. Save old versions of those four main system files (**config.sys**, **autoexec.bat**, **win.ini**, and **system.ini**).

2. Load on that big, potentially dangerous program, and if things do not go well…

3. Restore the old versions of those system files. Your computer will be configured the way it was before.

4. Call the product's technical support line and tell them what went wrong…but at least you can do it with a functioning computer!

The diagram to the right explains in four steps how to save an old version of your **system.ini** file in another directory, rename it **system.old**, and have it available if something goes wrong later.

But there's a catch. **You can't have two files with the exact same name in one directory.** You can't have two files called **system.ini** in your Windows directory. One thing you can do is copy your **config.sys** file, for example, to a new directory (copying leaves a version of the file where it was, and makes a copy elsewhere) and rename the one in the new directory **config.old**. Then, when the new program alters your **config.sys** file and messes things up, you just

1. Log on to the directory where you stored **config.old**.

2. Rename it **config.sys** by entering **ren config.old config.sys**.

3. Copy it back to your root directory. The **config.sys** that was created by the new piece of software will be erased, and the old one will be operative again. All will be as it was. Hooray!

## RENAMING A FILE WHEN YOU'RE IN WINDOWS

Windows makes it easy to rename a file, keeping both the new and old version on your computer before you go on to add a potentially temperamental program.

1. Load Windows.

2. Go to the **Main** group.

---

### HOW TO SAVE AN OLD VERSION OF YOUR AUTOEXEC.BAT FILE IN A DIRECTORY CALLED XTRAFILE

Enter these commands:
1) **md xtrafile** (to make a directory called XTRAFILE)
2) **copy autoexec.bat c:\xtrafile** (make sure you're in your root directory before you enter this)
3) **cd\xtrafile**
4) **ren autoexec.bat autoexec.old** (*ren* is the DOS command for "rename")

Later, if some program alters your autoexec.bat in a bad way,
1) Log on to your root directory (cd\), then enter the following commands:
2) **del autoexec.bat**
3) **cd\xtrafile**
4) **copy autoexec.old c:\**
5) **cd\**
6) **ren autoexec.old autoexec.bat**
7) Reboot your computer.

---

### YOU'RE GETTING READY TO INSTALL A NEW VIDEO CARD, AND YOU KNOW THAT CHANGES WILL BE MADE IN YOUR SYSTEM FILES

1) Make a directory called OLDINI.
2) Log on to your Windows directory.
3) Copy your **win.ini** and **system.ini** files to that directory.
4) Rename **system.ini system.old**.
5) Rename **win.ini win.old**.

Your video card is installed, but Windows won't load.
1) Log on to your new **OLDINI** directory. Make sure your **win.old** and **system.old** are still there and intact.
2) Log on to your Windows directory.
3) Delete **system.ini**; next delete **win.ini**.
4) Go back to your **OLDINI** directory.
5) Rename **system.old system.ini**; next **rename win.ini win.old**.
6) Copy **system.ini c:\WINDOWS**; next **copy win.ini c:\WINDOWS**.
7) Voilà! Windows can start.

3. Open **File Manager**.

4. Find the file you want to copy and rename. Click on it once.

5. Now go to the menu bar and select **File**. Scroll down to **Copy**.

6. You're given the option of copying a file and naming the copy something different. This is exactly what you want to accomplish. For example, the dialogue box will read **Copy autoexec.bat as**: You must supply the new name you wish to call your copy. You can call it **autoexec.old**, if you wish.

7. What you have done is created, *for your own safety*, a version of your **autoexec.bat** file called **autoexec.old**. Should your computer behave badly after adding a program or some upgrade, you can *restore the autoexec.old file*, renaming it **autoexec.bat**. After renaming it back again, your previous, tried and true autoexec.bat will be the one your computer starts up with. The other file is zapped, gone.

8. Call the company and describe what went wrong. If they walk you through an installation process, and the problem happens again, you STILL have this file called **autoexec.old** that can be renamed as **autoexec.bat**, allowing you to start up your computer in your old, tried and true way.

Have we met? My maker named me BANJO.PCX He wants to make a copy of me. But that copy must go into another directory. So he could type **copy BANJO.PCX c:\music,** but there has to already be a directory called music, or I won't copy.

Now I'm copied to a new directory, and my maker types **rename banjo.pcx banjo.old**. My new name is *banjo.old*, but do I care? Nope, 'cause on the inside, I'm still the same little ol' file. Ain't life grand?

Our, ah, strumming friend above is a note or two off. While it is true that she is the same file, no graphics program will open up a drawing called **BANJO.OLD**. She will have to be renamed again, back to **BANJO.PCX** before she can be useful. Luckily, you have me here to clear things up. Be seeing you.

To really restore your startup files to the way they were before a product changed them, you'll probably have to perform the above process on your **config.sys** file as well.

So to review, renaming files keeps the contents the same, but changes the title. Using the rename command can help you keep "good versions" of your four main system files available, should a new piece of software alter them. Another time you might need to put this skill to use is when you set up an automatic memory manager on your computer.

If you run the memory manager QEMM on your computer, for example, it makes permanent changes to your **autoexec.bat** and **config.sys** files. After QEMM is finished setting itself up on your computer, it will flash the message:

```
Your old AUTOEXEC.BAT and CONFIG.SYS files have been
   saved under the name AUTOEXEC.QDK and CONFIG.QDK.
```

(The name of their company is Quarterdeck.) The program saves the previous versions of these two main startup files so that if you decide QEMM's configuration is not working for you (perhaps some of your programs just don't run correctly), you can at least restore those old versions of your config.sys and autoexec.bat files, and try again from scratch. At least you won't have lost any ground, or be stuck with a computer that QEMM has hopelessly tampered with. This does not mean that QEMM is bad or reckless. It just means that QEMM has to try another configuration for your system, which it can do very easily. When QEMM flashes the above message, remember that the contents of those files are *exactly as they were before QEMM began messing with your computer*. Now, if you decide you want your old configuration back, you can **rename the .QDK files**. Renaming AUTOEXEC.QDK as AUTOEXEC.BAT will erase the work QEMM did. Same goes for your config.sys file, by the way.

Please note that you can rename a file anything you like, as long as you conform to DOS's rules of "eight dot three." You can rename MYTAXES.TXT to be IHATETA.XES, if you like. The file contents will be the same. But now, in a fit of hysteria, you created a file with the extension **.XES**. No word processing program will be able to open a file with that file extension. If you wish to vent your spleen and still have a workable file, you might have to settle for VERYMAD.TXT. The file will open with the same contents as it did when it was called MYTAXES.TXT.

**WHERE IS THAT STUPID FILE?**

# LOCATING FILES USING TIME-SAVING DOSKEY COMMANDS

## "I DIDN'T ERASE IT, SO IT MUST BE AROUND HERE SOMEWHERE"

## DOSKEY, AND THE WONDERFUL "WHEREIS" COMMAND

Put the DOSKEY "**whereis**" command in your **autoexec.bat** file, and you can find any file anywhere, as long as you know part of the name. *Now go get 'em!*

In two simple steps you can create a short and helpful command that will search your entire hard drive to find any file, simply by typing "**WHEREIS** [any filename of your choice]," such as "WHEREIS MYTAXES.TXT" or "WHEREIS MYPICT.PCX."

First, we'll set up the command on your computer. When we're done, the command will be part of your computer's regular operating procedure. We're going to edit your **autoexec.bat** file and make this command permanent.

1) Type **edit autoexec.bat**.
2) Place your cursor near the bottom of the file and create a new blank line.
3) Type **doskey**. (The DOSKEY program is now a permanent part of your startup files. You will not have to load it manually.)
4) Create another blank line under the doskey line. The blinking cursor should be at the beginning of that line waiting for you to type a new command.
5) Type **doskey whereis=dir /$1 /s /p**.
6) Save and exit.
7) The next time you reboot your computer, the "whereis" command will be in

1. Type **edit auto-exec.bat**. Hello, big, blue edit screen.

2. Using your mouse or arrow keys, scroll down near the bottom of the file. If you load Windows when you first turn on your computer (in other words, if **win** is the last line of your **autoexec.bat** file), scroll your cursor *before* that line.

3. Use the **End** key to scroll to the end of the chosen line near or at the end of the file. Press **Enter**. Notice you are now at the beginning of a blank line.

4. Type **doskey**. Press **Enter**. That's right, just type the word doskey, and press Enter.

5. You are now on a new, blank line in your **autoexec.bat** file, typing in the second phase of this command. Type as follows:

```
doskey whereis=dir /$1 /s /p
```

6. Go up to **File** on the menu bar. Select **Exit**. You'll be prompted to save the file. Do so. Now, reboot your computer.

Bernard here. The guy with the wand forgot to tell you that DOSKEY takes up some conventional memory. If you type **mem** and find that you have less than 570K free, adding DOSKEY might knock you below the amount you need to run your programs. Gotta run. Mom's making dinner. We're having lima beans.

Here's what you just did:

The first line, typing **doskey**, loaded a program into your computer that permits you to type one thing when you mean something else. Since we put the word **doskey** into your **autoexec.bat** file, the DOSKEY program is now loaded. The second line of the command makes the phrase **whereis** mean something special to your computer. In this case, the phrase **whereis** represents a string of letters that we don't want to have to type every single time. Instead, we only have to type **whereis**, and, because of DOSKEY, the computer knows what we mean.

Let's have a little fun. At the DOS prompt type

```
doskey apple=orange
```

What you've done is to tell your computer that, when you type the word apple and press Enter, you really meant to type the word orange. Try it. There you go, the computer spit out the word orange. Of course, you'll still see "bad command or file name," because orange is not a valid computer command. But now, lets make apple into something useful. Type

```
doskey apple=copy *.txt *.bak
```

Now, typing the word **apple** and pressing Enter will set in motion a useful little command: It will make backup copies of all your **.txt** files in whatever directory you are logged on to. (That's what **copy *.txt *.bak** does. As a sentence, the command would read: "Make a copy of every (**\***) file with a **.txt** extension, but change the file extension to **.bak**." If you ever wish to use your backup copy, just rename the **.bak** file. Change its name to the original **.txt** file extension, and then you can use it.) But with your DOSKEY command (which you named **apple**), you needn't type that long string every time. You only have to type the word **apple**. You may, of course, choose other words or memorable keystrokes besides apple.

DOSKEY can be used to create shortcuts to all kinds of commands. Here's another example. Many tutorials included in this book require you to edit your autoexec.bat file. Why type **edit autoexec.bat** every time? Make a DOSKEY command as follows:

```
doskey q=edit autoexec.bat
```

What happens now? Every time you type **q** and press **Enter**, your computer will type and carry out the command **edit autoexec.bat**. That command will work until you reboot your computer. To make it be permanent, you must type that exact line (doskey q=edit autoexec.bat) in your **autoexec.bat** file (after the command to load DOSKEY, of course). Remember the command to load DOSKEY is notoriously easy—just type DOSKEY—and if you followed the last tutorial, DOSKEY has been part of your autoexec.bat file for a few minutes. If you don't want to make DOSKEY part of your autoexec.bat file, just *type **doskey** at any time at the DOS prompt*, and voilà, the program is loaded.

One last extra-convenient DOSKEY command is to peer into any directory and look at the files that are "executable," or, the files that start up programs. Under normal circumstances, to view all executable files, you would have to type

```
dir *.bat
```

then watch the screen for the results, then type

```
dir *.com
```

watch the screen, and finally, type

```
dir *.exe
```

and watch again.

With DOSKEY, you may use the command separator. The *command separator* is the symbol that appears when you press the **Ctrl** key at the same time as you type the letter **T** (use the lowercase t when you type the command).

Simply type

```
dir *.bat | dir *.com | dir *.exe
```

What this does is group all three searches together into one command line. Make a DOSKEY command and stick it in your **autoexec.bat** file as follows:

```
doskey banana=dir *.bat | dir *.com | dir *.exe
```

After you reboot, any time you type the word **banana**, your computer
will go 'a searchin' for all the executable files in the current directory.
Pretty neat, huh?

## USING DOSKEY TO CHECK IF SOMEONE'S REALLY DONE HIS OR HER WORK

While DOSKEY is running, you can press the **F8** key, and the last 15 DOS commands entered into your computer will flash on your screen. The list will look something like this:

```
1)  CD\RUGRAT\ALIEN
2)  KINGQUES
3)  PINBALL
4)  CD\LETTER\GIRLFREN
5)  CD\REBLYELL\MIDNITE\HOUR
6)  CARDGAME
7)  WIN SOL
8)  WIN TERMPPER
```

> If **DOSKEY** is active, when you press the **F8** key, the *last 15 commands* typed on your computer will be on your screen. Pressing the **F7** key *scrolls backwards one command at a time.* Pressing **Enter** will operate each command just as if you had physically typed it. This saves finger wear and tear if you have been typing repeated commands.

and so on.

Then if some youngster tells you that he spent all night slaving on the computer over his term paper, you can show him this and ground him for the weekend!!! Actually, though, this command only tells you that these directories were accessed. It doesn't tell you how much time was spent playing those games. Junior very well could have spent most of the evening working on his paper.

# COPYING FILES

Copying files is easy. To make a copy of a picture file called **mypix.pcx**, first log yourself on to the directory where **mypix.pcx** is located, then decide where you want to send your copy. You cannot tell your computer: "I would like two exact versions of the same file right next to each other in the same directory." *You must specify that your copy exist somewhere else.* (You can get around this this rule by renaming a file, but leaving its contents the same, as discussed earlier.) You may send a copy of your file onto a floppy disk by typing

```
copy mypix.pcx a:
```

You may send a copy of your file to a different directory on the same drive:

```
copy mypix.pcx c:\oldpix
```

You can also send a copy of your file to a different directory in a different hard drive:

**`copy mypix.pcx d:\psd`**

But no, *you cannot copy a file to a CD-ROM*. CD-ROMs are "Read Only." Without special equipment, you cannot "write" to them.

## XCOPY IS BETTER

You may use shortcuts to copy groups of files to new locations. If you'd like to clear out last year's text documents, and archive them somewhere else, you may type

**`xcopy *.txt a:\oldfiles`**

You have used the wildcard * to tell your computer that ALL of the files with the .txt extension are to be copied.

You have also used DOS's program XCOPY rather than regular old COPY. XCOPY is faster for moving group files. XCOPY reads a group of files all at once before copying them, which is more efficient than repeatedly reading one file, then copying it, which is what regular old COPY does. And furthermore, when you use the regular **copy c:\*.\*** command to copy many files to a new location, and then you run out of disk space, after you're part of the way through, your computer will flash the message "insufficient disk space" part way through the operation. That's all. Start over. But since the XCOPY command reads all the files before it starts to copy them to the new location, XCOPY knows if it will need more than one floppy disk's worth of disk space to copy all those files. Therefore, when XCOPY has used up one disk, it merely asks for a new one and continues on its copying way, rather than quitting, like regular old COPY does.

> Pardon our duck crossing, but we couldn't think of a better way to remind you that when you are copying many files, use XCOPY rather than COPY. XCOPY copies all the source files to a buffer first, (rather than one by one) which is more efficient and speedy. Let's go, duckies!

XCOPY

# DOSKEY vs. BATCH FILES

I'm sick of having to type a command, wait, and then type another command. I want to type several commands in a row, and be done with it.

With DOSKEY you can! You can use the great
## COMMAND SEPARATOR

**1) Type your first command.**
For example, **del \*.doc**.

**2) Type** T (**t, really—don't capitalize it) while holding down the Control (Ctrl) button.**

**3) Type your second command.**
For example **copy tax.zip c:\archive**.

**4) Again, type** Ctrl+T.
You may group several commands in this manner. They'll be carried out one after the other.

For **DOSKEY** commands to work, the program must be loaded. Type the word **doskey to** load it. Simple as that.

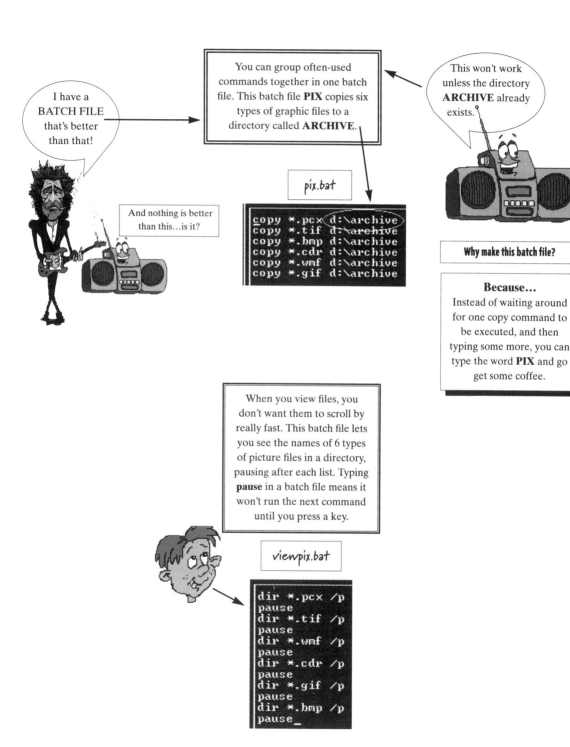

I have a BATCH FILE that's better than that!

You can group often-used commands together in one batch file. This batch file **PIX** copies six types of graphic files to a directory called **ARCHIVE**.

This won't work unless the directory **ARCHIVE** already exists.

And nothing is better than this…is it?

pix.bat

```
copy *.pcx d:\archive
copy *.tif d:\archive
copy *.bmp d:\archive
copy *.cdr d:\archive
copy *.wmf d:\archive
copy *.gif d:\archive
```

**Why make this batch file?**

**Because…**
Instead of waiting around for one copy command to be executed, and then typing some more, you can type the word **PIX** and go get some coffee.

When you view files, you don't want them to scroll by really fast. This batch file lets you see the names of 6 types of picture files in a directory, pausing after each list. Typing **pause** in a batch file means it won't run the next command until you press a key.

viewpix.bat

```
dir *.pcx /p
pause
dir *.tif /p
pause
dir *.wmf /p
pause
dir *.cdr /p
pause
dir *.gif /p
pause
dir *.bmp /p
pause_
```

```
C:\ZOOKEEP (MAIN DIRECTORY)

      SUBDIRECTORY
          PROGRAM FILE
          PROGRAM FILE
          DATA FILE

      SUB SUBDIRECTORY
          IMAGE FILE
          IMAGE FILE
          IMAGE FILE

      SUB SUB SUBDIRECTORY
          MORE IMAGE FILES
          MORE IMAGE FILES
          MORE IMAGE FILES
```

XCOPY has one other great advantage: It can copy from subdirectories. Consider copying the files from the diagram to the left. Rather than go to your new destination drive and manually recreate all those directories and transfer them group by group, you need only type the following:

> **xcopy zookeep a: /s**

Typing the above command tells your computer to copy the parent directory and all of its subdirectories and files to the new location.

## COPYING FILES FROM ONE FLOPPY DISK TO ANOTHER

If you have a file that you'd like to copy from one floppy disk to another, here's a little surprise: Even if you only have one floppy drive in your computer (some computers do have two floppy drive called **drive A:** and **drive B:**) your computer pretends it has a **B: drive**. For reasons not important enough to explain at this moment, you can use this imaginary **drive B:** to copy data from one floppy disk to another. Here's how:

1. Put the disk you want to copy from into your floppy drive. Now type

   > **xcopy *.* a: b:**

   (For this example, I'm showing how to make a copy of *all the data* on the floppy disk.)

2. Follow the on-screen instructions until the copying process is finished.

Having said all that, I want to point out that the faster and more reliable process is to copy everything from the floppy disk onto your hard drive, perhaps making its own directory on your hard drive in the process, and then putting the blank "destination" floppy disk in drive A:, and copying the files from your hard drive to the new disk. Here's why I like that method more:

- It's much faster. Trying to copy work from one floppy to another is going to be very tedious. The computer will repeatedly ask you to replace the "source disk" then the "destination disk," on and on until you don't care anymore. Copying stuff to your hard drive and back again to a floppy disk will take seconds.

One way to make a copy of a floppy disk is to be logged on to drive A: and type

`copy *.* b:`

and follow the on-screen instructions. Your computer will treat your blank disk **as if it were in drive b:** and copy everything from the first floppy disk on to

- It's safer for your data. Floppy to floppy copying has a higher error rate. Any transition of data involving floppy disks is going to carry higher risk of errors than working from your hard drive. Working from one floppy to another simply doubles that risk. So copy from a floppy to a hard drive, then back to a floppy again. It's faster and safer.

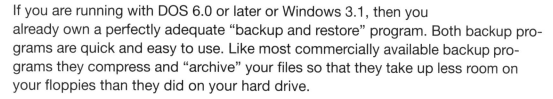

## BACKING UP FILES

You can make backups of your documents, your pictures, and all your family's computer projects by copying these files onto floppy disks for later use. You can restore them later, after you've bought a new, bigger hard drive, and you actually have the space for all of this archival nonsense. In the meantime, you need the room for the new programs you've just spent your paycheck on, so first, back up those old files, then kill 'em off!

If you are running with DOS 6.0 or later or Windows 3.1, then you already own a perfectly adequate "backup and restore" program. Both backup programs are quick and easy to use. Like most commercially available backup programs they compress and "archive" your files so that they take up less room on your floppies than they did on your hard drive.

If you have DOS 6.0 or later, simply type **msbackup** at the DOS prompt. Or, to use the Windows program,

1. Open **Windows**. Next you need to find the icon that starts the program.
2. Open the **Applications** group. If the icon isn't there, try the **Accessories** group.
3. Double-click on the icon to start the backup program.

4. Select the files you wish to back up. It's easy to double-check and make sure you picked up all the files destined for the slammer, and didn't include keepers by accident. Being able to view each directory helps me be a little more surefooted about my actions, which is important when I'm deleting files.

> If you are using DOS 6.0 or later, you may type **msbackup** at the DOS prompt to start a backup session.

(If you use the backup program from DOS 5.0, you do not have the advantage of viewing all the directories on your hard drive and picking off your choices with a mouse click. For a full discussion on upgrading your DOS version, see Chapter 2.)

5. The backup program prompts you for each disk, and a little line graph displays the progress of the backup.

The backup program displays how many files you've selected for backup, and will try to at least guess how many disks the backup will take. By my own experience, you'll need several more disks than the program initially asks for. The program also verifies the integrity of the backup as you go along, which makes your data safer. When you restore your data, the program knows exactly which disks to ask for, and asks you if you wish to restore all or only some of your backed up files. You are clearly guided every step of

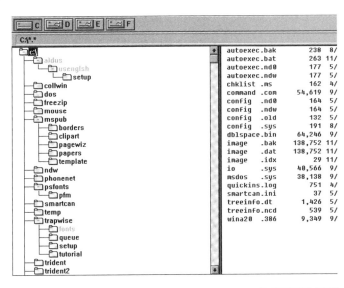

`C:\>backup c:\ *.* a: /s`

If you are using DOS 5.0 or older, you must still type backup commands. When you restore, you must specify the precise drive and directory, or you'll get the message **"bad command or file name."**

When you use the program in Windows, you see the backup "tree" style directory that makes it easy to view all your files. Anything previously backed up will appear in red. A black square appears by a file or directory you have selected for backup now. With very few mouse clicks, you can back up anything from your entire drive down to a single file.

the way, and I've never had a problem with this program. Best of all, it comes free with DOS 6 or Windows 3.1.

Now, after you've carefully backed up your files, labeled your disks and set them aside for the next millennium, you may delete them from your hard drive without worry.

# ERASING FILES TO SAVE DISK SPACE

There comes a time in every computer techie's life when the hard drive is full, full beyond overflowing, and it's time to say good-bye to those programs you are not going to use anymore, and after having backed them up for a time when you might want them again, you are going to have to erase them in order to have room for some new program you just bought that you know is going to eat up every inch of space you can find. You can cleanly erase an entire directory of files and their sub-directories by opening **Windows,** selecting **File Manager,** clicking on the game you wish to get rid of, and then pulling down the **Delete** command from the **File** menu. After asking for confirmation, Windows will erase the program's main directory AND every subdirectory.

If you are running DOS 6.0 or later, you can erase a program's directory and *sub-directories* by typing **deltree** [the name of the directory].

For example,

> `deltree zookeep`

In the above example, you would **log on to the root directory** (not the Zookeep directory), and type **deltree zookeep**. Mr. Computer will ask you if you are sure, and you may reply, "Why, yes, of course."

> **THE SCARY (AND PERMANENT) "DELTREE" COMMAND**

> And I can't be brought back to life with **UNDELETE,** either.

The **deltree** command should be used with discretion and caution, because most often, **you cannot undelete files that you have erased with DELTREE**. At the DOS prompt, type the command **help deltree** for a quick tutorial on this command.

Deltree **MANWALK** will eliminate a directory by that name, including all its files and subdirectories.

For a walk-through example of saving game files, and then erasing the game itself, let's look at Sierra On-Line's **The Island of Dr. Brain**. Once you have logged onto the SIERRA\BRAIN2 directory, type **dir**. All the files you see listed there were created by the makers of the game, except for these: **brainsg.001**, **brainsg.002**, and so on. *You made those files*. See, the games and learning adventures you are likely to buy are not designed to be finished in one sitting. Far from it. They like to imagine you and your family toiling away for 25 to 50 hours on one of these puppies, feeling like you really got your money's worth at the end. Woe to the creature who does not **save his or her game** at regular intervals. You don't want to have to start from scratch every time you play

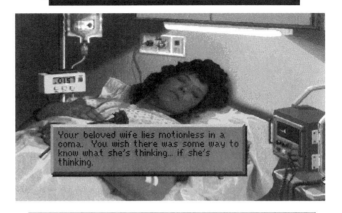

Screen from Sierra On-Line's **Police Quest 3**.

Your beloved wife lies motionless in a coma. You wish there was some way to know what she's thinking... if she's thinking.

Why get stuck here twice? Save those "saved game" files so when you load the game again later, you can also reload your saved games.

the game, right? So save your game at frequent intervals, especially immediately after a difficult sequence. And when you restore those saved game files, the program remembers where you are in the story line, the number of puzzles you have solved, your character's attributes, and so on. **You'll be plopped in right where you left off**, an important feature, if you EVER hope to see the ending.

But all good things must come to an end. You and your family have played **The Island of Dr. Brain** into the ground, and for the time being, are experts at Dr. Brain's homonym puzzles, circuit designing machines, and all the rest. It's time to take the game off of the hard drive to make room for something else. But before you erase it off of your computer, **save those "saved game files" on a floppy disk, and store that disk with the game disks**. Then, in the future, when you load the game on

I disagree. A real sleuth is not afraid to start from scratch. Besides, some computer games don't let you load on previously saved versions. They'd rather you use your noodle. Eh, Watson?

again, you may have immediate access to the puzzles and challenges that were favorites. Keeping your saved games around can be especially important with those complicated and multilayered role-play adventures like *King's Quest 6* and *Return to Zork.* They make 'em hard on purpose, and expect you to really sing for your supper. Only serious masochists want to go through all that torture twice. Saving your game gives you an entry point after those really hard bits, should you ever want one. (You will.)

So, when you take the game off of your computer, save the "saved game files" on a floppy disk first. Here's how:

1. Determine the file extension for the saved games. Most games and role-play adventures you are likely to pick up at the software store save each "saved game" as an individual file. See the diagram below for some examples that might help you recognize these files.

> It's easy to archive the "saved game" files in this directory.
> 1) Create a directory called "**SAVEGAME**."
> 2) Remain logged on to this directory and type **copy savegame.\* c:\SAVEGAME**.
> 3) You can now remove the game itself from your hard drive, and keep your saved games safe in a different directory, or copy them on to a floppy.

2. Put a floppy disk in drive A: Make sure it's formatted and ready to go.

3. Log on to the directory of the game you want to save files from.

4. Double-check the file extension used by all those saved games.

5. Type **xcopy \*.sav a:**. (The games referred to in this example have the **.sav** file extension. In your own practice, don't use **\*.sav** just because it's in the example. Replace **.sav** with the file extension that refers to the saved game files of the game you are copying from.)

6. Type **dir a:**. You should see the files you've copied.

7. Take out the disk, label it "Saved games from Dr. Brain," for example, and save it with your game disks.

8. You can now safely erase **The Island of Dr. Brain** from your computer.

Please note that you don't necessarily have to copy your saved game files on to a floppy disk. You can also make a directory on your hard drive called "brainsav," for example, and save them there. Saved

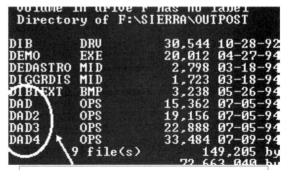

Viewing files of the game OUTPOST, one can spot the more personalized names that are probably "saved game" files.

game files themselves are usually only a few thousand bytes apiece, much less than the mammoth 5 to 20 million bytes of hard drive space usually required by the game itself.

# UNDELETING FILES

DOS is designed so that when you delete a file, it does not truly disappear from your hard drive right away. The file you erased will not entirely be gone until you load something that requires the space for itself. When you type **del mytaxes.txt**, that file is marked for destruction if you ever need that hard drive space. In the meantime, you can usually get it back if you change your mind. At the C:\ prompt, type **undelete**.

You will see a list of files that you might recognize as the names of files that you erased recently. (It's kind of like bumping into an old girlfriend at the supermarket.) You will notice that the first letter of the file is missing. If you wish to undelete that file, you'll need to type in the first letter of the file, press Enter, and all is forgiven. (Sure, as if life is that easy.) Your file is back. However, notice that also next to the file that you would like to restore is a comment on its condition: "excellent," "good," "fair," and so on. Obviously, your chances of retrieving your file are higher if it is in excellent or good condition.

The condition of your deleted file is determined by

- How long ago it was deleted, and
- How much action your hard drive has seen since the time of deletion.

```
     QUAKE    WRI     1152  5-26-94  2:32p  ...A
This file can be 100% undeleted. Undelete (Y/N)?n

     HISCHOO  WRI     3072  7-19-94  5:01a  ...A
This file can be 100% undeleted. Undelete (Y/N)?n

     FRONTPGE WRI     5888  1-07-94  5:33a  ...A
This file can be 100% undeleted. Undelete (Y/N)?n
```

Has a new file been loaded onto that sector? If so, then your old, deleted file could be damaged. If you only recently deleted that file, say, a moment ago, then immediately repent of your wicked ways—your file is probably undamaged.

**This undelete feature is standard on DOS 5 or later.**

## UNDELETE OPTIONS

There are two added levels of undelete protection available to you. By making a minor change in your **autoexec.bat** file, you may specify one of these.

1. Open your **autoexec.bat** file in the usual way, move near the bottom of the file and create a new line.
2. Type **undelete /T**.

This tells your computer to allow you to undelete the file without requiring you to provide the missing first letter. This method is called **deletion tracking**.

If you are a person given to great fits of ambivalence about the very notion of deleting files, you can choose the **delete sentry** method. To employ delete sentry,

1. Use the same directions as above, editing your **autoexec.bat** file and moving to a line near the bottom, clearing yourself a space.
2. Type **undelete /S**.

When you select **undelete sentry**, a portion of your hard drive is set aside to store those files that you have "deleted." They aren't really deleted at all. They're moved. To provide this level of undeleting power, sentry takes up a rather large chunk of your hard drive, and, if you are deleting files to save disk space, this rather defeats the purpose. If you leave your **autoexec.bat** file alone, and type nothing at all, and have DOS 5 or later, then DOS's standard **undelete** is operating on your system.

# Chapter 8

## You and Your Modem

# WHAT IS A MODEM AND WHAT DOES IT DO?

In its simplest definition, a modem is a unit that connects your computer to a phone line and allows it to talk to other computers around the country or the world. I have a friend who moved to northern Alaska to do scientific research. There is no way of finding his phone number. But because of his line of work, I know he's "on the Internet," which means I can reach him. Modems, the Internet, and online services like CompuServe have ushered in the era of instant global communication.

Here are a handful of tasks that a modem enables your computer to perform, especially if hooked up to one of the larger online services: You may send faxes, download files from thousands of sources, look into the archives of the Smithsonian Institute and copy articles and photographs that seem interesting to you, and play arcade games with someone in another state as your opponent. You can write a letter to 30 congressmembers at once, and set your computer to pay most of your bills automatically every month. You may also converse with people around the country who have similar interests to yours…all for the cost of a local phone call, plus whatever fee arrangement is set up with your online service. You may alert parents around the country to an upcoming congressional bill that will affect education in this country. You can peruse software for your computer and download as many programs as you like. You can also buy and sell

> People use their modems to do anything from share recipes with someone in a different state to download information about universities and colleges around the country. Software companies can give you product assistance or upgrades very quickly via modem. You can also download interesting articles on many subjects that are not available in the printed press.

shares of your favorite stock, and book a flight to anywhere, and a hotel as well, for far less than you normally would. Over your modem, you can determine if it's time to refinance your home, calculate the monthly payments you'd like to end up with, and download a huge file of lenders who are apt to do business with you.

After that, your kids can learn what majors are available in the colleges you can afford to send them to. Teenagers can also research which colleges offer the best education for their interests, and then quickly find out if the college of their dreams offers grants or loans. They can also contact and talk to other people around the country who have attended that college.

## THE BIG ONLINE SERVICES

The more elaborate benefits I'm describing come by subscribing to either America Online, CompuServe, or Prodigy, or by being "on the Internet." The first three services I mentioned are the most popular consumer-oriented networks that have connected their computer system to business databases, educational and government agencies, and dozens of information centers. These services function pretty much as an extension of your own computer, simply by plugging your phone into your computer by way of a "modem." You then pay the "online" host company (such as America Online, Prodigy, or CompuServe) a set fee per month, and you may have access to these huge databases and live services, and you may also "chat" with all

the other users of those services, sending each other notes, trading programs, sharing information back and forth, or getting information of mutual interest. These online services have banks of software programs that software companies and other users have simply left online for you to download and use. You may contact computer software companies with your complaints and comments and requests, and you'll find that they get back to you quicker than if you had merely "called and left a message." If you need "fix-it" software to make one of your programs run better, you can call the company and try to talk them into mailing it to your for free (sometimes they will, sometimes they won't), or you can access their "bulletin board" by modem, and download the program in five minutes…for free.

Some modems are installed *inside* your computer. There is no little black box, such as the one above. All you'll see is the phone jack in the back of your computer. Modems are rated according to speed of transmission: 2,400 bits per second (bps) is usually the slowest, and 14,400 bps is currently the fastest. (We can expect 28,800-bps modems in the near future, though.) This distinction is not as important as it sounds. Regardless of how fast your modem is, you are limited by the capabilities of the online service you are logged on to. Many companies have a limited amount of "fast lines." Also, if you have a 14,400-bps modem, and the person you are sharing information with has a 2,400-bps modem, all of your business with that person will be conducted at 2,400 bps.

One of the most surprising aspects of setting up a modem is how easy it is to do. Most modems come with a very intimidating manual that is written in the most obtuse computer-ese I have ever seen. You'd do well to put it aside and follow only the most basic instructions provided, and hope that those instructions will work for you. They almost always do. You probably won't have to change your modem's basic settings, and if you sign up with one of the online services I mentioned, they tend to take care of that for you. They provide live technicians that will hold your hand and walk you through anything difficult.

# THE INTERNET

## THE INTERNET STARTED AS A DREAM TO TEACH WORLD PEACE THROUGH COMPUTERS...NOT!

The Internet began in 1969 as a Department of Defense research tool to provide a flexible, almost phantom-like communication system to link computers at universities with those at other defense research centers. The network deliberately had no central location, so if a nuclear attack occurred, the new communication system would not be entirely decimated. As computers became more popular, so did the Internet. People began sharing research and data on many subjects, not merely military concerns. Since that time, the Internet has grown into a large "parent" network that links hundreds of smaller bulletin boards, networks, and network families. Today, the Internet includes government and quasi-government organizations, national and international news services, consumer outlets, and bulletin boards catering to any interest imaginable.

On the Internet, any individual may reach any other individual, network, bulletin board or service, as long as he or she knows the correct online "address." Network "traffic jams" abound and its unwieldy nature invites government regulation. But the Internet's free-for-all environment, its ever-mutating web of connectivity makes it one of the most fascinating and promising democratic institutions in the world. It would be a pity to turn it into an Amtrak. As things are now, you may, without leaving your chair, download an article on a particular subject of research from an obscure university in some other part of the world, read it, and drop a note to the author and solicit his or her response to your comment. This business is conducted between you and that person and no one has any say or jurisdiction over such communication. Such benign interlinking ought to be savored. It might not last forever.

Today it is not uncommon to see letters from individuals published in national magazines with their Internet address included, so that anyone who cares to may drop a line in response. Many do. Today, if you read in the paper that a particular university has developed a treatment for a disease, and if someone you care about has that disease, you may, on the Internet, quickly track down that university's research address and find out more information. This is not tomorrow talking. It's already being done, with all the casualness of opening a can of soup.

## YES, BUT HOW DO YOU GET STARTED WITH THE INTERNET?

One solution is to pick up SPRY's **Internet in a Box**, which is a user-friendly, easy to understand introduction to many Internet resources. **Internet in a Box** acts as a navigator, or a guide, and sets up a Windows-like "point and click" interface to help you access the networks and information sources that appeal to you. The product includes the *Whole Internet User's Guide,* which is one of the most helpful books on the subject. It also includes **Air Mosaic**, a real time-saving tool that allows you to browse the "Net" using a graphic interface.

## A LITTLE MONEY TALK

Spry's **Internet in a Box** is a great way to get moving quickly on the information highway, but please note that the sign-up service offered right out of the box will cost you $8.95 per month, *plus* $8.95 per hour. Let's do a little math: That $8.95 per month charge adds up to almost $108 per year, just for the privilege of being able to go online. Should you dare to actually use the "Net," let's say an average of 4 hours per month (it takes time to get acquainted, experiment, and discover the places you and your family enjoy spending virtual time), you're up to over $540 per year.

**Internet in a Box** includes alternate sign-up services that are significantly cheaper, and the *Getting Started* manual does a superb job of summing up the variables involved in selecting which Internet service to use. If at all possible, sign up with a service that provides you with a local number. Services that provide you with a "free" 800 number to log on to will generally charge more per hour. You pay them rather than Ma Bell.

## TIME-SAVING "NET-SURFING" HINTS

Since online time is expensive, do as many chores off-line as possible. Keep your keywords and addresses handy, so you won't have to look them up or search for them while the clock is ticking. And one of the first techniques you need to master is the art of selecting an item and downloading and saving it as a file to be dealt with later. Don't read in-depth online; just peruse, browse, download, and save. These techniques help keep those heart-stopping credit card bills to a minimum.

## WHAT DO YOU MEAN, TRANSFER PROTOCOL?

You've figured out your modem's baud or bps. But now, when you're ready to receive or send a file, the screen asks you to pick a transfer protocol. What's that? What do the choices mean?

- **Kermit**   Very slow, very accurate.

- **Xmodem**   Slow, accurate

- **Xmodem CRC**   Checks for accuracy as it goes along.

- **Zmodem**   Fast, fair accuracy, nice to use if you have a fast modem (9,600 bps or above). Cuts down on phone time.

## PROCEED WITH CAUTION

And now for the warnings: Hooking your computer up to a modem is hooking your computer up to the world. That means that more things can go wrong. You are now online to the world, and your computer can register new and unusual error messages that take time to figure out and solve. **You should have your virus detection software up and running,** since you are now open to more sources for potential "infection." I ought to point out, though, that computer online services like America Online check for viruses all the programs they make available.

Also, files and programs downloaded through your telephone line have the potential to be affected by a "noisy" line (static interference), and could induce your computer to behave in odd ways. Downloading something as touchy as a Windows video driver can be a risky undertaking, since you have no control over "airway noise" that could affect the driver's integrity in subtle ways. I should point out that I've seen very few problems of this sort, but **when you alter your computer's configuration utilizing a piece of software you have downloaded, make sure you provide yourself a "way back" to the way things were before**. Anything can happen. One way to minimize the risk of transmission problems is to have an extremely fast modem. The less time you spend on the air, the less time there is for interference to occur. But just remember that when you are online, you've got an open system, and the world is watching and listening to you. Things are different now.

Remember, too, that even if you have a super-fast modem, your transmissions are limited by the speed of the slowest partner. If you're set up for a blazing 14,400 bps, and your online service can only accommodate you with a 2,400-bps open line, then you will be downloading at the same slow speed as the rest of us tortoises.

# Here are five colleges and universities that allow you to get a degree online. You can earn an MBA without leaving your living room or depleting a forest.

**Boise State University,** 1910 University Drive, Boise, ID 83725. 800-824-7017, Ext. 4079. Master of Science in Instructional and Performance Technology.

**Connected Education Inc.,** 65 Shirley Lane, White Plains, NY 10607. 914-428-8766. Master of Arts in Media Studies with a specialization in Technology and Society. Offered jointly with the New School for Social Research.

**New Jersey Institute of Technology,** University Heights, Newark, NJ 07102. 201-596-3366. Bachelor of Arts in Information Systems.

**New School for Social Research, Distance Learning Office,** 66 W. 12th Street. New York, NY 10011. 212-229-5880. Courses in the humanities and social sciences.

**University of Phoenix,** 100 Spear Street, Suite 200, San Francisco, CA 94505. 800-388-5463. Master of Business Administration, Master of Arts in Organizational Management, Bachelor of Science in Business Administration, and Bachelor of Arts in Management.

Many home computer systems come with a peppy internal modem that will suit you just fine. See the two phone jacks in the back of your computer? One is for input, a phone line coming from your wall, and the other is for output, a phone line going to your phone. If your computer has two phone jacks, you need not purchase any special connectors or adapters in order to use both your phone and your modem from one wall jack.

# ONLINE CHATTING

Having conversations via modem, or "online chatting" is quite fun. Here's how chatting works on most of the major online services. You log on to a "chat line" and read the messages that are whizzing across the screen to get a feel for who is there. America Online has a quick way for you to find out who is on that chat line at the moment, and even obtain a few lines of personal information about someone on that line who seems particularly interesting. (Upon joining America Online, you are given an opportunity to fill out a "profile" that introduces you to any other curious member. Most members enjoy this opportunity to be anonymously candid. Some comments are downright hilarious.)

To jump into a conversation, just type any comment you wish. Someone already in that "chat room" will probably note your appearance. (The names of the new drop-ins are usually highlighted in some way.) Your typed-in comment (just press Enter when you're done typing) will appear instantly on the screen with the words of other participants. It's rather amusing to see how your typed comments blend in with the others. Inevitably, someone will respond to you, and you may either join the current conversational flow, or find yourself and a few others forming a subgroup discussing a certain topic. What makes this phenomenon particularly interesting is that the people you are talking to could be logged on from anywhere in the U.S. or Canada, all for the cost of a local phone call.

> Just like the bulletin boards you see in the library, online bulletin boards are places to post messages for other people to read. People leave notes about all kinds of subjects ranging from software problems to support group meetings and more.

At some point, a private message for you from one of the chatters will flash across your screen. This comment will not be read by the other people in the "room." You are given a chance to instantly respond, or ignore them and continue on with the group conversation. (Even online, you can quickly tell if someone is wearing a tiger-skin leisure suit and a gold medallion.) Some services such as America Online make it easy for people who are engrossed in a conversation to create a new room for themselves and their ilk. Two individuals may even establish a private line, where no one else is allowed to log on. (Can you imagine the wedding cake? "Forever Yours: 9,600 baud.") Spontaneous mutual interest groups form quickly and flourish very well in this newfangled virtual neighborhood. People are always sending each other helpful articles and downloading information back and forth, even if they don't know their real neighbor's names.

# The Lighter Side of Modem Mania

Here's an example of a Sunday afternoon's conversation in one of **America Online's** many "chat rooms" (the names have been changed. . .). Keeping track of the many threads of conversation can be quite a chore.

Commonly, you sit and watch and see what people are talking about, and if you like it, just join in. As soon as you type in a comment, it appears on everyone else's computer screen, as well as your own. People will address you by your screen name and comment on what you've said, if they care to. If you get bored, you can log on to another chat room. In this case, notice that Greenie can bring her own unique experience to this debate over "prayer in the schools." The people represented in this chat room come from all over the U.S.

| | |
|---|---|
| Online Host | You are now in room "News Room." |
| Paperclip | So much talk about the Constitution—and I have to teach it this week. |
| Allegro | Bonnie, are you referring to some sort of proposed "prayer" minute or something? |
| Bonnie | Nope, establishment of a state religion is unconstitutional. |
| **CAdelta** | **First Amendment was never intended to suppress religion; just keep a state religion from forming.** |
| **Gloria** | **Indiana is one of the few states I haven't been to.** |
| Geoff | If we don't use, we all lose. |
| **CAdelta** | **ACLU and courts have badly distorted the issue.** |
| **Gloria** | **Prayer should be allowed in school. Not mandated but allowed.** |
| MJJones | The First Amendment was also to ensure that religion did not suppress the state! |
| Aleboy | MJJ: Good point. |
| Allegro | CA, I'm in favor of separation; favor of Bonnie bemoaning the religious. |
| Ace | Amen, Gloria, equal rights. |
| *Tomcat* | *Time again for some guitar jammin'.* |
| Greenie | Our children have one hour of religion in public schools-optional off campus out of class time now. |
| *Tomcat* | *Drizzle Drazzle Drozzle Droll/It's Time For This One To Go Home.* |
| Ace | Greenie, what about the "Pledge"? |
| *CarmenSD* | *Aqualung, my friend.* |
| Allegro | Gloria, maybe…but I don't see any alternatives to a workable legal system. |
| **Gloria** | **No kidding, Simbie!** |
| *CarmenSD* | *Don't you start away uneasy.* |
| **oddball** | **Are you leaving** |
| *CarmenSD* | *You poor old sod, you see it's only me.* |
| Aleboy | Or is it Sot? |
| *CarmenSD* | *Nobody recognizes Jethro Tull lyrics.* |
| *CarmenSD* | *Am I too old or too young.* |
| Aleboy | Carmen: I did. |
| **Gloria** | **One nation, under God…** |
| *Snared* | *Jethro Tull Rules* |

# PKZIP FILE COMPRESSION

## ITTY BITTY LIVING SPACE: COMPRESSING AND UNCOMPRESSING PROGRAMS WITH PKZIP

PKZIP is a simple, inexpensive program that allows you to compress unused files and programs to a fraction of their normal size. This discussion could easily have been included in the chapter on how to save disk space, but since just about every file you download through an online service is going to be compressed through the PKZIP program, we'll deal with it here. PKZIP allows you to greatly reduce the size of any file. You can do this with a single typed command. Although you cannot use a "zipped" file, you can, at any time, rub Aladdin's lamp again, type one command, and expand the file to its usable size. The most basic PKZIP program comes with two files: PKZIP.EXE and PKUNZIP.EXE. The best way to use them is to place the two files in your DOS directory. Placing them there assures that both PKZIP and PKUNZIP will be accessible from any directory.

```
Volume in drive F has no label
Directory of F:\BARBWRIT

.            <DIR>          06-03-94  1:
..           <DIR>          06-03-94  1:
RESUME   TXT      1,926 05-28-94
SURVEY2  TXT      1,227 05-30-94
TERRINEV TXT      1,168 05-29-94
SURVEY   TXT      1,009 05-29-94
SURVEY3  TXT        986 05-30-94
RESUME   WRI      2,688 05-28-94
QUAKE    WRI      1,152 05-26-94
HISCHOO  PUB    170,496 08-14-94
TEDCLASS PPP    153,775 07-05-94  1
HISCHOO  WRI      3,072 07-19-94
FRONTPGE WRI      5,888 01-07-94
FRONTPGE TXT      5,235 01-07-94
MISC821  WRI     10,880 01-08-94
ISP      PUB     20,480 01-10-94  1:
REVIEW   PCX     30,935 01-08-94
REVIEWS  PUB    373,248 01-08-94
       18 file(s)        784,165 bytes
```

Before we use **PKZIP**, these files take up **784,165 bytes**. *PKZIP will store these files as one file, taking up about 75% less space.*

Here's an example of PKZIP's usage: If you have a directory full of picture files that you do not use very often, with PKZIP, you can easily compress all those files so that they would take up far less hard drive space.

First, log on to the directory that holds your unneeded pictures. Then type

```
PKZIP mypix.zip *.*
```

You have told the computer to compress everything in that directory (*.*) into a single file called **mypix.zip**.

Thinking of this command as a written sentence, the above PKZIP command line means

"Compress (**PKZIP**) into a file called mypix.zip (**mypix.zip**) everything in this directory (*.*)"

The PKZIP program would then "deflate" each file to its smallest possible storage size, and group them all together in one file.

You could then safely delete the original pictures, and keep the new file, called **myfiles.zip**. Obviously, you do not have to call it **myfiles.zip**, as any eight-character name followed by the .zip file extension will do nicely.

> Currently, the directory **BARBWRIT** holds 18 files. After using **PKZIP**, it will hold one.

```
     18 file(s)              781,165 bytes
                          68.665.344 bytes
F:\BARBWRIT>pkzip barbwrit.zip *.*
```

## UNZIPPING (RETRIEVING) YOUR FILES AFTER THEY'VE BEEN ZIPPED

Now, to return your pictures to usable form, type

> **PKUNZIP mypix.zip**

Sit back and watch. In a short time, your files will be restored.

## PKZIP OPTIONS

The PKZIP command recognizes wildcard commands. For example, you could type

> **PKZIP mypix.zip *.tif**

which restricts the compression action to files with the .tif extension. You may also use the PKZIP command to compress one particularly large file to its smallest possible size. If you have a single document called **mytaxes.txt**, and you would like to compress it, type

> **PKZIP mytaxes.zip mytaxes.txt**

Please note that the name of the file you are creating, mytaxes.zip, comes before the name of the file you are altering.

```
F:\BARBWRIT>
BARBWRIT.ZIP
```

FOR A COMPLETE VERSION OF **PKZIP,** WRITE OR CALL:
PKWARE
9025 N. Deerwood Drive
Brown Deer, WI  53223-2437
(414) 354-8699

To have access to the 18 files that are now zipped and compressed as BARBWRIT.ZIP, just type the **PKUNZIP COMMAND**:

**PKUNZIP BARBWRIT.ZIP**

and the original 18 files will be restored.

I have merely scratched the surface of the possible uses of this wonderful program, which is widely available on (and used by) online services like CompuServe and America Online. For example, by adding certain subcommands, you can tell your computer to update a compressed file by only adding to it the work that you have done since you last compressed the file group. In fact, PKZIP enthusiasts will howl that I have done you a disservice by touching on such a small portion of this great program. But you probably have better things to do than delve into the arcane reaches of every cool program you come across. (Don't you? Ahem. When was the last time you turned off you your computer?)

One important usage of PKZIP is uploading and downloading software. In order to minimize the time you spend online, **programs that are sent across modem lines are usually zipped**. It is often your responsibility to decompress the software you downloaded once you get off-line, and are incurring no further online expense. So having PKZIP on your computer can be very handy.

## THE HIDDEN COSTS OF GOING ONLINE

Some people use their modem more often than their telephone, but before you log on to one of the big online services, check out some of their hidden costs. With CompuServe, for example, the monthly charge only covers "core services." Downloading files, logging on to the Internet, or joining certain user groups cost you extra money. America Online is one of the few services that truly charge one flat fee per month. On America Online, after you use up your allotted number of hours, you are charged for the remainder of the month at a reasonable hourly rate. Prodigy is the oldest and most established online service, and is also fairly expensive. CompuServe has more "industry connections" than the other services. Almost every software company in the nation provides added support for their products through CompuServe. America Online is the most friendly towards the nontechnical user. It emphasizes chat lines and connections to more "layman's" news outlets like CNN and Newsweek. America Online does not cater as much to computer "techies" as CompuServe does. Their software library is smaller than the others, but growing. For all the services, finding a file or tracking down information online is usually quite easy. Most services have "keywords." (To reach Sierra On-Line at CompuServe, just type **go sierra** and you're there.) America Online has a Windows-like "point and click" interface to get you around.

# SOFTWARE BULLETIN BOARDS

If a particular software company doesn't have its own "kiosk" at one of the big on-line services, they can probably be reached on their own bulletin boards. (In the on-line lingo, a *kiosk* is a place you can log on to ask questions about a particular product.) **Most computer and software companies find it more convenient to leave extra features and upgrades available "via modem" rather than have to answer the phone all the time.** You'll find updated drivers, explanations of features that you didn't know you had, and free product upgrades available on modem bulletin boards as well as the big online services. Software companies provide bulletin boards where their users can share hints and tips, vent their frustrations, and trade files amongst themselves. If one user of a particular game has "gotten farther" than other people, he or she can leave a "saved version" of that game on that game company's bulletin board for other enthusiasts to download. Bulletin boards have given rise to a subculture of people who go well out of their way to research a problem for you, solve some quirky dilemma, or explain clearly how a particular product works. It's amazing how many good software features get left out of the manual. Software companies will cook up these wild products and send them to the stores with a cheesy manual, and leave it to the online fraternity to sort things out. For example, fanatical computer people love to show off the little "Easter eggs" they've dug up in a particular product. (Did you know that, while playing SimCity, if you press Shift and type the word "fund," you'll get $20,000 to help develop your city faster?)

# WHAT IS SHAREWARE?

There are companies and individuals who distribute neat little software programs, allowing you to download a program for free, try it out, and if you like it, send in a "user's fee." Computer magazines advertise these inexpensive gems, but most people pick up shareware online, by perusing the programs that sound interesting, and downloading the ones they feel are worthwhile. The folks who designed these programs include messages that pop on your screen from time to time and complain: "You are an unregistered user! Please register today!" The fees are reasonable—between $15 and $40. No one will call you or bother you or take your family hostage if you don't register your program. However, the "nag lines" will start to get on your nerves. And if you use the product, you're supposed to register it. Shareware requires a person to behave honorably, and pay the registration, or soon all these talented programmers will have to go work for Microsoft and type code, rather than come up with cool little programs that everyone can afford. These programs are developed by individuals who enjoy creating useful (or at least interesting) software. Once you download them through your modem, you may try them out, then read about what extra features the "registered version" contains. The creators usually make it worth your while to send in your $20 and obtain the extra features.

Shareware programs are good sources of simple utilities that get lost in the big, all-inclusive programs you're likely to find in the store. I use one to view all our picture files and convert them to different formats. We have another one that tests your knowledge of chemistry.

Online modem services like CompuServe and America Online often feature the Top 10 Most Popular Shareware Downloads each month. To the software makers, these accolades often amount to more than the financial rewards they can expect. The "top downloads" are usually programs like software to help you find and edit a particular file very quickly, or make your computer "recall" what it did last, as well as little tricks to allow your computer screen to display more text at one time. Also, you'll see quick and simple "back up and restore" programs, as well as little Windows doodads like the Greta Garbo Spell Checker, Lion King icons, and Elle Macpherson wallpaper for your desktop.

## IT'S CAMPAIGN SEASON! (HOLD YOUR NOSE)

Your modem can help cut the stink. Why watch those useless, negative campaign ads? Log on to the Internet, or one of the big online services and locate the news archives. Now type in as a **keyword** the name of the candidate or officeholder, and you will see a listing of articles pertaining to him or her. This way, you and your kids can find out what this person has been doing for the last four years, instead of having to take his or her (or the opponent's) word for it.

# Chapter 9

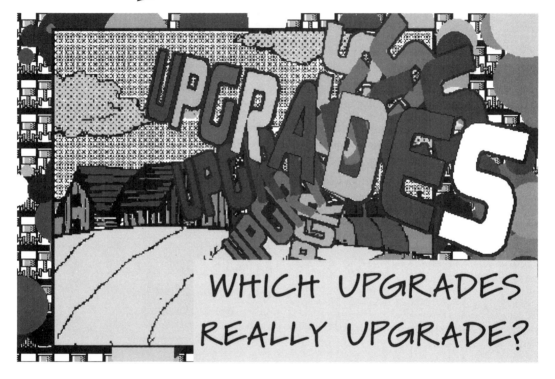

WHICH UPGRADES REALLY UPGRADE?

# THREE UPGRADES THAT CAN SEND YOUR BRAIN REELING

## THE "GETTING IN OVER YOUR HEAD" DEPARTMENT

We'd like computing to be easy. We'd like to spend a minimum amount of time fussing with the stupid manual, or on an expensive phone call to someone who might be able to help us. For the most part, setting up any of the learning games and software reviewed in this book should not be a major chore. But there are three system upgrades, or conveniences, available for your computer that will require you to learn some technical jargon, and require you to get more acquainted with your computer than you might otherwise have wished.

## SETTING UP A CD-ROM PLAYER BY YOURSELF

First, if you install a CD-ROM player by yourself (which in itself is not hard) you will have to learn about **loading devices high**. Running a CD-ROM player eats up about 40K of your lower memory, a phenomenon you might care nothing about until you start a program, and the screen says, "You need 34,987 more bytes free to run this program. Please unload any TSRs to free up more memory." (A TSR is a terminate-and-stay-resident program, like DOSKEY and Print Cache, that remains in memory even when inactive.) By typing **mem** you find out how much free memory you have. If you own a newer computer and have DOS 6.0 or 6.2, fixing this memory problem might be as easy as typing the word **memmaker** at the DOS prompt. You can pick up QEMM or 386MAX, which are two memory manager products that will probably fix everything for you. But to set up a CD-ROM player by yourself, be prepared

> **Vocabulary Tune-up**
>
> Q: What are buffers?
>
> A: Your CD-ROM driver needs small blocks of memory in which to conduct its background work while running a program. These blocks are called *buffers*. A higher number of buffers in the CD-ROM line of your **config.sys** file means your CD-ROM player will run more smoothly.

```
DEVICE=C:\DEV\MTMCDE.SYS /D:MSCD001 /P:300 /A:0 /M:64 /T:5 /I:10 /X
```

...and repeat that 10 times. Above is a typical CD-ROM line from your **config.sys** file. The M:64 refers to the number of buffers. Typically, CD-ROM programs you are likely to to buy will tell you to keep this number 32 or above. The I:10 refers to the "interrupt" assigned to your CD-ROM player. The /X tells your computer to load your CD-ROM player in upper memory. Please see your CD-ROM player's manual for the exact syntax employed by your player.

to crack open the manual and **learn about altering your config.sys and auto-exec.bat files**, adding more buffers, and other technical matters that you were trying so hard never to get bogged down in. See also the diagram at the end of this chapter for more answers to common questions people ask about their CD-ROM players.

## DISK COMPRESSION PROGRAMS

Another technical baddie is disk compression software. The drivers to run disk compression software also take up lower memory, and you'll probably have to learn "memory" jargon to deal with that. Newer versions of Stacker automatically "load high," leaving your memory allocation virtually unchanged. Indeed, you may run high and mighty with Stacker for a good long time, marveling at the extra disk space the program provides. Nonetheless, **disk compression is a complicated animal**. Your compressed drive is actually being stored in a "Host Drive," and is carefully put in place (mounted) when you boot up your computer.

Occasionally, if Stacker senses a sizable discrepancy between the estimated disk space available and actual file locations, **the Stacker program will cause your computer to refuse to load your compressed drive**, which leaves your computer "hanging" at startup…that is, no computer for the moment. Cruel as it may seem, this is part of a safety mechanism to protect your data. The program is in effect saying: "You can't use your computer until we figure out what's wrong." A good thing, really. Preventing you from writing more data to your hard drive until

Stacker will try to load itself "high" to avoid hogging lower memory. But your **config.sys** must include these four lines in the specified order:
```
DEVICE=C:\DOS\HIMEM.SYS
DOS=HIGH, UMB
DEVICE=C:\DOS\EMM386.EXE
DEVICEHIGH=C:\STACKER\STACKER.COM
```

The newest version of Stacker has tried to seperate you from the confusing world of typed DOS commands. All of your work-a-day chores maintaining your stacked drive can be conducted with a graphic interface: Pictures and easy-to-understand graphs have replaced arcane and exacting DOS syntax. This is nice, since I don't believe I would want the safety of all my data to rest on my typing skills.

the discrepancy is sorted out will prevent any real damage from being done. And actually, the problem is easily straightened out. The company's technical support number flashes on the screen, together with a promise that your data is safe as houses and not to worry about any little thing. Still, it's scary when your computer won't load, and you have to hop on the phone to ask somebody in another part of the world why that is so. This jolt to the heart might be more than you bargained for when you first decided to use compression.

### WINDOWS MULTITASKING

More technical "fun" arises when you decide to run multiple applications in Windows. If you stick to programs that don't use your sound card or programs that don't use large amounts of memory for graphics, you can probably carry on minimizing and switching and multitasking indefinitely. This is all quite fun, switching to a geography program for a few minutes, then back to a word processing program, then looking up something in *The Guinness Book of World Records,* then importing a small photo into a paint program. You can even run out to DOS occasionally, as long as you don't do anything too memory-intensive.

Trouble arises when two programs try to access your sound card simultaneously, or when the sheer number of open documents overwhelms available memory. Your computer might freeze up. Time to reboot, and how long has it been since you saved your work on that big project? After a crash, you usually have to defragment your drive to clean up any orphaned files, and then snoop around to find out which program was hogging your sound card or other resources. **These nerdly exercises can take up more time than you saved by your multitasking**. The Microsoft technical people are there five days a week to help you solve your crises, but there will be questions, questions, questions, and a disembodied voice telling you to do all these things that you scarcely understand. My family uses multitasking all the time, but, please, proceed with caution, and proceed, largely, with 8MB of RAM at least.

So unless you are extremely lucky or brilliant, be forewarned that the system upgrades discussed above are personal time-eaters. It will bring to mind how naive you were to believe that just because you spent the better part of $2,000 on the machine itself, all the science will be taken care of for you. Oh, well.

## DON'T BE THE FIRST ON YOUR BLOCK TO BUY ANY SOFTWARE OR HARDWARE

Getting dozens of programs to run well on your computer is not as easy as playing different cassettes in your tape player. When your child turns on the computer to run a favorite game, the program tries to figure out what kind of video card you have installed, what kind of sound card you have, whether you have a mouse, a printer, and if so, what kind. And finally, it need to know how much extra memory you've provided so that the program may manage its demands more efficiently. The people who write the program are aware of the **most popular** sound cards, video cards, printers, mice, and joysticks, and part of their job is to anticipate what you might have in your computer, and make sure their program can speak a language your computer's components can understand.

That's why each program you buy comes with different "device drivers," and will try to anticipate the kind of equipment you are running. If you buy something too new, or off the beaten track, the software makers might not be able to accommodate what you own. That's why, when it comes to buying computer components, you should stick to the mainstream. Buy the same darn thing that everyone else has, or you'll be stuck out on a limb. **The programmers are familiar with the main brands, and as long as you haven't gone out of your way to purchase components that are too exotic or hopelessly cheap, your computer's components and the programs you own will be able to talk nicely to each other**.

Companies who produce hardware peripherals for home computers (things like printers, sound cards, video cards, modems, and so on) usually try to standardize. But still, remember that it's best to purchase something that's very familiar to the rest of the industry. **Don't buy the "newest thing" until lots of other people have already done so**. The company that made the product needs time for the complaints to funnel in, and then they can get to work on the "upgraded version." And that upgraded version is the one that you want. Not the one that still has a few glitches to be worked out.

## PRODUCTS THAT CAN EMULATE THE POPULAR BRANDS

Regarding printers, for example, if you choose not to buy a very well-known brand, make sure the printer you buy will at least "emulate" one of the major brands. If a printer can emulate a famous make of printer, it can essentially fool your computer into believing it IS that well-known brand. For their part, most non–Sound Blaster sound cards can at least "emulate Sound Blaster," because the Sound Blaster card is what the software industry is used to having to work with. So if you do not buy a Sound Blaster sound card, make sure the card you buy can emulate one.

Software versions that end in the numeral zero (Windows 3.0, DOS 6.0) are often plagued with problems, while upgrades that end in any other numeral (Windows 3.1, DOS 6.2) are the **fixes,** and are less likely to have glitches.

## I'M A CUSTOMER, NOT A GUINEA PIG!

Regarding software, avoid products whose version numbers begin with 1 or end in 0. For example, a product called Discovery 1.0 will be Discovery's first appearance on the market. You, thrifty buyer that you are, ought to wait for Discovery 1.1 or 2.1 to hit the streets. Let them get the bugs out before you spend your hard-earned money.

# HARDWARE UPGRADES

## FIRST OF ALL, HOW UPGRADABLE IS MY COMPUTER?

If your computer is a "name brand" machine, meaning it was manufactured by a company that also makes household appliances, medical equipment, and so on, it might not be so easy to upgrade. Huge companies force you to return to their trough when you want a bigger hard drive or a faster CD-ROM player. You have to go and talk to them **and only them**, and it won't be cheap.

**The smaller firms that advertise in computer magazines usually produce computers meant for inexpensive upgrading.** The components are manufactured with the upgrade "slots" or "sockets" already in place. That foresight saves you a bundle. **In order to find out exactly which upgrades are possible, consult your computer's manufacturer and retailer.** In this regard, it matters greatly where you bought your computer. A small, storefront computer shop with one or two people on staff will give you more efficient and reliable service than a "computer superstore" where your machine can sit for days until somebody decides to open it up for a few minutes. A smaller store needs your repeat business. As far as Packard Bell is concerned, for example, your name is 1974A346T783. When you decide to upgrade, you need a knowledgeable person to sit down with you, ask some good questions about your computer and your goals, and then explain to you what the possibilities are. For this, you need a real person, not a supermarket. Check out the smaller shops when you want some computer work done.

## THE SIX BEST PLACES TO PUT YOUR MONEY

### A New Hard Drive

They're getting cheaper and faster, and you get two important system upgrades for one low price. (A 540MB or a 1 gigabyte hard drive costs less than half of what it used to. A computer repair facility can install it for less than $30.) Not only will you be getting more hard drive space, but the higher in size you go, the faster the access time. A 540MB hard drive has access times of 10 to 9 milliseconds, and a gigabyte drive is even faster, a difference you will notice as soon as you boot up. Windows programs love a large, fast, hard drive with lots of free space. And in general, a hard drive that has lots of empty space is more reliable, and your programs will run with fewer glitches. Also, today's

| 1 gigabyte hard drive holds 1 billion bytes | 170 megabyte hard drive (once considered quite adequate) **holds 170 million bytes** |
|---|---|

computers allow you to install additional hard drives, alongside the one you own now. One of our computers has four hard drives, totaling 2 gigabytes of space.

### A Hard Drive Controller Card

These "local bus" cards vastly decrease the time it takes for data from your hard drive to be accessed by your computer, which is by far the clunkiest process a computer must perform. A good hard drive controller card will allow you to set up as many as four hard drives in your computer, providing you have the physical space inside the tower and chassis itself. (Chassis size is an important consideration. Computer manufacturers tend to "cheap out" on the size of the "towers" they provide, meaning the whole big plastic thing that holds your computer's components.) A fast hard drive controller card ought to cost between $70 and $150.

### A Faster Computer

Upgrade to a 486. If you have a 486/33mHz, upgrade to a 486/66 or a 486/100. These improvements literally double or triple the speed of your computer on ALL your applications, not just some of them. You'd be surprised how inexpensive it is to upgrade your computer's CPU and motherboard to a faster speed. Check around. The costs of upgrading to a Pentium (586) computer tend to fluctuate, depending on which firms are trying to undercut each other's prices. Timing counts. Shop around before you make a big investment.

### A 15" or 17" Monitor

For a family computer, nothing adds more fun than a big monitor. An entire family can sit around a 17-inch monitor and be involved in what's going on up on the screen. No more crowding and shoving. (Somebody still has to watch the clock to see whose turn it is at the mouse.) Issues involving purchasing a new monitor are

- *Reducing screen flicker and eye fatigue.* If your monitor has a high refresh rate (the higher number is better) then you will notice less fatigue when looking at the computer image. You want a non-interlacing monitor. This feature, too, has to do with reducing eye fatigue. The monitor you buy should have .28 dot size, and nothing higher. This has to do with  the quality of the image. If an image is drawn with smaller dots (that is, .28 rather than .39), then the image reproduction is more accurate. It is worth the time to compare each monitor's ability to reduce flicker and eye strain.

- *Compliance with strict radiation output standards.* All monitors emit a small amount of radiation. Monitors that are "MPR II compliant" adhere to the strictest guidlines. This is important for young eyes who spend lots of time in front of the computer.

- *Power draw.* Fifteen and 17-inch monitors are usually "green," meaning that they have some kind of automatic "power-down" capabilities. This is very desirable, both for the environment and the electric bill.

- *Ability to display very high screen resolutions in Windows.* Most Windows software you are likely to buy for your kids will only run well in 640 × 480 dpi mode anyway. Plus, running at those higher dpi modes will slow your system down. Still, high resolution capability is a selling point that manufacturers push vigorously.

- *Viewing area.* A flat rectangular screen is more desirable than a rounded one, presumably because a flatter screen has a larger viewing area.

A good 15" monitor will probably cost you just over $300. A 17" monitor will be between $700 and $800.

## A FASTER VIDEO CARD

One computer peripheral you might choose to purchase is a video card. In the back of your computer is a slot with a small circuit board that controls the speed and quality of the images that reach your computer screen. Most computers come equipped with rather average video cards that will put text and some graphics on your screen in a reasonable amount of time. Large, full-color pictures and videos will appear soon enough, provided you aren't in too big of a hurry. If your program is attempting to run complex images, switching between video/audio segments and high-resolution animation, you must be even more patient.

If you find yourself waiting more and enjoying less, you might wish to invest in a fast video card. Computer magazines constantly review the different brands of "Windows accelerator cards," "super-fast graphics cards," and the like, and makers of graphics cards advertise heavily in those magazines. Each video card promises to deliver crisp and clear images to your screen at lightning speed, and indeed, purchasing one of these can make a big difference to your computer's performance.

High-speed video cards range from between $200 and $1,200. Features to look for are speed, compatibility with the software you own, memory, and how convenient it is to switch "modes." For example, running Windows in 65,000 color mode provides the best graphics. Nothing looks grainy, and images are clear and realistic. But some programs require you to run in 256 color mode, and will complain loudly if you try to run them in 65,000 color. You want a video card that allows you to quickly switch modes.

Another feature to look for is the amount of RAM thjat comes built in to the video card. Video cards come with 1, 2, or 4MB of RAM. Your Windows-based, graphics-intensive programs will run noticeably faster with a 2MB card, but purchasing a 4MB card does not mean the programs will run twice as fast. Four megabyte cards are a good deal more expensive, and some programs don't have the ability to take advantage of them. Two megabyte cards are sufficient. Most cards offer a 16-million color mode, supposedly matching the amount of colors the human eye may see. **I own a 2MB card, and selecting the 16 million color mode virtually grinds Windows to a halt.** (After all, you're asking your computer to process a palette of 16 million individual color values, rather than 256 or 65,000. My middling, unenlightened eyes cannot tell the difference between a 65,000 color screen shot and a 16 million one.)

The other issue regarding video cards is compatibility with the software that's out in the marketplace, the software that you are likely to buy at the store. Some programs just do not run with certain cards.

## VIDEO CARD TROUBLESHOOTING

Video card incompatibility may result in:

- A blank, black screen.
- Random color dots (pixels) strewn all over your screen.
- Screens with the text absent or distorted.
- A mouse trail that carves holes in your screen's image.
- Intermittent bad behavior, where it seems that your computer is just determined to ruin your day.

## USING YOUR NEW VIDEO CARD TO OBTAIN HIGH-RESOLUTION GRAPHICS IN DOS PROGRAMS

Most DOS programs provide their own generally compatible SVGA screen driver, but if you ever start a program and notice no text, off-colored images, or a blank screen, you'll need to

1. Exit the program.
2. Log on to the directory where your video card's software is located, for example, **C:\Hercules**.
3. Type the word **VESA**. (Some cards require you to type **VVESA** or **VESACOM**, and so on. Type **dir** and note the **.com** or **.exe** file that has the word VESA in it.) Typing this command will switch your video card to its own Super VGA mode,

and your program should run fine. You do not have to "off-load" VESA when you are done.

## CONFLICTS BETWEEN VIDEO CARDS AND AUTOMATIC MEMORY MANAGERS

Memory managers work their magic by finding regions of upper memory that are generally not used, and loading your basic operating software there. Sometimes video cards try to run in the same upper memory area, and your computer will behave very badly, giving you the old "black screen" treatment, or throwing you "out to DOS" in mid-program. Read your video card owner's manual very carefully. It probably comes with instructions on what to do if you are running QEMM or 386MAX and the like. Usually the instructions require to you **add a group of letters and numbers to a particular line of your CONFIG.SYS file**. These letters and numbers will appear nonsensical in nature, but **please type them in exactly**, and your programs and video card should talk to each other nicely again. These numbers are actually instructions to your memory manager to leave certain "pages" and "addresses" of upper memory alone.

## IF ONE PROGRAM IN PARTICULAR SEEMS TO ACT UP

Again, if after installing your new video cards you find that one of your programs misbehaves, **go look at the program's manual and find the troubleshooting section**. You'll probably find a paragraph or two telling you what to do if your screen acts funny. The program might be unable to recognize the "video mode" you are running in, and good software will usually come with a way to "force" the program to run in the VGA mode, sometimes by adding "-VGA" to the command line to start the program.

# DON'T STUFF NEW COMPONENTS INTO AN UNDERSIZED TOWER OR CHASSIS

When new controller cards, hard drives, and CD-ROM players are installed on your computer, components can end up sitting too close to each other. As circuit boards heat up, they expand slightly, and electrical current from one device can sometimes "hop" across to another, creating malfunctions. Needless to say, if your computer is turned on, and two of your components actually physically touch, both components can now be thrown into the trash. Go out of your way to ask the computer technician if things are getting a little crowded in there. If so, have him put all your computer's components in a new and larger "tower." Surprisingly, doing this shouldn't add more than $100–150 to your bill.

## "I HATE MEECES TO PIECES!"

If you and your family are giving your computer the real "art" workout, or if you just don't like using a mouse, one peripheral that might interest you is a "mouse pen." It replaces the familiar point and click mouse with an electronic pad and pen. When you press the pen on the pad, it responds like a left mouse click. Drag the pen across the pad, and you can draw lines and shapes that are simply not possible with a traditional mouse. A sophisticated *stylus,* as it is called, will respond to how

much pressure you use when drawing. More pressure means deeper and darker distribution of color, just like with a real brush or pencil. But the main difference is the dexterity. Painting with a traditional mouse is like playing piano wearing gloves. A high-quality stylus will run between $300 to $400. These are made by the CalComp, Wacom, and Kurta corporations. They are cordless, affording you even more freedom. The pads that come with them are generally 6" × 9" or 12" × 12", and

Yessiree! Perhaps a "pen mouse" is your thing.

fit comfortably in your lap. No more being chained to the table, bleary-eyed, hunched over your monitor. Ah, freedom. You may pick up the Acecad tablet and stylus for around $120. Say goodbye to pressure sensitivity, though, and they're not cordless. Styluses are an option, not only for computer artists, but for anyone who finds the action of using a pen more natural than operating one of those electronic rodents.

## BUYING MORE RAM: WHAT TO EXPECT

Be wary of buying more RAM to improve general performance. Some programs require 4MB or more of RAM to even run at all, especially programs run in Windows. For most programs, 4 or 8MB of RAM ought to be sufficient, and unless you have some need to keep three or four large programs open at a time in Windows, all with huge documents open in various states of development, you ought not to need 16MB of RAM. The upgrade from 8 to 16MB of RAM is expensive, and, unless most of your computer work is in Windows, specifically handling large files in multiple applications, your computer will not behave very differently when you jump from 8 to 16MB of RAM.

# SOFTWARE UPGRADES

## DISK CACHES AND SPEED DISK SOFTWARE

Products like **Lightning, PC-Quick,** and **Norton Speed Disk** all aim to improve your computer's performance by increasing the rate at which your computer processes information, specifically, by creating a "cache," a little storage area where your computer can place the data that you will be asking for next. Once again, it's a way to avoid your computer having to reach back onto your hard drive to retrieve information, which is always the slowest way of doing things. These programs work better with repetitive tasks, such as loading up the same document over and over again, running spell-check over and over again after a few minutes of editing, or printing the same document repeatedly. I know some people who swear that one or more of the above products made a real difference in performance. At different times, I've tried various disk cache programs hoping to speed up my computer, and never noticed a difference in speed or performance, although I suspect if you took out your stopwatch and timed the loading of one of your longer documents or programs, the stopwatch would record some difference. My advice is to take the $50 you would spend on one of the above and put it in your piggy bank until you can afford a faster hard drive.

## USING DISK COMPRESSION TO PUT OFF BUYING THAT NEW HARD DRIVE
### (It Almost Works)

Compression programs squeeze your files as close together as possible on your hard drive, and will report this space saving phenomenon to you as "extra disk space." That means if your real, physical hard drive is 120MB, if you run Doublespace or Stacker on your computer, it could report that your total disk space is now 200MB. These programs actually send up a graphic display of your wayward files being routed into efficient little squares, neat and tidy. You will indeed have more disk space available. In that sense, these programs work. You will notice that your computer runs a little slower, though, especially in Windows. And after you load on a disk compression program, your computer will never again accurately report how much disk space you have available. It will report only *estimated* disk space.

When you type

```
dir
```

at the DOS prompt, one bit of information you obtain is the amount of free disk space, expressed in **bytes free**. After your run either Doublespace or Stacker, that number is no longer accurate. Your compression program has made it so that when you look at that bottom number, you are now reading an estimate. **The real amount of disk space is invariably less than that number says.** It's just a disadvantage you learn to live with. How much less? If it says I have 6 million bytes left, do I have 4 million, or merely a few hundred thousand? This is important if you want to attempt to load on a new program, and are unsure about how much hard drive is left. At the beginning of the install process of most programs, the screen will say,

### You must have ___ bytes free disk space

They don't mean maybe. It really better be there. After running compression programs, you'll never again be sure how much disk space you have left. But there are some available guidelines: Both Doublespace and Stacker, when estimating free disk space, assume they had been able to perform the highest possible compression ratio on your files. What you need to keep in mind are these facts:

♦ Word processing files compress very well, and more than likely, your compression program did its best work on these files.

♦ **.Exe** and **.sys** files compress okay, although data and program files compress a little less.

♦ Compression programs can't do that much with graphics files. Images and digitized videos just don't lend themselves well to the process. Videos especially, if they are on your hard drive, are probably already as compressed as they can get.

♦ Most learning games are already very efficient in the way they use your hard drive space. Regarding most of the new, graphics-intensive learning games reviewed in this book, there just isn't much left for a compression program to work with. So remember that if you have lots of graphics-based learning games, and your compressed drive says you have, lets say, 9 million bytes of disk space left, cut that in half. You probably have closer to 4 million free.

## COMPRESSING ONLY THE EMPTY SPACE ON YOUR HARD DRIVE

There is a way to enjoy the advantages of disk compression with little risk. Doublespace and Stacker 4.0 allow you to compress the **empty space on your existing drive,** treating that empty portion of disk space as an entirely new drive, assigning it a new letter name. This is a an excellent option that I highly recommend, because it allows you to leave your **operating software like DOS or WINDOWS uncompressed**, while still letting you party down with more disk space than you had previously. You should do this, obviously, while your disk is still fairly empty, and you will notice that the size of your new drive is still substantially larger than "the empty space on C" you began with. The hard drive space savings involved here are even worth deleting a few programs before you begin. This will give you a bigger wad of space going in to the process, and much more going out. (I only trust my compressed drives with programs that I have backed up and readily at hand, not the ones whose original floppies I haven't seen in a while and I'd have to tear apart the house looking for if something went wrong.) Here's how you would do this:

1. Delete several programs from your hard drive. Delete only those programs you have handy, the ones you can load back on again in a short time with minimal hassle. What you are doing is creating a large block of free space for your compression program to work with.

2. Now start your compression program. Select the **Compress Only the Free Space** option.

3. When the program is done, it will report to you some extravagant and glorious number of free disk space. It won't be as big as all that, but it will be significantly more than you had before.

**By compressing only the free space on your drive, your system data is kept out of harm's way, away from the compression process, while you still get the fun of more disk space.** Although manufacturers of compression programs insist that the program is safe, horror stories abound. I, for one, do not want to be up all night reloading data from my floppy disks because my DOS and Windows and everything else went down with the ship. Still, the allure of "free disk space" is quite compelling. By compressing only the empty portion of your drive, you can have your cake and eat it, too.

# WHAT IS OS/2?

DOS and Windows are not the only ways to run a computer. IBM has developed an operating system called OS/2. Its value is mainly for people who insist on printing out a long document at the same time they are downloading a file, while simultaneously editing a brochure while playing King's Quest VI. In other words, the goal is serious multitasking. OS/2 carries out big and complicated jobs with fewer complaints than Windows. It crashes less often, owing to a piece of sharp technology called **preemptive multitasking**. In Windows, when you have several programs open, even those programs that are not being used at the moment are using your system resources and memory. With OS/2, the program you are using at the moment can have access to all the resources it needs. OS/2 appears to do away with DOS entirely, and there is no more typing of DOS commands to get things done. To copy files or move them, you click on icons and drop them in appropriate sections of your screen. OS/2 is truly another world. OS /2 also frees us from the limitations of DOS file names. You may name a file anything you like, up to 256 characters.

On the downside, OS/2 takes up 25 to 40MB on your hard drive. Also, some software manufacturers will have to provide you with new drivers to allow their programs to run with OS/2. There are still even a very few programs that do not run with OS/2 at all. Standard disk compression does not work with OS/2, although the Stacker Corporation does produce a disk compression program specifically for it. But most important, **OS/2 will run very slowly unless you have 16MB of RAM**. If you do have the 16MB of RAM, and find yourself always using your computer to do about six things at once, then hang on to your hats. You've never seen anything like OS/2.

## WHAT ABOUT THE NEW VERSION OF WINDOWS?

Windows 95 promises a **preemptive multitasking environment** similar to OS/2's. Such a development will probably be worth the $50 to $100 that the upgrade will cost.

# WHAT IS A PRINT CACHE?

There are third-party products you may buy that will set aside a portion of your hard drive or RAM memory as a storage area for the projects that are headed for your printer. These products speed up the printing process, and get you back to work on your computer quickly, rather than make you wait forever and ever while your printer finishes its job. The idea is that your computer's print drivers are capable of speedily sending data, but your printer can't receive it fast enough, which causes a gridlock, and keeps your computer busy while your printer and the project you are printing are slowly talking to each other. If part of your hard drive (or RAM, if you've got it to spare) is set aside to facilitate this laborious process, the printing work could be going on while your computer's main resources are already returned to you. I have noticed that products like Laser Tools **Print Cache** and Zenographics **Super Print** do significantly cut down print time, and get us back to work sooner.

## WHAT ABOUT LONG FILE NAMES?

For your Windows programs anyway, View Software's **Long File Names** frees you from the "eight character" rule. No more naming files

```
C:\DOCUMENT\termpper.wpd
```

for example. From now on, you can call it

```
C:\DOCUMENT\Study of penguins after an oil spill
```

if you so choose. You may use capitals, commas, periods, and spaces, any combination up to 256 characters. Long File Names does not change your file itself, and thus, it is a very safe product. Your file will still have its "DOS-legal" eight-character name, but the file name will be linked to Long File Name's own File Manager, which provides it with its new, extended moniker. Long File Names does not work with every single Windows program on the market, but each new release increases the number of Windows programs compatible with it. The product has no affect on Windows programs that are not compatible with it. Long File Names has not disrupted my Windows working environment or caused errors. Nor have I found it to hog memory or system resources, as some Windows trinkets do. In fact, I have found Long File Names to be not a trinket but a tool. The $29 it cost was a good investment.

## WINTER, SPRING, SUMMER, OR FALL

One final word on upgrades of any type. Before you do anything big with your computer, either a hardware upgrade like an additional hard drive, or installing Stacker or Doublespace, for example, it sure helps to have someone you can call who has done it first. It pays to have a "computer buddy," someone who is "farther along" (read: poorer from having spent more money than you have yet) and can help you with the inevitable conflicts, errors, and glitches that will arise. It's impossible for a hardware manufacturer or a software company to anticipate every single combination of components that their product will be called upon to operate with. It's actually a wonder this stuff works as well as it does, when you consider how many different types of systems are up and running with thousands and thousands of different hardware combinations and configurations. So be prepared to ask someone for help. "'T'ain't no shame in it."

## COMMON QUESTIONS PEOPLE ASK ABOUT THEIR CD-ROM PLAYERS

CD-ROM Issues...

Oh, you already knew that?

1. Even if a game "is on CD-ROM," it is still going to load some files on to your hard disk. In fact, this is desirable. Unless you have a quadruple-speed CD-ROM player, any game that runs exclusively from CD-ROM would go too slowly. A good CD-ROM game will load the program files onto the hard disk, just like any other game would do, but would still use the CD-ROM to provide those huge video and sound files whenever they are needed. Those are the files that are too big for your hard drive. A one-minute video with narration can be as large as 10 million bytes. Good CD-ROM games have $1/2$ to 2 hours of video, music, and sound. Having access to those huge files is the beauty of multimedia. But you don't want the program itself to be run exclusively from your CD-ROM. Too clunky. Bah!

2. When you first start up your computer, your CD-ROM drive needs to be told where to find two very important files, or it won't start up. In your **config.sys** file, there must a reference to the CD-ROM driver. Your CD-ROM config.sys line should look something like this:

```
DEVICE=C:\DEV\MTMCDE.SYS /D:MSCD001 /P:300 /A:0 /M:64 /T:5 /I:10 /X
```

Secondly, in your **autoexec.bat** file, there needs to be a reference to your CD-ROM's Microsoft extensions. The line should read something like this.

```
C:\DOS\MSCDEX /D:MSCD001
```

Please see Chapters 7 and 10 of this book for details.

3.  In your **autoexec.bat** file, be sure to check the "buffer allocation" in your CD-ROM line. It is usually the number right after the "M" (M:64, for example). Check your CD-ROM's manual for details. A higher number of buffers provides more storage areas for your CD-ROM program to keep data until the game requires it. Your CD-ROM software will run smoother if you have allocated enough memory buffers in this fashion.

4.  These days, most CD-ROMs that come preinstalled with your computer will run off of your sound card. (So do CD-ROMs from the big "multimedia kits" that include speakers, a sound card, and free CD-ROMs thrown in.) When a CD-ROM player "runs off of your sound card" that means it can use the same "interrupt" as your sound card, and it means that you don't have to install a special CD-ROM card in its own slot. This arrangement keeps things simple, which is highly desirable in the home computer biz. The CD-ROM players of this sort will be attached to the sound card itself by two cables.

5.  By installing a SCSI (pronounced "skuzzy") sound card, you can set yourself up with a quadruple-speed CD-ROM drive, and a one-gigabyte hard drive (a one-gigabyte hard drive is capable of holding a billion bytes of data). If that sort of upgrade sounds expensive, it is, but it won't be for long. Prices are falling fast. In the computer world, today's luxuries have a way of becoming tomorrow's reasonably priced necessities.

6.  Even when a CD is cued up properly and ready to go, your CD-ROM player will occasionally complain as follows:

```
CR101 not ready reading drive,
(A) Abort? (R) Retry? (F) Fail?
```

Just press R a few times, or F and start again, and your drive will eventually figure out that there is a CD in position requiring its services. Especially after replacing one CD with another, CD-ROM drives are just plain slow to get off the ground. Such occurances will not affect performance once your program has started.

7.  If your computer came with a good 16-bit sound card, or you went out and bought one yourself, you can play regular CDs in your CD-ROM player. In

Windows, open the group that was set up by your sound card, and you'll probably see a program item called "Jukebox," or a similar name. These little programs usually set up a tool bar that looks like the front of a standard CD player.

8. Conversely, some CD-ROMs allow you to play the game soundtrack on a standard CD player. If so, the manual will say so explicitly. Don't just experiment unless you were planning to buy new speakers anyway.

9. Regarding Windows-based CD-ROM programs, you might notice that the desktop icon set up for the program will disappear, being replaced by the generic DOS Program icon. Don't be alarmed. Your program will still work. Sometimes, when Windows boots up and cannot find a valid path for a program, it will not draw the icon. Windows is searching your CD-ROM drive just as if it were any other drive, and, not finding the exact CD-ROM in place for that program, it will not display the icon. When you attempt to set up the icon again (which in itself is no problem), Windows might display the message:

> **The following path might not be available for future Windows sessions. Proceed anyway?**

Just say yes and carry on.

10. When starting a CD-ROM-based program, Windows might complain

> **Cannot read from Drive X**

(X being your CD-ROM drive, whatever letter it is.) Just click on the Retry button a couple of times or go to File Manager and click on your CD-ROM drive. Either of these stratagies will convince Windows that your CD-ROM is indeed correctly in place, and the show will go on. The problem is that most CD-ROM drives (and drivers) are a bit slow to get moving, and Windows will register this clunky behavior as an error. Not to worry. Carry on.

11. At the time of this writing, quadruple-speed CD-ROM players are starting to hit the market. These CD-ROM drives do not operate at twice the speed of your double-speed CD-ROM drive, nor are they four times as fast as the now-obsolete single speed CD-ROM drive. Quadruple-speed CD-ROM drive users will notice faster access to their CD-ROM data, but not nearly as dramatic as the name of the product suggests.

# Chapter 10

# A COMPUTER IN TROUBLE IS A TEMPORARY THING

THE DIAGRAMS ON PAGES 192–194 MIGHT PROVIDE ENOUGH INFORMATION TO SOLVE YOUR PROBLEM. GLANCE AT THEM FIRST.

I work at a hospital taking care of babies who are born prematurely, often with lung disease and various ailments of underdevelopment. Every so often, my friends of childbearing age ask to hear about what I do, and I say, "Come back in about 20 years, when your children are safely grown and I won't be responsible for you lying awake worrying about what could go wrong."

If your computer is working well, I should perhaps tell you, "Don't read this chapter." After glancing at the next few pages, you'll swear off computers faster than you can say "general protection error." But actually, the primary message here is that you can fix things, and not only that, **your kids can be in on the process**, watching you work through the problems, offering suggestions, and doing some of the figuring with you. Think of it as family time—putting together a 5,000-piece puzzle of a sheer white snow bank. It's fun, it's challenging…well, on to the specifics.

## AN OUNCE OF PREVENTION

The nicest thing you can do for your computer is to **run a defragmentation program every couple of weeks**. If that sounds intimidating, it shouldn't. All that's required of you is to type the word **defrag** at the DOS prompt. That's it. (If you are running DOS version 5 or lower, you have to purchase a defragmentation program. If you are running DOS version 6 or higher, **you own a defrag program**. The **Norton Utilities** come with a very good one, as does Central Point's **PC-Tools**.) Why do you need to defragment your files? The space on a hard drive is divided into "clusters" and "sectors," as shown in the diagram below. When your computer pulls up certain files and alters them, adding or subtracting data and then putting the files back later, the computer doesn't always put the file back exactly where it found it. Remember, your hard disk is a physical machine that must rotate around towards a particular location. This process is not 100% accurate.

**File 1** is not fragmented. Each segment follows neatly after the other. File 1 is "contiguous."

**File 2** is fragmented. File segments are spread all over.

Now if you were to go into the directory that stores the program SimEarth, for example, and type **dir**, you will see all your game files listed neatly in a row. But in reality, some of your game files will be spread to the far reaches of your hard drive, and are not in the same physical location as the other files. If your hard drive is severely fragmented, the problems you will encounter are

1. Programs running very slowly, or programs "hanging up" (not responding to your mouse-click) at certain frames.
2. Random error messages occuring.

Defragmentation programs, as much as is possible, will return files to their proper place. At the C: prompt, type the word **DEFRAG**, and the program will direct you the rest of the way. The Defrag program will find those far-flung files and store them closer to the programs to which they belong. The program will try to place all your files in contiguous blocks, which means putting them all in a row without empty spaces in between. During the process, the program displays a satisfying graph that shows a block of clean and free disk space, growing ever larger, while your program file blocks are stacked up neatly in a row. The DOS DEFRAG program is not perfect, and the **Norton Utilities**, among others, are more thorough, but the DOS DEFRAG program is free.

### LIMITATIONS TO DOS'S DEFRAG PROGRAM

However, If your hard drive is 540MB or larger, then DOS's DEFRAG program might not work. Even if it starts up, it could stop in the middle of the job because the drive data is just too big for DOS's program to store in its memory buffer. You'll need to invest in the **Norton Utilities** product (which is not such a bad idea anyway) or perhaps Central Point's **PC Tools** program, which is also quite good. One way or another, you need to regularly defragment your hard drive, or drives.

There's a lot of activity going on inside your computer: You move the mouse and at the same time the sound card plays music, and all the while your hard drive and CD-ROM drive load program data, and so on. To cope with these various demands on system resources, each piece of hardware is assigned an *interrupt number* (IRQ#), *DMA channel,* and *hex number.*

### TROUBLESHOOTING: LOOK FOR SOFTWARE CONFLICT FIRST

When your computer appears to be "broken," it probably isn't. There is probably a line in your **autoexec.bat** or **config.sys** file that told your computer to do something it couldn't do, or perhaps two of your computer's "devices" are competing for the same "interrupt," DMA channel, or high memory area. **Ninety percent of your computer problems are going to be software conflicts.** Not broken software or bad disks, but programs that have a hard time talking to each other and making allowances for each other's existence on your computer. If your motherboard or CPU were to truly "break," you would know it immediately.

Some computer problems require you to patiently strip back your computer's peripheral toys (CD-ROM player, modem, etc.) until you discover the offending device.

You don't need to physically unplug your CD-ROM player or mouse. Just find the appropriate line in your **autoexec.bat** or **config.sys** file and *remove that line of text.* As far as your computer is concerned, if a device is not referred to in one of these files, the device doesn't exist. You don't have to delete the line completely, though. Just put the word **rem** at the beginning of the line, and your computer will ignore that line's instructions for the time being.

If a video segment of your new CD-ROM game appears cut in half, who is accountable for that error? You call up the company that made the game, and they will blame your video driver. You call the company that manufactures your video card and perhaps they will help you edit your config.sys file so that the game will know how to send a full video image to your screen. The list to the right shows the technical support phone numbers

> Keep these technical support numbers near your computer:
> 1) Your computer's manufacturer
> 2) Your sound card's manufacturer
> 3) Your video card's manufacturer
> 4) The store that sold you the computer
> 5) The software makers whose products have been giving you the most problems

you ought to have handy by your computer. Since most of the problems you'll encounter are **software conflicts**, there probably is a very simple solution available.

## USING DIAGNOSTIC SOFTWARE TO DETECT HARD DRIVE ERRORS

As I've said before, your hard drive rotates mechanically, and it can "go bad." If you are ever using a program on your computer and a sudden message flashes on the screen:

```
Bad Sector. Fatal Error on Drive C:
```

you've just been given a strong indicator that your hard drive could be failing. Also, if a program's activity virtually grinds to a halt at the same point every time you use that program, this, too, is an indicator of a failing hard drive. This process often happens gradually, and you will get some warning before cryin' in your beer that you lost all your data.

> You start a program, and the screen reads "Sector Not Found," "Bad Sector," "CRC Error," or "Fatal Error on Drive C."
>
> Your hard drive has bad clusters and is damaged. You may run a disk utility like Norton to try to isolate the bad sectors. Programs like these will try to move data away from the damaged portions of your drive. Even in these situations, data can be saved. Either way, it's time to buy a new hard drive.

Sudden surges in electrical current can cause clusters on your hard drive to "go bad." Also, abruptly turning off the computer can damage your hard drive. The disk's surface develops imperfections where data is stored. This could be an isolated event, causing few problems. or could be a sign of impending "disk failure," the possibility of which should be taken very seriously.

It does happen. You can purchase software that scans the surface of your disk, slowly searching out imperfections. These programs, like the Norton Utilities, will mark off these bad clusters of disk surface, making sure they are not used again. Some programs will attempt to rescue the data on these bad disk clusters, and move it elsewhere. **But if you own DOS 6.0 or later, you already have a program that will search your hard drive for bad clusters, and isolate them somewhat, allowing your programs to "work around" the damaged area.** Admittedly, DOS's disk checking features are not as advanced as the programs you pay extra money for, like Norton or PC Tools, but they do work.

**Type SCANDISK at the DOS prompt every couple of weeks**, **or after any unusual occurrence on your computer**. If you do not have DOS 6.0 or later running on your computer, then you should type "CHKDSK /F" instead of SCANDISK.

(If you don't know what version of DOS is on your computer,
type **ver** at the DOS prompt, and the screen will tell you.)

These programs make sure the files on your hard drive are reasonably close to where they should be, and are not mixed together in some way that makes your programs unworkable. SCANDISK or CHKDSK /F also search your hard drive for files that are not properly associated with any program. When a program, usually a Windows program, closes as a result of an error, it leaves "orphaned" files lying around, unfinished work that you were not given a chance to properly close because some program suddenly stopped working. SCANDISK will search your hard drive for "lost clusters," various misappropriations and errors in file size reporting. Orphaned files, or "lost allocation clusters," can cause a variety of computer errors, from screens "hanging up" to programs ending abruptly.

Anyway, back to SCANDISK and disk-checking software. After having run through the process of checking the integrity of your files and directories, these diagnostic programs will then ask if you care to save the lost, unknown files, or just blast them off your computer and be done with it. Unless you know a bit about converting a lost file to usable data, go ahead and tell the computer to trash the bad file segments. No harm done. These files are not part of your computer's operations, but simply pieces of lost work or badly fragmented and unusable files. After an event of this sort, it's a good idea to run your Defrag program to prevent further trouble.

**At the end of DOS's basic SCANDISK operations, you're given the option to start a disk cluster check**. If you suspect a hard disk error, go ahead and answer "yes." Go get a cup of coffee and come back in 10 minutes to a half an hour, depending on how big your hard drive is, and what your computer's speed is. The results of the "cluster examination" will be displayed on your computer screen. The results will stay up there until you tell them to go away, so don't worry about staying away too long and missing the diagnosis. If the SCANDISK program detects a bad sector on your disk, believe it. It's for real. The program will go ahead and try to move your files around the bad cluster area so that little data is lost. But unfortunately, if your hard drive has a bad cluster, its pretty much time for a new hard drive. Bad cluster problems can spread, and can cause further damage to your data.

One step of self-protection you might wish to take is purchasing one of the popular "system diagnostic" software packages, or "disk utilities" as they are also called. **Norton Utilities 8.0** can be picked up for just over $100, and if your hard drive is physically damaged, Norton's can almost always isolate the damaged area, recovering and removing files from the bad sectors and placing them elsewhere. Norton Utilities have recovered data from floppy disks that have been all but submerged in water. The package also comes with a program that monitors your system "integrity": Is your CPU failing? Has your RAM gone "bad"? Norton Utilities, as well as Central Point's **PC Tools,** provide good "online" help to walk you through assorted system errors and fix what can be fixed.

---

### Rebooting Your Computer

There are three ways to reboot your computer:

- A "soft reboot" is done by pressing **Ctrl+Alt+Delete**. Your computer restarts from the point at which DOS loads. Try this first.

- If the soft reboot doesn't work, you can try the **Reset** button on the hard drive. This "hard reboot" starts your boot process at the very beginning and is a little harder on your components than a soft reboot.

- Avoid using the power switch to reboot your computer. Having to turn your computer off and on again is a sign of a badly fragmented (and over-filled) hard disk. If you are forced into it, run your disk scanning utility afterward to check for fragmented files.

## BASIC TROUBLESHOOTING STRATEGIES

If you notice your computer is starting to behave in a generally unpredictable way, with error messages of various kinds springing up where none were before, there are some things you ought to do:

1. Back up your data (see Chapter 7).

2. **Think from the ground up.** Ask yourself, if your computer were to crash, do you have floppy disks around from which you could reload your programs if you had to? Did Uncle Fred return the programs you let him borrow? Well, borrow them back. Make backup disks of everything that's important to you. Prepare for the worst. It is especially important that you make sure you have your original DOS disks around. You know, the ones that came with the computer. What about your Windows disks, screen driver disks, and mouse and printer drivers? Start thinking, "If everything crashed, do I have what I need to rebuild?"

3. Pinpoint the nature of the problem. Does the screen run too slowly? Does the program freeze up when a sound kicks in? Did the problem begin as soon as you turned the computer on? Write down any on-screen messages—that will be a big help if you call technical support.

4. Recall what you did last: **Before all this started....What was the last new thing you set up on your computer?** Did you recently install a new **peripheral device,** such as a CD-ROM drive, a sound card, a hard drive controller card, or new mouse with extra features like programmable buttons? Or, did you

### Day of Disaster Checklist

1) What was the last upgrade or new program I added to my computer?

2) Does the problem occur all the time or only in certain programs? In DOS, or in Windows only?

3) Run a virus check right away.

4) Have I backed up all my data?

5) Have I run SCANDISK or a similar program to rule out hard drive errors?

6) When the problem presents itself, what are the EXACT screen messages I am getting?

7) Do I have a boot disk? If not, make one.

8) Are there liberal amounts of orange-flavored cola oozing from the keyboard?

recently install a **program that took the liberty of placing itself in your autoexec.bat or config.sys files**? (These programs are called TSRs. Some TSRs are DOS's own SMART-DRIVE, print cache programs, "speed disk cache" programs, and so on.) Did you recently compress your hard drive space by using Doublespace or Stacker? These modifications can sometimes present problems. So remember, it's important to **determine what is the most recent modification you made to your computer before the problem began**.

5. **Rule out your sound card and other peripheral devices.** Simplify and streamline your computer's configuration step by step. This will help isolate the problem. A good rule of thumb is to disable, one by one, each of your computer's "extras," then, run the program that gave you the most problem. For example, try using the offending program **with your sound card disabled**. This can easily be done by rerunning the install or "setup" procedure that comes with any game, and this time, when they ask you about the sound card, select "NO SOUND CARD" as your option, or answer "PC SPEAKER ONLY." Now play the game. Does it run well (but without sound, of course)? Try that same procedure on another game, running the set-up program again, and directing the game not to use the sound card. Does that game now work? Voilà! You have isolated the problem. That's half the work. Now dial the technical support number that came with your sound card, get a sandwich, wait on the phone, and they should be able to help you…once it's your turn. This same "process of elimination" procedure applies to other devices as well. Disconnect or "rem out" your modem, your mouse pen or even CD-ROM player, and try using the program that created the problem. We'll look at the "rem" command in a moment.

> ## The Screen Freezes
> Either while your computer is making a sound, or, right where there ought to be a sound, the picture on your screen stays exactly the same no matter what you do, and you have to reboot.
>
> The culprit is probably your sound card. More than likely, your "interrupt" or "DMA channel" needs to be reselected. Some other device, perhaps a CD-ROM player or a disk cache, is accessing your computer along the same pathway as your sound card. See Chapter 5.

## CHECKING LOWER MEMORY AVAILABILITY

If you've made no changes in your computer's configuration, and you notice less lower memory available than there used to be, something's wrong.

At the C: prompt, type **mem**. Look at the bottom two numbers. **Are they lower than the last time you looked at them?** If you have 580K conventional memory, you ought to be able to run any program. If you have less than 580K, then why?

Did your computer fail to load something into high memory? Is there a cache or buffer that is not off-loading when it should, and therefore, hogging your conventional memory?

If you have DOS 6 higher, **try running Memmaker again**, or if you have QEMM, try running "Optimize" again. You can get back that extra conventional memory you need to run your programs. (For 386MAX users, run "Maximize" again.)

Programs like QEMM can configure your memory usage in many different ways. Go back and try again, and this time, select a different option. For example, with QEMM, perhaps you need to avoid using the Stealth mode. Other automated memory managers have their own methods of "cloaking" your devices and loading them in a high memory area. These programs will try to place **every single device in an upper memory area**. Perhaps your computer would run with fewer glitches if **some of your devices remained in lower memory**. One of the memory manager options will work for you, but it might take some experimenting to find the most stable arrangement.

## DID CERTAIN PROGRAMS NOT WORK AFTER YOU INSTALLED STACKER OR DOUBLESPACE?

Hopefully, when you set up your disk compression program, you did not compress your *entire* hard drive. It's a good idea to leave part of your drive uncompressed, because, among other reasons, certain programs just don't run well on a compressed drive. Read carefully the portions of this book that deal with compressed drives (Chapter 9), and read the manual that came with your disk compression program to learn how to *uncompress part of your hard drive.*

Now, back to the programs that didn't work well on your compressed disk. Reinstall them, but this time, put them on the *uncompressed* part of your hard drive. Do they work now?

---

### A NOTE TO QEMM USERS:
### ERROR MESSAGES SUCH AS EXCEPTION 13 AND 21.

If you are using a DOS program, and it quits suddenly, and your screen is filled with a message from QEMM telling you that what just happened to you wasn't their fault, there are only two portions of that message you need to concern yourself with. First, what "Exception" number is it? Write that down. When you call QEMM to report the error, they will need to know what the Exception number was.

Secondly, see that big glob of numbers and letter in the middle of the screen? Those are memory page addresses. Write them all down exactly as you see them. When you're done with that, call QEMM, tell them what happened, and they may be of some help, but they will more than likely suggest that you call either the maker of the program that crashed out on you, or the maker of your video card.

Ultimately, what will happen is a technical support person from one company or another will help you construct an "address exclusion" line to be placed in your **config.sys** file. This line, which will be dictated to you exactly, will tell QEMM to avoid using certain regions of upper memory, because one of your programs (or your video card) also seeks to use that same region.

---

# IT'S PROBABLY SOMETHING IN YOUR AUTOEXEC.BAT OR YOUR CONFIG.SYS FILE

## MAKING A BOOT DISK

Many computer problems result from too many devices crammed into your startup files. (The diagram following this section shows an overly cluttered autoexec.bat file.) One way of simplifying your setup and isolating the problem is to make a boot disk. Most "children's" software produced since 1992 comes with instructions on how to make a boot disk, and some companies like Sierra On-Line have a program with each game that will make a **clean boot disk** for you ("clean" meaning the disk doesn't have extras loaded onto it, just the basic commands and files required to get your computer running). All you need is one floppy disk. **It is good to keep a clean boot disk on hand.** A boot disk will help you get started even if some conflict has occurred with your regular startup files on your hard disk. If you have a boot disk, you may start your computer and begin searching for what the problem is. A clean boot disk helps you eliminate devices that could be causing "lock-ups," video problems, and a host of other errors.

## USING THE REM COMMAND

Programs labeled TSR take up part of your precious lower memory, and can cause problems. Even if a TSR's memory usage is not a problem, the fact that a particular TSR is loaded before or after another program can cause problems. **It's amazing how often removing one or two lines from your autoexec.bat or config.sys can solve problems.**

You have a handy command for temporarily disabling lines in your autoexec.bat and config.sys files without erasing them altogether. Just place the word **rem** (followed by a space) in front of the line you wish to disable. After "remming" out a line, you can reboot your computer, and try to load the problem program, reproducing the situation that caused the problem. If the program now works, you can either keep that line "remmed" out or erase it entirely. There are no bad effects of having several remmed-out lines in your startup files.

## USING THE F8 KEY

If you are running DOS 6.0 or later, you have a "hot key" at your disposal to remove lines from your startup files while your computer boots up. You can see the effects of removing certain lines right away, rather than waiting to reboot again. Here's how it's done:

1. When your computer is booting up, as soon as you see the screen read: "Loading MS-DOS" (or "Starting MS-DOS"), hold down the F8 key.

2. Your computer will load your config.sys and autoexec.bat files **one line at a time,** and ask if you want to load the next line or not. You may type **y** or **n** for each line.

If you suspect one of your peripheral devices, perhaps SmartDrive or your CD-ROM, is a problem, watch the screen carefully, and **when it's time to load one of the devices you suspect might be a problem, just type "n," for no**. Now try to load the program that was giving you such grief. Does it work now? You've found your answer.

After you've isolated the offending device, or program, call the manufacturer's technical support line and tell them the symptoms.

### The Screen Went Black

When you tried to start a program, all you got was a black screen.

The program you are starting does not recognize your video card. You might be able to fix this by typing a couple of extra letters after the command to start the program. Please see the game's documentation. Also, call the video card's maker and ask them to send you the most recent driver for that card.

# The REM command

You can disable each "extra" device, one at a time. Now, with one device disabled, go and start the program or play the game that was most often giving you trouble. Does it work now? If it does, then you've at least isolated the "problem" component that was interfering with your other programs. Keep trying. You can do this as effectively as if you had paid some technician to do it for you.

**rem** here to disable your CD-ROM player.

**rem** here to disable SmartDrive.

Here's a grammar checking program that might not need to be in your PATH. **Use the backspace key to remove it.**

Fastopen, Print Cache, Sidekick, and DOSKEY are all great programs, but loading them all might be like taking blood pressure medicine with a glass of wine. They might not mix. **rem** these puppies for the moment.

```
                                    AUTOEXEC.001
C:\DOS\mscdex.exe /d:mscd000
C:\DOS\SMARTDRV.EXE 2048 512
C:\DOS\emm386.exe
SET BLASTER=A220 I5 D1 T4
SET SOUND=C:\SBPRO
C:\SBPRO\SBP-SET /M:15 /VOC:15 /CD:15 /FM:14
@ECHO OFF
PROMPT $P$G
SET PATH=C:\DOS;C:\QEMM;C:\WINDOWS;C:\MOUSE;C:\BAT;C:\KIDDESK
C:\QEMM\LOADHI /R:3 SHARE
SET GMKW5=C:\GRAMATIC
C:\DOS\MOUSE
SET TEMP=c:\Temp
fastopen c:=50; d:=50 /x
pcache
sidekick
doskey
```

Use the **rem** command to disable any device you suspect might be interfering with other stuff on your computer. *If you find that the device was not the cause of the problem, then remove the word rem.* No harm done. Honest.

*You will have to comb through your config.sys file as well.* For example, above, you **remmed** out the CD-ROM *extensions*, but your config.sys file will still try to load your CD-ROM *driver*. It must be **remmed** out as well. Remember that any changes you make will not be in effect until you reboot your computer.

I don't feel so good.

# VIRUSES

Computer viruses, like their human counterpart, do their dirty work by reproducing codes that will lead to the system's devastation and destruction. They can ruin a few of your programs or corrupt your entire system, depending on the virulence of the virus(es) that have wormed their way into your darling machine. They are written by mean people who desire to do mean things. One day, they got me.

## ABNORMAL PROGRAM TERMINATION

For a couple of weeks, I had noticed that a few of my kids' favorite programs had been "hanging up" after the first screen. They were not particularly complex programs, and they had never given us trouble before. That should have been my first clue of what was amiss, but since I had just installed DOS 6.0, Windows, and a CD-ROM player in the space of two weeks, I was hoping the system would just sort itself out. Clue two came when it seemed a few more programs were exhibiting weird behavior upon starting up.

I defragmented my drive, hoping that would help. Perhaps some .exe files had strayed to distant places on my hard drive, and needed to be placed closer to their respective programs. Still problems, and now a few more of them, but nothing seemed to add up. The errors didn't look like "sound card errors" or "memory errors" or anything else I was familiar with. I was not happy. I had heard some scary rumors about DOS 6, especially regarding the Doublespace program, which I had just installed on my computer. Since I had done so many upgrades on my computer at once, I did not look forward to stripping everything back and starting over.

# Fixing Stuff Is Easy!!

## The Hard Part Is Figuring Out What Went Wrong

That, my friends, is an important lesson: **Don't add lots of upgrades at once, because if problems occur, you won't know which new toy is creating havoc.**

The next day, my daughter called me downstairs to report that a third of all our computer programs were reporting "abnormal program termination" when we tried to run them. I was advised to "wipe my hard drive," meaning start over, remove all programs, "format" my hard drive and load everything on from scratch, this time with DOS 5, the tried and true workhorse, not DOS 6 with all its risky features. I loaded the programs again, but guess what? **A virus can walk right across your floppy drive, and infect "fresh" disks.** Whoda' thunk it? I didn't. I took the computer to the shop, whined and fretted and assumed I was looking at a several hundred dollar repair job. I described the symptoms to the technician who said, "Sounds like you've got a virus." He ran a virus check program on my computer which revealed exactly two nasty bugs that were programmed to rewrite my **.exe** files and destroy them. That's exactly what they had done. He sold me a $30 **virus protection program, which I ran on all of my floppy disks, as well as my hard drive**. Most of them worked again, because the virus that got my computer was not particularly virulent. Some viruses will send your system crashing to the floor without a reprieve, I have since learned. That antivirus program is now permanently loaded onto my computer, and will alert me if a virus is detected. If you buy lots of software, an experience with computer viruses is probably in your future. Stay protected.

If you are running DOS 6.0 or higher, there are three levels of virus protection available to you. First of all, you can periodically check you computer for viruses by typing **msav** at the DOS prompt. After this, follow the on-screen directions. Your second option is to load DOS's antivirus program into your startup files. Just place the command **msav /p** in your **autoexec.bat** file. From then on, your computer will check your entire hard drive for viruses every time you start your computer. Putting this command in your autoexec.bat file will add between one and two minutes to your reboot time.

For the highest protection: Add the command **vsafe** to your **autoexec.bat** file. This program requires a hefty 44K of memory (which would, for example, knock your available conventional memory down from a comfortable 590K to an anemic 546K). What this program does is flash a warning message on your screen whenever a virus is detected. The program then offers to take care of the problem for you. ("Do you want me to hurt him *real bad*, boss? Jus' say da' woid!")

> If your computer has a virus, and you put a disk in your floppy drive, the disk you just put in could get the virus. This means that, even if you get the virus off your computer itself, the virus still exists on your floppy disks, and can reinfect your computer. To truly rid yourself of a computer virus, you must run the antivirus program on all your floppy disks, as well has your hard drive. So remember: Viruses can walk across floppy drives and infect fresh disks.

On the downside, many, many changes in your computer's configuration can look like a virus, at least as far as this program is concerned. Installing new software often trips the alarm, terminating the installation process. No fun at all. Windows can be especially touchy with **vsafe** running, especially…need I say it?…in hi-color video modes. (What a surprise!)

You do have the option of **turning vsafe off for the time being. Simply type the command vsafe /u** at the DOS prompt, and the program is gone, either until you reboot or until you type **vsafe** again.

The **vsafe** program also gets cranky if it is not the most recent TSR loaded on your computer, which can create a small crisis if you run Print Cache or DOSKEY occasionally as needed.

I find it sufficient to simply type **msav** from time to time, especially after loading new software. Too many TSRs (and vsafe is one) lead to a temperamental computer, that's what I say. But don't forget to check for viruses every once in a while, or you'll be sorry.

# FLOPPY DRIVE AND FLOPPY DISK ERRORS

Below are a few common floppy drive disk errors and their solutions.

When you put a floppy disk in your drive and the screen displays

```
Cannot read from drive a: Abort? Retry? Ignore? Fail?
```

This is what could be wrong:

1. **The disk could be defective.** A surprisingly high number of floppy disks have imperfections on their surface, which render them useless. The percentage of defective floppy disks is especially high if you buy bulk mail order disks by the hundreds. Some floppy disk companies are just not very careful about the quality of their disks.

2. **Your disk might not be formatted to work on your system.** To fix this, type

   ```
   format a:
   ```

   at the DOS prompt. If the disk gives you any kind of grief at all regarding this process, just chuck it. You don't need bad, or even *possibly* bad, disks holding data that might be important to you.

3. **The disk might be defective.** If you are loading a program from floppy disks, and during the installation the screen  reads: "CRC error" or "Data error reading

Drive a: (or b:") or "Sector Not Found," that means that the disk the company gave you is defective. Call for another disk.

4. **The disk's density might be incompatible with your floppy drive.** If your floppy drive only supports double-density disks, and you attempt load a program with high-density disks, you will get error messages. Very few home PCs manufactured since 1992 support only double-density disks (disks that contain 720K of data, rather than 1.44MB). But it does happen. Almost every program you buy at the software store will require you to have a high-density floppy drive in order to load it. Did you go to the computer store and buy a box of floppy disks and forget to notice whether the box had HDD or DDD written on it? The box looks the same, the disks are shaped the same, but high-density disks store twice as much data as double-sided double density. If your computer has a double-density disk drive, meaning it may only read double-density (720K) disks, and you just bought a game that says "high-density disks enclosed," then call the company to arrange for them to replace your disks with the kind you can use.

Before you buy a program that provides high-density disks, make sure your floppy drive supports them.

"**CRC error**," "**Data Error Reading Drive a:\\**," and "**Sector Not Found**" are all indicators that the disk itself is bad. Get the company to send you another

5. **Look for system conflicts.** Floppy drives do malfunction, but before investigating that, check if if your sound card, scanner, or other peripheral device is incorrectly configured. These "system conflicts" could be interfering with the functioning of your floppy drive. This problem should be looked at by someone qualified to run a thorough check on your whole system.

Here's an easy error message:

`NON-SYSTEM DISK ERROR: please remove disk and press any key.`

You left some sort of disk in your floppy drive, and when your rebooted the computer it tried to boot up from the disk, just like it was supposed to do. When the computer realized that the disk in your drive wasn't a bootable system disk, it sent you an error message. All you have to do is remove the disk and press a key. The computer will continue starting up from the hard drive. But if you are like me, seeing the word "error" flash across the screen when your computer starts is like a couple shots of espresso in the morning. Excitement like that I don't need.

## "THE DANG THING WON'T TURN ON"

If, when you turn the computer on, almost nothing happens, it could be that your computer has failed to detect the kind of hard drive you have, and won't continue booting up until you set things straight. This is actually quite easy to fix. Detecting the size, type, and configuration of your hard drive is one of the first "self-checking" steps your computer puts itself through when it first turns on. Usually right after identifying the video driver, you'll see a notice on the screen saying "press F2 to enter setup" or "press spacebar to enter setup." At this point, your computer is auto-detecting your hard drive. If your computer "hangs" right there (does not proceed and appears to "freeze up") you need to press F2 or the spacebar or follow whatever directions you were given to enter the hard drive setup program for your computer. Once you're in the setup process, selecting "auto-detect" will almost always be enough. The screen will report that it detects your hard drives, and will prompt you to save these settings and exit the setup program. Before you exit, make sure the "detected" size of your hard drive is correct. Most often, you will not have to worry about cylinders and sectors and such. The auto-detect program simply needs a little help detecting the correct drive. Your computer should then boot up correctly. There are many causes for this problem. If it happens more than once or twice, take it to the shop. As they say, "It's a hardware problem."

# BE CAFEFUL WHAT KEYS YOU PRESS WHEN YOUR COMPUTER IS BOOTING UP!

## OTHER UNPLEASANT EXPERIENCES WTH THE F2 KEY

Sometimes anxious little fingers grow tired of waiting for the stupid computer to boot up in the morning. They assume that pressing extra buttons will speed things along. Anyway, it couldn't hurt, right? These little fingers end up pressing F2, the Delete key, or spacebar, and accidently entering your computer's CMOS setup mode. This setup program is necessary for installing new hard drives and floppy disk drives, but otherwise, entering CMOS setup should be avoided. CMOS setup is accessed very easily, just by pressing a key, and suddenly, the screen is blazoned with unfamiliar and intimidating instructions. If CMOS setup is accessed by accident, don't panic. Just use the arrow key to select "exit without saving," and get out of there. No harm done. However, anxious little fingers in the morning may trounce on a few buttons before finding the one that says "exit." Fear of dad coming down the stairs and finding them monkeying in no-man's land can cause youngsters to lose common sense. If the wrong buttons are pressed, anxious fingers might accidently select the wrong floppy drive. Then exit, reboot. Here comes Dad.

"Hi, Dad. Nice morning, huh? Be a chum and go make us some french toast."

All goes well until later in the day when you try to use your floppy drive. You keep getting messages saying "Unable to read drive A," or perhaps saving data to **drive A** just doesn't work. You will not get a message that says, "Your kids screwed around this morning and are covering their furry little tracks. Look at the reported size of your floppy drive, dummy. Interesting, isn't it?" No, you'll have to figure it out for yourself. If you notice your hard drive acting funny, type **MSD**, then press the **Enter** key, and see what it says about your floppy drive. Do you have a 3$^1$/$_2$ inch 1.44MB A:\ drive? Most people do. But does MSD report that you have a 5$^1$/$_4$ inch 1.2MB A:\ drive? You don't? Then somehow, setup was altered, and not surprisingly, you cannot work with your **drive A** if the computer believes you own something different than you really do. (Kind of like the IRS.)

Actually, in all fairness to the children of the world, your computer can simply fail to detect your floppy drive, and carry on through your computing day believing something entirely false about itself. This misreporting can happen for no apparent reason other than the moon is blue in June. If it happens more than once in a long while, haul the computer back to where you bought it and get the "CPU battery" replaced. This a hardware problem. Let someone else fix it.

Earlier I mentioned using the program **MSD** to see how your computer detects your floppy drive. MSD is a system reporting program that lists vital info about your computer's components. MSD is new to DOS 6.0. If you don't have DOS 6.0, you'll have to use another method of tracking down what kind of floppy disk your computer thinks you have. Try formatting a disk in drive A. What does it say? "Formatting 1.2MB disk on drive A" ? WRONG! BUSTED! (You don't have a 5$^1$/$_4$-inch 1.2MB floppy drive, you have a 3$^1$/$_2$-inch 1.44MB, remember?) Now, reboot your computer, and immediately press whichever key is specified for entering CMOS setup. It probably won't use the phrase CMOS setup,

## My Computer Started Going Really Slowly

1) Perhaps the program you are using demands more horsepower than your system can give. Check out the program's requirements.

2) If your hard drive is more than 85% full, your computer will take more time searching for data. Take stuff off or buy a bigger drive.

3) A DMA ERROR will cause your computer to behave erratically, but will not necessarily stop everything dead in its tracks. Check for conflicts between devices.

but specifying this setup key is the very first instruction that your computer spits out when you first turn it on. It has to be. It can't go far in life without detecting a hard drive and a floppy drive, can it? Having pressed this key, go find a selection that reads something to the effect of "basic CMOS setup." You will see your floppy drive listed there, joyously reporting to all the world that it is a 1.2MB A: drive, when you know very well that it isn't. Use the Arrow keys to move the **A drive** selection line, and use the PgUp and PgDn keys to select the correct type of floppy drive, which is 1.44MB $3^1/_2$ inch. Press **Escape** to go back to the main screen, and select **Save Settings and Exit**. Reboot and your computer is now through with its identity crisis.

# WINDOWS TROUBLESHOOTING

## JOIN THE WINDOWS WALKING WOUNDED

**If all your DOS programs work okay, but Windows has problems,** start asking yourself questions about your Windows setup. Are some of your drivers conflicting, competing for the same IRQ? When your computer began acting up, what was the exact error message on the screen? **Try to reproduce the error, then write down the error message, even if it makes no sense to you, get it on paper, exactly, and then call the Windows technical support line.**

## CHECKING WINDOWS'S MEMORY AND SYSTEM RESOURCES AT A GLANCE

Windows errors often happen because of too many drags on system resources.

1. From the Program Manager screen, click on the world **Help** on the upper bar of the screen. A pull-down menu will appear.

2. At the bottom, you'll see the phrase "About Program Manager." Click on it.

3. At the bottom of the About Program Manager box, you'll be told how much available memory you have, plus a message:

```
XX% System Resources Available
```

The XX is there in place of a number. What percentage of free system resources do you have? Is that number less than 50%, meaning that you have less than half of your system resources available to run programs? Please see Chapter 4 for a look at some of the situations that could reduce your available system resources.

If you've gotten error messages and unexpected shutdowns while in Windows, there's a handful of simple tips you should know. And remember that, as a registered Windows user, you are entitled to three months of free technical support from Microsoft. Their technicians are generally patient and knowledgeable, and a call to them is usually worth the time.

First of all, if you attempt to load Windows (by typing **win**), and Windows doesn't load, you might be able to start Windows by typing **win /s** instead. Typing **win /s** starts up Windows in Standard Mode rather than Enhanced Mode. Sometimes, for a variety of complex reasons, Windows Enhanced Mode will not load, but Windows Standard Mode will. To find out if you are running in Enhanced or Standard Mode,

> ## In Windows, I get lots of general protection errors, and other programs misbehave unpredictably.
>
> Your computer's programs have different ways of accessing upper memory blocks and RAM. They seek specific "Pages" and "Addresses" and if your video driver or memory manager is already using that area, or "memory page," your computer could freeze, or force you to quit the program. To fix this, look in the manual that came with your video card, hard drive controller card, or memory manager, or call their support line, and find out the "Page Exclusions" to place in your **config.sys** file. This will often solve the problem.

1. Click on the word **Help** on the Windows opening screen title bar.
2. Drag your mouse pointer down to the line "About Program Manager." Click on that line.

Down near the bottom, you'll see the description "Enhanced Mode" or "Standard Mode." Even after changing to Standard Mode, you will probably notice the memory pinch pretty soon, but at least you'll be up and running. Call Microsoft's technical support for advice, and review Chapter 4 of this book.

## MSVIDEO.DLL: SAME NAME, DIFFERENT DATES, DIFFERENT FILE (KEEP BOTH VERSIONS AVAILABLE)

Video for Windows utilizes a module called MSVIDEO.DLL. The makers of Video for Windows update their drivers occasionally, to smooth out performance and to remain compatible with the newest software. Certain older games cannot use the newest version of MSVIDEO.DLL, but I had to snoop around to discover the problem because error messages do not always tell you exactly what is wrong. In one case I opened a program, an interactive video game called Quantum Gate. The error message said "CANNOT LOAD VIDEO #$^$#*" I had no idea what was wrong. I logged onto the drive that contained the game files, and noticed it came with a file called MSVIDEO.DLL. The files was 35,987 bytes. Now I examined the file by the

| MSVIDEO | DLL | 124,416 | 11-19-93 |
|---------|-----|---------|----------|
| REG | DAT | 3,545 | 9-02-94 |
| MPLAYER | EXE | 117,536 | 6-24-94 |

| MSVIDEO | DLL | 119,072 | 6-24-92 |
|---------|-----|---------|----------|
| REG | DAT | 5,861 | 9-11-94 |
| MPLAYER | EXE | 33,312 | 11-1-93 |

Are your eyes open, Watson? Those are NOT the same files.
Yes, they have the same name, but the file SIZE is different, as well as the
date. It seems that newer software has been along and updated these files, sometimes for the better, but
not always. *Some newer versions of important files like MSVIDEO.DLL will not run with older
programs.* This is another reason to keep older versions of your system.ini and win.ini on hand. **When
trouble arises, always go back to the last "ini" that worked well for you.** At least you can get off the

same name in my Windows root directory, and it was 123,387 bytes. I realized that
when Quantum Gate was loading its necessary drivers into my Windows directory,
it must have noticed that there was already a driver called MSVIDEO.DLL, and decided not to reinstall a driver by the same name, even though the drivers were substantially different. So it was up to me to replace the newer MSVIDEO.DLL with the
older version whenever I wanted to play Quantum Gate, then put back the newer
version the rest of the time.

## HOW TO CHANGE YOUR WINDOWS VIDEO DRIVER FROM DOS

At times, you'll realize that the video driver that is currently loaded on Windows is
preventing you from even being able to start Windows at all. If only you could
change to a more generic, safer video driver **from DOS,** without having to go into
Windows to make the adjustment. Well, you can!

1. Log on to the Windows directory. Don't try to load Windows (by typing win),
   just type **cd\windows**.
2. Type the word **setup**.

You can change your video driver. Video drivers for Windows can be very temperamental, and not permitting you to start Windows is just one of the bizarre and
unpleasant quirks that video drivers exhibit. To change this system setting, select
the word **Display**. You'll see a scroll-down menu, and you should scroll down until
you see the selection "VGA." Just plain old "VGA" without any other words or
numbers next to it. Select it. What you've done is selected the most simple and

unembellished Windows video driver on your system. If you try to start Windows now, it might very well work. If this does work, you might want to get on the phone to the company that made your video card, or whoever sold you your computer. They might show you a way to edit your **system.ini** or **config.sys** file to solve the problem. But at least you're not locked out of Windows in the meantime.

## TWO TIPS FOR WINDOWS FOR WORKGROUPS 3.11 USERS

If you are using Windows for Workgroups 3.11, there are two important points to remember:

1. You can't start Windows for Workgroups 3.11 in Standard Mode. Starting Windows in Standard Mode (typing win /s instead of win) is how you would normally start Windows if your "swap file is corrupt," or if something is otherwise wrong with your Virtual Memory settings.

   In Windows for Workgroups 3.11, you must type **win /d:v** instead of win /s.

2. Windows for Workgroups 3.11 has a special feature allowing you "32-bit file access." This feature, which is set in the 386 ENHANCED section of your Control Panel, can increase the speed and efficiency of many Windows applications. Some computers do not permit 32-bit file access, or permit it only under certain conditions, and some computers will ignore the command to use 32-bit file access for a while, but then suddenly…Windows won't start. What to do? Again, from DOS, go to your Windows directory, and type **edit system.ini**. The big, blue DOS edit screen appears. Scroll down to the [386 ENHANCED] section of the file. Find the entry: 32-BIT ACCESS=ON. Just make it say 32-BIT ACCESS=OFF. Windows might start now.

### THE COMPUTER WON'T LET ME SAVE MY WORK

The Computer Won't Let Me Save My Work

When you try to save your work, the program tells you it can't save your file.

Your TEMP file may be full, or your hard drive is so fragmented, it can't find enough *contiguous* space to work with. If you have a different drive available, save your work there, or on a floppy disk, if possible. Then quit the program, delete everything in your temp file, and defragment your hard drive.

### THE UNKINDEST CUT

Have you ever been working on a very important project and saved your work, only to have your computer crash during the middle of the "save" process? Not only do you lose the work you've just been doing, but if you have a previously saved version of the same file, with the same name, your previously saved work can be ruined as well. This is why I always save a project under a slightly different name than the version I'm working on. It's good to have a "new one" and an "old one" as a back-up, in case something goes wrong.

Many Windows troubleshooting tips can be found in Chapter 4 of this book.

The next few pages are diagrams designed to explain troubleshooting at a glance. They are great for posting on the refrigerator so you can wake up each morning and wonder why you ever started any of this. Following those are detailed instructions on how to make a boot disk.

# CALLING CUSTOMER SUPPORT
## THE FINE ART OF BEING PUT ON HOLD

The highly competitive nature of the software biz means that sometimes products are sent to the store before all the bugs get removed. Software manufacturers try to recreate every condition a new product will encounter BEFORE it's in the hands of consumers, testing all the possible computer configurations and options that we, the people, have running in our living rooms. Extensive pretesting is a big job, and sometimes software companies are tempted to put stuff out on the shelves and wait to hear from us if something doesn't work.

Smart companies have installed an "800 number" to field your complaints, and if their product doesn't work on your system, they will "walk you through" a modified installation process, or send you the updated version of the product in question.

But when you call, you will be put on hold. If you have a speaker phone, you can probably wash half a sink full of dishes while the elevator music entertains you. (Microsoft has long wait times, but the hippest music. They even announce what you're listening to.)
Finally, a voice!
    A real, human voice!
        Don't faint.
            "May I help you?"

And that was Tom Petty's "The Waiting," which is what YOU'RE doing!!

Telephone technical support folks are usually prepared to spend enough time with you to solve the problem. Computer people love to fix things, and their curiosity is easily aroused. As a last resort, they will usually issue you a refund, but not before trying everything else first. Be patient. For these people, software that won't work creates feelings of profound loss. Be in front of your computer when you call, or you'll spoil all their fun and also they can't be of much service.

> **You WILL be put on hold, but the tech people haven't forgotten about you. When they pop on the line all breathless and full of questions, be prepared to tell them ALL about your computer.**

⇒ **Information to have available when you call for technical help:**

1. Your computer is a (example: 486 /33)
2. Sound card?  (Sound Blaster, Pro Audio)
3. CD-ROM drive? (Panasonic, Sony)
4. Recently installed new video card? (Hercules, Diamond Viper)
5. How much lower (conventional) memory do you have? (At the DOS prompt, type **mem** to find out.)
6. How much RAM do you have?
7. Are you running QEMM or Memmaker, and so on?
8. Are you using disk compression such as Stacker or Doublespace?
9. What upgrades or new features were added to your computer recently?
10. Did the screen "freeze," or "hang while loading"?
11. Were the colors wrong, or were the screen colors garbled?
12. Does your printer work?

THE TECHNICIANS WILL PROBABLY WANT TO MAKE CHANGES TO YOUR *AUTOEXEC.BAT, CONFIG.SYS, SYSTEM.INI,* OR *WIN.INI* FILE. IT WILL SAVE TIME TO HAVE THEM BACKED UP FIRST.

Have your autoexec.bat
and config.sys files handy,
and be prepared to edit them.

*ALSO*

Have the disks available for the program you are calling about.
They might ask you to reinstall the software entirely,
or just "run the setup" again, which means
reselecting the sound card, video mode, and so on.

Most problems on your computer are software issues. The solutions are usually simple to implement. It's just a matter of talking to people who know what they're doing.

# BOOT DISK INSTRUCTIONS

## STEP 1

## FORMATTING THE DISK

PLEASE NOTE: Even if your disk has been formatted, we must format it again, this time, as a SYSTEM DISK. To do this, add the /s switch to the format command. Type

```
format a:/s
```

Some popular diagnostic software won't let you use the word "format." Rather, a password is assigned for your protection. Please read the manual that came with the **Norton Utilities** or Central Point **PC Tools,** if such software is resident on your system.

## STEP 2

## LOCATING THE MOUSE DRIVERS

Your boot disk can direct your system to look up the mouse drivers where they already are, which means you can copy the mouse line from your **autoexec.bat** and **config.sys** files exactly as they are, or you can copy your mouse drivers to the boot disk itself, and have your startup files load them from there.

There are two types of mouse drivers available, **mouse.sys,** which must be loaded in the **config.sys** file, and **mouse.com** which must be loaded in the **autoexec.bat** file. You do not need to load both mouse.sys and mouse.com. Since mouse.sys uses less conventional memory, go ahead and use that one. Therefore your auto-exec.bat does not need to refer to your mouse, since your config.sys already does.

### a) Locating the mouse drivers

If you do not know where the **mouse.sys** or **mouse.com** files are located on your system, the command below should help in locating them. Type

```
dir \mouse /s
```

This command will cause the computer to search all subdirectories for a file called **mouse**. If it locates a file called mouse, it will display the path where the mouse files are located. For instance, if the mouse.sys file is located in the C:\MOUSE> directory, the system will display

```
Directory of C:\MOUSE
MOUSE SYS 55160 03-10-92 3:10a
MOUSE COM 56408 03-10-93 6:00a
```

Please note that if you own a Genius Mouse, for example, the files might be located in a directory called **GMOUSE**. Mouse manufacturers often have unique names for mouse driver directories.

**b) Copying the mouse driver**

Once you have located the mouse driver, copy it to the boot disk. In this step, we will assume that the mouse drivers were located in the C:\MOUSE> directory as shown in the step above. To copy the **mouse.sys** file to the boot disk, type the following at the C:\> prompt:

```
copy c: \mouse\mouse.* a:
```

*If you have a CD-ROM player, you need to include a line referring to your CD-ROM extensions. Please read the following carefully.*

## STEP 3

## CREATING THE CONFIG.SYS FILE

Now log on to drive A and type the following:

```
COPY CON CONFIG.SYS (The cursor will drop down
    one line.)
DEVICE=C:\DOS\HIMEM.SYS
DEVICE=C:\DOS\EMM386.EXE RAM 1024
```

Adding RAM 1024 will allocate 1MB of RAM as Extended Memory, or EMS. Unless you are very certain that your programs do not use EMS, please include the line RAM 1024 right after the EMM386.EXE command as shown.

If you are certain that your programs do not need EMS, and are running low on RAM and would like to wring every drop possible out of your system, then you may type the following add-on command after your EMM386.EXE line: **NOEMS,** which means No Extended Memory allocated.

```
DEVICE=C:\DOS\EMM386.EXE NOEMS
DOS=HIGH,UMB
FILES=30
BUFFERS=20
STACKS=9,256
```

*If you have a CD-ROM player, you must include its driver in your config.sys. Follow these directions very carefully or your CD-ROM player won't work.*

### Locating the CD-ROM Device Driver

Along with MSCDEX extensions, the CD-ROM also needs a device driver. This driver is loaded in the CONFIG.SYS file. To determine the correct CD-ROM device driver, at the C:\> prompt type:

> **`TYPE CONFIG.SYS | MORE`**

Note: The | is called a "pipe" command and is created by pressing SHIFT and \ (backslash) at the same time.

Now look for the line that contains information about your CD-ROM drive. It will look something like the examples below, but NOT exactly:

```
DEVICE=C:\DRV\CDROMDRV.SYS /D:MSCD001 /P:220 or
DEVICEHIGH=C:\DRV\CDROMDRV.SYS /D:MSCD001 /P:220 or
DEVICEHIGH /L:14652 =C:\DRV\CDROMDRV.SYS /D:MSCD001 /P:220
```

Your line may differ from the ones listed above. In the space below, write down the CD-ROM device driver line EXACTLY as it appears:

> `DEVICEHIGH=`_____

Finally, your "mouse line" can go near the bottom of the file. Make sure you type DEVICEHIGH, or your mouse will be taking up precious lower memory that you need for your programs:

> `DEVICEHIGH=MOUSE.SYS`

*Special note for MS-DOS 6.0 users who have compressed their hard drive:*

If you're using Doublespace or Stacker, add the appropriate line listed below.

### For Doublespace, add

> `DEVICEHIGH=C:\DOS\DBLSPACE.SYS /MOVE`

### For Stacker 3.1, add

> `DEVICEHIGH=C:\STACKER\STACHIGH.SYS`

### If you have Stacker 4.0 and DOS 5.0 or earlier, add

> `DEVICEHIGH=C:\STACKER\STACKER.COM`
> `DEVICE=C:\STACKER\SSWAP.COM`

If you have Stacker 4.0 and DOS 6.0 or later, then Stacker loads a Stacker-aware version of DOS's DBLSPACE.BIN very early in the startup process. Please see your Stacker 4.0 manual for directions on making a boot disk.

Complete the file by pressing the F6 key.

## STEP 4

### CREATING THE AUTOEXEC.BAT FILE

First, create an **autoexec.bat** file by typing:

```
COPY CON AUTOEXEC.BAT (The cursor will drop down
     one line.)
SET COMSPEC=C:\COMMAND.COM
PROMPT $P$G
PATH=C:\;C:\DOS;C:\WINDOWS;
```

**Locating the MSCDEX CD-ROM Extension**

MSCDEX is the Microsoft extension for CD-ROM drives. It must be loaded in order for your CD-ROM drive to operate. The following steps should assist you in locating this file on your system. To locate MSCDEX, at the C:\> prompt, enter

```
TYPE AUTOEXEC.BAT | MORE
```

Now look for the line which loads "MSCDEX." This line should look something like one of the following lines:

```
C:\DOS\MSCDEX /D:MSCD001
LH C:\DOS\MSCDEX /D:MSCD001
LOADHIGH /L:14429 \DOS\MSCDEX /D:MSCD001
```

Your line may differ from the ones listed above. I've provided a space for you to write down the line EXACTLY as you see it. The LH means "loadhigh" which tells your computer not to use up conventional memory loading your CD-ROM extension.

```
LH_____
```

If you are using the **mouse.com** file to load the mouse, add the following line to the **autoexec.bat** file:

```
LH MOUSE.COM
```

Complete the file by pressing the F6 key.

**NOW REBOOT YOUR COMPUTER
WITH YOUR BOOT DISK IN DRIVE A.**

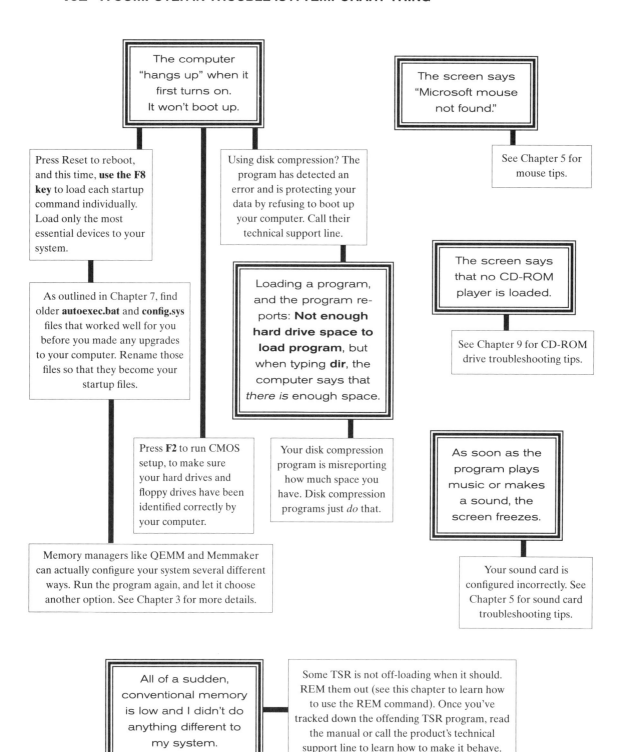

The computer "hangs up" when it first turns on. It won't boot up.

Press Reset to reboot, and this time, **use the F8 key** to load each startup command individually. Load only the most essential devices to your system.

As outlined in Chapter 7, find older **autoexec.bat** and **config.sys** files that worked well for you before you made any upgrades to your computer. Rename those files so that they become your startup files.

Press **F2** to run CMOS setup, to make sure your hard drives and floppy drives have been identified correctly by your computer.

Memory managers like QEMM and Memmaker can actually configure your system several different ways. Run the program again, and let it choose another option. See Chapter 3 for more details.

Using disk compression? The program has detected an error and is protecting your data by refusing to boot up your computer. Call their technical support line.

Loading a program, and the program reports: **Not enough hard drive space to load program**, but when typing **dir**, the computer says that *there is* enough space.

Your disk compression program is misreporting how much space you have. Disk compression programs just *do* that.

The screen says "Microsoft mouse not found."

See Chapter 5 for mouse tips.

The screen says that no CD-ROM player is loaded.

See Chapter 9 for CD-ROM drive troubleshooting tips.

As soon as the program plays music or makes a sound, the screen freezes.

Your sound card is configured incorrectly. See Chapter 5 for sound card troubleshooting tips.

All of a sudden, conventional memory is low and I didn't do anything different to my system.

Some TSR is not off-loading when it should. REM them out (see this chapter to learn how to use the REM command). Once you've tracked down the offending TSR program, read the manual or call the product's technical support line to learn how to make it behave.

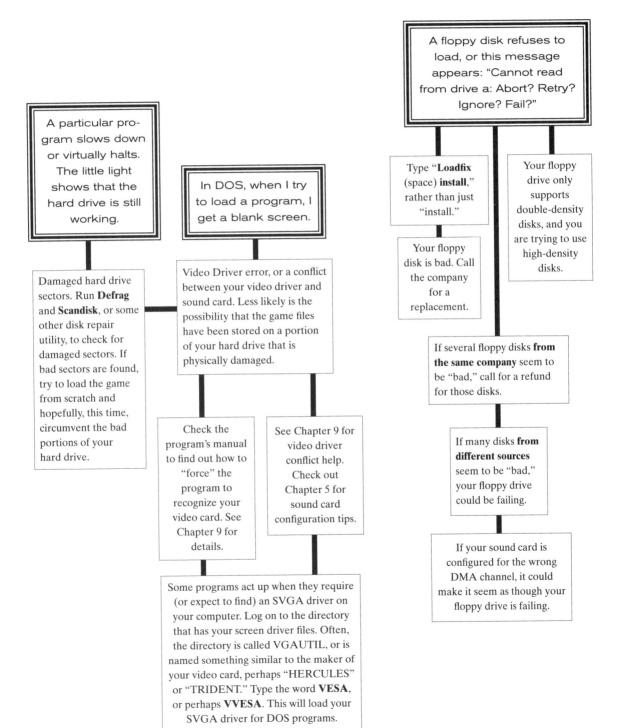

A floppy disk refuses to load, or this message appears: "Cannot read from drive a: Abort? Retry? Ignore? Fail?"

A particular program slows down or virtually halts. The little light shows that the hard drive is still working.

In DOS, when I try to load a program, I get a blank screen.

Type "**Loadfix** (space) **install**," rather than just "install."

Your floppy drive only supports double-density disks, and you are trying to use high-density disks.

Damaged hard drive sectors. Run **Defrag** and **Scandisk**, or some other disk repair utility, to check for damaged sectors. If bad sectors are found, try to load the game from scratch and hopefully, this time, circumvent the bad portions of your hard drive.

Video Driver error, or a conflict between your video driver and sound card. Less likely is the possibility that the game files have been stored on a portion of your hard drive that is physically damaged.

Your floppy disk is bad. Call the company for a replacement.

If several floppy disks **from the same company** seem to be "bad," call for a refund for those disks.

Check the program's manual to find out how to "force" the program to recognize your video card. See Chapter 9 for details.

See Chapter 9 for video driver conflict help. Check out Chapter 5 for sound card configuration tips.

If many disks **from different sources** seem to be "bad," your floppy drive could be failing.

If your sound card is configured for the wrong DMA channel, it could make it seem as though your floppy drive is failing.

Some programs act up when they require (or expect to find) an SVGA driver on your computer. Log on to the directory that has your screen driver files. Often, the directory is called VGAUTIL, or is named something similar to the maker of your video card, perhaps "HERCULES" or "TRIDENT." Type the word **VESA**, or perhaps **VVESA**. This will load your SVGA driver for DOS programs.

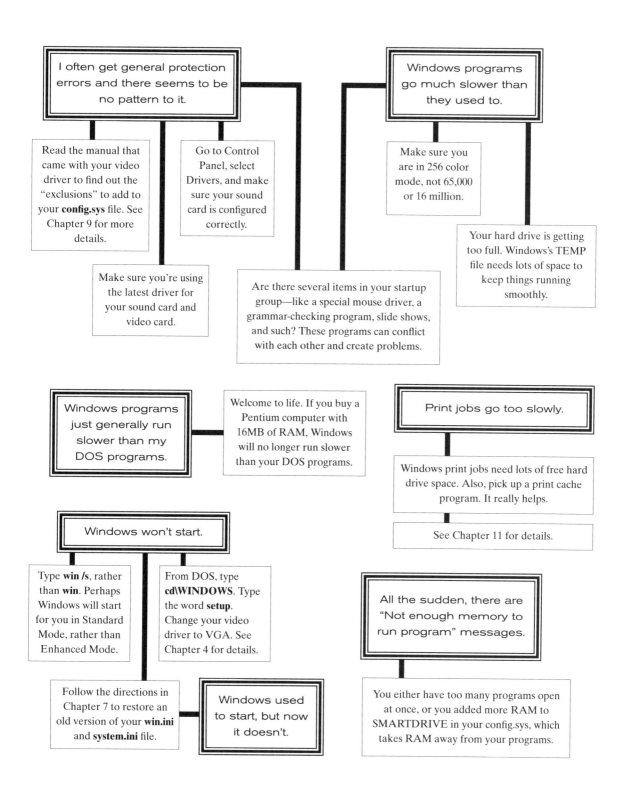

**I often get general protection errors and there seems to be no pattern to it.**

Read the manual that came with your video driver to find out the "exclusions" to add to your **config.sys** file. See Chapter 9 for more details.

Go to Control Panel, select Drivers, and make sure your sound card is configured correctly.

Make sure you're using the latest driver for your sound card and video card.

**Windows programs go much slower than they used to.**

Make sure you are in 256 color mode, not 65,000 or 16 million.

Your hard drive is getting too full. Windows's TEMP file needs lots of space to keep things running smoothly.

Are there several items in your startup group—like a special mouse driver, a grammar-checking program, slide shows, and such? These programs can conflict with each other and create problems.

**Windows programs just generally run slower than my DOS programs.**

Welcome to life. If you buy a Pentium computer with 16MB of RAM, Windows will no longer run slower than your DOS programs.

**Print jobs go too slowly.**

Windows print jobs need lots of free hard drive space. Also, pick up a print cache program. It really helps.

See Chapter 11 for details.

**Windows won't start.**

Type **win /s**, rather than **win**. Perhaps Windows will start for you in Standard Mode, rather than Enhanced Mode.

From DOS, type **cd\WINDOWS**. Type the word **setup**. Change your video driver to VGA. See Chapter 4 for details.

Follow the directions in Chapter 7 to restore an old version of your **win.ini** and **system.ini** file.

**Windows used to start, but now it doesn't.**

**All the sudden, there are "Not enough memory to run program" messages.**

You either have too many programs open at once, or you added more RAM to SMARTDRIVE in your config.sys, which takes RAM away from your programs.

# Chapter 11

# GETTING ALONG WITH YOUR PRINTER

# PRINTER FACTS

The three basic kinds of printer technologies that most consumers come across today are dot matrix, bubble jet, and laser printers.

Dot-matrix printers are given away for free with "home computer systems," and you soon discover why. The output looks bad, and your neighbors will think you bought a jackhammer for Christmas. The ribbons for dot-matrix printers need to be replaced far more often than the corresponding ink cartridges required for bubble jet or laser printing. Laser printers do great work, but are fairly expensive. Bubble jet printers represent a middling, happy compromise.

A printer capable of an attractive, full-color ouput for family and semi-professional use will cost around $550. If you don't need color printing, just about the same amount of money can buy a higher quality, black-and-white laser printer. There are lots of creative and fun things a family can do with a color printer, but all the color printers that fall into the $500 to $600 price range are bubble jet. Print jobs will take longer, and the quality will be a slight cut below laser printing. If black-and-white (or grayscale) printing suits your needs, you can spend as little as $300 for a bubble jet printer and come away feeling fairly satisfied. As you move up in price range, what you are paying for is the speed of the print jobs and the accuracy of the printed page (no blurring, no fuzziness, no smudgy look to the pictures and images).

Unless your livelihood depends on top-quality printed work, most households carry on quite nicely with printers that fall into the $500 to $600 price range.

But why should you own a printer? Will it sit there and collect dust, or become a family obsession for a month and then forgotten? That depends how creative you are at finding uses for it. Many educational programs readily access the printer, and can become a family fad for a short time and never used again.

Broderbund's **Kidpix**, MECC's **Storybook Weaver**, Maxis' **SimCity,** and Davidson's **Headline Harry** are just a few of the programs that allow users to print out good representations of their work. Some programs like Davidson's **Zookeeper** and **Word Attack**

Types of commercially available printers:

- **Dot Matrix**   Inexpensive, noisy, not very good quality in black and white or color. Cost: $200 to $400.

- **Ink Jet, Bubble Jet**   Middle price range, acceptable quality in black and white and color for most non-professional uses. (The Epson Color Stylist printer is very good.) Cost: $400 to $650.

- **Laser**   Professional quality, "publishable" print jobs. Cost: $500 to $1,200.

- **Dye-Sublimation and Wax Thermal-Transfer**   Quality full-color printing for the rich and famous. Cost: $1,000

**Plus** print out colorful, personalized plaques showing off a student's accomplishments on the program. Programs like The Learning Company's **Creative Publishing Workshop** are made so that preteen children can type and spell check and print out reports, and even add a few graphics to spruce them up. But kids can exhaust the most obvious uses of the printer fairly quickly, and ignore it long before you feel you've gotten your money's worth. Without some creative parental prodding, even stellar programs like Broderbund's **Print Shop Deluxe** can languish from disuse.

## MAKE YOUR PRINTER PART OF THE FAMILY

But don't despair. Here are a few extra uses that make it worthwhile to keep a printer around. Use these suggestions as a springboard for discovering fun ways to incorporate the printer in family activities.

Creative fun with your printer and a moderately priced paint program like Corel PhotoPaint. This is a grayscale screen shot of a full color original.

### IT'S A BIG, BIG WORLD

Using most any commercially available drawing program, you can import a map from an atlas program such as **World Atlas** by Mindscape and print it out any size you wish. A good map program such as World Atlas allows you to save your maps as .PCX files, which is a universal format recognized by all decent drawing programs. Have your child pick a part of the world or country of interest, and go to the Save File option. Now have her name it mymap.pcx, or something else meaningful (the usual DOS rules for filenames apply here).

After saving, leave the atlas program entirely, and turn on the drawing program. Painting programs like Corel PhotoPaint have a "Poster Option" (sometimes called a "Tile Option"), which allows you to print out your file (in this case a map) *any size you wish*. We have the kids print out a huge map of a country or continent (even in black and white, this is effective), and have them write in the cities, draw in the mountain ranges and rivers, and label oceans and neighboring countries. Most drawing programs are quite capable of printing out a map large enough to stimulate the imagination of a child. The kids can write and draw large, not being confined to the usual thumbnail sizes of the features shown on most commercially available children's atlases. The way print programs accommodate objects larger than a single page is by printing them over several pages.

After the printing job, you may have to supervise the cutting and pasting, or else your child's atlas creation could resemble a Picasso painting. When they are done, the kids will have created a map that takes up half the dining room floor, if they so desire. They can cut out images from magazines that could be associated with the country whose map they've printed out, and paste the pictures on the map. Of course, your child can use the drawing program to color his or her map before printing it out, or import images like tigers, cable cars, mountains, or any of the thousands of clip art images available with most drawing programs. Using the Tile Fill feature found in programs like CorelDRAW, a child may select a picture of a boat or an image of water, save it as a Tile, then click on the "Ocean" portion of the map he or she selected. **Now watch the boat or image of water fill up the map's entire Ocean segment, leaving the land untouched. This is an amazing effect, and it creates wild results even when printed out in grayscale.**

## WHAT A BOD!

The activity I just described—saving a map from an atlas program as a .PCX file, then going into a drawing program and playing with it and printing it out extra large—well, that idea doesn't only apply to atlases and maps. Take a good anatomy program like Software Marketing's **BodyWorks,** which also stores diagrams of the body as .PCX files. You can open those up in a drawing program, and have the kids alter them and print them out extra large for cutting and pasting. Have them print it out themselves, color it, and show it to Mom at dinner.

## STAR LIGHT, STAR BRIGHT

There are many good astronomy programs that allow you to export space photos in a format that most drawing programs can recognize. Again, after naming and saving your star map or planet photo, exit the astronomy program and open your drawing program. Any halfway decent drawing program can open the planet or star map file, and the kids can color or add special effects or just go straight to the print menu if they wish, and select "Poster," or some corresponding command that allows the program to print out extra large. Most of the ideas I've described here would work fine printed as simple "line art," since outlines of the objects allow the kids to go to work filling in the areas themselves.

## WORLD SCRABBLE

We developed a variation on the game Scrabble. We printed out large cards with the countries of the world, each containing a few facts about each country that we thought might be important to know. Instead of passing out the Scrabble letters, we pass out country cards, four at a time. In order to form a word on the playing board, you may dip into the letters as you wish, but you may use only words pertaining to the countries you have in your hand. As soon as you use a card, put it down in front of you and take another. Points are awarded for letters used, as usual, plus we've included a point system for using the right country cards to complete an entire continent. Of course, this variation need not be limited to geography studies. One can just as easily print out pictures and facts pertaining to famous inventors or composers. Children need more vivid and memorable connections to the dreary facts and figures fed to them at school. Creative use of the printer, by you and them, can make the initial $500 investment well worth it.

# THE HIDDEN COSTS OF OWNING AND MAINTAINING YOUR PRINTER

Even after making your initial investment, color printing at home will not be free. Your costs will be between 8¢ and 25¢ per page, depending on how much of your page is covered with ink. This cost is far below color mimeographing, but you still must caution the kids not to go crazy with their flyers, banners, homemade comic strips, and class projects.

You may purchase glossy, almost "photographic quality" paper to print out pictures that have highly detailed artwork in them. Art stores often carry this kind of paper. Itwill cost you around 17¢ per sheet. Name-brand paper that is of this same quality can run 50¢ to 60¢ per sheet. Shop around before you buy.

## MAINTAINING YOUR PRINTER

**Keep up with your printer's recommended maintenance**. Become familiar with your printer's cleaning procedure. Take the time to learn the safe way to replace the ink cartridges and how to "power down" the printer at the end of the day. Over time, dust can settle into the ink nozzles, making your "first project of the day" a bit of a waste, so do invest in a dust cover. And as you can imagine, consumer-grade printers you are likely to buy at computer stores are not made out of tungsten steel. One drop from a flimsy shelf could result in a visit to the repair shop.

Also, printers, like computers, cannot be turned off any old time. Check the manual that came with your printer. The eight or nine pages that discuss your printer's basic upkeep are usually written in plain English. It's worth reading at least those few pages. If you are wondering, by the way, why the rest of your printer manual is full of such confusing technical jargon, it's because back before everybody had computers, you had to actually program the printer itself to do relatively basic functions like change fonts and print double-spaced documents. Nowadays, people look to their word processing and desktop publishing programs to run the actual print job, so now you need not memorize your printer manual's technical jargon. But you still need the manual to teach you how to

- Insert the printer head (which you have to do when you buy a new printer or a new printer head)
- Do a thorough cleaning of your print nozzles
- Do a quick cleaning of your print nozzles
- Put your printer in standby mode and properly replace the ink cartridges

**Your printer is *the* piece of computing equipment most likely to need service while your warranty is still valid, so send it in.** You'll be glad you did. Outside of cleaning the print nozzles and making sure the paper and print cartridges are properly inserted, there is very little "self-service work" you can perform on your printer should it begin to act up. So get it to the shop on time, while everything is still covered.

The most obvious sign of a problem with your printer is poor print quality: poor ink distribution, color reproduction gradually getting way off, or the page appearing smudgy and blurry. But, no, if print jobs take too long, it's probably not a mechanical problem with your printer. How long it takes to print something has more to do with your computer and the software you are using, rather than the printer itself.

## SELECTING PAPER FOR YOUR PRINTER

When you purchase paper for your printer, there are some options. Stationery stores sell paper in various thicknesses, or "pounds." Twenty-pound paper is standard, but your finished product will look better if you buy **24 pound paper** instead. Thicker paper means less "ink spread." Images and text look sharper.

Also, for color printing, the paper you buy should be very bright white. The whiter and brighter the paper, the better your printed colors will look. Remember that high-quality printer paper has a "good side" for printing. Make sure the brightest side is facing up.

**Speed Up Those Print Jobs!!**

**Cure the Lazy Printer Blues**

Products like Laser Tool's **Print Cache** and Zenographic's **SuperPrint** really do get your work printed faster. They set aside a portion of your hard drive (or RAM, if you like) as a permanent area for your print work to be routed. You'll notice a smoother job with fewer stops and starts.

Printing out a big document requires lots of disk space, sometimes ten times the size of the document itself. What's worse, the free disk space usually has to be "contiguous," meaning "all clumped together in one group of free space." So if you are printing a large piece of work, and your computer freezes up during the process, or goes very slowly, lack of free disk space might be the reason.

## WHAT IS A PRINT CACHE?

There are third-party products you can buy that will set aside a portion of your hard drive or RAM memory as a storage area for printing projects that are headed for your printer. These products speed up the printing process, and you get back to work on your computer quickly, rather than wait forever and ever while your printer finishes its job. The idea is that your computer's print drivers are capable of speedily sending data, but your printer can't receive it fast enough, causing a gridlock that keeps your computer busy while your printer and the project you are printing are slowly talking to each other.

If part of your hard drive (or RAM, if you've got it to spare) is set aside to facilitate this laborious process, the printing work can be going on in the background while your computer's main resources are already returned to you. I have noticed that products like Laser Tools' **Print Cache** and Zenographic's **SuperPrint** significantly cut down print time and get us back to work sooner.

# Q & A WITH MR. PRINTHEAD

I HAVE A PRETTY GOOD COLOR PRINTER,
AND YET THE COLORS ON MY COMPUTER SCREEN
LOOK MUCH BRIGHTER AND CRISPER THAN IN MY PRINTED PRODUCT.
HOW COME?

Your computer creates colors by combining shades of red, green, and blue, which is referred to as the RGB color mode. But when your printer combines cyan, magenta, yellow, and black ink to produce the colors seen on your printed page. To account for the difference in color modes and to account for the fact that everybody has a different video card/monitor/printer combination than everybody else, some of the better graphics programs will **"calibrate" your printer** to output colors that look reasonably like those you see on your monitor. You may also "gamma correct" your monitor. If you own **CorelDRAW**, Adobe **Photoshop**, Micrographics **Picture Publisher**, or some similar product, please see the manual that came with your software for instructions on how to match your printer's output with what you see on the big screen.

IN WINDOWS, PRINTING TAKES TOO LONG. WHAT CAN I DO?

Yesterday's term paper printed out just fine. All 80 pages, zip, all printed in 20 minutes. But today, my daughter's colorful newsletter project won't print. The hard drive is working. (At least the little green light that shows my hard drive working is going on and off as it should.) I go make a cup of coffee, come back, still nothing is printed. I take the dogs to the park. Come back. Still nothing's printed. What's wrong?

For starters, **anything with color is going to take longer to print than even large amounts of black-and-white text**. And programs like Microsoft **Creative Writer** that invite kids to rotate text, fill drawings with one color blending into another, or explore any other zippy artistic feature is going to greatly increase your printing time. **For a printing job to take hours is not necessarily a malfunction with your computer.** In fact, it probably isn't. If that hard drive indicator light is blinking on and off, registering activity, then your computer is working. **Do not reboot or turn off your computer when your hard drive activity light is blinking. Serious and expensive disk errors can occur.** If the print job is just taking too darn long, and you're tired of waiting, press Escape,

> If a special effect takes a long time to render itself on your screen, it will probably take a long time to print as well.

or whatever button is indicated to stop the printing job. **(Pressing Escape will not instantly give you access to your computer. It even takes time to stop an aborted print job.)** Let the computer do its job. Don't get impatient and start pressin' buttons.

But, well, now what? This was supposed to be a quick project, and it's turned into a big, time-consuming mystery. You have a few options. First, if speed is what you're after, **make sure your Windows video mode is set to 256 colors, and no higher**. Certainly not to 65,000 or 16 million colors. Those high-color modes are for printing highly precise work, not for your average newsletter, flyer, or school banner. Reducing your color mode to 256 colors is the single most important step you can take to print documents out quickly. And you certainly don't need 65,000 colors to do some really good work. If you know the brand name of your video controller card, Windows automatically sets up an icon for it, so you can quickly click, see

### Printing Your Important Stuff on Somebody Else's Fancy Printer

1) Find a local, computer-friendly print shop that has a high-quality printer. Find out the brand name and model number of the printer.

2) Obtain the "Windows driver" for that printer, or the "generic driver" that emulates it closely enough. Load the driver for that printer onto your computer and, from Windows Printer Setup, select it as your printer.

3) But when you choose your Output, don't select LPT 1 like you normally would. Instead, select **Print To File**.

4) When you finish your document, you'll be printing it onto your hard drive instead of to paper. The file will be called a .prn file. You'll be prompted to name the **.prn** file just like you would name any other computer file. The result IS your printed work. (It'll go much faster than printing to paper.)

5) Copy that .prn file to a floppy disk, and take it to the print shop.

## PRINTING TO FILE (.PRN)

6) Put the disk in their computer. Copy it to their hard drive. *You do not have to load their publishing or word processing programs.* Type

```
copy myfile.prn lpt1 /b
```

(Don't call it *myfile*, call it whatever you named it.)

7) What you've done is used their computer to copy your printed file directly to their printer. The layout, font choices, and everything about your document will still be what it was at home on your word processor or publishing program. At home you "printed" your work to this fancy printer you could never really afford. Now at the print shop, you are merely "copying the file" to their printer.

how many colors you are running, and switch modes if necessary. If you find that you are at a higher-color mode, switch to 256 (8-bit) colors. You will be prompted either to restart Windows or continue with your work. Select **Restart Windows**. If you don't know the name of your video card, or cannot quickly find an icon on your Windows desktop to reset your color mode, then **exit Windows, and log on to the Windows subdirectory.** Next, type

> `setup`

You'll see four lines of information, one of them being your video mode.

- ■ If it says 256 colors, leave it alone.
- ■ If it says 32,000 or more, click on that line, and you'll be given a list of options.
- ■ Scroll down to select 256 color, 640 × 480 dpi.

Another step you can take to reduce your printing time is to tone down some of the wilder artistic effects you or your children (probably your children) employed. Also, reduce the number of pictures used in your project. **Using several fonts, especially "frilly" or artsy fonts greatly increases print time.** Reducing the amount of text will not substantially shorten print time, unless the text is oversized and rotated on the page and has sparkles all over it.

**Print jobs need lots and lots of hard drive space.** Your computer needs to spread its image data into its individual components, like colors used, size, number of fonts used, and so on. Your available contiguous disk space must be five to ten times the size of your file itself, so if your project is 700K, your available contiguous disk space must be 3.5 to 7MB. Defragmenting your hard drive before a large print job is usually a good habit to form. Using a "print cache" program can quite often reduce the print time, but it will not replace taking the steps outlined above.

THE SCREEN LOOKS OKAY, BUT MY PRINTED PAGE HAS DROP-OUTS.

If your print job has erratic errors, such as words and paragraphs dropping out for no apparent reason, your first step ought to be to restart Windows with its very own "plain Jane" VGA driver. Video drivers often cause confcts between what the screen shows and what the printer prints. Using Windows's most simple, unembellished driver will help reduce points of conflict. Please see Chapter 4 for instructions on how to change video drivers. Chapters 5, 9, and 10 have additional tips for dealing with your video driver.

# Chapter 12

# HUNTING AND PECKING THROUGH THE BEST WORD PROCESSING AND DESKTOP PUBLISHING SOFTWARE

# WHAT'S THE DIFFERENCE?

We'll get started by outlining some of the differences between word processing software and desktop publishing software. The distinctions are less important than they used to be. Many people get by quite well with only one or the other, rather than needing both.

Generally speaking, word processing software concerns itself with the document text, fonts, spelling, margins, and page length. If your document requires a table of contents and an index, good word processing software can whip them out almost automatically. Word processing programs can quickly organize footnotes and page headers and can make sure your document has a uniform appearance from beginning to end.

Desktop publishing (DTP) software is geared more to dealing with the look of the page itself; importing graphics, like pictures and artistic text to spruce up your work; and providing special effects that add pizzazz to your final product. Desktop publishing programs turn your paper into a magazine.

These days, word processing software comes packed with special features that used to be more the domain of desktop publishing products. And conversely, the newer desktop publishing programs come equipped with spell checkers and thesauruses. You might not need two separate packages.

# WORD PROCESSING PROGRAMS

**WordPerfect**, Microsoft **Word**, and Lotus's **Ami Pro** are pretty much the final answer regarding word processing programs. They have recently fallen below the $100 price range, if you do some shopping around through mail-order services like MicroWarehouse. All three have every imaginable feature for editing documents of all kinds and lengths. They are fine for professional and home use, and come with good built-in tutorials so that beginners won't be left wandering in the dark. Essentially, word processing programs are to typewriters what jet planes are to cars.

The high-powered word processing programs, such as Word and WordPerfect, even offer some DTP-like capabilities: You can import some graphics, put your text into columns, create tables and borders, and so on. You can create a nice-looking newsletter, for example, without having to venture into DTP Land.

But if you're creating a long document with lots of pictures or graphs, or if you want to do fancy things like rotate or skew your text, you're going to want the strength of a DTP program.

# DESKTOP PUBLISHING PROGRAMS

Later in this chapter, I talk about specific DTP programs. First, though, I want to go over a few features these programs have in common. Think of this section as a primer to the manual that comes with your publishing program.

## WORKING WITH OBJECTS

For starters, most DTP programs get you working with "objects." Your project is a series of "objects" that you can manipulate, resize, move, and color. There are text objects, pictures, headlines, and border art, all of which you can select and then manipulate or edit.

Thinking of text as an object is a new concept to many people. Imagine a box around the words you've typed—the boxed text is an object. If you decide you'd like to leave extra room on that page for a picture, for example, you can "shrink" the amount of room your text appears in by shrinking the size of the box. Now, since you've made your text box smaller, not as many words will fit in it anymore. So where did your words go? Your desktop publishing program stores those words that can no longer fit in the select box. As soon as you create a new page, or make a new text box, your extra words will spill into the new box, or page. Almost all desktop publishing programs have this feature of allowing you to resize and reposition your text blocks without losing the words you've typed. The extra words are never lost. They are merely repositioned by you at a later time, on a different page or column.

There are so many features to DTP programs, and differences (some subtle, some not) among them, that I'm not going to explain how to use them. Refer to your manual, check out the online tutorial if the program has one, and/or buy a supplemental "how-to" book about the program. Also, play around with the program to explore all those features. I use Microsoft **Publisher** a lot, and on the next page is a screen showing some common DTP items, such as text blocks and drawing tools.

## IMPORTING TEXT FROM OTHER PROGRAMS

DTP programs are designed for you to import text from word processing programs. It's usually easier to compose text, especially long pieces of text, in a word processing program, and edit it there, too. Then you can import your polished prose into the DTP program to lay out and liven up with pictures and so on. After all, that's what DTP programs do best.

# Publish your own newsletters, resumes, brochures, wine lists, flash cards, stories, games...

Work-in-progress using the Microsoft **Publisher** program. The big line after the question mark is the cursor's current position. Any typing will begin at that point, using the selected font and size.

**Replace This With Your Headline** means that when you type in that square, that "placeholder" will disappear and be replaced with your words, at headline size.

**LIFE ON MARS?** is the currently selected **text block**, as indicated by the surrounding small black boxes.

Click here to select a picture. Before importing, you may use your mouse to create a box showing where you want the picture to fit, like the car in this newsletter.

You can draw lines, shapes, "speech bubbles," arrows, and boundaries surrounding your text blocks.

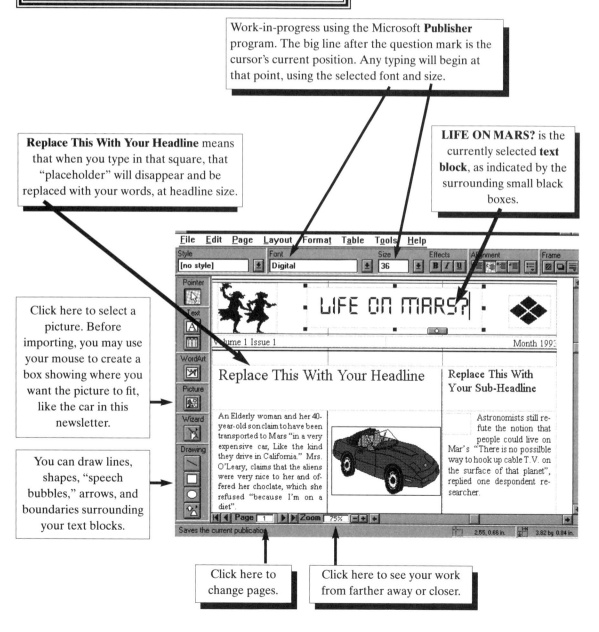

Click here to change pages.

Click here to see your work from farther away or closer.

## SAVING YOUR WORK AS A STYLE SO YOU CAN APPLY IT TO OTHER PROJECTS

Most DTP programs have a way for you to save your personal favorite combinations of font, size, letter spacing, number of columns on a page, and such. Setting up and saving your favorite set of options is called a *style.* Save your work as a style and you can quickly apply that style to any project you undertake in the future. **That way you don't have to assemble each project from scratch.** Look up at the tool bar, and you'll probably see a menu of style options, such as name style, copy style, and so on. Learn more about style options from your program's manual. They are time savers.

## TEMPLATES

Another big time saver is the use of templates to get your project started, which all the good DTP programs include. A *template* is a set of placeholders on your page. One placeholder near the top of the page, for example, might be the perfect size for a headline, and **all you need to do is type in your chosen words, and not have to fumble with creating a frame.** The next placeholder on the page might say, "Place your picture here." You would then select a piece of clip art or some other picture, and the size and angle and placement would be taken care of for you. The same goes for the body text, which is the main portion of text for your project. Most programs include templates for brochures, posters, cookbooks, resumes, business cards, birthday cards, banners, and term papers, to name only a few. The better DTP programs help you get to work quickly and give you a sense of accomplishment rather than leave you floundering around trying to make things work. Later, you can explore the program and tap its deeper potential.

## FONTS

Fonts are the various styles of type that you use with your DTP or word processing program (see the diagram on the next page). The choices go on forever. When you make a document in Windows, you have access to *TrueType fonts*. These fonts retain their clarity and exact shape no matter how large or small you print them. Have you ever seen a photograph enlarged beyond the point of clarity? The edges get jagged, the shapes indistinct. For a photograph to look good, you cannot enlarge it much beyond its original size. The same rule holds true for the pictures and letters you print out from your computer, except when you use TrueType fonts. They will look clean and clear whether you print them out at 6 points (very small) or 172 points (banner size). For most documents, use TrueType fonts whenever possible.

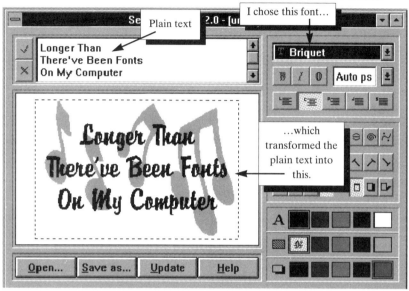

Serif's **Type Plus** gives us an opportunity to see a bit of plain text before we select a nice font for it. Type Plus allows you to put a graphic behind your words to create headlines or poke fun at your favorite love ballads.

# HOW TO SELECT THE BEST DESKTOP PUBLISHING PROGRAM FOR YOU AND YOUR FAMILY

## DESKTOP PUBLISHING PROGRAMS FOR DOS

The trouble with desktop publishing from a DOS program is that you don't have access to TrueType fonts, or to Windows's usually superior printing capabilities. TrueType fonts are like a common "pool" of letter styles that just about all your Window's programs have access to. If you purchase a DTP program for DOS, you will be limited to the fonts (and the printing options) that expressly come with that program. Also, many DOS publishing programs do not include some of the most important features I described above. Many DOS fonts have the problem of losing their sharpness when shrunk too small or expanded too large. There are DOS font editors available, and there are collections of DOS fonts that you can buy that will work around this problem, but the process is not as convenient as such tasks are in a Windows program.

## WHICH ONE OF THESE PRETTY BOXES?

In purchasing a desktop publishing program, your hardest task will be remembering what your own priorities are, looking for the product that has most of those, and sticking to your decision. If you buy a program that's flashy but complex, you will find yourself longing for the days when pen and paper were all you ever needed. Standing in a software store staring at all the pretty boxes, you might find yourself drawn to the product with 125 true type fonts and a built-in espresso maker. But when you are home writing a paper, and it's time to select a font…okay, start selecting…20 minutes later, your eyes are glazing over, and the example letters are starting to look like bats hanging from trees. You might find yourself wishing you didn't have so much to choose from. So keep your own priorities in mind. What if you wrote a paper with a footnote that is supposed to be at the bottom of the page, but the program didn't tell your computer exactly where the page break should be, so all along you've been putting your footnotes in the wrong place? Make sure your desktop publishing program will repaginate automatically. You could spend lots of money on a program that will give you ultimate control over letter kerning and spacing of letters, but comes without a good spell checker. If children will be the main users of your DTP program, make sure it imports pictures from other formats easily, and make sure it's easy to use.

**Before you go to the software store and get mesmerized
by the rows and rows of desktop publishing software,
write down the four or five features that are the most important to you,
grab an intelligent looking salesperson, give him your list and put him to work.**

## THE VERDICT IS IN

If you are in the market for a good desktop publishing program, the biggest bang for your buck is either Microsoft **Publisher** or Serif's **Page Plus**. Page Plus is not available in the stores; you must send away for it. Please see the appendix for a list of company addresses. Both Microsoft Publisher and Page Plus log in at less than $100, and can churn out good looking documents for the home user or the semi-professional. You don't need Quark Express or Page Maker 5.0 to make a good brochure, flyer, invitation, business card, or newsletter. The two programs I mentioned are easier to use than the high-end programs, and will cost hundreds of dollars less. Both Microsoft Publisher and Page Plus can be mastered quickly. Neither have taxed my computer's resources greatly, or have caused many general protection fault errors that are common to programs that employ multiple fonts and graphics. Both these programs run fast, and the results of your hard and careful editing will show up on your screen pretty quickly.

Both employ the use of multiple text frames, allowing you to add and edit text to each framed-off portion of your document without affecting the rest of your work on that page. If you type too much and the current framed-off area that you are typing into becomes filled, simply make a new text frame elsewhere on that page or on a new page, and your overflow text will be there. Both programs allow quick access to the features you want to keep handy, such as magnifying your document, changing font sizes and color, and adding special effects like drop shadows and gradient fills. Both programs make it easy to browse through the available clip art you might want to include with your text.

You may quickly add pages, copy one text style to another, and import text from many document formats. Microsoft Publisher provides a very comprehensive built-in tutorial to acquaint you with just about every feature of the program. You may work with cue cards, which are little messages that pop up and explain where to go next with your document and what to do if you are having problems. Microsoft Publisher has a feature called Page Wizard, which prompts you to type in the headline and main text entries for your document and perhaps select some artwork. Then Page Wizard will paste everything in the right place. Publisher's templates are very easy to use. Just put your cursor in the frame you wish to put text, delete the text place-holder, and start typing. Your words will appear on your screen the correct size and style for that template.

Microsoft Publisher lets you adjust the fit of your text as it wraps around any picture you place on top of it. In some programs, the text wraps around the entire picture frame, creating a very artificial block-like appearance. Microsoft Publisher lets you move the wrap-around text as close to the picture itself as you like, not merely its frame. This makes for a very professional looking document. It's very easy in Publisher to make changes to small parts of your text, such as centering the lead paragraph but leaving the rest alone. The CD-ROM version of Microsoft Publisher comes with a hefty selection of clip art, all easily accessed through a categorized online browser. It's a snap to add a border, align objects so that they line up exactly, and move and resize any object. Microsoft Publisher's cue-card hints are genuinely helpful and do not over-explain. Publisher has one very irritating drawback, how-ever: You cannot rotate most objects, tilting them slightly to the right or left. Putting pictures or text blocks at a slight angle is a standard eye-catching technique. It makes your documents stand out. Too bad they omitted this one. I ought to point out that Page Plus will perform four-color separations (a process required for high-end printing of documents), whereas Microsoft Publisher does not.

## HONORABLE MENTION

Microsoft **Creative Writer** is a program for kids to use, full of splashy features, such as the ability to press a button and make the title of your story automatically take on a zany shape. You may punctuate your story with sound effects (not relevant to the printed version of your story, obviously), and you can even put your story "in code" so only a chosen friend can read it. There's an online spell checker, and you have access to all the fonts stored on your Windows system and to the program's cute, full-color clip art. You can import any Windows-compatible picture into the story, and the text will wrap neatly around it. Creative Writer also provides drawing tools so that you can illustrate your story by hand. Perhaps the most fun and unique feature is a little juke-box machine that will spit out a story idea (there are 3,000) for your child to expound upon and illustrate for a few paragraphs. These little teasers are clever enough to stir up the embers of a little creative thought.

On the downside, you know that any program of this nature will run slowly, simply because it's in Windows and utilizes sound effects and multiple fonts. Kids love to accessorize, and will surely put several wild fonts in their stories, lots of pictures, and cool sound effects just for fun. Not surprisingly, the computer will grind to a halt, inevitably, before Junior has saved the final version of his story he's been working on all afternoon. **Consider this an 8MB-of-RAM program, on a fast computer, unless you want to subject your children to much frustration.** Printing out the stories has not proven entirely glitch-free either. One suggestion: Encourage the kids not to use the sound effects very often. The program's other

"Rules"

1. Follow what leader says unless it is wrong.

2. No walking barefoot.

3. Do not tell passwords to outsiders.

The author's daughter uses Microsoft **Creative Writer** to maintain civil order at the local treehouse level. Did Thomas Jefferson start this way?

functions will run smoother without being dragged down by your computer having to making frequent trips to access your sound card.

## THE LEARNING COMPANY'S CREATIVE PUBLISHING WORKSHOP

**Creative Publishing Workshop** is perhaps the best and easiest handling DTP program for kids. It's not overloaded with features, and what's available is helpful, not overwhelming. There's an easily accessible spell checker, a thesaurus, even online punctuation advice. You may insert pictures wherever you like in the text, and the text automatically "wraps around" the picture. Creative Publishing Workshop also helps kids design a bibliography. I'd recommend it for ages 9 through 14. Kids will quickly exhaust the clip art that comes with the program, but Creative Publishing Workshop permits the importing of any Windows-supported graphic file, such as .PCX or .BMP.

# Chapter 13

## THE PICASSO INSIDE
### Making Art with Your Computer

# SIX TYPES OF COMPUTER ART PROGRAMS

In this chapter, we'll take a closer look at some of the more popular computer art programs and explore the features they have in common. Hopefully, this will make it easier to see if any of these programs are right for you.

## DRAWING

There are programs that allow you to adjust line length and the width of your drawing strokes with great precision, and allow you to rotate, expand, or shrink objects. These programs let you combine and blend shapes and curves to your liking, color them, add text to these objects, and even permit you to treat letters and numbers as artistic objects themselves. The best known drawing programs are **CorelDRAW**, Micrographics **QuickDraw**, and Denebar **Canvas**.

## PHOTO EDITING

Then there are photograph editing programs, such as Adobe **Photoshop** and Aldus **Photostyler**. With them you can take a photograph from any source, replace colors in the photograph with your own choice of shades and hues, add objects to the photograph that weren't there before, and run the photograph through various filters. For example, some photograph editing programs let you create the impression that the picture is a reflection on a drop of water or a shattered mirror. You can take a photograph of yourself and place your image on top of a shot of Mount Everest, without obvious paste marks or jagged edges where the photo images meet.

One warning when working with these programs: There is a loss of quality when you try to make the photo bigger than its original size. A 6″ × 6″ color photo on the computer screen does not translate into a 6″ × 6″ color printout. Heartbreak and disappointment await the poor soul who expects his medium-priced color printer to painlessly duplicate what his hands have just created on the computer screen itself (more on this later).

## ARCHITECTURAL DESIGN

Next, there are architectural programs, also known as CAD (computer aided design) drawing. With these programs you can type in the measurements and dimensions of an object you wish to draw, such as a room or a bookcase, and see the objects rendered as three-dimensional pictures. You may also design your object surface by surface, block by block, drawing in the lines yourself, asking the computer to set everything to scale for you. Not only may you add color to your objects, but you can tell the computer to color it in such a way that the light reflects on the surface to suggest shadows and a 3D surface. Creating a design with realistic and dramatic lights and shadows is something a computer does very well. The most expensive industry-standard CAD program is **AutoCAD**, followed by some surprisingly well-featured imitators, such as **3D Design Plus**. CAD programs are not intuitively driven fun art programs for an evening of noodling around. You must read the manual and be willing to learn some math. Programs like SoftKey's **KeyCad** and **3D Design Plus** are appropriate for the casual user and can give a child a great head start in construction design and related careers.

## PAINTING

Next are the paint simulation programs. Software such as Fractal Design's **Painter 2.0** and Fauve **Matisse** do a great job of providing you with "paint brushes" that simulate the effects of real oil paint, water colors, felt tip markers, various types of pencil tips, and acrylics, as you "paint" them on your "canvas" with your computer's mouse or stylus. The kinds of paint media are infinitely adjustable, so the styles of brushes and paint selections offered to you when you first start up the program are merely the beginning. **Paint programs tend to be very intuitive to use**, and after mastering a few "point and click" operations, you can be on your way to creating some startlingly interesting artwork. Paint programs also allow you to alter the "canvas," including options such as bumpy paper, wet paper, and wood, all "at the touch of a button," as they say.

## ARTISTIC TEXT

Now let's look at some artistic text rendering programs, like Pixar's **Typestry** or Crystal Graphic's **Flying Fonts**. Programs like Typestry will take any true type font string—a word, a symbol, or a single letter—and apply special lighting effects to it, including spotlights, shadows, colored lights, and distancing effects. These programs also change the letters into three-dimensional objects like stone or shiny metal or varnished wood (to name only a few), so that a simple word becomes a work of art. The results are similar to the movie company logos. (Typestry also allows you to animate your words and special effects, so you may watch your own logo charge at you from a distant point somewhere out of deep space, or gyrate like Elvis Presley.)

### FRACTAL LANDSCAPE DESIGN

Last, I'll mention "virtual landscape" programs, like **VistaPro**. These programs re-produce natural settings like trees and mountain ranges, rivers, and valleys, and allow you to fiddle with the images. You can adjust the vantage point, camera angle, snow line, ruggedness of the mountains, and so on. You may start with a classic natural wonder like Earth's moon or Half Dome, Yosemite, and go crazy from there. These programs use fractal technology to "paint" worlds that look like they really could exist in nature (fractal technology draws pictures using millions of tiny repetitive shapes, much as occurs in the natural world, like rocks and leaves and water drops), but the fun begins as you start reshaping and recoloring according to your own whim. Morro Bay can become Mars with a few deft strokes. You can add unearthly textures and patterns, creating a unique visual world.

## GENERAL TIPS FOR THE BUDDING COMPUTER ARTIST

### IMAGE QUALITY ISSUES

As far as your computer is concerned, most of your artwork consists of millions of colored dots, sometimes called *pixels,* that are assigned a numeric and color value. Your computerized photo or painting is rendered as dots per square inch (dpi), and the way these dots are blended across a color palette give your picture its appearance.

## SCREEN SIZE VS. PRINTED SIZE

One surprise in store for the fledgling computer artist is the size of the printed ma-terial compared to the size of what you see on the screen. The first time you print out a nice, bright, full-screen image, you will probably wonder what went wrong. The printed image will be very small. Why is that? Your computer screen generates pictures at images of 72 or 96 dpi (your TV renders about 34 dpi). Your printer out-puts at 180 or 300 dpi. Since your image is generated according to its number of dots per square inch, **the same number of dots covers a larger area on your screen than on your printed page**. Your printout will be $^1/_3$ or $^1/_4$ the size of the same image on your computer screen. Therefore, to ensure that your final printed product is not miniscule, keep in mind that your on-screen image should fill more than the screen itself.

# ENLARGING YOUR COMPUTER ARTWORK

Not surprisingly then, computer art and publishing programs allow you to enlarge your pictures. And when you tell your computer to enlarge your photograph or painting, your magic machine will create the new dots for you, using a fancy algorithm to compute a larger piece of art. **However, your art will look more grainy and less sharp as a result of enlargement.** Computer art programs come with a dazzling array of tricks to help you restore lost clarity, and with careful editing, you can pull off a moderate enlargement without bad results. Still, the loss of quality after enlarging is sometimes quite obvious.

# WORKING WITH GRAYSCALE IMAGES

Well then, why not just start with a nice 6″ × 9″ photograph and forget about resizing? Because such a photo, especially a color photo, will often take up 5 or 6 megabytes of space on your computer, and editing it will almost surely grind your system to a halt. This is why many projects rendered on a computer end up utilizing very little color photography or artwork with complicated blends from one color to another. Grayscale artwork, a technique that allows you to use sharp and complex images but discards the color information, is less taxing to your computer. A 6″ × 9″ grayscale image will not require nearly as much computer horsepower as the same sized color image. Using grayscale art does not confine you to mere black-and-white line art or stick images. A grayscale image has shaded areas, shadows, and depth, and can be very complex, with 256 shades of gray. These images can look quite professional and sharp. You also don't have to worry about those memory-hungry color images crashing your computer every time you try to edit them.

# VECTOR-DRAWN IMAGES

The next main category of computer artwork is vector-drawn images. These are images made by **CorelDRAW,** Micrographics **Draw,** or clip art that is created for the purpose of being resized. These images are not saved on your computer as millions of colored dots, but as a series of curves, lines, angles, and areas of simple, solid color. Rendered well, these drawings can be beautiful and very effective in your documents or as stand-alone artwork. The real beauty in working with these pictures is that **they may be resized without any denigration in quality.** When you make a vector-drawn image bigger, you aren't asking the program to reinterpret the blend of colors across a larger area, which makes for a dull picture. Rather, the program just recalculates the angles and curves and line lengths for the new size you've requested. This is an exact process, and the results still look sharp, no matter how big you go.

# PICTURE FILE EXTENSIONS

You can identify the kind of picture you are working with by its file extension. Certain files can be opened and edited only in their own programs, but there are a host of standard file extensions common to many different art programs. You may save and open your artwork in many Windows-compatible file extensions, such as .PCX, .BMP, .TIF, and .TGA, to name a few. Most good art programs can work and edit artwork in these and many more formats, but if you have a program that is picky (Pixar Typestry's Glimpse can only create new backgrounds for you from the .BMP file format) there are a number of simple, inexpensive programs available **that will convert files from one type to another very quickly**.

# THE BEST COMPUTER PAINTING PROGRAMS

## FRACTAL DESIGN

In the past, computer art looked uninspired and sterile, full of technical perfection fresh off the calculator. Three products by Fractal Design—**Painter 2.0, Sketcher, and Dabbler**—have put an end to all that. Their specialty is recreating the experience of a brush on canvas, with all of its sloppy randomness. No two paintings will ever look the same. Oil, water colors, charcoal, and soft pencils all look like the real thing. You can change the canvas, too, since the program allows you to paint over many surfaces, such as pebbles, bricks, rice paper, or embossed woodcuts. You can control how "drippy" your water colors can look once you apply them on paper. Do you want the painting to look like your brush is saturated with paint, or kind of dry and airy? Should the colors you use blend with the colors already on your page, or paint over them as if they weren't there? Besides having dozens of artistic brush styles that respond like the real thing, there are special effect brushes that blend and move colors and textures around in many unique and unusual ways. You can "record" your painting strokes, then, when you are finished with your painting, press "stop record" and "the machine" will do the whole thing again, allowing you to first re-adjust the brush to your liking, perhaps using more bristles, showing more of an acrylic look, looking more "goopy" and painterly, whatever you like. Why not mix your brush color with a random tint from another hue, as if, in a fit of impressionistic frenzy, you decided not to clean your brush in between strokes.

# A BUNCH OF DOTS

Many art and graphics programs give you tools to resize images, even up to the size of a full printed page. But the image will suffer in quality if you expand it too much. Your software uses complicated algorithms to keep the dot ratio the same and maintain image quality, which works up to a point. The best bet is to try to start out with a large image at a high dpi.

Image at **180** dots per square inch

**Vector-drawn images,** like CorelDRAW (**.cdr**) art or clip art that is made for resizing will not look jagged and blurry when they are stretched. They are saved and restored as a series of shapes and curves, which can be accurately recalculated at a larger size.

Images can be saved in many different formats, and fortunately, most art programs can work with pictures of many file types. Some common file extensions are .pcx, .bmp, .tif, .wmf, .tga, .gif, and .jpg.

| | |
|---|---|
| **.TIF** | Used by both IBM-compatible and Macintosh computers |
| **.BMP** | Windows bitmap format |
| **.GIF** | Popular format for modem transfer of images |
| **.JPG** | For compressing large images |
| **.PCX** | The format most common to both DOS and Windows programs |
| **.WMF** | Can be stretched without much loss of quality |

Image at **72** dots per square inch

The more dots per square inch an image has, the higher quality it is. I don't have that many dots.

You should print out documents with **artwork** at **300 dpi** (*dots per square inch*). Documents **without pictures** can be printed out at **180 dpi** and still look good.

You can also work with the professional art technique of creating masks or friskets for your painting. In this process, you cut out areas of your painting to be protected, while you paint over other areas, then remove the mask from the protected area. (Imagine working with stencils or templates.)

Fractal Design's main product is **Painter 2.0,** which includes brushes, pens, crayons, pencils, and the ability to create just about any drawing device you can think of. **Sketcher** provides pencil and pen tools for lifelike drawing. **Dabbler** is a full-featured paint program for older children.

## FAUVE MATISSE

Fauve **Matisse** might not have all the features that Fractal Design's Painter 2.0 has, but it's nearly $200 cheaper, and has a couple of features that Painter doesn't. One helpful tool, not available in any program below the $400 range, is the ability to cut a piece out of one painting, drag it over to another, enlarge it, distort it, recolor it, paint over it, place it anywhere you like on the document, but still have it remain as

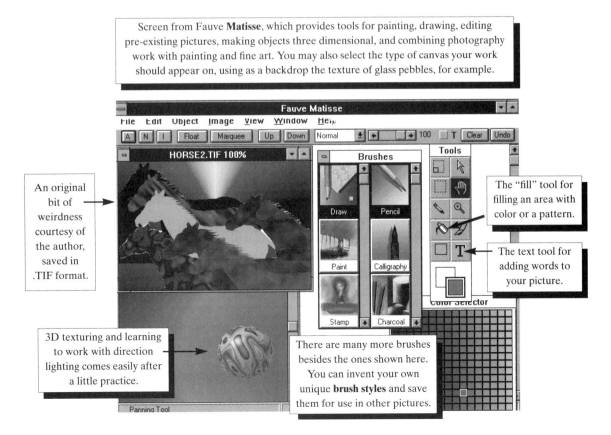

Screen from Fauve **Matisse**, which provides tools for painting, drawing, editing pre-existing pictures, making objects three dimensional, and combining photography work with painting and fine art. You may also select the type of canvas your work should appear on, using as a backdrop the texture of glass pebbles, for example.

An original bit of weirdness courtesy of the author, saved in .TIF format.

The "fill" tool for filling an area with color or a pattern.

The text tool for adding words to your picture.

3D texturing and learning to work with direction lighting comes easily after a little practice.

There are many more brushes besides the ones shown here. You can invent your own unique **brush styles** and save them for use in other pictures.

a stand-alone object even after you close the program and open your painting again at a later time.

In Fauve Matisse you can edit and reshape all the "floating" objects of your painting at any time. Such versatility is not provided with Painter 2.0, unless you want to pony up an additional $89 to purchase their add-on, known as Painter X2. Newer versions of Fractal Design's Painter will include this ability, but still make a much larger dent in your pocketbook than Fauve Matisse does. I personally love Fauve Matisse's default color palette. It is bright and punchy, allowing you to get subtle later on by mixing shades. Like Painter 2.0, you can change paper textures at any time, and control the sensitivity of your brush's response to the texture. You do not get nearly as many brush options as in Painter 2.0, but Matisse comes with two collections of filters that quickly bring endless lighting and texture possibilities to your canvas. Using a lightly tinted airbrush over textures like "straw" or "wood shavings" is an especially nice touch. You may also import your own pictures, using them as textures or as fill patterns.

# Chapter 14

# COMPUTERS AND EDUCATION

**WILL EDUCATIONAL SOFTWARE GET ANY BETTER?**

**SOME POSSIBLE IMPROVEMENTS**

**AMERICA'S SCHOOLS, THE BUSINESS COMMUNITY, AND COMPUTERS**

**STUDY RECIPE FROM WINSLOW MANOR**

The price of a very adequate computer, CD-ROM player included, is now roughly one-third the cost of a year's tuition in a private school. As this fact becomes more widely comprehended, we will see an increase in the quality and variety of educational software.

## WILL EDUCATIONAL SOFTWARE GET ANY BETTER?

Software still tends to be designed by male post-graduate students who spent a good part of their youth reading Famous Monsters in Filmland and still got A's in everything. Not surprisingly, much of the software for kids, even games with learning value, leans heavily towards killing and maiming. Software writers tend to do their most imaginative programming on fantasy role-play adventure games. (You are the sole survivor on a strange planet. You are a hero on a forgotten continent.) But this is changing. People of all shapes and sizes (and social agendas) are writing software programs today. For future releases, software companies are trying to reach beyond the familiar set of story lines and game ideas. Translation: In the future, the academic software won't be so boring.

## SOME POSSIBLE IMPROVEMENTS

### LOOKIT ME! I'M ON LEVEL 6!

Hopefully, the talent to create believable fantasy worlds, with their own rules of play and game assumptions, will be used to create an environment in which children could learn about important characters in history and begin solving real world problems. Kids could learn about the lives of Clara Barton, Jane Hull, Sojourner Truth, and other remarkable historical characters through software that retells their stories utilizing all the riveting technology that has been put into torpedoing space aliens.

Why shouldn't educational programs display as much imaginative pizzazz as the adventure games? Why not a program, rendered in realistic 3D, in which a child assembles a car engine? Or a "Junior Architect" program in which kids assemble different kinds of structures using the terms and materials that a general contractor would have to know? How about a game in which a child works in a courtroom, each time picking a different legal career to sample; one day he or she could be a lawyer, questioning witnesses, selecting a jury, discussing with the opposing attorney the evidence that will be discussed, and finally, going to trial. The next "day" he or she could be a court reporter, a judge, or an attorney for the opposing side. Imagine a game in which your child, as a doctor, listens to the complaints of sick people, then retires to the research lab, looks up various afflictions, hits on the diagnosis, prescribes medication, and carries out the treatment? Should the difficulties in designing such programs be daunting for an industry that has presented us with 5,000 ways to slay dragons?

## AND I GOT 10,000 BONUS POINTS FOR ISOLATING THE RIGHT GENE!

Another way in which computer games could stimulate real world creativity is to examine a real problem and work toward a solution. Take the disease multiple sclerosis, which generally affects women between the ages of 26 and 40, women who, at some time in their lives, lived in a cold environment. In multiple sclerosis, the body's immune system attacks the protective layers (*sheaths*) that surround the nerve fibers. The process is like scraping the insulation off an electric cord, short-circuiting it; the "short-circuited" nerves can no longer send messages to the muscles. No one really understands what causes multiple sclerosis. To create a computer program that lays out in visual form the facts of this disease, how it attacks the body and who gets it, and setting up a workshop to experiment with and propose possible solutions would require no more technology than fantasy simulations already employ. Think about the millions of intelligent kids who spend their afternoons learning how to jump through a series of caves without getting hit by a lightning bolt. Couldn't we use the familiar computer-screen medium to stimulate thought on problems with more substance?

Using imaginative computer programs, children can examine many of the thorny issues facing society today, such as what to do with repeat offender criminals, or how to reform of the welfare system. In each case, kids can learn the basic rules, laid out visually and attractively through the computer game. These rules would resemble our society and how it works. A child could then prescribe new solutions, try new ideas, and tinker with the various assumptions in the games model. **In the process of winning the game, kids could discover new approaches to some old problems, the same problems that they will have to respond to as they grow up in the world.**

Does all of this sound too sophisticated and high-tech to be available to us ordinary people?

The gargantuan, multilayered "action-simulation" games that kids are already addicted to are made possible by a complex core of artificial intelligence. Artificial intelligence provides the reasoning, the underlying assumptions, and systems of logic that make these simulations so realistic. Programs of this nature are necessarily large, requiring incredible amounts of disk storage space and RAM access.

Today, since CD-ROM drives and super-fast computers are almost as prevalent as toasters, programs with a sophisticated core of artificial intelligence can be as accessible as Madonna's next album. Of course, until a short time ago, only well-funded think-tanks like the Rand Corporation or university research teams had access to such complex models of real-life situations. But times are a changin'.

# AMERICA'S SCHOOLS, THE BUSINESS COMMUNITY, AND COMPUTERS

## HEY SCRUB, COME OVER HERE AND CLEAN MY BOOTS!

Computers will play a large role as Americans seriously rethink school as we know it. Nobody's happy with the current school system. Parents feel schools are a breeding ground for bad behavior, students feel they are being herded like cattle, and the business community complains that, after more than 12 years of full-time academic training, students are totally unprepared for "the real world." Half a century ago, there were many approaches to elementary school education in this country. Now we have one: Six or seven hours a day spent away from home with peers and a handful of overworked teachers. As more mothers join the work force, what we call "school" has become a baby-sitting accommodation, and has little to do with creating an optimal learning environment to prepare children for life. Two or three intensive, quality hours at school, followed by computer lessons at home, would prove more valuable than spending all day in class, worrying about how everyone else is dressed or what ninth-grade creep is lurking in the hallway. Parents are alarmed at how fast kids grow up, and how quickly friends at school become more important than family members. Well, what can parents do to reduce the sheer number of hours that kids spend at the O.K. Corral? Are there other options?

Later I will discuss home school as a possibility, but for now, I'd like to point out that a home computer could be a viable link between the student and the classroom, vastly decreasing the requisite number of hours that must be spent on campus itself. If a student had a PC and a modem at home, the teacher could interact with his students—**many students at once**—via computer. Does this sound ridiculously expensive? Check out the lower computer prices, and compare them with how much tax money is spent per year on a single student's education. Students could attend school for fewer hours each day, while doing a good deal of class work at home, via modem. Teachers could interact individually with students via modem regarding their progress and areas where improvement is needed.

Also, a large percentage of school costs are paper, that is, books, written work, and tests. Education via modem and software would take a huge bite out of paper costs. A game like **Math Blasters** provides fun and excellent drill exercises for kids from grades one through six. Its entire database is stored on two floppy disks or one CD-ROM. Compare that to the mountains of paper generated by doing math drills over a child's time spent in the same number of grades.

## OF COURSE I KAN DIKTATE A LETTER!

Computers could also go a long way toward bridging the gap between students and their future employers. Educators often complain that America's business community pays little attention to our country's young people. Students graduate not knowing what kinds of careers are available to them. And it's true— there is little contact between schools and private industry. Corporate representatives are leery of spending their "time-is-money" hours braving spit wads and snickers just to explain what a "key grip" does for a living. But surely, from the safety of Chevy Chase Drive, they could design a (profitable) interactive learning game that features various careers in their respective industries.

## SHOOT YOUR TELEVISION

But this book ends where it began: with a plea that just about anything that can drag the kids away from television is worth the time and the effort. The section below shows you how to mix your computer, some of the newer software, and a child's eager mind for some fun, creative learning. If it seems to be just too darn much work on your part, and perhaps redundant work as well, since your child leaves home every day supposedly to learn such skills, remember that your own curiosity and willingness to try new things will do more to stimulate a desire to learn than any curriculum. Go show them that you, together, as a family, can master this stuff. You're not licked yet.

## STUDY RECIPE FROM WINSLOW MANNER

1. Explain to your child that, in order to pick a study topic for that day, you will browse through a program on the computer together, and discover something

interesting. Pick a program with many topics to choose from. Especially for younger children, pick a program with a large multimedia component, videos, music, and varied narrative styles. You should position yourself to the side of the computer as chief notetaker, suggesting topics and helping narrow down the subject matter to something manageable.

For now, you have the pen and paper, and your child has the mouse. As you read the articles and watch and listen, point out to your child the pertinent information, and help him or her zero in on data that's digestible for your child's age group. Make sure to break up the encyclopedic text entries with attention-grabbing bells and whistles.

2. After 20 to 30 minutes of this, you should have on your paper eight to ten vivid, short, and informative sentences that you've gleaned from browsing the material. (Obviously, adjust the amount of time involved and number of sentences to your child's age and capabilities.) It also helps to select one photo from your reference program and import it to the Windows Clipboard.

3. Open a word processing program and select a nice, big font for the child to work with, and zoom in so the typed text will appear nice and big. Select Paste from the menu bar so that the picture appears at the top of the paper. Make sure it's the picture your child believes is most representative of the subject at hand.

4. To the best of your child's abilities, have him or her type in all or part of each sentence, with you offering some assistance as needed. Keep the sentences separate, random, with double-spaces in between each one. The point here is not to get bogged down in spelling or exact syntax, but to maintain the threads of interest, and keep things moving.

5. Print out the document with the random, unconnected set of sentences and the picture.

6. Have your child read the sentences carefully and assemble them into a brief essay on the subject. First, he or she should pick the best order for the sentences by numbering them. You may give hints, but your child should establish the sequence that he or she believes would make sense to another reader of the work. If you give help, be sure to explain your reasoning.

7. Now have your child compose the sentences in paragraph form, either by hand, or again on a word processor, as you see fit.

8. What will keep this kind of assignment fresh is the serendipitous, unhurried, and exploratory nature of it. As much as possible, have your child call the shots.

## WE HOMESCHOOL OUR CHILDREN

It comes out sooner, rather than later, "Gee, your kids are home a lot." "You're always going places with your family." "Why does your downstairs look like a schoolroom?"

Finally we tell them: "We homeschool our children."

"How do you do that?" Initially, people look at us as if we've just confessed to making moonshine in our basement. Every question we answer seems to raise more questions. Is this legal? Should we be nominated for sainthood or reported to the local authorities?

So let's cut to the chase:

- There are many educational organizations that offer oversight for people who wish to homeschool their children. They provide standardized testing and supervision, which are important tools to make sure your kids are up to (or above) grade level in all subjects.

- There is a large variety of textbooks available to homeschooling families, far more than are available to public school students. Picking textbooks for public schools is a very political process. The books must be approved by large committees, and the only textbooks that make it through the process are the ones that offend no one. In order to please everybody, the committees end up selecting books that are bland and general and superficial. That's why public school textbooks are so unbelievably boring. (Ask your kids, if you can't remember from your own school days.) Such limitations do not exist for homeschooling parents who select textbooks for their children. Homeschool textbooks come with teacher's guides so parents can refresh themselves on the subject at hand.

- Successful homeschooling depends on parents finding athletic activities for their children, since the built-in physical education class is no longer available. Creative field trip planning is also a must. Teaming up with other homeschooling parents makes these outings more fun.

- Currently, the population segments most likely to homeschool are families in rural areas where farming chores require the labor of every person in the community, including children (the potato harvest cannot wait for midterms); and religious fundamentalists who do not want their children being taught that humans came from monkeys. However, there are plenty of free-spirit parents among the ranks, those who believe that a rigid classroom structure stifles creativity in children. It's always quite a spectacle to watch these groups get together over the common agenda of home education.

■ Us? Well, we do it because we live in an area where the public schools are submerged in gang warfare and good private schools are priced astronomically. Our work schedules make it possible to be home often, provide good lesson plans, and make sure they get done. I'm surprised more parents don't home school. One mother asked if we would help her set up a homeschool plan for her first-grade daughter, who, on school property, was left dangling over the edge of a second-story building by a classmate.

Public school teachers rightfully complain that they are expected to be counselors, social workers, policemen and drill sergeants, and only secondarily does any teaching get done. Homeschooling—even for one year—is a way for parents to enjoy their kids again. Why let 'em grow up to be strangers? Have one parent take a year off and try something really different. What better way to get reacquainted with your kids before they are, once and for all, beyond the reach of your best intentions.

# Chapter 15

# REVIEWS OF THE BEST EDUCATIONAL SOFTWARE

**Imagination is more important than knowledge.**

*—Einstein*

*Personal Note*

**All stories are true; some of them actually happened.**

*—Madeleine L'Engle*

When I was 11 or so, my friends and I hung out at the home of a retired taxi driver who always had a game going. By that I mean Clue, Risk, Parcheesi, various unkosher versions of gin rummy, and he taught me to play a mean five-minute chess. As he sat with his blanket draped across his lap, he would talk endlessly about game strategies. "Next time, you do thus and so, thus and so," he would demand, as if our life depended on it. When it came time to leave, he would follow us to the door with even more instant replays, critiques, and arcane strategy devices. My friends and I grew older, went on to discover guitars and girls and the world at large, and I never gave games another thought until I had children of my own.

As a young man, I would occasionally walk into a room full of grown people who were howling with laughter over charades or Monopoly, and I just didn't get it. I could not suspend disbelief, allow my imagination to take over and "buy in" to the game's premise. I could never make it seem that important to me. But I looked upon their silliness with a secret envy.

Having kids made me think again about my retired taxi-driver friend, about the role of imagination and a child's ability to create an airtight world equipped with its own rules and systems of logic, inhabited by people who create rainbows and laser beams with the wave of an arm, people who wear magic rings and can fly and cast spells. It all came back to me. When you're five years old, learning to fly is simply a matter of sending mom shopping for magic breakfast cereal. Sooner or later, she'll bring the right box home.

> Now you have kids of your own, a computer, and the unfinished business of your own childhood…a chance to get excited about some stupid game.

As we become hard-drinking businessmen waddling into our fourth and fifth decade, I wonder where all that imagination goes. It sure disappears during adolescence, during which time a person must cling to his peer-group's code of behavior with a rigidity that would make any Nazi bleat with delight. For teenagers, all that freedom is really no freedom at all. When I think about the people who created and designed the games I'm about to review, I like to imagine them as people who never lost touch, who kept that world alive, alive with Aslan the Lion, Middle Earth and Mordor, Wilber the Pig and Charlotte, Harold and the Purple Crayon, Famous Monsters in Filmland, and of course, that special secret bedroom Where the Wild Things Are. Imaginary friends might go away for a few years, but they shouldn't disappear altogether. Now you have kids, a computer, and the unfinished business of your own childhood, a chance to get all excited about some stupid game.

The creators and programmers of these games have submitted to the doubly difficult task of dreaming up a wild idea, compressing it down to some ridiculously tedious computer code, and making the fun part re-inflate in your child's mind. As you wade through these reviews and try to pick out the games that are right for you and your family, keep in mind that very little of what was attempted by these game makers has ever been done before. So go have a blast. Maybe your mom will finally bring home the right box of breakfast cereal.

## HOW TO CHOOSE A GAME FOR YOUR CHILD

It's hard to tell from looking at a box if a learning game is going to be right for your child. In reviewing the following children's software selections, I've found that the reading skills demanded by the game are the most obvious factor in making a game either over a kid's head in one case or patronizing and silly in another. In order to buy your child a piece of educational software, you need to know if the program will be right for his or her skill levels. Many games you can buy say things like "ages 3 to 103" on the box. This is not helpful information. An 11-year old might not appreciate an "Aquarium" program that turns out to be a glorified coloring book of exotic fish. Conversely, your first grader probably couldn't tackle a full-throttle anatomy and physiology program, even if the box is plastered with colorful skeletons.

What different skills does your child need before he or she can enjoy a particular program? The natural breaks in the groupings tend to cluster around the *five levels of reading skills* I've laid out below. Every game reviewed here will be placed in one of these categories.

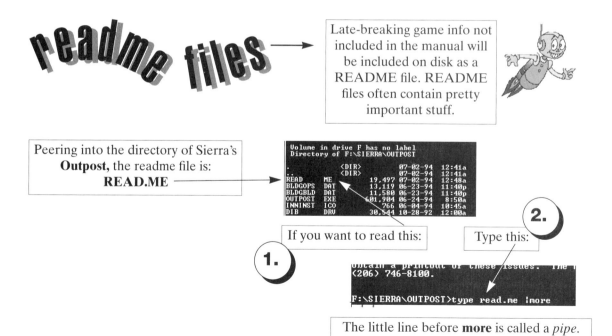

**readme files** →

Late-breaking game info not included in the manual will be included on disk as a README file. README files often contain pretty important stuff.

Peering into the directory of Sierra's **Outpost,** the readme file is: **READ.ME**

```
Volume in drive F has no label
Directory of F:\SIERRA\OUTPOST

.              <DIR>          07-02-94  12:41a
..             <DIR>          07-02-94  12:41a
READ     ME         19,497  07-02-94  12:48a
BLDGOPS  DAT        13,119  06-23-94  11:40p
BLDGBLD  DAT        11,580  06-23-94  11:40p
OUTPOST  EXE       601,904  06-24-94   8:50a
INNINST  ICO           766  06-04-94  10:45a
DIB      DRV        30,544  10-28-92  12:00a
```

If you want to read this:

Type this:

**1.**

**2.**

```
obtain a printout of these issues.  The
(206) 746-8100.

F:\SIERRA\OUTPOST>type read.me ¦more
```

The little line before **more** is called a *pipe*. Find the straight-up line on your keyboard. This command means the same as **/p**.

## NO READING REQUIRED

For example: Broderbund's **Treehouse**, Binary Zoo's **Mystery at the Museum**.

These games have gone out of their way to make a learning game that would be totally appropriate for pre-readers. They would supplement any written instructions with nodding heads and smiley faces for "Yes," or frowning faces for "No," or would have a audible, speaking voice give directions that would ordinarily require reading. Please note: The games in the No Reading Required category do have written text on the screen, and some of it is quite interesting and descriptive. But the games in this category section require no reading in order to operate and enjoy.

## BEGINNING READERS

For example: MECC's **Word Munchers,** The Learning Company's **Treasure Mountain**.

Games in this section will encourage and require the ability to read simple three to five-letter words. Words in these games will follow simple sentence structure and the paragraphs will be brief, non-abstract, usually involving simple observations from nature and animals, household items, and ideas familiar to young children.

## GROWING READERS

For example: Sierra On-Line's **Ecoquest**, Broderbund's **Where in the U.S.A. is Carmen Sandiego?**

Consider this clue from one of Carmen's mysteries:

Looking for Saffron for his magic potion,
He went to an Island in the Atlantic Ocean.

These games will have word play and humor that would go over the head of most of the youngest readers, even those precocious kids who

It's 1897, the U.S. is in a major depression, and with MECC's **The Yukon Trail** you can join the "Stampeders." The game takes you from Seattle way up north to Dawson City, where you try your luck at mining for gold. You must make good decisions and face many perils along the way. Gambling was a way of life along the Yukon Trail, so in this simulation, card sharks and "games of chance" abound. If you'd rather your children not be exposed to this aspect of pioneer life, you can disable it. (If only real life were half this easy.) **Yukon Trail** has more multimedia features than its worthy predecessor, **Oregon Trail**, but the format is very similar.

could make out all the words. These games would encourage more conceptual reading, introducing unfamiliar ideas from other cultures, story lines and dialogue that require a small amount of abstract reasoning, ideas like catching on to a case of mistaken identity, overhearing a conversation and thinking it's about you when it really isn't. While games in this category push vocabulary skills and unfamiliar ideas, they tend to avoid long, complicated paragraphs.

## GOOD READERS

For example: Knowledge Adventure's **Science Adventure 2**, Sierra On-Line's **King's Quest 6**.

Very similar to the category above, but to enjoy these programs, your child must feel comfortable with reading several paragraphs at a time, be able to pick up the subtle implications, get the jokes, and apply what was read later in the game.

## ADVANCED READERS

For example: **Multimedia Encyclopedias**, Magic Quest's **Time Trek**, D.C. True's **Shadow President**.

These games require the same level of reading skills that are required in traditional reference tools such as encyclopedias.

## YES, BUT WILL THEY PLAY IT?

Where applicable, I will point out if a game does not seem to be "age-appropriate." For example, there are several excellent spelling programs available that provide word lists for more advanced readers, packed with words like "parsimony" and "ambidextrous," but the game play is still geared toward a very young child who enjoys bright and cheery happy-face cartoons. The words might be right for seventh or eighth grade, but no 13-year-old would be caught dead playing that kind of game. In this case, I would point out that although such a program might be capable of teaching certain skills, it's too cartoony for a big kid.

Mission UFO requires you to look up an exact number in the manual each time you start the game. Unless you have memorized exact interplanetary distances in kilometers, don't ever throw it away.

Please note that your kids may enjoy certain learning games even if much of the reading is over their heads. For example, no harm is done in attempting to solve the Tower of Hanoi puzzle in Sierra On-Line's **The Island of Dr. Brain**, even if you cannot read the explanation and history of the game that pops up when you're finished solving it. Be assured that some reading skills will be acquired just by osmosis, by being exposed to all the writing on the screen. The guide above refers to the minimum skill needed to get through the game. For example, an eight-year-old would be hard pressed to get much out of **Turbo Science** or The Learning Company's **Time Riders in American History**, simply because if you take too long, you'll always lose. Quite frustrating.

Software companies are releasing more products as CD-ROMs because

1) CD-ROMs can hold more music, narration, and video than disks can.

2) *CD-ROM games are actually less expensive than floppy-disk games.*

3) **You can't make copies of CD-ROM games and give them to your friends.**

## LETTING OLDER KIDS TEACH THE YOUNGER ONES

One phenomenon I've enjoyed watching is what happens when an older child teaches a younger child to use a computer game. This often works better than having an adult be the teacher. The people that developed these games have a lot of imagination, and children respond to that very quickly. Younger kids seem to catch on faster if there's an older child to compete with and learn from.

## REPLAY VALUE

I will also comment, where appropriate, on a game's "replay value." Spending $20 to $60 on a game that will be zipped through once and forgotten does not seem like a worthwhile investment. The best games are those that combine educational value with playability. You want them to keep at it, to keep trying, and move on to the higher levels.

On to the games, shall we?

## SOME FAVORITES

First, here's a handful of our family's favorite games.

### TURBO SCIENCE

The game is a race against other animated characters. As your science skills improve, you are pitted against smarter opponents. You answer science questions, and you may purchase high-tech modes of transportation around the racetrack by answering correctly. Answer poorly and you must walk. The questions are not merely listed. You are whisked away to familiar environments in which the scientific phenomena going on around you is bracketed or highlighted. Multiple choice questions regarding the phenomena appear on the screen. The game is lively and never boring. The music is fun and the characters are simply a scream. **Turbo Science** comes with a surprisingly broad and well-written science handbook. During the question phase, you may pause the game and look up the answers you need. Getting to the heart of the game is quick and learning takes place from square one. On your mark…get set…Good reading skills. High replay value.

Very exceptional music

A very, very good game

Screen from The Learning Company's 256-color **Treasure Math Storm**, an excellent math program for young kids. The game is reviewed on page 262 of this book.

### TIME RIDERS IN AMERICAN HISTORY

A rather colorful villain named Dread has taken to rewriting American history, broadcasting unlikely spins on some of America's most cherished events and personalities. You are part of a team of students who must dig through computerized archives of events in America's past and piece the truth together, beat nasty Dread to the punch, and broadcast the truth. Facts are built on cumulative knowledge: Kids can't select the correct event unless they truly understand the related facts. Built in to the sequence of broadcasts and counter-broadcasts is a clever story line that makes the kids want to keep going to find out what happens next. Good reading skills. High replay value.

Highest learning value

Works OK on an older computer

## SIMCITY

Design a city. Watch it flourish or die, depending on your skills. Your game starts out as a clean slate or as one of several urban scenarios. You then add (or bulldoze away) residential, commercial, and/or industrial areas. You raise or lower taxes, learn to live within a city budget, try not to shortchange essential city services in your quest for "growth." You have graphs available to track various urban "quality of life" markers…but the most amazing aspect of this program is how easy it is to enact everything I've just described…and more. As you plan and build, your screen is constantly reflecting your new urban environment, giving you quick feedback on the changes you've enacted. Growing readers. High replay value.

Screen from Mavis' **SimCity**, one of the oldest computer simulations.

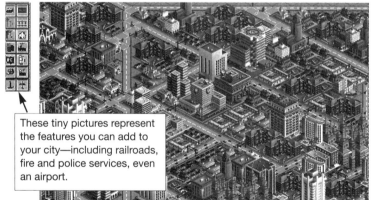

These tiny pictures represent the features you can add to your city—including railroads, fire and police services, even an airport.

A very, very good game

Good strategy game

## WORD ATTACK PLUS

There is no shortage of spelling exercise games, some that allow you to input your own spelling list, which means that your kids can practice their spelling using words of your choosing. **Word Attack Plus** is a series of five activities that test a child's knowledge of words in every way imaginable. This program emphasizes definitions, spelling, and correct word usage in sentences. It does not deal with phonics such as recognizing short vowel sounds and diphthongs. A major plus is that you may input short phrases—"cave drawings," "medical technology," AND their definitions, then send the kids through five colorful and engaging activities to learn them. A big plus for **Word Attack Plus** is its replay value. Because there are several activities built around your chosen word list, kids don't get bored. Growing readers.

Highest learning value

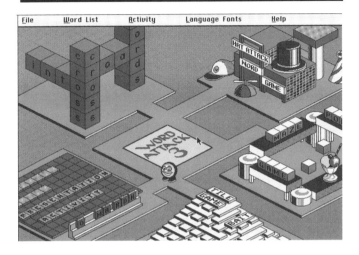

Screen from Davidson's **Word Attack Plus**. The game offers five activities to check spelling, sentence use, and comprehension.

## DANGEROUS CREATURES

Some subjects lend themselves very well to the wandering pace of Microsoft's **Exploration Series** CDs. To explore often means to take your time. (Running this program on a 386 computer will indeed increase your sympathy for naturalists who sit patiently in the middle of nowhere waiting for something to happen.) Programs like these, which provide four or five different paths to access information about any of nature's most scary beasties, are not for the soul in a hurry. Produced in conjunction with the World Wildlife Fund, **Dangerous Creatures** serves up a full platter of video clips, identification games, guided tours, and interesting articles about the endangered world of wildlife on earth. There are enough bells and whistles to keep early readers busy and learning for many hours, while at the same time, **Dangerous Creatures** is worth having on hand as a reference tool. Each animal photo is

Screen from Microsoft's **Dangerous Creatures**. Just about every word or image you click on will take you someplace interesting.

surrounded with bright red hypertext links, leading to brief narratives, videos, and games that are all worth digging around for. There is no central listing of all the resources at your disposal. You'll just have to go exploring. Beginning readers. High replay value.

Good use of video

Requires CD-ROM

Requires fast computer

## TREASURE MOUNTAIN

The Learning Company's **Treasure Mountain** hails back from the 16-color days, when, if you shelled out extra for an 80MB hard drive, you were considered silly or too rich. **Treasure Mountain** weighs in at less than 800K, but for four to six-year-old computer trekkers, **Treasure Mountain** is probably one of the best. You must wander around a mountain in three different environments, and at each level you gather objects that interest you. Under the objects is a single descriptive word, such as "Big" or "Three" or "Flowers." Your child picks up more objects to obtain more clues, and soon, a phrase will fall into place, such as "Five little pinecones" or "Two Big Sleds." That phrase tells him or her what object to look under to obtain a shiny gold key, and the key takes the player to the next level. After three such challenges, you've arrived at the snowy uppermost regions of **Treasure Mountain**, where you take on the Master of Mischief. You are rewarded with a toy and are given a fast trip back down the mountain, where you may store your reward game after game. The music is quite nice, and the graphics are clear and uncluttered. Beginning readers. Very high replay value.

Works OK on an older computer

A very, very good game

## HARRY AND THE HAUNTED HOUSE

Mark Schlichting's interactive book for very young children is part of Broderbund/Random House's **Living Book** series. The computer screen becomes a page of the book. The story is read aloud page by page; however, click on a character, and he or she will talk, play around, or elaborate further on the story. Click on any object on the screen and something fun happens. Young kids can spend hours at a time exploring the story rather than simply reading it. If you have a fairly fast computer, when your child clicks on an object, the effects are instantaneous. Page transitions are quite smooth as well. Each Living Book disk comes with the story told in at least two languages. **Harry and the Haunted House** can be run in either English or Spanish. Living Books, which include **Just Grandma and Me** (*Lil' Critter*, remember?, by

Screen from Living Books interactive
**Just Grandma and Me**, by Mercer Mayer.

It's Lil' Critter with Grandma, and yes, that's Japanese in the lower right-hand corner. Each interaTctive book from the Broderbund/Random House series **Living Books** can be run in more than one language. I understand that the Japanese is narrated quite fluently.

author Mercer Mayer) are first-rate learning entertainment for young children. No reading required.

Requires fast computer

Requires CD-ROM

Highest learning value

Very good story

## CAPITOL HILL

You've just been elected to Congress. You must meet your peers, hire staff, walk through the halls of Congress, and select the office space that will be your home away from home during the length of your term. You vote on bills, read letters, and answer phone calls from constituents back home. You get a guided tour of the House and Senate chambers and the Capitol building. **Capitol Hill**, a CD-ROM program presented by Mindscape, is a seamless learning experience. Click on a statue in the main rotunda, and a gentleman who's been giving tours of the Capitol for 30 years begins telling you about the statue you've clicked on. Real members of Congress pop into your office from time to time (in the form of smooth little video clips that fill up about $^1/_4$ of your screen) and offer sage advice. People obviously worked hard on this CD, ensuring that a child gets a broad picture and a good sense of what it's like to live and work on Capitol Hill. Moving around from screen to screen and switching activities is a breeze. The photography and movies are large and clear enough to create for a child a believable impression of actually walking around the place and interacting with people. The bills you vote on as a freshman congressperson, and the people you get mail from are gleaned from real-life

Requires CD-ROM

Good use of video

Highest learning value

situations. All budding political animals should sink their eyeteeth into this one. Despite the potentially dense subject matter, a child who reads on the fourth or fifth grade level won't feel out in the dark on **Capitol Hill**. Fair replay value.

## WHAT IS A ROLE-PLAY INTERACTIVE ADVENTURE GAME?

You are the character on the screen. You must explore every place you can get to. You must talk to all the people you meet, pick up everything you find along the way, put all your clues together and figure out what to do next. If someone extends some kindness to you, return the favor. Seek out the people whom the other characters direct you to. Use your imagination. Interactive role-play adventures are like movies or books with many possible endings, depending on how well you fare. You may wander into one plot branch, and meet up with the main plot again later in the game. Interactive role-play adventures are never played the same way twice. Every choice you make brings about a slightly different story twist from previous journeys.

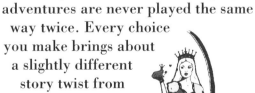

Find out more about interactive role-play adventures on page 315.

## GRAMMAR GAMES

The best games for teaching kids rules of punctuation and general grammar is Davidson's **Grammar Games**. It includes four arcade-style activities that neatly hone in on most basic grammar, and it also shows your kids a good time. (My kids actually play this game on their own. As far as they are concerned, it doesn't have the smell of schoolwork.) The game has a "save the rain forest" theme, and the sentences used in the exercises display an unusual amount of interest and intelligence. The activities range from proofreading entire paragraphs for grammatical errors to correctly punctuating sentences. Appropriate for children ages 7–12.

## KING'S QUEST 6

Playing this interactive adventure with full-voice support is by itself reason enough to purchase a CD-ROM player. But even playing the disk version, **King's Quest 6** is one of the best. You are Alexander, a prince smitten by the memory of a princess in a faraway land. You travel to the four islands that make up this land, and a story of genuine substance and literary worth unfolds. I was surprised, not at the second-to-none animation, which everyone expects

## Personal Note

You're probably thinking, "Where'd these guys get all that software? Have they actually played those games? Do they just sit around and play games all day? Are they independently wealthy, crazy, or both?" Well, read on:

A little third-grade girl comes over to our house after school for tutoring. When Rosa (not her real name) first came, she could confidently read sentences like "Tim Can is a tin can," but that's about all. She could not count out change from a quarter. Rosa is not dim or slow, and she had been going to school for those appointed three years plus pre-school. But Rosa fell between the cracks. Her parents are from El Salvador, and Spanish is the only language spoken in her home. At school, it's easy for her to get lost during lessons.

We live near downtown Los Angeles, and we "home school" our children. There are lots of kids like Rosa in our neighborhood, most of them older than third grade, and they sometimes come over to get extra tutoring or spend entire days here "when the schools are off-track." The schools here are not so good. The teachers try very hard, but are fighting an uphill battle. As soon as the "student to teacher ratio" drops down below 35 kids per teacher, the teacher is assigned more students, so he or she can "work more efficiently."

The work of tutoring four or five kids at a time is not that different from two or

from Sierra On-Line, but by the extremely well-written script and characters that were keenly realized in the literary sense. Sierra knows the value of a well-turned phrase, and has proved that interactive adventures need not be merely a series of colorful shoot-'em-ups. Good reading skills. High replay value.

Very good story

Very exceptional music

Good strategy game

## MERCHANT COLONY

It's the eighteenth century and the world is your oyster. As a member of the British merchant class, you charter sea vessels of various sorts, and set up profitable outposts all over the New World. Before leaving Liverpool, you must think about what you want to accomplish when you arrive at Bombay or Cathay or Seward, or wherever you have chosen to direct yourself. Each "colony" has its own raw materials that you may develop profitably. You must select the right kind of settlers and ship's crew to accomplish those goals. You may purchase as many ships as you are able, and you may borrow outrageous sums of money from usurious Old World scoundrels, but if you go broke, the game's over. The amazing thing about this game is how little reading there is. Young children may play it with a reasonable notion of what's going on, yet it's sophisticated enough for older kids to learn a few economic principles.

The other amazing thing about this game is that it costs about as much as a medium pizza, excluding the tip. Pick it up before Impressions repackages it and triples the price. In **Merchant Colony**, the maps refer to the nations of the world by their seventeenth and eighteenth century names; for example China is Cathay, and Eastern Canada is Stewardsville. Beginning readers. High replay value.

Highest learning value          Works OK on an older computer

## ZOOKEEPER

This one's a bit of a classic. You're in charge of a zoo. Poorly mannered creatures enter the zoo and disrupt the animals' environment. The animals are being fed the wrong food, and are being left to languish in the wrong environment. You are led to an animal's area and must correct the problems. When you've fixed things, the animals clamor about as if you were some sort of demigod. (It's for the younger kids, okay?) If you're not sure about how to fix the animals' surroundings and feed them correctly, click on a friendly robot and get some hints. The first few "cases" require no reading, but after that, you're guided by two or three sentences. Beginning readers. High replay value.

A very, very good game

three. The older ones help the younger ones, and thus, their earlier lessons are reinforced. Computers help in a big way. Because of my work schedule, and because of success in some other fields, my wife and I are able to arrange a workable plan for schooling the kids, picking out the best software and seeing how it works for the different groups and ages of children.

Our school day consists of me running up and down the stairs totting a cappuccino and a half-eaten croissant, setting two or three kids up at the computers while the others are at their writing desks. After an hour, we rotate everybody around. We own three computers, which are rarely unoccupied. We've got a big chemistry set, lots of maps and workbooks, and for P.E., we take the dogs to the park and run 'em till they're exhausted. There are lots of nearby museums, workshops for kids, and noteworthy field trip possibilities. No, we don't charge money, because we're doing it for our own kids anyway, and they enjoy the tutoring quite a bit, so money seems beside the point. If this sounds like a lot of fun, it is, and having all the software really helps.

So that's why we have so many learning games on hand. Sounds expensive? Not compared to Rosa's case, in which taxpayers have already ponied up more than $15,000 dollars to put her as far as third grade, and they don't have much to show for their investment. Computer learning games, if chosen correctly and applied with a thoughtful lesson plan, are a bargain.

## READ AND ROLL

**Read and Roll** teaches kids to read for meaning, and it works. They are tested on paragraph comprehension and are rewarded by getting to play a little arcade-style bowling game. It sounds silly, but you try getting young children to sit still for multiple-choice questions for hours at a time! The graphics are a little dull. **Read and Roll** is an old program updated recently for VGA graphics. But something about the layout keeps kids involved. Perhaps it's because they keep the print size nice and big. The newer programs that emphasize graphics have made the size of the words so small that children have a hard time reading them, and their eyes get tired. So don't be surprised if, after an initial fascination with a new razzle-dazzle program, they go back to an older one like **Read and Roll**. Good reading skills. High replay value.

Highest learning value

## ECOQUEST: THE SEARCH FOR CETUS

Save the whales. And the rest of the ocean while you're at it. This role-play touches on enough issues to generate half a semester's "environmental curriculum" for young kids and pre-adolescents. You learn about various kinds of ocean pollution, sea life, great and small, interdependence of underwater animals, civic responsibility in the face of a crisis, even how to train a dolphin and not scare it away. You're a young boy, and you live with your dad, oceanside, as he investigates a new treatment for the effects of oil spills on sea life. You befriend a dolphin, and are led to his underwater world, where you come face to face with an ocean environment in deep crises. You meet many sea creatures and learn how they interact and survive. For children ages 6 to 11, I rate this as one of the best. The CD-ROM version is full-voice, and the interface is fast and easy. Good reading skills. (CD-ROM version requires no reading.) High replay value.

SCREEN FROM SIERRA ON-LINE'S
ECOQUEST: THE SEARCH FOR CETUS

Very good story

IN THE UNDERWATER KINGDOM OF ELURIA, A YOUNG BOY, ADAM, MUST CONVINCE THE FISH TO WORK TOGETHER AND SAVE THEIR CITY.

A very, very good game

Highest learning value

## SIMFARM

Your computer screen becomes an ordinary strip of land that you've selected by pointing at a particular region of the United States, and voila! You are there, staring at your farmhouse, your piece of land, and $40,000 in the bank. The climate and soil quality of your land are dictated by the region of the United States you choose at the outset. (Actually, you may alter these to your liking, decreasing or increasing wind speed, yearly rainfall, and the like) There's a little town nearby that will prosper as you do. Surrounding the main screen are boxes for you to click on and select your task: plowing a field, planting crops, purchasing farm equipment, even betting $500 on your cousin Jed's horse to win at the horse show! There's a farm bureau in town to advise you on what to plant, how often to fertilize, and so on. You may choose from 32 crops, plant and harvest, replant or change crops, or give the land a rest. You can even invest in crop "futures," examining the crop's past financial performance, and from there, try to make a ton of money. (Do farmers ever really make a ton of money?)

The amazing thing about **SimFarm** is how quickly you can make changes, buy more land, sell and buy farm equipment, automate your harvest and planting, spray pesticide, etc. You can see your results almost instantaneously, or slow down the speed of the game to allow more lazy afternoons on the front porch. With the speed set on high, it seems that all you ever do is spray fertilizer to the point of diminishing returns…just like real farming! You may indeed go bankrupt or switch to hog farming if it turns out you've got a black thumb. You may raise other farm animals as well, build fancy roads into town and borrow obscene amounts of money from the bank and watch the tax collectors come and take it all away. At times, you'll forget it's all a game until you look at your clean, computer-fatigued hands and fingernails. Beginning reading skills. The font on the screen is small and the youngest readers might not bother trying to decipher it.

Highest learning value

Good strategy game

## PEPPER'S ADVENTURES IN TIME

**Pepper's Adventures in Time** teaches "learning by contrast" and it seems to work. Re-create a situation in America's history by painting its opposite, then bring the two together. It's funny and instructive. Pepper is a nine-year-old girl living in a modern suburb. Weird Uncle Ed is upstairs trying to invade the mind of Benjamin Franklin and reduce him to a vapid "Peace-Child" who preaches non-involvement in anything. Through this device, Weird Uncle Ed hopes to rule the world. Pepper and her dog Lockjaw stumble on to Ed's plans and are whisked back to the

Colonial era as Ed starts his time machine 'a-rollin'. Pepper finds herself in eighteenth-century Philadelphia talking to a populace under the spell of an incense-burning sort of "dead-head" named Ben Franklin. Pepper must talk sense to the citizens, reminding them of the good sense Ben Franklin used to make before "whatever happened to him" happened. Remember Benjamin Franklin's 13 proverbs, some of his most famous pithy common-sense sayings that got printed in Poor Richard's Almanac? Well, now they're twisted into justifications for abject mellowness, peace, love, and Indian tapestry. Pepper must sort out the correct proverbs of Ben Franklin from the phonies, redistribute them to the citizens and help them choose an appropriate course of action.

If my explanation seems tedious and overly complex, let me point out that Sierra has managed to make it all a ton of fun, and kept the gameplay within the range of a second to fifth grader's reading vocabulary. There are clever plot twists, all the characters are richly drawn, and the dialogue is satisfying and quite funny. If your child misses a point of strategy and history goes awry, a huge British flag comes down, Pepper is shown (in modern day) singing "God Save The Queen," and a hint flashes on the screen, advising you how to adjust your strategy and save the course of history. Pepper is set in six acts, and after each, Ben Franklin gives you a 10-question pop quiz on his life and times. (When he asks you "Which famous composer wrote music for the Glass Harp?" don't select Danny Elfman.) Throughout the game, you have available a "True or False" icon so that you may point and click at any object on the screen and guess whether such an object or state of affairs existed in Ben's time, or in modern time. After clicking, you are told whether your answer was correct or not, and why. Returning Ben to his senses involves learning to assemble his famous electricity-seeking kite on his behalf, piece by piece, hoping to jolt his memory. Teaching this important period in U.S. history to youngsters need never be boring again.

Good reading skills. High replay value. Sierra On-Line has attempted to make the vocabulary appropriate for the reading skills of younger children

A female heroine

Very good story

Highest learning value

## WHERE IN THE WORLD IN CARMEN SANDIEGO?

Ten years after its first release, The **Carmen Sandiego** series is still one of the best computer programs for teaching children geography. The premise is simple. In each round of play, Carmen and her V.I.L.E. henchmen have stolen a world landmark, and you, as a professional detective, must follow her trail of clues, interview people

Screen from Broderbund's **Where in Time is Carmen Sandiego?**

People along your sleuthing way present you with clues based on historical personalities and events. Even big and smart people lose the game if they guess without looking things up.

in countries where she might have gone, and figure out from the clue "where Carmen and her gang will show up next." The clues are facts about the country, ranging from the elementary, "She went to a landlocked country north of China" to questions requiring some research. The makers provide an excellent geography reference guide to speed you on your mission. Deciphering the clues faithfully will lead you to Carmen's gang and the stolen goods. If you don't know your geography, you'll end up on a wild goose chase and time will run out. At this point, "the Chief" (your boss, you know) appears on the screen, chiding you for letting her slip away.

Along the way, some of the people you interview will recall a fact or two about the crook himself (or herself), "She had auburn hair," or "He read Latin American novelists." The game allows you to make note of these factoids, and when gathered sufficiently, you may obtain a warrant for the arrest of who you believe stole the goods. There's always an instructive element in deciphering the clues, and my children have pummeled many a coffee table having correctly nailed the location only to find out they've obtained a warrant for the wrong person. Carmen has expanded her horizons over the years, and you may now purchase **Where in Europe**, **Where in the U.S.A.**, **Where in America's Past**, and finally, **Where in Time** and **Where in Outer Space...Is Carmen Sandiego**. Over the years, the graphics get cuter and more lively, and the most recent addition, **Where in Outer Space** comes with an online reference guide to the solar system, but the basic format has not changed. Good reading skills. High replay value.

Works OK on an older computer

Highest learning value

Screen from Sierra On-Line's **Lost Secret of the Rainforest**. As the story develops, you can use an "eco-scope" to identify people and objects in the environment. The emphasis is on various pollutants, agricultural methods, indigenous art forms…and, oh, yes, the game itself is quite a lot of fun.

## LOST SECRET OF THE RAIN FOREST

It's eco-conscience, non-violent, clever, and witty, and even comes with a point and click glossary of words and phrases relevant to saving the "lungs of the earth," that is, the rain forest. Besides all that, it's a good story: A young boy visits Latin America with his painfully politically correct father, who has just arrived with a plan to help Brazilian tribesmen develop and market their own nature-friendly yet profitable products. Young "Adam" is transported to the middle of the rain forest. He interacts with nature's beasts, solving a number of follies with an evenhanded kindness that would warm the heart of a Franciscan monk. Packed with Sierra's usual awesome graphics, as well as their educational products' standard themes of interdependence and mutual cooperation. Good reading skills. High replay value.

Very exceptional music

Very good story

## MATH BLASTERS

The trouble with math and young children is that numbers don't have little faces, numbers don't sit up and smile at you and say good morning. How can we make numbers and math equations less abstract to young children? **Math Blasters** has arrayed dozens of

It's Davidson's **Math Blaster: In Search of Spot**. Use your jet pack to fly up and complete the sequence.

clever animations and colorful games to make math equations more fun. In **Math Blaster: In Search of Spot**, you don't merely add or subtract, you blast the correct answer out of the sky while hovering over the moon in a jet pack. In another activity, you float upwards towards the correct answer while dodging space litter, like old cola cans and rotting fish bones. Then squeeze correct math answers through a conveyer belt whilst compacting the offensive debris into recyclable compost. I was charmed. The problem for me is that throughout this process, the equations themselves still seem relatively abstract. What IS "6 times 3 equals 18?" What does it look like? How about a little animation portraying 18 laser beams being divided among 3 space aliens, resulting in 6 lasers per alien? Still, the **Math Blaster** series brings new life to a familiar childhood drudgery. The series extends up through algebra and geometry, and **Math Blasters Mystery** is a game introducing a child to the concept of solving for one unknown (What does n equal if it's less than 10 and more than 8?) while looking under pieces of furniture in a room. The **Math Blaster** series provides fun math instruction for ages 6 through 12. Beginning readers. High replay value.

Highest learning value

A very, very good game

## STORYBOOK WEAVER

With this program, your child may actually assemble an illustrated story. Beginning with a title page, you may select border art and font style. The following pages are divided into text and picture segments. Your child may compose four or five sen-

tences of text per illustrated page, and then may get to work choosing from preset selections of scenery, creating the mood for the story to come. Kids can pepper their stories with objects found in nature, people (both mythical and real), forms of shelter such as castles or log cabins, and other bric-a-brac. These features make composing short stories especially rewarding for children.

There is no "free-draw" mode available. You must make do with the items and situations the makers have provided for you, and although

The main screen is where your stories are constructed. You populate your stories with the people, objects, animals, and environments found on the toolbar to the right. The bottom screen is for your text. Kids can change the look and size of any object.

there is provision to resize and flip objects to face the other direction, objects can begin to look a little funny if you tweak them beyond their intended proportion. Your child may also assign little snatches of music to open and close the story. The program is compatible with a hefty list of popular printers. Children often daydream about pasting up their stories into books, and with **Story**book **Weaver**, they can do it easily. No reading required. High replay value.

Works OK on an
older computer

## KIDPIX

Two years after purchasing **Kidpix**, our children are still discovering new features in it. This is the most entertaining drawing program for young children. You only get sixteen colors. There is no color blending or shading. You cannot "edit" curves or lines, to reshape them to your liking. **Kidpix** will never teach anyone about the subtle side of art, but, jeese, is it fun. Children can draw fairly simple shapes and forms and recognizable objects and then, by applying a couple of the many widgets and doodads that **Kidpix** comes packed with, they can transform their pictures into the most bizarre abstract landscapes.

Screen from Broderbund's **Kidpix**, which is a full-color painting program for young children.

Saving and loading pictures is easy and quick. Your kids can pull out a picture they worked on a year ago and play with it some more, and save the new and the old version, which is standard procedure around our house. Text may be added to the drawing. **Kidpix** comes with "stamps," little predrawn figures that you may paste throughout your drawing at will. You may alter and redraw your own

THE MENU BAR GIVES YOU LOTS OF BRUSHES, SHAPES, FILL TOOLS, PENCILS, AND SPECIAL EFFECTS TO WORK WITH. THERE ARE HIDDEN PICTURES THAT YOU'LL NEVER KNOW ABOUT UNTIL YOU COMBINE CERTAIN TOOLS.

KIDPIX gives you lots of stamps, which are small color pictures that you can add to your own. If you make a mistake, just click on the "undo guy" and he'll trash it. The eggbeater is a lot of fun.

stamps. You may also "cut" a portion of your picture, and "paste" it somewhere else…even in a different picture. In this case, the old advertising claim, "For children 3 to 103" really does apply. Beyond words like "save" and "load" on the menu bar, no reading is required to play **Kidpix**. You may also type words into your stories. High replay value.

A very, very good game

Works OK on an older computer

## PRINT SHOP DELUXE

It must have been hard to design a printing program that's flexible and high-quality without putting it beyond the grasp of the youngest family members. Most commercially available printing programs are awash in "options" and would send the average 10-year-old scurrying for her crayons. Broderbund's **Print Shop Deluxe** has opted to provide a product that's perfect for designing birthday cards for grandma, and creating ads for garage sales, but please, don't use PSD to design a resume for the job of your dreams. You get 30 fonts, six of which may be shrunken and enlarged with remarkable precision, but they are not up to snuff for business use, except, perhaps, to offer free popcorn in the lobby during intermission.

You get lots and lots of graphics, square graphics that truly retain their integrity when shrunken or enlarged. You also get attractive borders, a big selection of backgrounds, pre-made templates that spare you the work of organizing your page layout, if you so desire. **Print Shop Deluxe** provided enough special effects to keep things interesting, such as the ability to rotate both graphics and blocks of text and text color blending and shadowing. You may adjust color density of all objects, backgrounds, graphics, and text blocks. This is handy if your printer doesn't quite deliver what's up on your computer screen, which is often the case. **Print Shop Deluxe** does not provide many of options found in its more upscale neighbors on the software shelves. You may not select objects or text blocks you've created and paste them into another project. **Print Shop Deluxe** will not automatically create a new page for you just because you've typed too much text to fit on one page. These limitations, however, help keep the product accessible to young users. Broderbund also sells "add-ons" for Print Shop Deluxe with extra graphics for various applications. There is now a CD-ROM version of **Print Shop Deluxe**, featuring extra fonts and extra graphics. Growing readers.

Works OK on an older computer

Chapter 12 tells you more about other desktop publishing programs. Chapter 11 talks about managing your printer.

## FINE ARTIST

Released as a companion to Creative Writer, which, as part of Microsoft's "Home" series, hopes to serve notice that Bill Gates and his company don't just do Offices. Broderbund's **Kidpix**, Fractal Design's **Dabbler**, and Microsoft **Fine Artist** have each carved themselves a special nitch in the "software-for-young-artists" department. **Fine Artist**'s leg up is the strong tutorial presence built in to the program. Good thing, too. **Fine Artist** has so many features that a youngster could easily get lost without the little tutor "Maggie" on screen to lead the way. When you first load the program, kids are given a quick teach-in on defining and using an object's "positive and negative space" when drawing. This is followed by a fast run-through on how to design a picture

The pictures on pages 260 and 264 were done with Microsoft **Fine Artist**, by Larisa Steward.

using perspective, defining the picture's "vanishing point," and using it to help set up your objects. That being done with, you are whisked into an "art studio," given the choice to either design a sticker, a cartoon strip, or make a multimedia slide show. Pains are taken to demonstrate the procedural aspects of setting up cartoon frames, text bubbles, how to add sounds to your slide show, etc.

Beyond any of these extras, the regular old "drawing program" aspect of **Fine Artist** is nothing to sneeze at. There are plenty of strange and wacky brushes, special painting effects, and interesting textures that kids can quickly add to their drawing. **Fine Artist** includes a healthy selection of clip art, making it easy to add predesigned pictures to drawings. These little black-and-white line drawings (which may be colored by brushes or filled with color) are more spirited and humorous than the usual frogs and sunflower paste-ups that get thrown in to kid's art programs. **Fine Artist** seems less temperamental than its sister product, Microsoft **Creative Writer**. (Since **Fine Artist** was released a few months later, one hopes that future versions of **Creative Writer** will be less apt to freeze up on the screen and die, which the current release does far too often.) You get more than 30 colors to choose from, and dozens of "fill patterns" to choose from. Editing features included being able to resize objects, move them around freely, moving them forward, backward, or closer or farther from your vanishing point. **Fine Artist** is a worthwhile, friendly creation from Bill the Conqueror and his ambitious friends. Good reading skills. High replay value.

Requires fast computer

A very, very good game

## SCIENCE ADVENTURE 2

One of the best "new and improved" projects by Knowledge Adventure, this program is certainly the broadest. This CD is FULL: 644MB of science simulation workshops, videos clips, sounds, unusual photo libraries of all kinds of science phenomena, great and small, with clear and concise spoken narratives. **Science Adventure 2** opens by placing you in a rotunda, surrounded by doors that lead to the various activities. One such activity is using a microscope to pull up a slide of a red blood cell, examine an aspirin tablet, the AIDS virus, or dozens of other interesting molecules. Play with a set of prisms to discover more about the nature of color and light. To learn about the nature of sound waves you are taken to a close-up performance by a full orchestra. There's a science museum, with "rooms" divided by subject matter. Click on an exhibit to hear and see more about it. Bored with the room you are in? Walk through the wall to the next one. In the "Bogus Science" game, you are standing in a science gallery, discussing science facts with the people around you, and you must identify the one who says something false. You may also cruise down the lanes of scientific discovery, eavesdropping on some of science's most famous mistakes. Can you redirect the thinking of the day and get discoveries right? This CD has enough on it to keep anyone busy for weeks. No reading required, but the concepts would be over the heads of most kids below fourth grade. High replay value.

A very, very
good game

Good use of
video

## THE AMAZON TRAIL

You fall asleep one night, and in your dreams, an ancient world beckons. You awaken and are sent on a journey through time, down the Amazon River, beginning at its mouth in Benin, Brazil. You stop along the way, interviewing the many kinds of people who live (or have lived) along the Amazon. You'll talk to a "Rubber Baron" who, in the 1800s, turned huge swaths of jungle into his personal rubber plantation. You'll talk to researchers, scouring the Amazon's plant life for cures to a number of diseases. You talk to Teddy Roosevelt, who, after his presidency, visited the Amazon frequently, championing its preservation. There are hundreds of different Indian tribes along the Amazon's waters, and you'll meet them, barter for goods, and learn the skills to stay in their good graces. But your main mission in **Amazon Trail** is to wind your way back to the 1500s and bring the Inca King some "cinchona," which contains quinine, the cure for malaria. To obtain food for your journey, you and your guide must fish, learning to distinguish the edible from the poisonous. You may dock your vessel at will, and search the jungle for important items, such as plants that have medicinal properties. You also have a camera for photographing whatever interests you. Perhaps the greatest feature in **Amazon Trail** is the online encyclopedia, instantly accessible at any time. It will provide you with a brief description of all the people, plants, animal life, villages and tribes, and goods for bartering that you will encounter throughout the game. It also audibly pronounces every word you look up, a real plus, since there are hundreds of languages and dialects to be heard along the **Amazon Trail**. One of the best. Good reading skills. High replay value.

Very good
story

## TREEHOUSE

Lots of activities here for 4- to 9-year-olds. A gopher leads your child to a treehouse, which is really a launching pad for a myriad of music games, animal classification, a little theatre, a road-race game that teaches kids how to make change, and other hidden features. The highlight is a well-thought out music workshop, where you create your own melodies on the instruments of your choice, learn to recognize note sequences, and play back well-known melodies as well as your own creations on various instruments at various tempos. The animal game teaches children to classify hundreds of different creatures according to their living patterns: Is the "secret animal" nocturnal? Does it have lungs or gills? Fur or scales? How many legs? By process of elimination, you child selects the correct animal. For a product with so many activities included, the screen layout of **Treehouse** is remarkably uncluttered and easy to work with. This one requires very little parental guidance, and most children can usually jump right in. No reading required, but **Treehouse**'s components include written text in small, unintimidating doses. High replay value.

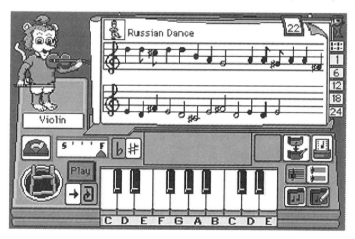

Works OK on an
older computer

A very, very
good game

A longstanding children's favorite, Broderbund's **Treehouse** is packed with activities. The above teaches melody and instrument recognition. Using the keyboard pictured above, kids can also create their own tunes.

## SPELLBOUND

This is one of the very best spelling programs for children of all ages. After choosing (or writing) a spelling list, your child works the words through five different activities, including a crossword puzzle, filling in the blank letter, and ultimately, a spelling bee. Your child's character is shown on the screen with two spelling bee "opponents," and the moderator asks the contestants to spell words. (The moderator's voice is audible.) One by one, either you or the opponents are eliminated. If you win, you move on to a citywide, statewide, and finally, a national spelling bee, complete with the White House and Capitol Building in the backdrop. **Spellbound** comes with multiple lists of words sensibly organized into categories that aid memorization. You may also compose your own spelling list, or type in your child's spelling list from school. The CD-ROM version of **Spellbound** provides more audible cues and spoken words, and not as many flashed word exercises. Beginning readers. High replay value.

Works OK on an older computer

The best software for very young children is reviewed later in this chapter.

## MATH BLASTERS

The trouble with math and young children is that numbers don't have little faces, numbers don't sit up and smile at you and say good morning. How can we make numbers and math equations less abstract to young children? **Math Blasters** has arrayed dozens of clever animations and colorful games to make math equations more fun. In **Math Blaster: In Search of Spot**, you don't merely add or subtract, you blast the correct answer out of the sky while hovering over the moon in a jet pack. In another activity, you float upwards towards the correct answer while dodging space litter, like old cola cans and rotting fish bones. Then squeeze correct math answers through a conveyer belt whilst compacting the offensive debris into recyclable compost. I was charmed. The problem for me is that throughout this process, the equations themselves still seem relatively abstract. What IS "6 times 3 equals 18?" What does it look like? How about a little animation portraying 18 laser beams being divided among 3 space aliens, resulting in 6 lasers per alien? Still, the **Math Blaster** series brings new life to a familiar childhood drudgery. The **Math Blaster** series extends up through algebra and geometry, and **Math Blasters Mystery** is a game introducing a child to the concept of solving for one unknown (What does n= if it's less than 10 and more than 8?) while looking under pieces of furniture in a room. The **Math Blaster** series provides fun math instruction for ages 6 through 12. Beginning readers okay. High replay value.

Works OK on an older computer

## MATH ACE

**Math Ace** provides more levels of math instruction than any other program I've seen on the market today. You can be working on simple subtraction, then switch to algebra-trig or geometry faster than you can say "polynomial." The game play is simple: You are presented with a picture of a computer circuit

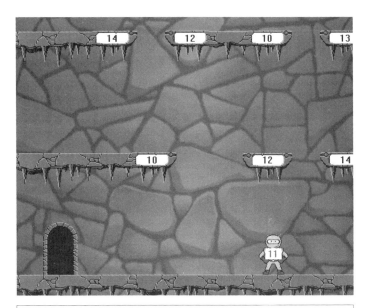

Screen from Davidson's **Math Blaster: In Search of Spot.** In the above activity, the number on your back falls between the numbers shown on two of the cave ledges. You can only float to the top of the cave if you fly between the appropriate ledges.

board being devoured by a computer virus. You isolate and contain the virus by answering a number of math problems correctly and quickly. Every few questions, you are thrown into a little game that involves calculating simple angles, teaching you, for example, how to eyeball what the trajectory of an object shot into the air at 60 degrees might look like. **Math Ace** comes packed with two very excellent features: An online glossary to many math terms, complete with example problems to clarify the definitions. The game also includes a practice lab, in which you work on a particular kind of problem over and over again, until you get it right. You may then return to the game. The lab provides drill-like consistency with enough variation to keep you awake. **Math Ace** aces most of the competition, and if you have to pick one math program for your children, try this one.

Beginning readers okay, but the math lab and tutorials would require reading at about the fourth or fifth grade level. High replay value.

Requires fast computer

A very, very good game

Two Screens from The Learning Company's **Outnumbered**

What's going on in the TV station? You'll have to solve word-math problems to find out.

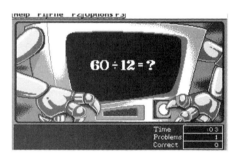

"Telly" will only give you clues if you answer his pop quizzes correctly.

## OUTNUMBERED

For teaching word math problems, **Outnumbered** is one of the best. You wander around a television studio trying to chase down the bad guy, and are faced with a number of word math problems along the way. The math skills covered seem right for first through fourth graders, and happily, the look of the game and the way it plays suits the same age group. Every so often, this television-shaped robot appears from nowhere, pins you to the wall and treats you to a little math quiz. There they are, 11 plus 9, 15 times 3, 24 divided by 3, and on and on…and only 5 to 10 seconds to answer each one! Seldom have I seen kids try so hard to nail this stuff.

Parents may set the skill level for both the word problems and the drills. Beginning readers. High replay value.

A very, very good game

## TREASURE MATH STORM

Easy beginning math for ages 5 through 9, this is a colorful game from The Learning Company, who seem to understand the kind of games young children will want to play over and over and over again. Is it the friendly smiles on all the little characters? The simple palette of bright colors that eschews subtle shades and pastels of any sort? The problems are varied, clearly presented, and not very hard. There's simple, object-oriented multiplication, addition and subtraction, and plenty of happy little snowmen and smiling tea-pots to entertain and enlighten. Very little reading required. High replay value.

## REAL WORLD MATH

**Real World Math** is a dream of a program for any math-resistant child. Math problems are presented as part of the workday routine of a busy airport. To complete the game, you must earn "flight time" by learning about the different jobs involved in getting airplanes off the ground and returning them safely to earth at the appointed hour. You learn about scheduled maintenance, establishing flight paths by using coordinates, and planning and purchasing supplies without overstocking or running out. These problems are all presented in a breezy, uncluttered, friendly interface that encourages the mastery of one or two skills before moving on. Always on screen is a gauge reporting how much more flight time you need to reach the next level. All math problems are narrated clearly and carefully. Most of the characters are cartoon-rendered, so your computer's resources are left free to handle the game action and narrative smoothly. The cartoons are not cute animal faces, and thus will not offend a 13-year-old who's having trouble with math in his or her own real world. Good reading skills.

## OPERATION NEPTUNE

Using an underwater game of search, a child must navigate ocean waters, avoid the usual scary monsters, locate the missing pieces of a space vehicle gone awry, and along the way, learn some applied math. **Operation Neptune** poses word problems only, so a fair amount of reading is required. A child must correctly calculate remaining fuel, subtract weights and measurements and solve for one unknown. The game is colorful, kids love it. **Operation Neptune** will not sit idly on your hard drive. Good reading skills. High replay value.

Some of the best games might not be available at software stores. Unfortunately, most retail outlets carry only the most current titles. Call or write the software company itself to get a copy of older products that interest you. Addresses and phone numbers of many software manufacturers whose products can be found in the Appendix.

## SIMEARTH

Like its sister Sim, **SimCity**, **SimEarth** is one of the original multiple-outcome science computer simulations. There is much detail to keep track of, so keep your eyes open, searching all four corners of that computer screen for signs of new life on your personal version of Earth. You made your planet, now you have to lie down and burn (or freeze) in it. Your job is to make your planet work, allow all species of animals to develop and become permanent residents of our planet, not a shaky evolutionary experiment ripe for extinction during the next ice age. On the main screen, you watch all natural phenomenon occur, such as tidal waves, comet crashes, and new species evolving.

When a new species evolves on your planet, its arrival is announced on the screen, in the form of a nice smiling dinosaur or crustacean or mammal, and so on.

However, just because a species makes a biological appearance on your version of Earth, there's no guarantee it will stay there. If your atmosphere has too little (or too much) oxygen, or is too hot or cold, you'll get an on-screen announcement such as "Mass extinctions are occurring." And your new species will disappear from the screen.

You may alter many features of your planet's environment by simply pulling down a menu and clicking on a box. Such high-brow features as "earth-cloud albedo" and "earth core heat" are yours to adjust by pulling a lever. You may also play with the rate at which new species evolve into other species, the rate at which animals reproduce, rainfall, "greenhouse effect," and rate of $CO_2$ consumption, to name only a very few. Luckily, **SimEarth** comes with a plain-English manual that is both helpful and entertaining, falling somewhere between a biological thesis and outtakes from Rowan and Martin's "Laugh-in." There are lots of charts and bar-graphs that readily report your planet's progress.

Later in the simulation, human disasters loom as large as nature's variety, and you must encourage peace and combat famines. Don't let those two tribes go to war! In this later mode, you may manipulate human energy allocations by a flick of the switch, just as readily as you fussed with planet temperature and oxygen consumption rates previously. This means you may decide how much human energy ought to go toward science, philosophy, leisure, and "progress," and so on. High points towards philosophy means fewer wars, for example. For some modern-day Godzilla fun, try dropping in a few dinosaurs in the modern era, or send tidal waves to disrupt civilization like some cranky deity. If you play mean, you'll have to put up with "Gaia," a little planet-shaped icon that resides in the corner of your screen and smiles at you with puppy-eyed affection when you are nice to the planet, and

Screen from **From Alice to Ocean**, the story of Robin Davidson who walked across Australia on foot. The CD-ROM chronicling her journey is reviewed on page 291 of this book.

glowers when you're bad. This simulation is second to none for introducing difficult biological concepts to youngsters, such as the interdependence of animals and the environment, and the ability of computer simulations to give you a headache when you play them too long with the lights down. This is a complex, multilayered computer simulation and would intimidate most children under the sixth grade. Good reading skills. High replay value.

## THE AMAZON TRAIL

You fall asleep one night, and in your dreams, an ancient world beckons. You awaken and are sent on a journey through time, down the Amazon River, beginning at its mouth in Benin, Brazil. You stop along the way, interviewing the many kinds of people who live (or have lived) along the Amazon. You'll talk to a "Rubber Baron" who, in the 1800s, turned huge swaths of jungle into his personal rubber plantation. You'll talk to researchers, scouring the Amazon's plant life for cures to a number of diseases. You talk to Teddy Roosevelt, who, after his presidency, visited the Amazon frequently, championing its preservation. There are hundreds of different Indian tribes along the Amazon's waters, and you'll meet them, barter for goods, and learn the skills to stay in their good graces. But your main mission in **Amazon Trail** is to wind your way back to the 1500s and bring the Inca King some "cinchona," which contains quinine, the cure for malaria. To obtain food for your journey, you and your guide must fish, learning to distinguish the edible from the poisonous. You may dock your vessel at will, and search the jungle for important items, such as plants that have medicinal properties. You also have a camera for photographing whatever interests you. Perhaps the greatest feature in **Amazon Trail** is the on-line encyclopedia, instantly accessible at any time. It will provide you with a brief description of all the people, plants, animal life, villages and tribes, and goods for bartering that you will encounter throughout the game. It also audibly pronounces every word you look up, a real plus, since there are hundreds of languages and dialects to be heard along the **Amazon Trail**. One of the best. Good reading skills. High replay value.

Very good story

Screen from MECC's **The Amazon Trail**. The people you meet along the banks of the Amazon are valuable sources of information and trade goods.

Workman Publishing's **Brain Quest** and David Macaulay's **The Way Things Work**, two long-time staples of educational bookstores, are now available to computer users. **Brain Quest**—those ubiquitous boxes of colorful flashcards which have been a godsend the the hard-traveling parent who needs hours of entertainment for the kids in the car—makes a smooth transition to the computer screen. But since half the fun was tossing the box of cards into your purse or backpack and popping questions out at a moment's notice, I'm not sure I see the point of making **Brain Quest** into a computer program.

**The Way Things Work**, however, is all about, well, how things work, as in move, spin, expand, bend...everything from clocks to toasters to nuclear power plants gets a thorough exam in Macaulay's mammoth book. But sitting with it in your lap and explaining to your child how this stationary diagram would look if it were in motion, or actually working, has always been a chore. Expanding the book into a computer program, with animations and videos is, therefore, a perfect idea. With the program, you see the gears rotate, the oars row, and the plutonium... well...chain react, I guess. This CD-ROM product is put out by Dorling Kindersley Multimedia.

## LOST SECRET OF THE RAIN FOREST

It's eco-conscience, nonviolent, clever, and witty, and even comes with a point and click glossary of words and phrases relevant to saving the "lungs of the earth," that is, the rain forest. Besides all that, it's a good story: A young boy visits Latin America with his painfully politically correct father, who has just arrived with a plan to help Brazilian tribesmen develop and market their own nature-friendly yet profitable products. Young "Adam" is transported to the middle of the rain forest. He interacts with nature's beasts, solving a number of follies with an evenhanded kindness that would warm the heart of a Franciscan monk. The game is packed with Sierra's usual awesome graphics, as well as their educational products standard themes of interdependence and mutual cooperation. Good reading skills. High replay value.

## VOYAGER

Trying to strike a working balance between arcade action and anatomy lessons, the people that brought you **Autoworks** and other very instructive software pieces have come up with a rather smart and playable game. Essentially, your child is shrunk to the size of a pin and sent inside the human body with a mission to blast out bacteria and viruses. Your child is told, "The culprit is somewhere near the semicircular canal," for example. In order to locate the "semicircular canal," kids are given some anatomy charts to study, and these charts are **Voyager**'s greatest strength. **Voyager** found a way to lay out lots of information without overloading the screen or the sensibilities of an easily distracted child. The body part labels are easy to read, and some worthwhile study is possible in between beaming down and blasting microbes to kingdom come. Your child is armed, legged, dangerous, and is wading around in someone's sub-arachnoid hematoma right about now. Bodywork's **Voyager** gives new meaning to the question, "Should I let you into my heart?" (I don't know. Maybe you shouldn't.) Confident fifth grade readers could tackle this game without assistance quite easily. Sans coaching, younger kids could settle in to the shoot-'em-up portions of the game and possibly fake it through the learning parts. The rest of us could enjoy it when no one else is looking. Good reading skills.

## TURBO SCIENCE

The game is a race against other animated characters. As your science skills improve, you are pitted against smarter opponents. You answer science questions, and you purchase high-tech modes of transportation around the racetrack by answering correctly. Answer poorly and you must walk. The questions are not merely

listed. You are whisked away to familiar environments in which the scientific phenomena going on around you is bracketed or highlighted. Multiple choice questions
regarding the phenomena appear on the screen. The game is lively and never boring. The music is fun and the characters are simply a scream. **Turbo Science**
comes with a surprisingly broad and well-written science handbook. During the
question phase, you may pause the game and look up the answers you need.
Getting to the heart of the game is quick and learning takes place from square one.
Good reading skills. High replay value.

## THE DISCOVERERS

Based on the IMAX movie *The Discoverers,* this CD-ROM is a very pleasurable
stroll through the garden of, well, human discovery. We look at Magellan's voyage
across the oceans, Newton discovering the nature of color, and radar astronomers
recording the magnetic shadowplay known to us as the aurora borealis. What civilization first discovered eclipses? How? How did the scientists at JPL simulate
those exhilarating "moving" topographical maps of Venus? You wander through
the caves of Altimira, Spain, getting a close-up view of the earliest cave drawings.
You may also explore the "talking" artwork of four ancient civilizations through
dramatizations of creation legends and sundry ancient myths. The CD contains a
free-running, condensed version of the IMAX movie itself, complete with the Arab
astronomers predicting a total eclipse, and one of Magellan's wary investors, quip-
ping that the explorer's ships would most certainly be devoured "by monsters…with
four arms."

But as the movie plays, click anywhere on the screen to go to another relevant film
clip, narrated text, or illuminating sideline of some sort. The wonder of this program
is its breadth. Hypertext links in the movie can send you back to the beginning of
time, or to an interesting glimpse at the future. And truly, you may stop anywhere
along the way an smell the roses. The links make more sense, and carry more of
a viewpoint and story line than the usual hypertext sludgeworks. Knowledge
Adventure CDs sometimes go overboard in trying to include activities for everybody; hence, some Knowledge Adventure outings seem too "kidsy" for adults and
way over the heads of children. But **The Discoverers** maintains a layman's accessibility without become trite. I've noticed two major improvements: Many different
voices are employed in reading narration, acting out dramatization, and as guides
through the various activities. You know longer feel as if you are listening to one
long commercial for K-Mart.

Secondly, and this is great for kids, as the narration is being read aloud, the written text scrolls automatically. You may also select a clear and large font for children's reading ease. They took the time to render everything gorgeously, and even the playing-card-style "name the discoverers" game looks like a jewel. **The Discoverers** is a must-have for CD-ROM owners who have kids. Because all text is narrated, good reading is not a must. Children as young as 5 would be fascinated by the subject matter. Fair replay value.

Requires
CD-ROM

Good use of
video

## OCEANS BELOW

Screen from Mindscape's
**Oceans Below**

A team of two friendly and informative deep-sea divers escort you on an underwater tour of planet Earth. Go anywhere, as long as it's deep and wet. Learn all about diving equipment, and after you've selected the locale of your next plunge, your instructor always imparts sage wisdom about safe diving tips before you go under. See film clips of hundreds of sea animals, all in their own environment. Find underwater treasure, or examine relics of WWII battleships submerged near the Fiji Islands in the South Pacific. You may examine selected sea animals closely. **Oceans Below** packs enough data to round out a detailed report on oceanography, diving, or underwater life forms. It truly imparts a sense of the diversity of sea life, and after playing this game, you'll never think of the undersea world as a uniform mass of fish. Very little reading is required, since all the text is clearly and carefully narrated. Fair replay value.

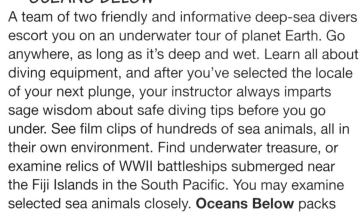
Good use of
video

Requires
CD-ROM

## ABOUT "KNOWLEDGE ADVENTURE"

**Science Adventure**, one of the very first Knowledge Adventure games released in 1991, sported a photo of Isaac Azimov on the box. Azimov wrote hundreds of books, fiction and non-fiction, on subjects ranging from biblical archeology to robotics, and was said to possess automatic recall, the ability to recite from memory whatever he had most recently read. Not surprisingly, **Science Adventure** and the other early Knowledge Adventure computer learning programs were probably more fun if you possessed similar abilities. You could read about the man who invented the first primitive computer (a Mr. Babbage) and bone up on neighboring galaxies and black holes, and learn who King Ashirbanipal was and all about the Mede-Persian empire dominating the known world circa the eighth century BC. You get some photos and rather gratuitous sound effects, and you get lost in a hurry, navigating the threads of logic that connect the articles to each other. All of the early Knowledge Adventure programs have a main screen that features a globe in the upper left-hand corner. To learn about a particular part of the world, rotate the globe with a click of the mouse, zoom in or out, and click on your area of interest. You may click on a time line, pick your favorite era in history, and limit your globetrotting to that particular age. And in order to really put these programs through their paces, you'd better be nearly as smart as Mr. Azimov.

Hoping to draw in those of us who are a little softer upstairs, later products by the Knowledge Adventure people, such as **Dinosaur Adventure** and **Space Adventure,** incorporate more multimedia resources, such as video and audio clips. **Dinosaur Adventure** features movies of dinos at war, and contains a dinosaur recognition game with a friendly narrator and decidedly non-raptoresque music. **Space Adventure** comes packed with planetary goodies such as computer-generated "film footage" of Venus, assembled from the Magellan spacecraft's databanks. All Knowledge Adventure games feature hypertext links: Click on any active text bubble that interests you and be whisked off to learn something new elsewhere in the program. Self-motivation is a necessary feature for enjoying any of the Knowledge Adventure series programs. To enjoy the older programs, your child must already be curious about the subjects at hand, and able to absorb lots of facts and figures without too many blinking lights to make the whole process seem like Nintendo. A child who's not sure what he or she wants to learn about will be left scratching his head, wondering what to do next. These programs push you out of the nest and expect you to be aggressive and curious.

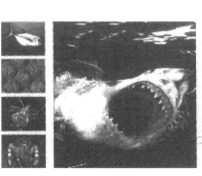

The newest flock of Knowledge Adventure programs, such as **Speed Adventure**, **USA Adventure**, and **Undersea Adventure** lead you by the hand more easily, dividing the screen into well-defined activities, but still retain the kind of "open-ended" quality that has become Knowledge Adventure's trademark. There are more film clips and multimedia goodies than ever. **Speed Adventure** includes a program that, if you can guess how fast a particular animal or machine can travel, your computer screen becomes the "eyes" of something

Screen from Knowledge Adventure's **Undersea Adventure**.

traveling at the speed of your correct answer. **USA Adventure** comes with film clips from famous events in American history. **Undersea Adventure** lets you dissect various sea creatures, or you may cavort with them in a virtual underwater environment. Most of the activities found in the Knowledge Adventure games can be tackled by those who possess fourth or fifth grade reading skills. Each game comes with an on-line reference library for those who would like to conduct more in-depth research.

# PHYSICS

## THE INCREDIBLE MACHINE

Not an understatement. Did you ever want to teach your children about gravity and friction and inclined planes, or how one gear can turn other gears, thereby performing a greater degree of mechanical work? Try putting that into words that a young person will understand. Don't bore them with science lectures yet. First, show them **The Incredible Machine**. You use various mechanisms, from teeter-totters to windmills to small motors and electric switches that turn on light bulbs. Your job is to get any number of mechanisms to work together to perform a task. The task something like, "make all four basketballs fall in a hoop," or "feed the cat some lunch." To get your child acquainted with the workings of the dozens of doodads that come in **The Incredible Machine,** there are more than 100 preset puzzles, in which the goal is spelled out at the beginning, and the mechanisms at your disposal (say, a magnifying glass, a superball, and some rope) are ready in the screen margins for your child to insert where he or she sees fit. Now you can talk to them about Isaac Newton and the apple. Good reading skills. High replay value.

Very exceptional music

Good strategy game

## GIZMOS AND GADGETS

That Master of Mischief returns to plague little brains with new puzzles and contraptions. **Gizmos and Gadgets** teaches young children some principles of elementary mechanics and takes a stab at very basic physics. In order to turn on a light bulb, kids must "assemble" a circuit board, placing the components in the correct order. To assemble a simple go-cart, your child must select the correct pieces, applying a little knowledge of kinetics and friction reduction and how placing a small gear

Computing doesn't have to be a chore. Learn some time-saving tricks to reduce the drudgery.
**See Chapter 7**

within a large gear will reduce work, making the go-cart more efficient. Simple mechanics and physics are two areas of science that children can grasp and work with long before they are able to explain to a bunch of grown-ups what they already know to be true. This game enhances a child's understanding of simple machines like wedges and inclined planes, and lets them see those ideas put to work in real life. Beginning readers okay. Fair replay value.

Highest learning value

## TURBO SCIENCE

The game is a race against other animated characters. As your science skills improve, you are pitted against smarter opponents. You answer science questions to purchase high-tech modes of transportation around the race track. Answer poorly and you must walk. The questions are not merely listed: You are whisked away to familiar environments in which the scientific phenomena going on around you is bracketed or highlighted. Multiple choice questions regarding the phenomena appear on the screen. The game is lively and never boring. The music is fun and the characters are simply a scream. **Turbo Science** comes with a surprisingly broad and well-written science handbook. During the question phase, you may pause the game and look up the answers you need. Getting to the heart of the game is quick and learning takes place from square one. Good reading skills. High replay value.

## SCIENCE ADVENTURE 2

One of the best "new and improved" projects by Knowledge Adventure, this program is certainly the broadest. This CD is FULL: 644MB of science simulation workshops, video clips, sounds, and unusual photo libraries of all kinds of science phenomena, great and small, with clear and concise spoken narratives. **Science Adventure 2** opens by placing you in a rotunda, surrounded by doors that lead to the various activities. One such activity is to use a microscope, examine an aspirin tablet, the AIDS virus, or dozens of other interesting molecules. Play with a set of prisms to discover more about the nature of color and light. To learn about the nature of sound waves, you are taken to a close-up performance by a full orchestra. There's a science museum, with "rooms" divided by subject matter. Click on an

Curious eyes can examine many different specimens with **Science Adventure's** microscope.

exhibit to hear and see more about it. Bored with the room you are in? Walk through the wall to the next one. In the "Bogus Science" game, you are standing in a science gallery, discussing science facts with the people around you, and you must identify the one who says something false. You can also cruise down the lanes of scientific discovery, eavesdropping on some of science's most famous mistakes. Can you redirect the thinking of the day and get discoveries right? This CD has enough on it to keep anyone busy for weeks. No reading required, but the concepts would be over the heads of most kids below fourth grade. High replay value.

A very, very
good game

## DANGEROUS CREATURES

Some subjects lend themselves very well to the wandering pace of Microsoft's Exploration Series CDs. To explore often means to take your time. (Running this program on a 386 computer will indeed increase your sympathy for naturalists who sit patiently in the middle of nowhere waiting for something to happen.) This program, which provides four or five different paths to access information about any of nature's most scary beasties, is not for the soul in a hurry. Produced in conjunction with the World Wildlife Fund, **Dangerous Creatures** serves up a full platter of video clips, identification games, guided tours, and interesting articles about the endangered world of wildlife on earth. There are enough bells and whistles to keep young readers busy and learning for many hours, while at the same time, **Dangerous Creatures** is worth having on hand as a reference tool. Each animal photo is surrounded with bright red hypertext links, leading to brief narratives, videos, and games that are all worth digging around for. There is no central listing of all the resources at your disposal. You'll just have to go exploring. Beginning readers. High replay value.

Requires fast
computer

Requires
CD-ROM

Good use of
video

## ZOOKEEPER

This one's a bit of a classic. You're in charge of a zoo. Poorly mannered creatures enter the zoo and disrupt the animals' environment. The animals are being fed the wrong food, and are being left to languish in the wrong environment. You must correct the problems. When you've fixed things, the animals clamor about as if you were some sort of demigod. (It's for the younger kids, okay?) If you're not sure how to fix the animals' surroundings and feed them correctly, click on a friendly robot and get some hints. The first few "cases" require no reading, but after that, you're guided by two or three sentences. High replay value.

Works OK on an older computer

## CIPHER

There are really three aspects to this game. First, there's some category recognition: mountains, islands, gems, flowers, many natural occurrences. Next, it's a "What's-my-animal?" research puzzle, where you must match a number of clues to the appropriate mammal. You've got an online reference guide of mammal facts for just such an occasion. Then, with the remaining time, you must unravel a code, replacing incorrect letters with the right ones, sort of like a game of hangman, but extended to a paragraph, rather than a single word. Tanager's **Cipher** isn't seen much in the stores anymore, perhaps because it defies categorization, but I recommend it. The game moves fast through a variety of activities. **Cipher** will increase reading skills for most second through fourth graders. Even children slightly above that range will probably not find it sappy or overly cartoonish, and are apt to learn a bit about the animals. Good reading skills. High replay value.

Good strategy game

## ODELL DOWN UNDER

**Odell Down Under** is produced by MECC, one of the oldest and most established software companies. This underwater simulation teaches kids what it's like to be a fish and have to survive in ocean water infested with predators, unhealthy water, and/or scarce food. You may choose to be one of a 100 or so fish, and you are provided with a couple of paragraphs of data about the sea creature you have chosen to embody. Use your mouse to direct that fish through the water,

There are techniques that you as a parent can use to increase the learning value of these games. For example, if you child is playing a game with lots of spoken dialogue or text written on the screen, have him or her write down five words that are unfamiliar, then look them up in a dictionary, or bring them to you for clarification.

up or down, right or left; if your fish has a special ability (like a blowfish being able to puff itself up, or an octopus emitting ink) then pushing the space bar activates this ability. Children hungry for an ego boost will find themselves playing most often as the great white shark, rather than the tiny shrimp angler. What gets you most often though, is the futile search for that dang cleaner fish. Quite often, playing as one of God's less robust offerings, if you do escape becoming a meal for a barracuda, you succumb instantly and unceremoniously to tail rot. Uggh! Beginning readers okay. Fair replay value.

# OUTER SPACE

### WHERE IN SPACE IS CARMEN SANDIEGO?

As with the rest of the Carmen Sandiego series, you don't catch the crook until you master a bit of knowledge of the subject at hand. **Where in Space is Carmen Sandiego?** differs from her predecessor by including an online glossary of relevant space facts. The first few Carmen games hit the street back when 286s were considered fast. But in order to play **Where in Space?**, a minimum 386 /33 computer is recommended…by me anyway. Good reading skills (small text on the screen). High replay value.

### UFO

You hop about the nine planets, seeking a UFO. Clues pop up, bits of knowledge that lead you to the next planet in your search. For example: The planet in question "was visited by the Mariner spacecraft," or "is made of mostly gas and ice." This game has good clear graphics, a very uncluttered screen, and encourages second and third grade level reading skills. Your child may keep score and print out the results of his alien-catching escapades. Beginning readers okay. Fair replay value.

Highest learning value

Works OK on an older computer

### SPACE ADVENTURE

Part of the Knowledge Adventure series, **Space Adventure** provides lots of little info-nuggets about all things celestial and astronomical. **Space Adventure** was one of the first of the Knowledge Adventure series released on CD. The written articles are not narrated, such as with later Knowledge Adventure works like 3D Body Adventure. There's lots of marvelous footage of space walks and surface photography of Saturn and Venus, as well the historic moonwalk "The Eagle Has Landed" film clips. Good reading skills. Not much replay value after you've gone through the highlights once or twice. Excellent reference tool, however.

# U.S. HISTORY AND CURRENT AFFAIRS

## WHERE IN THE U.S.A. IS CARMEN SANDIEGO?

The original **Where in the U.S.A. is Carmen Sandiego?** is the only one that my 8-year-old son can play by himself. You know why? Because the text is really big and easy to read. The deluxe SVGA **Where in the USA?** made the screen fonts smaller to make room for their more impressive animations. "The Carmens" teach geography like no other program available, and this program passes on important U.S. history facts, too. Good reading skills. High replay value.

Screen from Broderbund's original **Where in the U.S.A. Is Carmen Sandiego?**

## OREGON TRAIL

**Oregon Trail** is one of the oldest learning computer games on the market, and was updated in 1992. The role-play begins in 1849: You and your family must travel from Independence, Missouri, to Willamette Valley, Oregon, recreating the famous westward trek of our sturdy pioneer ancestors. You may play as a farming family, which merely means you have little money at the outset, and ensures that you and your intrepid family will be doing lots of hunting along the trail in order to get food. Riding the trail as a carpenter and his clan affords you more of a margin for error, and the loss of a yoke of oxen to thieves won't bankrupt your family and set you to wandering in the cold until you starve. As a banker, you begin with $1,600, making the Oregon trail a veritable king's highway. First, you name all the people in your family, and choose the time of year you wish to leave. Strategy is important here, and, as with all choices you make along the trail, there's a handy "more info" button to make you wise. You must stop by the general store at the head of the trail, with a friendly store manager on hand to advise you. Spend wisely, for seldom will purchases have such vast implications on your livelihood. As you travel the trail, check your progress on a map, and if your family's health looks poor, stop to rest for a few days. Should you wait out bad weather, or press ahead? Talk to people at different campsites and outposts along the way, go hunting, or make purchases, although the prices will be higher than they were back in Independence, Missouri. Hardships abound, and you'll get to see just how prepared you and your family are to face them. As you approach Willamette Valley, you must approach over land, or navigate the potentially treacherous Columbia River. Each choice has its benefits and perils. Good luck. The CD-ROM version eliminates some of the need for reading, but not all. Beginning readers would enjoy this game. Fair replay value.

Highest learning value   Works OK on an older computer   A very, very good game

## TIME RIDERS IN AMERICAN HISTORY

A rather colorful villain named Dread has taken to rewriting American history, broadcasting unlikely spins on some of America's most cherished events and personalities. You are part of a team of students who must dig through computerized archives of events in America's past, piece the truth together, beat nasty Dread to the punch, and broadcast the truth. Facts are built on cumulative knowledge: Kids can't select the correct event unless they truly understand the related facts. Built in to the sequence of broadcasts and counter-broadcasts is a clever story line that makes the kids want to keep going to find out what happens next. Good reading skills. High replay value.

Highest learning value   Very good story

## NEWSWEEK INTERACTIVE CD

Like the magazine itself, **Newsweek Interactive CD** is a collection of stories and events that fall under the category of "current affairs." This CD focuses on two issues. One is the changing roll of the United States as a superpower. What do we do with all those weapons now that there is no Soviet Union to train them on? The other focus is a video/news-article entitled "The Secret Life of Animals," which reviews current research on animal consciousness: Do cats think and feel or merely chase mice? Nobody would ever accuse *Newsweek* of going heavy on the academics, but in this case, this CD's slick readability really pays off. Children as young as eight and teens through early college could all profit from spending a few hours at the computer with this one. The foreign policy article

Screen from Newsweek's Interactive CD-ROM. Can Bowser think, reason, or merely redesign U.S. foreign policy?

includes several scenarios which place you at the helm in a time of crisis. After hearing from your advisors, you must decide your course of action. Later events either validate or repudiate your actions. The "animal article" is accompanied by some unique film footage that brings the issues to life quite nicely. One of the nicest features of **Newsweek Interactive CD** is that the on-screen text is large enough for children to read comfortably. Good reading skills.

Requires<br>CD-ROM

## AMERICA ADVENTURE

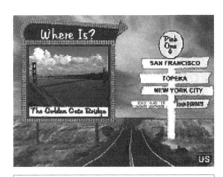

This newer product of the Knowledge Adventure series has a handful of historic U.S. moments captured on film, a narrated "What is the capital of…" game, and a fun doodad in which one president's face gradually fades into the next one's, while quotes from each president kind of whirl around you like some weird historical vortex. Some activities here for even beginning readers. Most appropriate for fourth grade through junior high. Fair to low replay value.

Screen from Knowledge Adventure's **America Adventure**.

## THE PRESIDENTS

Since CD-ROMs hold so much data, it's tempting to go look up as much material as possible on a subject, especially a subject old enough to be public domain, write it to a CD-ROM disk and market it as a program. I put off purchasing this CD-ROM for a long time, thinking it would tell me more than I ever wanted to know about Grover Cleveland's left big toe. I'm glad my family picked it up. You do get film clips, radio broadcasts, photos, and lots of interesting data on each American president, but you also get a breakdown on how the voting went state by state in each election, and a discussion of the issues surrounding each presidential election. There's a brief video, showing the sequence in which each state joined the Union. Most of the articles you'll read in **The Presidents** include hypertext: Click on a key word, and an extended explanation pops up, or you might be whisked off to a related article. Good reading skills. Fair to low replay value, except as a reference tool. If a word is unfamiliar, you may click on it and the word's definition will appear on the screen.

Requires<br>CD-ROM

# Preeeesenting

## AN INTERVIEW

WITH A REAL LIVE
SOFTWARE
DESIGNER

(They Don't Bite unless
You Provoke Them)

**Lorelei Shannon is a software designer with Sierra On-Line. She designed and wrote *Pepper's Adventures in Time*, an interactive role-play adventure that teaches children about Benjamin Franklin, and she wrote dialogue for *The Dagger of Ammon Ra*, one of Sierra's most popular interactive mystery games. She grew up in Mesa, Arizona, and has degrees in both art and English. This interview was conducted over the phone in early February, as Ms. Shannon was working on Sierra's upcoming *Phantasmagoria*.**

**Winston Steward:** Many people still think of software games as a "guy thing." Two of the big projects you've been associated with, *The Dagger of Ammon Ra* and *Pepper's Adventure in Time*, have female heroines. Over the years, have you gotten mail from female computer users who appreciate how you've opened things up?

**Lorelei Shannon:** Yes we do. Particularly from young girls. They feel left out, and there are so many extremely violent video games that are directly marketed at boys, I think they're delighted to find things that are, if not *aimed* at them, that at least *include* them.

**W.S.** Did *Dagger of Ammon Ra* and *Pepper* take a lot of research? You make it seem quite effortless, but it's seldom as easy as it seems.

**L.S.** For *Dagger of Ammon Ra*, I just did some of the writing. I know Bruce Balfour, the designer on that one, did a lot of research on Egyptology. With *Pepper*, we did a lot of research. There were about two months of research before we even started the project, and after that, we had a consulting historian, a woman named Victoria Cornell, come in and help during the production. We wanted to be accurate.

**W.S.** My son and daughter learned about Ben Franklin's innovations and inventions from *Pepper's Adventures* at least a year before such topics appeared in their school curriculum. Role-play adventures like the kind you've written can make difficult concepts accessible to young children. If you could pick another historical person to work an adventure game around, who would it be?

**L.S.** Something we were considering doing is sort of a pastiche of female inventors and scientists and people like that. We were going to have Pepper trying to decide what she wants to do with her life, and meet various female journalists, scientists, and so on.

**W.S.** Like Madame Curie, for example?

**L.S.** Yes, people like that. Another project we're considering is a history of flight, which, of course, would include Amelia Earhart and other famous female pilots.

**W.S.** Isn't the youngest pilot ever to fly across the Atlantic an 11-year-old girl named Vicki Van Meter?

**L.S.** Yes, that's right.

**W.S.** So you're not just doing *Phantasmagoria*? You have other irons in the fire?

**L.S.** Well, that's all I'm doing right now, but I've always got lots of ideas ready, and now, I'm in the same state with Bright Star, which is Sierra's educational division. I'm hoping to be able to work with them, because I always enjoy doing children's software.

**W.S.** Sometimes the dialogue you've brought to the games has been quite touching and almost poetic. What's it like for you to write games in a market still dominated by laser bombs and battle scenes? Do you think people really appreciate the dialogue you compose?

> In doing *Pepper*, we went around and around about whether there would be too much text. We actually brought in a bunch of children and watched them play. And they enjoyed it! They liked the funny parts, and they actually went ahead and read the touching parts.

**L.S.** Well, I think they do. I'm primarily a writer—that's what I do most of the time, and I think children really like to read. In doing *Pepper*, we went around and around about whether there would be too much text, and would children actually read it. We actually brought in a bunch of children and watched them play. And they enjoyed it! They liked the funny parts, and they actually went ahead and read the touching parts.

**W.S.** Down here in Hollywoodland, script writers often complain that by the time their script makes it up to the big screen, the words they labored over are so butchered that they can scarcely recognize their work. Are you happy with how your words finally look (or sound) once they become part of the computer game as a whole?

**L.S.** Yes, we have a tool called a message editor, and it actually goes from my fingers into the software.

**W.S.** Ooh, nice.

**L.S.** Yes. I'll bet script writers wish they had them.

**W.S.** Tell us about Sierra's upcoming educational titles, especially those you have something to do with. Are there any more adventure games in the works, similar to *Pepper* or *Ecoquest*?

**L.S.** I know we're working on an update of our classic game *Mixed Up Mother Goose*, but beyond that, the people at Bright Star handle our educational titles.

**W.S.** We purchased Bright Star's *Yobi's Spelling Tricks* when it first came out, and to this day, I still think that my kids learned more early vocabulary, grammar, and sentence structure by osmosis, from playing the interactive adventure games.

**L.S.** You know, I've always felt that way. I think that when kids actually enjoy something and play it and pay attention to it, they're learning more than if their parents say, "Sit down and play this."

**W.S.** Can you give us a really good definition of a Sierra "role play interactive adventure game"?

**L.S.** I think that the heart of a Sierra interactive adventure game is the fact that it's got a lot of story, a lot of humor, and a lot of fun. Our puzzles are unique.

**W.S.** As the designer, are you the first person to put the story together or do you come along after things are storyboarded by someone else, and then you add dialogue, and so forth?

**L.S.** I come up with everything. I come up with the basic plot ideas, character ideas, and puzzle ideas. The original sketches are done from my basic description of the characters. The artist and I work together to come up with something that we both really like. At Sierra, the designer really does drive the production throughout. Our designers try to create products with a specific vision in mind. We don't design "by committee."

## PEPPER'S ADVENTURES IN TIME

**Pepper's Adventures in Time** teaches "learning by contrast" and it seems to work. Re-create a situation in America's history by painting its opposite, then bring the two together. It's funny and instructive. Pepper is a nine-year-old girl living in a modern suburb. Weird Uncle Ed is upstairs trying to invade the mind of Benjamin Franklin and reduce him to a vapid "Peace-Child" who preaches non-involvement in anything. Through this device, Weird Uncle Ed hopes to rule the world. Pepper and her dog Lockjaw stumble on to Ed's plans and are whisked back to the Colonial era as Ed starts his time machine 'a-rollin'. Pepper finds herself in eighteenth century Philadelphia talking to a populace under the spell of an incense-burning sort of "dead-head" named Ben Franklin. Pepper must talk sense to the citizens, reminding them of the good sense Ben Franklin used to make before "whatever happened to him" happened. Remember Benjamin Franklin's 13 proverbs, some of his most famous pithy common-sense sayings that got printed in Poor Richards Almanac? Well, now they're twisted into justifications for abject mellowness, peace, love, and Indian tapistry. Pepper must sort out the correct proverbs from the phonies, redistribute them to the citizens, and help them choose an appropriate course of action.

If my explanation seems tedious and overly complex, let me point out that Sierra has managed to make it all a ton of fun. The

Pepper and her dog Lockjaw failed to keep the American Revolution on track. She is singing "God Save the Queen" here.

gameplay is within the range of a second to fifth grader's reading vocabulary. There are clever plot twists, all the characters are richly drawn, and the dialogue is satisfying and quite funny. If your child misses a point of strategy and history goes astray, a huge British flag comes down, and Pepper is shown (in modern day) singing "God Save the Queen," and a hint flashes on the screen, advising you how to adjust your strategy and save the course of time. Pepper is set in six acts, and after each, Ben Franklin gives you a 10-question pop quiz on his life and times. (When he asks you "Which famous composer wrote music for the Glass Harp?" don't select Danny Elfman.) Throughout the game, you have available a "True or False" icon that you may point and click at any object on the screen and guess whether such an object or state of affairs existed in Ben's time, or in modern time. After clicking, you are told if your answer was correct or not, and why. Returning Ben to his senses involves learning to assemble his famous electicity-seeking kite on his behalf, piece by piece, hoping to jolt his memory. Teaching this important period U.S. history to youngsters need never be boring again. Good reading skills. High replay value. Sierra On-Line has attempted to make the vocabulary appropriate for the reading skills of younger children.

Very good story

Very exceptional music

A female heroine

A very, very good game

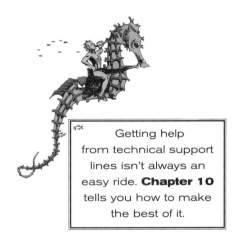

Getting help from technical support lines isn't always an easy ride. **Chapter 10** tells you how to make the best of it.

## 20TH CENTURY ALMANAC

It didn't take long for the software industry to figure out what kinds of data can be stored on CD-ROMs. Ninety years of historical bric-a-brac has been sitting in film canisters and the musty archives of the news bereaus. Some truly important, some trivial, but who's to judge? With CD-ROMs you can put it all on, and let the buyer be the curator. In the case of Mindscape's **20th Century Almanac**, the buyer must wade through five CDs, and try not to get bogged down in the minutiae. We always say that this has been an eventful century, and this collection lets you see, read, and hear just how eventful. Remember Nixon's resignation speech? Troops returning from Vietnam? The Challenger liftoff? Mahatma Gandhi giving a speech? "The Big Three" at Potsdam? Your favorite "old movie" clips? Run **20th Century Almanac's** "On this day in history" feature in your **autoexec.bat** file, and when you turn on your computer in the morning, you'll see a little article or video clip about an important event that happened on that date in a previous year. Fortunately, the Almanac's creators set up several ways to search for a particular event. Search for it alphabetically, on a time line, by subject catogory, or viewing format (film, photo, text, sound clip). The interface is easy and smooth. **20th Century Almanac** is one of the few CD-ROM products I've found that are worth owning even if you have an underpowered computer. Fifth grade through adult. Moderate replay value.

Requires CD-ROM

Good use of video

## DINO'S U.S. GEOGRAPHY

This is a simple and colorful multiple choice game that teaches elementary geography, such as recognizing U.S. states by their shape, and selecting capitals of states from a group of three choices. No typing is needed. The playing board is bright and clearly laid out, and takes less than 1MB of hard drive space. The four menu choices appear on the opening screen in big friendly letters, which helps young players to find their way back to square one and choose another activity. Beginning readers.

## HEADLINE HARRY AND THE GREAT PAPER CHASE

Do you know the names of all three of the Apollo 11 astronauts? How about the year *and the month* that the Beatles performed at Yankee Stadium in New York? You are a reporter sent somewhere in the U.S. to cover a story. The story is actually a chapter out of U.S. history. You go from city to city, interviewing people and narrowing down the facts. Here comes the clever bit. People along the way will feed you facts pertaining to *three* stories, and you must weed out the facts you don't need. There is a data sheet that you must fill in with appropriate people, places, and times. Your facts and figures must be pretty straight. After you've saved the day and unearthed the central story, you may then print it out with your byline and show it to mom. Another twist: As a reporter, you are competing with the *Diabolical Daily*, a rival newspaper with callous disregard for the facts and a taste for ruining Headline Harry's day. Happy hunting. On the downside, the

**Screen shot from Davidson's Headline Harry. The game is actually in 256 colors.**

**Headline Harry and the Great Paper Chase** teaches geography skills by linking them to current events. As a reporter, you are sent to a specific region of the United States. You interview people and track down enough facts to establish a viable story. These news stories are actually major events of the last 25 years, such as Hurricane Andrew and the 1980 eruption of Mount St. Helens.

data sheet you must fill out in order to complete the game is not very flexible in dates or titles of events. "Moon Launching," for example, will not do. Neither will "Launching of Appollo 11" or "America goes to the moon." You must type "Mission to the Moon," exactly. You must type precisely what the programmers were thinking when they developed the game. Still, this game is fun and informative. Good readers (long passages).

A very, very good game

Highest learning value

Good strategy game

## CAPITOL HILL

You've just been elected to Congress. You must meet your peers, hire staff, walk through the halls of Congress, and select the office space that will be your home away from home during the length of your term. You vote on bills, read letters, and answer phone calls from constituents back home. You get a guided tour of the House and Senate chambers and the Capitol building. **Capitol Hill**, a CD-ROM program presented by Mindscape is a seamless learning experience. Click on a statue in the main rotunda, and a gentleman who's been giving tours of the Capitol for 30 years begins telling you about it. Real members of Congress pop into your office from time to time (in the form of smooth little video clips that fill up a small part of your screen) and offer sage advice. People obviously worked hard on this CD, ensuring that a child gets a broad picture and a good sense of what it's like to live and work on Capitol Hill. Moving around from screen to screen and switching activities is a breeze. The photography and movies are large and clear enough to create for a child a believable impression of actually walking around the place and interacting with people. The bills you vote on as a freshman congressperson and the people you get mail from are gleaned from real-life situations. All budding political animals should sink their eyeteeth into this one. Despite the potentially dense subject matter, a child who reads on the fifth or sixth grade level won't feel out in the dark on Capitol Hill.

Requires
CD-ROM

Highest learning
value

## TYPING TUTORIALS

### MAVIS BEACON TEACHES TYPING

Mavis Bacon produces the best computerized typing instruction program, suitable for fifth grade and up. The CD-ROM version of Mavis' tutorial amounts to having your own personal typing teacher (and a good one) hovering nearby, computing scores, dropping hints, and suggesting areas of improvement. Good reading skills.

### MARIO TEACHES TYPING

The little red man who caused "Nintenditis" to be listed as a genuine medical condition afflicting young males has found a niche in the world of education. Yes, typing really IS a question of "eye-hand coordination," and Mario's here, ready to teach even his youngest disciples how to type. He's patient as a saint, and doesn't scold you even if you slip below three words per minute with a 67% error rate. He merely bellows cheerfully, "Maybe you should try again!" Colorful typing drills may be set for one or five minutes in duration, after which Mario is seen pointing at a chalkboard announcing the statistics of that round. As your child's skills improve, the typing drills get more varied and less repetitive. Growing readers.

## TIMETREK

This game is a test of history knowledge, and the player must be able to read single paragraph text bubbles at about the fifth through eighth grade level. Sample question: "When was the Norman Conquest?" followed by multiple choice answers. To play the game, you select one of 20 squares that appear on the screen, and you are whisked away to a map or a group of pictures or a time line. A question appears on the screen, and you must point and click at the correct answer. Not as dry as it sounds, **TimeTrek** makes up with charm and good humor what it lacks in high-tech graphics. The "time searches" are creatively thought out and varied enough to keep the interest level high. **TimeTrek** imparts broad knowledge of world history, ample enough to keep most young people scratching their heads right through junior college. Good reading skills.

## SHADOW PRESIDENT

You're the president, you negotiate with the nations, big ones, small ones, friendly and hostile, weak and strong. The Presidential Advisory Team is a mouse-click away, feeding you data regarding a particular country's standard of living, type of government, military might, level of religious fervor, etc. You must decide what kind of relationship is desirable with each nation, then gauge their response. Your choices of action range from encouraging economic cooperation to assassinating heads of state. To play **Shadow President**, you must have strong reading skills. The layout draws you into the action and decision-making right away, but the text is an odd shade of red against black, and can be tiring on the eyes. There is a good balance between getting feedback from the action you initiate and having to respond to a crisis somewhere. This game tosses you in circa 1991, allowing you to wage your own version of the Gulf War, with the obvious benefit of hindsight. The information database employed by this game is exhaustive, or at least it feels exhausting when you try to read it all. Memorizing one-third of the facts and figures presented in this program would indeed turn you into an expert of sorts. ("But President Johnson, we've been bombing them for five years!") A very good online tutorial helps you get started. Good reading skills.

## MARIO IN TIME

Once again I'm forced to say something nice about a computer program associated with that decomposer of children's brains: Mario the Plumber. In accociation with Mindscape, **Mario in Time** has virtually no arcade sequences. The evil villain is collecting important objects from history and Mario must return the objects to the correct person in the correct year. Objects include a prop from a Shakespearean play, a piece of type from the Gutenberg printing press, and a lense from Galileo's telescope, to name only three out of the more than 20 historical situations explored here. The player must meet people along the way and gleen information from them before being allowed to coast on in and return the object in question. That's the good part of this game: There's no faking it. For a child to be able to complete the sequences, he or she must genuinely read the information in question, understand it, and complete a little essay on the subject at hand. Children love this game. It's colorful and fast-paced and intelligent. A child who plays **Mario in Time** can't help but learn something. Growing readers.

Very good story     A very, very good game

## MULTIMEDIA WORLD HISTORY

Published by the quasi-governmental Bureau of Electronic Publishing, the label says that the organization exists "to enrich and empower through multimedia." The group obviously has access to some old historical film footage, such as a clip from the first time the United Nations critized South Africa over the issue of apartheid (the late 1950s). The whole project cries out for some creative reworking of the way the information is presented. There's some interesting stuff here that ought not to have put us to sleep twenty minutes into it, which is what really happened. **Multimedia World History** includes lots of animated maps of important events, treks, campaigns, and so on, but were all narrated by one man. This makes for suddenly heavy eyelids or the realization that going out for a hamburger would be really fun right about now. The CD comes with scads and scads of historical texts, details of Charlemagne's campaigns through Europe, the Gupta Empire in India, and, you know, making this stuff compete with MTV takes some real doing. I look forward to the revised version. The videos are all thumbnail-sized, a problem that can be partially fixed by adjusting the setup of your Windows MCI video driver.  Advanced readers.

Requires
CD-ROM

## RECESS IN GREECE

Morgan Interactive's **Recess in Greece** is a broad primer to classical Greek legends, geography, and language, but the characters are all cartoon animals, except for Hermes the Messenger, who, in the 1995 rendition, rides a Harley Davidson and looks like a biker.

The story begins with you, the main character, as a young child in school questioning whether it's necessary to learn about Sparta, Athens, Troy, and so on. Suddenly you are whisked off to ancient Greece to retrace the steps of Homer's *Iliad*. To follow the story you must make strategic decisions based on your knowledge of the objects, alphabet, and traditions of your new world, which are taught to you along the way through various puzzles, pop quizzes, and narrative videos. Growing readers.

## ASHES TO EMPIRE

The screen greets you with the outstretched hand of a hungery mother and child, Stravinski's Firebird Suite revs up in the background, and news flashes of civic unrest scroll by. Breakdown. Decay. An empire that sounds remarkably like the Soviet Union has breathed its last. Ancient ethnic rivalries and old grievences could escalate into war at any second, and you must get these people to talk to each other again. You must negotiate with mechanics, engineers, doctors, radar techinicians, military men, and all manner of decent folk, get their support, help them…and be deemed worthy of their help. As you become a more popular leader, it becomes easier to win people to your side. You must learn to negotiate wisely, not give away resources or political support too cheaply, and not make promises you cannot keep. You mark your travels on a map, and must make contact with all the different groups that hold sway in a particular community. Then, quickly, move on to the next community. There are some rather gratuitous gunning and shooting sequences you must deal with as you plow your way from point A to point B. Again, because **Ashes to Empire** is graphically intriguing and fun to watch and manipulate the

"But I can never seem to find these programs at the stores."

Software stores only carry the latest titles. At the end of this book is a list of all the software manufacturers mentioned, including their addresses and phone numbers. They'd be happy to deal with you directly.

Just because a game is old doesn't mean it's no longer valuable. Newer is not necessarily better. Plus, the older titles tend to make a smaller dent in your pocketbook.

I've also included a list of "discount houses" and software wholesale outlets that specialize in older products.

various choices, remarkably young children can pick up what's going on, long before learning to spell the word "negotiate." Good reading skills (long passages).

## MARIO IS MISSING

This tidy geography game successfully blends big and little, teaching children surprisingly detailed facts and figures about historical landmarks found in 25 cities throughout the world, and yet the cities are framed within their respective countries and continents, helping a child to understand the vastness of the world. This game has a natural momentum that encourages kids to memorize a few important facts about the part of the world they find themselves in because they must answer a few questions before they're allowed to move on and gather more clues. The CD-ROM version of the game gives a child a detailed look at a number of international treasures, and gives a generation raised on shopping malls an understanding of what is timeless and ancient.

Characteristically, Mario the Plumber leaps and hops across your computer screen, but perhaps because kids associate him with a game of quick action, the memorization involved doesn't seem so tedious. Everything a child needs to know in order to answer the questions correctly is readily available in the little worlds where Mario and his brother have landed, but the kids have to find it, and learn it. One round of **Mario Is Missing** is considerably longer than one case of Where in the World is Carmen Sandiego?, so expect to spend at least two sittings visiting each place.

You are Mario's brother, Luigi, and you find yourself in a famous city. The famous landmarks in the city are closed, and are replaced by boarded-up storefronts marking where the landmarks used to be. The player must help himself to a fact card explaining the landmark's significant features and history. The landmarks have been stolen by. . .well, a small army of evil turtles (yes, turtles—particularly loathsome ones, I imagine) and Luigi must find them. He wanders the city, asking people he meets if they've spotted the evil turtles holding the national treasures. Once Luigi catches up to a villian (several in every city) they hand over the loot. Luigi must return the landmark's identifying feature. On his way to the appropriate location, Luigi will meet several people, and will have a chance to ask them some facts about the landmark and its feature, which he is carrying. Luigi does well to inform himself, because he cannot return what he found unless he proves to the guards that he knows certain facts about the landmarks and the city itself. Once all the city's landmarks are in place, Luigi may leave and continue his search for his brother elsewhere in the globe. **Mario Is Missing** is the perfect Trojan Horse for some real learning.

Highest learning value

(Quickly, now. Who deployed the Trojan Horse, Greece or Troy? Play this game to refresh your memory.) Good reading skills (long passages).

## FROM ALICE TO OCEANS

In 1992, Robin Davidson, along with photographer Rick Smolan walked from the center of Australia to the Indian Ocean. With this CD, you get to go along. The trip is beautiful, harrowing, funny, and exaspirating, but mostly, there are camels. Robin is a remarkable woman, and this retelling balances her inner and outer journey, and I'm sure that seldom has a visit to Ayers Rock provoked such hand-wringing and inner turmoil. Rick's photographs provide a stunning backdrop for Robin's journey, while the camels plod along agreeably, fending off tourists and wild boars. With this CD, you can start at the beginning of her journey and wade through, drop in for a day, or travel from one point on the map to another. Along the way, a coffee cup will appear at the bottom left of the screen. Click on it for an "aside," either a related piece of Australian history or a photography tip by Rick. The CD runs smoothly, and the interface is simple and enhances your enjoyment of the journey.

A female heroine

Very good story

Requires CD-ROM

## CIVILIZATION

This game divides the growth of civilization into phases, and during each phase, a nation or civilization will acquire a new ability, such as the ability to work with metal instead of wood, the development of monotheism, or the codification of written law. As you tromp around the screen in the form of armies or settlers or pioneers, you establish cities, and after a time, the possibility to push your civilization towards these various advances presents itself up on the screen. You may read these three or four well-written paragraphs at your leisure, and discuss them with your children, as there is no time constraint. At the game's outset, you may choose your favorite empire, and begin to forge your own path from barbarism to feudalism to democracy. If you decide that monarchy is your thing, for example, and wish to continue ruling in kingly repose, your civilization's wise men appear more frequently, relentlessly presenting you with the tools your society needs to get out of the dark age, for cryin' out loud. Better use 'em or hordes of Visigoths or Conquistadors will descend and devour.

You may choose how many other nations or nation-states you feel like tangling with throughout your game. The more civilizations are involved, the more strategy you must muster to negotiate to your advantage and keep threats of war at bay, or at least, in your favor. As you move your settlers or militia around the main screen area, you may receive on-screen "help" messages giving you strategic advice, such as where to begin a city or mine for minerals. Or, in an arrogant swipe at your advisors, you may discontinue these messages if you like.

Since the process of settling cities and exploiting resources can be rather automatic, the pleasure in this game comes from reading the little blurbs about the steps of a civilization's advance, deciding what skills your empire ought to invest in next, and watching the "known world" expand as your empire succeeds. There are no "battle scenes" to speak of, only a blustery close-up of somebody rather large and foreign challenging you to battle. If your society prevails, progress can lead to the "nuclear age" (oh, joy) and beyond into some sort of idealized society. There is good information about each advancement a society can make. The strategies are quite involved, and more than one book is available teaching you this game's deeper secrets. My eight-year-old son began exploring this game as a series of battle moves around the screen, but attentive reading is essential to advance your worlds, so he has become acquainted with the finer points of feudalism and chivalry, the Magellan voyage, and the Manhattan project. Learn or die. Good reading skills (short passages). High replay value.

## ANCIENT LANDS

Microsoft's "Home" series is a signal that the mammoth company does not want to be known only for their business products. They've put out a CD-ROM that displays and catalogues 2,000 paintings from the Museum of London. They have products that allow you to browse leisurely through the archives of Strauss and Beethoven, to name only a couple composers. And now, we have **Ancient Lands**. They seem to be striving to provide a comfortable stroll through man's early history, stopping here and there to examine major events, everyday lifestyles, archaeological discoveries relevant to the age in question, and perhaps a look at the technology of the times. **Ancient Lands** is a little thin. The information presented is a bit obvious and commonplace. The emphasis is on multimedia technique, rather than new information on the subject. **Ancient Lands** sets you up to explore Rome, Greece, and Egypt. That's it. No China, no India, no Native Americans, no Incas, or Aztecs. It doesn't take long to hit the top rung of the program's apparent knowledge base. The artwork is exceptional, rivaling most elementary school history books in illustrative quality. The video sequences make you wish you had rented Ben Hur and got some popcorn. Growing readers. Decent replay value.

Requires fast computer
Requires CD-ROM

## WORLD ATLAS

**World Atlas** is a terrific atlas program that lets you select any area of the world, either as a political map or a topographical map, then select information about that region of the world or country, its agricultural output, standard of living, number of hospitals per 1,000 people, major export products, and so on. All of the above information is available as a bar graph or a chart, which you may print out or save as a printable document. The maps themselves may also be printed out in full color. You may also compare one country's state of affairs with another's, or assemble your own cross-section of nations to suit your particular research project. Countries may also be grouped together according to international organizations they belong to, such as OPEC or the Organization of American States. For added fun, select a country and **World Atlas** will play its national anthem, although many of the melodies suffer in the translation from ethnic passion to synthesized quarter notes. **World Atlas** provides extensive written information about the world's nations, but very little reading is required to enjoy its other features. High replay value.

## RISK

Remember the board game Risk? Global domination, armies challenging armies at a role of the dice? The more continents you control, the more armies you obtain, and thus you may conquer further? Well, now budding Alexander the Greats no longer need leave their computer screen (it's probably a safer place for them) to go a'conquerin'. I make my kids pronounce the name of a region of the world before they lay their imperial hands on it, which is not hard for "southern Europe," but takes some practice for "Irkutsk" (a region of Russia). The computer remembers the rules for us, reminds us whose turn it is, and counts out the new armies correctly, disregarding the protests of angry Junior Generals in the heat of a military campaign. Good reading skills. Available for Windows or DOS. The Windows version has larger writing, and is easier on young eyes. High replay value.

## MULTIMEDIA WORLD ATLAS

Since most CD-ROM encyclopedias come with a decent world atlas, why would you want this one? In Mindscape's **Multimedia World Atlas**, you get 150 video clips from cities throughout the world. You hear pronunciation of all major cities. You have a huge database from which to compare vital statistics of the nations of your choice. The program provides you with several styles of "markers" that you may leave on the map, and you can write a note to yourself in the "notepad" reminding you what they represent. (My kids leave a marker on the map for every place they have made some notable geographic discovery in their studies.) The program also includes hundreds of pictures from all over the world. With **Multimedia World Atlas**, you may convert currency from one country to another, instantly. There's a utility to help you print out giant wall maps, and make a slide show of the maps and graphs of your choice. You can also attach any image of your choice to the maps in this program (BMP, PCX and GIF format). Mindscape also provides on-line audio help. Click on something, select help, and you'll hear instructions on how to make use of what you've selected. Growing readers.

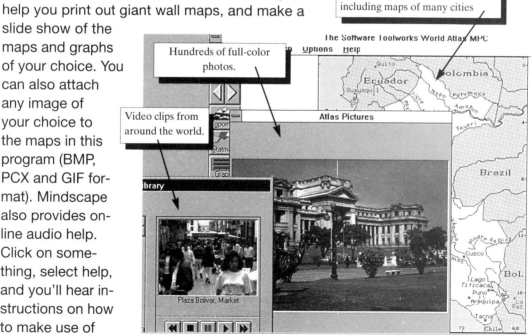

Political and topographical maps, including maps of many cities

Hundreds of full-color photos.

Video clips from around the world.

The Software Toolworks World Atlas MPC

Atlas Pictures

Plaza Bolivar, Market

There's more here than full-color videos and pictures. With this atlas, you can compare statistics between nations, and chart your findings in graph form. Mindscape has provided an impressive database to work with.

## MERCHANT COLONY

It's the eighteenth century and the world is your oyster. As a member of the British merchant class, you charter sea vessels of various sorts, and set up profitable outposts all over the New World. Before leaving Liverpool, you must think about what you want to accomplish when you arrive at Bombay or Cathay or Seward or wherever you have chosen to direct yourself. Each "colony" has its own raw materials that you may develop profitably. You must select the right kind of settlers and ship's crew to accomplish those goals. You may purchase as many ships as you are able and borrow outrageous sums of money from usurious Old World scoundrels, but if you go broke, the game's over. The amazing thing about this game is how little reading there is. Young children may play it with a reasonable notion of what's going on, yet it's sophisticated enough for older kids to learn a few economic principles. The other amazing thing about this game is that it costs about as much as a medium pizza, excluding the tip. Pick it up before Impressions repackages it and triples the price. Good reading skills (short passages). In **Merchant Colony**, the maps refer to the nations of the world by their seventeenth and eighteenth century names; for example, China is Cathay, and Eastern Canada is Stewardsville. High replay value.

Highest learning value

## More General Science and Anatomy

## THE ISLAND OF DR. BRAIN

You have applied to be the assistant to Dr. Brain, ensconced on his own island, kind of a candied-apple-Caribbean tropical paradise. Before Dr. Brain hires you, there are dozens of puzzles to solve. When you solve one, Dr. Brain audibly congratulates you, explaining the skill you've just mastered, and presents you with a plaque. When the game ends, Dr. Brain rates your various skills, and suggests areas of improvement. These puzzles are not merely "logic brain-teasers" or Rubic's Cube affairs. You learn homonyms and synonyms, physics, chemistry, molecular weights, computer circuit analysis, and how to program a robot using simple commands. There's a music section, where you learn note value by hearing a note, by seeing it, and by

Screen from Sierra On-Line's **The Island of Dr. Brain**, a collection of puzzles that teach science, math, language skills, music, and art recognition, and even how to program a robot. Pictured above, the largest mug holds alcohol, the cup in between holds water, and the smallest holds mercury. Do you know which cup would weigh more?

playing it in a short composition. There are a couple of puzzles that teach you "X-Y coordinates," or mapping skills, and even a crossword puzzle, matching English words with Spanish, French, or German, your choice. Good reading skills (short passages).

Highest learning value

Very exceptional music

A very, very good game

## 3D BODY ADVENTURE

In college I had the greatest biology teacher. Not only could he teach, he could draw. As he cheerfully imparted his thoughts on basal ganglia and the ten groups of facial nerves, his hands furiously worked the chalkboard. Anatomy and physiology as seen through neo-impressionistic dots and dashes. He understood what the Greeks called "the body beautiful," and as a result of of his enthusiastic impromptu renderings, I chose medicine as a career. To serve a new generation of thinkers and tinkerers, Knowledge Adventure has come out with **3D Body Adventure**. You may view any part of the body at any angle, with as much complexity as you desire, building from the basic skeleton up to nerves, blood vessels, muscles and tendons. Remember those old 3D comic books? If you read while wearing the provided "3D glasses," the images seem to pop off the page. **3D Body Adventure** provides the glasses, and, yes, those red-blood cells and strands of DNA really jump out.

Hypertext links lead you down the trail of medicine, physiology, and Knowledge Adventure's rather nifty space age anatomy lessons. For the youngest kids, they throw in a flashcard game, matching body parts with their names. There's a game of "doctor," wherein you identify the patient's condition, then race through corridors of veins and nerve cells, lung tissue, or vertebral columns and zap out the offending toxin. All the written text entries are narrated, so kids can learn the pronunciation of the terms used, not just the spelling. **3D Body Adventure's** data base is far from complete, though. I searched in vain for an article on muscular adduction vs. abduction, an anatomy topic that can be most obtuse without some good pictorial aids. Nonetheless, **3D Body Adventure** is a three-dimensional thrill ride through the adrenal cortex. Never has mitral valve stenosis so closely resembled an attraction at Disneyland. **3D Body Adventure's** big claim to fame is the fact that, as you slide through the brain's nerve fibers and take pot shots at strands of rabies viruses (I'm not exaggerating), the media you are floating through are photographic reproductions of the real thing. So put on those "3D" glasses and slide down the pike. This is not a test. Growing readers okay.

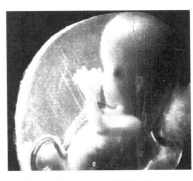

Screens from Knowledge Adventure's **3D Body Adventure**. Knowledge Adventure's chief strength is its knack for obtaining unusual photos and video clips.

Requires
CD-ROM

Requires fast
computer

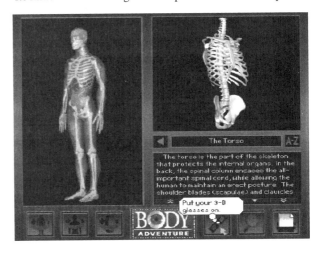

### BODYWORKS

**Bodyworks** is like having a well-illustrated anatomy book on a computer. The screen is divided into two parts, the human body on the left, and descriptive text on the left. Click on any part of the body you wish to study more in depth, and the text will change, offering more in-depth options. You may print out pictures of various organs (if that's your thing), and there are a few animations, such as a short cartoon of the actions of the heart, lung, and diaphragm. This program's outstanding feature is the ability to look anywhere in the human body quickly, and zip down for a more detailed view of many functions and structures. It's all here: Most, if not all of the hundreds of bones in the human foot are appropriately labeled, and click and your happy skeleton is literally reduced to bundle of nerves, all named and labeled. This program makes bonehead anatomy more attractive, if not easier. While **Bodyworks** provides lots of descriptive text and explanatory notes, a pre-reader may certainly enjoy exploring the well-drawn, three-dimensional appearing diagrams. Anyone curious about anatomy will enjoy this program. The accompanying text seems to be geared towards sixth grade and up.

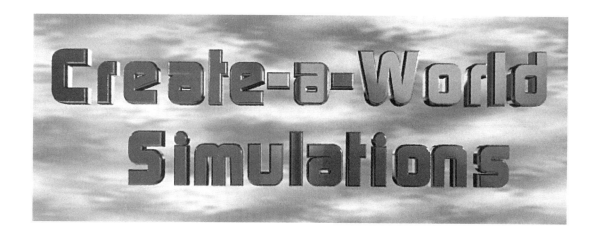

## SIMCITY

Design a city. Watch it flourish or die, depending on your skills. Your game starts out as a clean slate or as one of several urban scenarios. You then add (or bulldoze away) residential areas, commercial and/or industrial areas. You raise or lower taxes, learn to live within a city budget, try not to shortchange essential city services in your quest for growth. You have graphs available to chart various urban "quality of life" markers…but the most amazing aspect of this program is how easy it is to enact everything I've just described, and more. As you plan and build, your screen is constantly reflecting your new urban environ- ment, giving you quick feedback on the changes you've enacted. Good reading skills.

Good strategy game

## OUTPOST

Sierra should have thought twice about producing a simulation without people in it. Even after one masters all the technical manipulation necessary to survive in a new galaxy, your world is still dark and barren, except for the structures you have built yourself. Having colonized a new planet, you make buildings of various types. Beyond that, **Outpost** is a technically intriguing game, but without much heart, which is unusual for Sierra. The gameplay becomes cranky once you get past the introduction. A thriving planet of colonies is hard to come by in **Outpost**. Cursed by inadequate documentation in a rush to get it to the shelves, the game doesn't include several of the main features referred to in the manual. You cannot build monorails, roads, or trade with colonies. To get the REAL instructions on how to run this thing, you must call Sierra, or download related documents from a modem bulletin board, CompuServe, America Online, and the like.

**Outpost** runs something like this: You are one of the last few people remaining on Earth. You must leave to colonize a planet near the star of your choice in some other part of the galaxy. You must pick a star, a new home planet, choose what sort of satellites you will send before you arrive with the humans. Once on your planet, you must build structures like power plants, waste processing facilities, agricultural domes, places for people to live, all connected with an imposing but necessary tube system. Your colony must also expand underground to survive. You must mine for resources, and build the kind of structures that will genuinely improve the quality of life for your new world. Keeping the colonists' moral up is a real chore, and so is the quest for adequate resources so your planet doesn't die. You may, however, cheat. Press Control and F11 to give your colony unlimited resources. Press Control and F12 to boost your colonists' morale rating to the maximum. The animations that pop up from time to time, as well as the opening sequences, all look like a million bucks (they were) and will tax your computer's resources considerably. The box says you need 4MB of ram to run the game, but in all honesty, make that 8MB. Think of **Outpost** like interplanetary **SimCity** with twenty-first century graphics. One last point. Our family has always looked to Sierra's games for a dollop of good humor, but Sierra's classic wit and clever banter are in short supply in **Outpost**.

Requires fast computer

Good strategy game

Requires CD-ROM

## THEME PARK

Kids design their own amusement park. The amount of detail that you have control over in this game makes it truly one of the best simulation games you can buy. Very little is left up to chance. And another important feature: After a child makes a decision, whether to build a particular ride, or add more salt to the french fries, or speed up the roller coaster to frightening levels…the feedback is almost instantaneous. There's no sitting around and wondering if your decision was implemented. There are dozens of rides to build, and a child must decide what features to add to the rides. This is done quickly and cleanly with a few mouse-clicks. The amusement park grows before your very eyes, and park visitors zip around from ride to ride, to restaurants and balloon shops, and at any time, you may click on a park visitor and find out his or her state of mind, hours spent inside your park, and, most importantly, how much money he has left to spend. **Theme Park** is one of the most visually alluring computer games I've ever seen. You can even click the magnifying glass on one of the rides you've built and "ride" it yourself. The animation is first-rate and original. There's a business angle to **Theme Park** as well. Competitors are either trying to

Screen from Bullfrog's **Theme Park**. The above represents just one tiny corner of your park layout. You make the paths, rides, and food stands; hire personnel; and get your fingers in every possible decision about managing an amusement park of this sort. By the way, look up. Your snake ride is smoking.

buy an interest in your park, or outdo your park's strengths. If you do well financially, you may take your profits and build another amusement park somewhere else in the world. In **Theme Park**, you hire employees—lots of them. They must keep your park clean, keep the rides in top shape, and entertain the kids as they stroll the grounds. (They even pass out umbrellas during rainstorms.) But in **Theme Park** (as in real life), employees demand raises. You must negotiate with your workers, and, with nerves of steel, meet some of their demands without giving away the store. If all of this sounds too technical for younger kids, I must point out that **Theme Park** sweeps you into each scenario with clever animations, not a screen full of jargon and text. One of the best. Growing readers okay.

Very exceptional music

A very, very good game

## SIMHEALTH

The future of public policy debate lies in programs like **SimHealth**. Rather than yammer on in ignorance about the health care choices facing our country, people can play this simulation, picking one or two of the program's built-in scenarios, and then (if you're so dang smart) design your own, playing as a Canadian-style socialist or raving free-marketeer. Watch your city succumb to tuberculin squalor if you make the wrong choices. High-tech surgery for the few or vaccines for all: The choice is yours. **SimHealth** runs in 16 colors and is no big deal to look at, but it is laid out for a pleasant and informative go at designing urban public health systems. At the outset of the game, you establish your health care priorities, answering policy questions along a continuum of values and ideals. I have never seen a program that laid out political choices along a visual, four-point spectrum. The effect is interesting. You then implement policies, using up political chips, disappointing some groups,

Good strategy game

and pleasing others. At the end, you are treated to a graph of how your policy decisions have either met or fallen short of those ideals. Good reading skills.

## SERF CITY

Noting the success of **SimCity**, it seems that all the companies are trying their hand at simulations. But of all the programs I've seen, **Serf City** provides the most human touch. Set in the middle ages, your goal is to develop an enduring little community of serfs, complete with iron foundries and tool making, guard huts, warehouses, bakeries, and fishermen. The game takes up less than 5MB of space on your hard drive, so it is cartoony and a bit kidsy. Still, it's nice not to have to fuss for an hour just to make a game work the way the box says it should. You must develop mines, hone the skills of your knights, leave plenty of land for farms, build a few ships, keep your roads open, and sit back and watch your serfs hard at work. Kids will love the fact that, as soon as you give "the order" to begin building something, the people get to work almost immediately. You see the people right away on the screen, enjoying their duties in the sunlight. **Serf City** is cheerful. The music invokes a happy day in the court of some English earl. Carry on, good fellow, carry on! Good reading skills.

## ALIEN LEGACY

I think many strategy games are hopelessly underutilized. Kids often crack only the first layer of activity, but beneath the surface are all these other angles that might really make the game come alive and seem more worthwhile. But the game's other features remain buried because no one can figure them out. For example, kids can get stuck exploring only the surface of one planet, and not be properly introduced to the other components of the game. Some strategy games have an "online tutorial" to whiz you through the different "worlds" or stages of development you will encounter in the game. **Alien Legacy** is the only strategy game that has a story line designed to specifically get you acquainted with the game's higher functions. This is quite neat because, as a result, none of the programmers' good intentions and hard work go to waste. Like **Masters of Orion** and **Outpost**, **Alien Legacy** begins with you as the captain of a space station full of Earth's last survivors. You must choose a planet, or group of planets, populate the heavens and judiciously expand your reach into the stars. Each colony must receive its share of start-up resources, but afterwards, each must make its own way or die on the vine. You lead exploration teams who scour new planets for precious resources of various types. You must also direct the flow of scientific discovery, deciding where to put your research dollar, and predict what sort of inventions would be the most fruitful for your planets and colonies to concern themselves with. You start small and expand quickly, and **Alien Legacy** gives you plenty of time to get your bearings before various kinds of challenges present themselves. Along with **Masters of Orion**, **Alien Legacy** is one of the best of its kind. Good reading skills.

Requires fast computer

War scenes

Very good story

## DETROIT

Wanna make a car? Do product research? Design it? Learn about your market and sell it? **Detroit** is one of those all-encompassing simulations that brings you face to face with every step in the process of marketing a product. In this game, you pick the year you wish to begin working in. Then select the part of the world that appeals to your business sense. Do research and get technology on your side. Put the car together, test drive the thing, and foist it off on an unwary public. **Detroit** is visually appealing, and the game is set up to get you moving and creating without having to memorize a bunch of baffling commands first. A fun and believable simulation, but challenging, too. Good reading skills.

## SIMCITY 2000

A much more in-depth simulation of urban planning than its predecessor, **SimCity 2000** gives you a good deal of control over your city's fate: Which industries should you, as mayor, encourage? Should you provide free clinic services? Become a nuclear-free zone, pass an anti-pollution ordinance? You don't just build a power plant; you must select from several kinds, each with their own advantages and disadvantages. You may name most of your city's structures, and personalize buildings and parks with little pop-up signs, if you choose to. **SimCity 2000** operates on a more three-dimensional model than does **Simcity**. Good reading skills.

Good strategy game

A very, very good game

Microsoft Windows 3.1 has many hidden benefits. Computing is more fun once you've cracked their mystery. See Chapter 4.

## KIDCAD

A child may build a house, three-dimensionally rendered, with building blocks of dozens of shapes and sizes. He may then "zoom in" to view his creation from many different angles, inside and out. Problems with this game are that the blocks must line up perfectly or the whole structure is lopsided, and the entire program runs too slowly. **Kidcad** requires Windows. At the time I reviewed the game, I had a 486/33 with 4MB of RAM, configured optimally for **Kidcad**, and the program still crawled. Problem number three is that the entire premise does not really improve on a child getting out his own building blocks and toy animals and building his own city, AWAY from the blinkin' computer, for a change. Very little reading required.

Requires fast computer

# Spelling and Language Skills

## READ AND ROLL

**Read and Roll** teaches kids to read for meaning, and it works. They are tested on paragraph comprehension and are rewarded by getting to play a little arcade-style bowling game. It sounds silly, but you try getting young children to sit still for multiple-choice questions for hours at a time! The graphics are a little dull. **Read and Roll** is an old program updated recently for VGA graphics. But something about the layout keeps kids involved. Perhaps it's because the print size is nice and big. The newer programs that emphasize graphics have made the size of the words so small that children have a hard time reading them, and their eyes get tired. So don't be surprised if, after an initial fascination with a new razzle-dazzle program, they go back to an older one like **Read and Roll**. Growing readers okay (long passages).

Works OK on an older computer

## WORD ATTACK PLUS

**Word Attack Plus** is a series of five activities that test a child's knowledge of words in every way imaginable. This program emphasizes definitions, spelling, and correct word usage in sentences. It does not deal with phonics such as recognizing short vowel sounds and diphthongs. A major plus is that you may input short phrases like "cave drawings" and "medical technology" AND their definitions, then send the kids through five colorful and engaging activities to learn them. A big plus for **Word Attack Plus** is its replay value. Because there are five activities built around your chosen word list, kids don't get bored. Growing readers.

A very, very good game

## WRITER RABBIT

**Writer Rabbit** is proof that a learning program doesn't have to be a digitally roto-scoped fully voiced talkie with 256 colors in order to be fun. All the animations here are basically line drawings, but the activities are well thought out. **Writer Rabbit** teaches sentence structure (who? did what? where? why? when?). Find the "Who" in this sentence. Find the "Did what" in this sentence. Find the "Why." After the child has mastered a few sentences, she or he incorporates them in composing a short story that may then be printed out. Growing readers.

## WORD CITY

Kids must save **Word City** from surrounding invading viruses before they waste the place. To block the virus's advance, you must perform a variety of language-use skills, including recognizing adverbs, finding synonyms, spelling words correctly, and paragraph reading comprehension. The game layout is fun, fast, and keeps kids jumping at those word problems to advance their score. **Word City**'s big strength lies in the variety of activities presented in rapid sequence. No one can fall asleep on the job playing this game. The Quest Corporation, who also made the game **Math Ace**, has brought a creative approach to some very familiar territory. Growing readers.

Highest learning value

## WORD MUNCHERS, NUMBER MUNCHERS, SUPER MUNCHERS

You go around the screen and eat words. Or numbers, when appropriate. A screen is divided into 36 squares, and at the top of the screen is a directive: "4-legged animals" or "words with a long a sound" or "multiples of 16." With those instructions in mind, you zip around the squares and press the space bar in order to "eat" a correct answer. You rack up points for swallowing little squares that meet the stated criteria. Things get complicated when another carnivorous creature appears on the screen, one that has you in mind. You must avoid landing on a square where he is, and be careful of squares where he has just been. He alters a square he is on, changing its number value, or the name of animal or city or country or word that was just written on it. This game makes for quick category recognition skills, not to mention reading and quick multiplying and adding, as well as promoting the ability to walk around squares and avoid little monsters. Growing readers.

If you like one of these games, and you don't see it on the shelf at your local software store, refer to the list of software companies and sales outlets at the end of this book. They can send you just about any product you're interested in, often for less money than you'd pay over the counter.

Works OK on an older computer

## READER RABBIT 2

This second outing for Mr. Reader Rabbit is much better than its predecessor. Skills taught include matching words with long and short vowel sounds, alphabetization, and picking homonyms and synonyms from a list of possible choices. **Reader Rabbit 2**'s animation is appropriate for the same age group that is developing the above skills. Growing readers.

## SPELLBOUND

One of the very best spelling programs for children of all ages. After choosing (or writing) a spelling list, your child works the words through five different activities, including a crossword puzzle, filling in the blank letter, and ultimately, a spelling bee. Your child's character is shown on the screen with two spelling bee "opponents," and the moderator asks the contestants to spell words. (The moderator's voice is audible.) One by one, either you or the opponents are eliminated. If you win, you move on to a city-wide, a state-wide, and finally, a national spelling bee, complete with the White House and Capitol Building in the backdrop. **Spellbound** comes with multiple lists of words sensibly organized into categories that aid memorization. You may also compose your own spelling list, or type in your child's spelling list from school. The CD-ROM version of **Spellbound** provides more audible cues and spoken words, and not as many flashed word exercises. Growing readers.

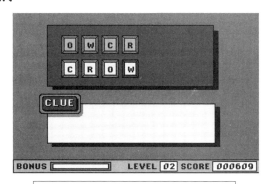

Highest learning value

## STICKYBEAR

The **StickyBear** series of spelling and math programs are perfect for preschool through second grade children. The program is simple to run, low on memory requirements, and thus you don't need a mega-computer or tons of available hard drive to run it. Most of the **StickyBear** games involve a child using the arrow keys to guide **StickyBear** across blocks of numbers or letters; the child presses the space bar to select the correct character. **StickyBear** games have been around a long time, from the era of 16-color computer screens, but the puzzles appear crisp and brightly drawn and

No youngster would be intimidated by **StickyBear's** big, cheerful letter and number exercises.

have a sharp, three-dimensional look that helps keep children interested. **StickyBear** is more fun and effective than a good deal of the fancy VGA affairs out there that actually cost more but offer less. Beginning readers.

## MIDNIGHT RESCUE

**Midnight Rescue**, along with Davidson's **Read and Roll**, appear to be the only comercially available children's software games that directly test a child's ability to read and comprehend *several* paragraphs of text. Comprehension skills tested here would challange a 7-year-old and not bore the average fourth grader. To solve a mystery and win the game, you must read several brief essays and remember a few details *exactly*. If you have read with good comprehension, you will correctly identify the culprit at the end of the game. Having done this, the villain, Morty Mischief, disappears into smoke and justice is served. As with others in The Learning Company's Super Solver series, the main character wanders through colorful corridors under some kind of time constraint, and must enter a room to solve a challenge. The "exploring" aspect makes it a good deal more fun than sifting through pages of paragraphs at a time. The added colorful pizzazz makes **Midnight Rescue** a fun way to test kids' reading comprehension skills. Good reading skills (long passages, but the paragraph content might seem a little nerdy to anyone over 11).

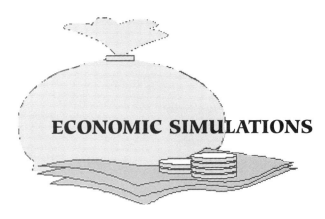

## ECONOMIC SIMULATIONS

## CAPITALIST PIG

This program is sadly misnomered, since nothing in this game is irreverent toward, let alone critical of, Adam Smith's favorite economic system. The box art shows a pig in a business suit, greedily feasting away on his underlings, ah, er, employees, I guess. The game itself does not criticize capitalism, but, on a small scale, clarifies its mechanisms. **Capitalist Pig** packs clever lessons about supply and demand, cash flow, yearly profits margins, getting the most for your advertising dollar, and even the stock market. The game manual includes an extremely well-written narrative about a boy who opens a lemonade stand. His little business grows quickly, and he encounters all the trials and tribulations explored in the computer game itself. The vocabulary would not frighten away your average fourth grader, and since its lessons are carried in the story of a lemonade stand, the manual makes for an appropriate reading lesson for any pre-teen budding entrepreneur. It deserves to sell well, for it enlightens much even in small doses. Good reading skills.

Good strategy game

Highest learning value

## JONES IN THE FAST LANE

Remember the game "Careers" in which you would move around the game board earning a predetermined number of points (happiness points, wealth points, and fame points), dealing with life events that come your way through the roll of the dice? **Jones in the Fast Lane** is similar, except instead of fame points, you must seek out a certain amount of higher learning, that is, college. You buy food, pay your rent, go to work, get a degree, treat yourself to some stereo equipment, and avert disasters, which are announced as a newspaper is flashed on the screen. A nice feature is that, occasionally, the news will flash "INFLATION INCREASES," and sure enough, your paycheck, though looking fatter, doesn't go as far. Conversely, when a recession hits, your pay shrinks. Thus **Jones in the Fast Lane** led to a good deal of table talk with my young children about the late '70s and what it meant to buy a house paying 17% interest (weren't those great years?). To go to college, you choose a major, and are afterwards are employable as an engineer, if appropriate, or a manager or a teacher. Everybody you deal with appears on the screen as a digitalized mini-videoclip: Your landlady in beebop shades yells, "Stop sniveling!! I'll give you another month to pay." The boy at the hamburger stand asks "Would you like some french fries with your fries?" And just like in real life, your wages are garnisheed if you fall too far behind. Good reading skills.

Good strategy game

Requires CD-ROM

### Learning Recipe

Here's a fun game you can play with your kids. Give them a quiz, perhaps 10 questions, on a subject that they are learning at school. Make the quiz a bit on the hard side. Now, somewhere in their room, hide partial answers, or clues to some of the question on the quiz, perhaps under a chair or a pile of books. Or leave a clue saying the name of a computer program that will help them find the answer to a question on their quiz. Give them points for answering the questions correctly, as well as for finding the clues.

## RAGS TO RICHES

This game plants you in a seedy New York office as an amateur stock trader. You start with a small staff: a secretary, a "runner" who does your bidding on Wall Street for you, and a "headhunter" who finds you good financial talent. From there you wander down to the newspaper stand and read the trades, watch the ticker-tape for trading tips, and "do lunch" with the illicit "inside trader" of your choice. Of course, with skill, luck, and acumen you can become a big shot. This game even provides your own shopping mall to spend your millions in record time on useless trinkets. **Rags to Riches** is a must for the Michael Milkens of tomorrow. Good reading skills.

## THE TREEHOUSE

There are lots of activities here for 4- to 9-year-olds. A gopher leads your child to a treehouse, which is really a launching pad for a myriad of music games, animal classification, a little theatre, a road-race game that teaches kids how to make change, and other hidden features. The highlight is a well-thought out music work-shop, where you create your own melodies on the instruments of your choice, learn to recognize note sequences, play back well-known melodies as well as your own creations on various instruments at various tempos. The animal game teaches children to classify hundreds of different creatures according to their living patterns: Is the "secret animal" nocturnal?" Does it have lungs or gills? Fur or scales? How many legs? By process of elimination, your child selects the correct animal. For a product with so many activities included, the screen layout of **Treehouse** is re-markably uncluttered and easy to work with. This one requires very little parental guidance, and most children can usually jump right in. No reading required, but **Treehouse**'s components include written text in small, unintimidating doses.

## TREASURE MOUNTAIN

The Learning Company's **Treasure Mountain** hails back from the 16-color days, when, if you shelled out extra for an 80MB hard drive, you were considered silly or too rich. **Treasure Mountain** weighs in at less than 800K, but for 4- to 6-year-olds computer trekkers, **Treasure Mountain** is probably one of the best. You must wander around a mountain in three different environments, and at each level, you gather objects that interest you. Under the objects are a single descriptive word, such as "big" or "three" or "flowers." Your child picks up more objects to obtain more clues, and soon, a phrase will fall into place, such as "five little pinecones" or "three big flowers." That phrase tells him or her what object to look under to obtain a shiny gold key, and the key takes you to the next level. After three such challenges, you've arrived at the snowy uppermost regions of **Treasure Mountain**, where you take on the Master of Mischief. You are rewarded with a toy and are given a fast trip back down the mountain, where you may store the loot you've been rewarded with for saving the day game after game. The music is quite nice, and the graphics are clear and uncluttered. Beginning readers.

## PETER PAN

EAKIDS' **Peter Pan** actually begins with six painting and drawing tools, each cleverly animated, introducing themselves to your child. After explaining their purpose, they remain in the foreground of the screen, and quickly, the familiar story of Peter Pan unfolds. The well-rendered animation features bright faces and very ethereal landscapes. Whenever Peter finds himself in a crisis, one or more of the art tools in the foreground will turn around and face you. Your child may choose an art tool, and use it on Peter Pan or near the area of what threatens him. Rather automatically now, the art tool begins to either redraw or erase or paint or otherwise alter the situation in Peter's favor. Perhaps Hook's sword turns into a banana, perhaps the sky is redrawn to cause a quick thunderstorm. Here's the lowdown: In about 90 different situations, a quick application of art skills allow Peter Pan and Tink and the Lost Boys to live another day. This orients very young children to see the power of the brush and the pen unfold before them, rather than only seeing the finished, typeset product. Another plus: You may instantly replay the recent scene of the story, chose a different art tool, and watch a different solution to Peter's problems unfold. The game can be quite inspiring for ages 3 to 7. Beginning readers.

Screen from Westwood's **The Legend of Kyrandia**.

## THE LEGEND OF KYRANDIA

The Brothers Grimm meet Sesame Street. This is not an insult. Lots and lots of kids like Sesame Street. Of all the adventure role-plays on the market today, Westwood's **The Legend of Kyrandia** is probably the least intimidating. In terms of game difficulty, or story complexity, there is nothing here that would discourage the most novice of novices, although playing it, any kid over the age of 12 might feel like he is being force-fed marshmallows. **The Legend of Kyrandia** is a gentle fairy tale, and except for the squirrel who becomes toast in the opening cartoon, nothing here would disturb the sleep of even the jitteriest of young children. **Kyrandia** is exceptionally well-drawn and painted, and bids you to enter its caves and forests for some good-natured exploring and dragon slaying. The sound track is one of the best I've heard from any computer game ever, and completes **Kyrandia's** gentle spell and exquisite calming atmospherics. Good reading skills.

Very exceptional music

## ECOQUEST: THE SEARCH FOR CETUS

Save the whales. And the rest of the ocean while you're at it. This role-play touches on enough issues to generate half a semester's "environmental curriculum" for young kids and pre-adolescents. You learn about various kinds of ocean pollution, sea life, great and small, interdependence of underwater animals, civic responsibility in the face of a crisis, and even how to train a dolphin and not scare it away. You're a young boy, and you live with your dad, oceanside, as he investigates the a new treatment for the effects of oil spills on sea life. You befriend a dolphin, and are led to his underwater world, where you come face to face with an ocean environment in deep crisis. You meet many sea creatures and learn how they interact and survive. For children 6 to 11, I rate this as one of the best. The CD-ROM version is full-voice, and the interface is fast and easy. Good reading skills (CD-ROM version requires no reading).

A very, very good game

## KIDPIX

Two years after purchasing **Kidpix**, our children are still discovering new features in it. This is the most entertaining drawing program for young children. You only get sixteen colors. There is no color blending or shading. You cannot edit curves or

lines to reshape them to your liking. **Kidpix** will never teach anyone about the subtle side of art, but, jeese, is it fun. Children can
draw fairly simple shapes and forms and recognizable objects
and then, by applying a couple of the many widgets and doodads
that **Kidpix** comes packed with, they may transform their pictures
into the most bizarre abstract landscapes. Saving and loading
pictures is easy and quick. Your kids can pull out a picture
they worked on a year ago and play with it some more,
and save the new and the old version, which is standard
procedure around our house. Text may be added to the
drawing. **Kidpix** comes with "stamps," little predrawn figures that you may paste throughout your drawing at will.

**Chapter 11** tells you
why a printer can
double your family's
computing fun.

You may alter and redraw your own stamps. You may also "cut" a portion of your picture, and "paste" it somewhere else…even in a different
picture. In this case, the old advertising claim, "For children 3 to 103"
really does apply. Beyond words like "save" and "load" on the menu
bar, no reading is required to use **Kidpix**. You may also type words
into your stories.

A very, very
good game

## MYSTERY SOLVING AND LOGIC PUZZLES

### MYST

Everybody's talkin' 'bout **Myst**, an elegant world of puzzles and logic designed by
Cyan, Inc. You will meet no people in **Myst,** brook no conversations, but you will
quickly figure out that the buttons and levers you play
with on one side of the island will effect what happens
elsewhere. **Myst** is huge. It goes on and on, and the ex-
plorations are rather breathtaking. Good reading skills.

Good strategy
game

Requires
CD-ROM

### GOBLINS 1, 2, AND 3

The makers of **Goblins** must provide happy employment for many European illustra-
tors. Produced in France by the Coktell Corporation, and distributed in the U.S. by
Sierra On-Line, the different rooms within the seven worlds in **Goblins** are a sight to
behold. The paintings are so other-worldly and lavish that you think they are going to
pop out of your computer screen, or else you'll pop in to them. In **Goblins**, you play
the part of two characters. They must cooperate, doing everything in sync, or nothing will work. While one is distracting a noble citizen, another takes the sausage.
While one coerces a saxophone player to play, the other must catch his note in a net.

Goblins Winkle and Fingus do not speak, but make terribly endearing nonsensical noises, now appropriated regularly by two children I know when they don't want to eat their dinner. **Goblins 3**, released only on CD, has characters who, upon entering a new world, explain their goals and what you must do to get them out of this mess. **Goblins 3** is so beautifully and richly painted that you feel compelled to jump in to your computer screen and join the fun. Each room within a world has dozens of objects to lift or throw or balance or carry away and use elsewhere, and odd people or animals to taunt, manipulate, or befriend. Very little reading required.

## SHERLOCK HOLMES CONSULTING DETECTIVE

**Sherlock Holmes Consulting Detective** sets up your investigating day as a series of locations to visit. You thumb through your address book and figure who might deserve a good looking up. When you click on a person to visit, you're treated to a little movie that acts out Holmes' visit with that individual. This game moves fast, and the intuitive interface keeps things interesting. When you think you've solved the case, mouse-click on "the Judge," and you get your day in court. If you're wrong, it's back on the street for you.

Good strategy game

Requires CD-ROM

## THE LOST FILES OF SHERLOCK HOLMES

A number of Sherlock Holmes enthusiasts must be computer programers. Programming causes the same sensory responses in the human brain, no doubt. **The Lost Files of Sherlock Holmes** is one of several interactive role-plays involving Sherlock and the good Doctor Watson, the Baker Street irregulars, and the intrepid Lieutenant Lestrade, all true to form and in keeping with the characters found in the original Sherlock Holmes short stories. Read that box carefully. **The Lost Files of Sherlock Holmes** requires a hefty 30MB of hard drive, which is far more than any product I can think of, except for the hard-disk version of **CorelDRAW** or **Return to Zork**. You will find yourself working hard to solve this mystery simply so you may again have access to your computer for other things. **The Lost Files of Sherlock Holmes** features an exquisite rendition of Victorian London, the shops, avenues, houses, back allies, theatres, "dark satanic mills," and so on. The screen layout is brimming with detail, but is clear and crisp. (Except for the London fog. The London fog is not crisp.) below the action scenes themselves are "text buttons" with actions at your disposal, such as "Pick up", "Use," "Walk," "Open," and so on. You simply click on the action you wish to choose, and then click on the object or person on the screen you wish to perform it on. The mystery that unravels here is thoughtful and smart, vintage Sherlock Holmes. Good reading skills (long passages).

## CLUE

If you've ever considered picking up the computerized version of the board game "Clue," let it be said that they've kept it true to the original. It's certainly nice to have a computer to take up the slack as that "third player," which **Clue** requires. There are no game pieces to pick up afterwards, or cards to stuff in envelopes and hope that nobody sees. The nice machine always remembers whose turn it is, it never cheats, and you can set the computer opponent to play under par or downright ruthlessly. An animation is shown when a character investigates a room, and the computer program keeps track of the rules of play better than most humans would care to, especially when looking for a rationale to claim victory. With **Clue**, you have to be able to read fast, short bits of information.

Works OK on an older computer

## CHALLENGE OF ANCIENT EMPIRES

Go spelunking (cave exploring) in search of pieces to an ancient puzzle. Turn secret panels on and off by shining a beam of light at just the right angle. Timing always counts as you leap from one sheer wall to another, without getting zapped by some underground meanie. Find all the pieces, make it out alive, and identify a treasure from another time, such as the Rosetta Stone or a ziggurat from Sumer. These logic and strategy puzzles are as varied as they are addicting, but **Challenge of Ancient Empires** is no mere Rubic's Cube. Even the youngest spelunkers will learn a little history along the way. Growing readers.

A very, very good game

Works OK on an older computer

## EAGLE EYE MYSTERIES

Think of this as a multimedia Encyclopedia Brown. You are part of a team of young "detectives," who solve neighborhood "crimes." You compare stories, look for inaccuracies and inconsistencies, examine evidence, look up things in the library, and when all your ducks are in a row, you select a culprit. If correct, you are rewarded by having an article written about you and your team of young sleuths in the daily paper. The game comes with 50 mysteries to solve.

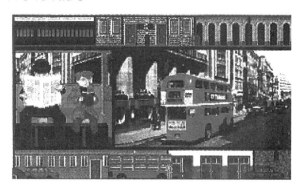

Screen from EAKIDS **Eagle Eye Mysteries in London**. Carry on like Encyclopedia Brown whilst touring England.

You zip around the city on your skateboard, interviewing victims and potential culprits. The game is fast-paced and colorful, a nice feature since **Eagle Eye Mysteries** involves lots of reading, mostly "text bubbles" and clues annotated by hypertext. Another nice feature is that not only must you select who did it, you must point out five facts to support your reasoning. To solve the mysteries correctly in the London version of the game, you must learn some habits of daily English life. These are rather interesting in themselves. Good reading skills. The CD-ROM version of **Eagle Eye Mysteries in London** is pleasantly eccentric and fun.

Highest learning value

Very good story

## MYSTERY AT THE MUSEUM

This is a colorful set of logic puzzles, similar to the object manipulation exams that are part of IQ tests for children. The objects appear three-dimensional on the computer screen, and are attended by Edison, a squeaky-voiced little mascot who applauds furiously whenever your child solves a puzzle. There are memorization games like "concentration" and star constellations to name appropriately. Most objects bear some connection to exhibits found in the Smithsonian museums in Washington, D.C. Very little reading required.

## MUSEUM MADNESS

What MECC's **Museum Madness** has going for it is variety. All the exhibits at a large urban museum have run amok, and a child is called upon to set everything right. There's zoology, botany, anatomy, a little chemistry and physics, even history and math skills, all rolled into a series of clever puzzles and problems. **Museum Madness** has high replay value because none of the puzzles are that similar to each other. It's not like a child can "get the system down" and whiz through the rest of the exhibits without doing much thinking. This game keeps kids awake. The makers of **Museum Madness** have put together a unique and thoughtful program. There's lots of on-screen reading, appropriate for children as young as 9 to play without assistance, but still possesses educational value for kids as old as 13. This game has especially high educational value.

## ULTIMATE DOMAIN

Mindscape's **Ultimate Domain** is a complex, "create-a-world" strategy game that requires much planning and forethought. You start small. Very small. The population of your little village grows quite slowly. Each time you think you are getting ahead, half the town's population is quickly dispatched into the next life by a spot of cold weather. Winter is serious business in this game. Still, once you've conquered the elements and figured out how to stay alive from season to season, this game flourishes into one of the most complete simulations available. Although planning and complex figuring is a must, ultimate domain does not require much reading. Nor are you merely organizing little blips and blobs on a screen. An exclusively CD-ROM-based game, **Ultimate Domain** makes good use of multimedia.

# The Best Interactive Role-Play Adventures

### KING'S QUEST 6

Playing this interactive adventure with full-voice support is reason enough to purchase a CD-ROM player. But even without one, **King's Quest 6** is one of the best. You are Alexander, a prince smitten by the memory of a princess in a faraway, shadowy land. You travel to the four islands that make up this land, and a story of genuine substance and literary worth unfolds. I was surprised, not at the second-to-none animation, which everyone expects from Sierra, but by the extremely well-written script and

Alexander "meets death," and must procure the release of King Calihan and his wife in order to win his lady fair.

characters that were keenly realized. Sierra knows the value of a well-turned phrase, and has proved that interactive adventures need not be merely a series of colorful shoot-'em-ups. Good reading skills.

### SPACE QUEST 4 AND 5

While spoofing just about every sci-fi icon in firing range, hero Roger Wilco manages to save the universe from galaxy-hopping toxic waste pirates, or is sent to the future by a son he has yet to conceive, to save his home planet Xenon from a computerized

*Cool Games for the Price of a Pizza*

Educational software doesn't have to be expensive

## 5 WORTHWHILE PROGRAMS FOR UNDER $20

**DesignWare™**

Hey, Trev, you've got to help me!
Which one of these is correct?
Choice 1:
Grandma, do you want to rollerskate?
Choice 2:
Grandma do you want to rollerskate?

DesignWare's **Junior High** is an English Teacher's dream: Imagine a game that reviews grammar skills that somebody would actually want to play!

## ALSO CHECK OUT. . .

Sierra On-Line's **Jones in the Fast Lane** (page 307), **Merchant Colony,** by Impressions (page 246), and EuroPress' **Learning Adventures with Sammy Spy** (page 327).

**DesignWare™**

You are offered a bribe not to write a story on corruption.

You lose $157 in pay!
Press [ENTER] to continue.

Screen from MECC's **Word Munchers**

| Level: 1 | | /eer/ as in deer | | | |
|------|-------|-------|------|-------|-------|
| air | glare | purge | herb | clear | snare |
| tier | scare | jeer | bare | snare | year |
| beer | fear | clear |  | mare | gear |
| pare | sheer | beer | clear | care | veer |
| here | curb | serf | deer | nurse | sear |

Score: 0

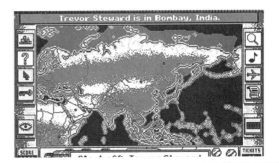

Trevor Steward is in Bombay, India.

PC Globe's **Bushbuck** is a geography scavanger hunt. It provides hours of fun and learning and we paid $14 for it.

world gone awry. Those dark inter-stellar outposts of your favorite Ray Bradbury novels have been replaced by shopping trips to the "Galaxy Galleria," where you dress in drag and clean out your ex-girlfriend's bank account. After battling a sea slug, you must replace your spacesuit at the "Big and Tall Alien Store." Short on cash? Then flip some burgers at "Monolith Burger," but don't stay too long or you'll be made assistant manager! Star Trek lovers might be offended since Roger Wilco's loyal shipmates seem more intent on playing paddle tennis and filing fingernails than patiently awaiting orders. If you'd like to see an overstuffed trash bag floating through space being sucked into a "Garbage Scow"…all to the intro-ductory bars of "2001: A Space Odyssey," then the Space Quest series might be for you. But today's jokes could become tomorrow's ecological crises. Earthlings are dumping "waste in space," even today. How long until it floats back? Good reading skills (long but unintimidating passages).

Very good
story

## THE DAGGER OF AMMON RA

The vain academic celebrity, the femme fatal, the furious international diplomat, the inexplicably rich "countess," and the boozy Irish detective…they're all here, and others, locked in a museum, while mysterious murders pile up, and you're a cub reporter for a newspaper who must find out "who dunnit." It's 1926, era of the speakeasy and America's fascination with the ancient and exotic. A big-time Egyptian archeology exhibit has come to New York's famous Leydendecker Museum. There's talk of the improper removal of artifacts from the home country, Egypt, and of course, an ancient curse. Laura Bow is Sierra On-Line's spunkiest heroine, passing up a secure position with her daddy's newspaper in New Orleans, for a shot at the Big Apple. Once in the Leydendeker, Laura must follow her nose, unearthing clues in the most unlikely places. Along the way, she learns hieroglyph-ics, fumbles with secret panels, and walks in on ancient Egyptian cult rituals. This is a good program to hone inductive reasoning skills. There is on-screen violence, but **The Dagger of Ammon Ra** is such a fun, campy period piece that it's hard to take the vio-lence very seriously. Good reading skills. Adult situations.

A female
heroine

Violent scenes

Very good
story

The "Icon bar" is activated when you move your mouse to the top of the screen.

In adventure games by Sierra On-Line, you must move your mouse to the top of the screen, which reveals a row of possible options, such as "walk," "take," "look at," and "talk to." Further to the right are objects you may use from your "inventory."

## THE QUEST FOR GLORY SERIES

The title **Quest For Glory** did not attract me. I suppose I pictured a battlefield littered with the bodies of the enemies of the Throne, and our hero standing alone to savor his bloody victory in Shakespearean repose. By the time my kids nudged me towards the box with the picture of the blond dragon slayer, I looked a little closer and thought I'd give it a try. The games follow a familiar pattern of activities. A quick animation sets up the premise, outlines the beginning of the story and introduces a couple of characters, including you, the persona you adopt. After this, you're left on your own, your inventory packed with a few essentials for "survival," and you must wander the lands, talk to everyone, ask all the questions you can, tell people you meet a little bit about who you are, and find out how they might help you on your quest. Leave no stone unturned and pick up everything not nailed down.

The writers have a keen sense of the world of a sojourner. In an era before phones or regular mail, a hard-traveling visitor brought news of the outside world and unusual items for trade, and could dispel superstitious notions of life beyond the city's walls. These are interesting shoes for a young person to put wear. Sierra has a knack for putting pep into even the minor characters you meet along your adventuring way. They sparkle with more personality than your average pixilated proto-being. Sierra role-plays also pack a genuine substance into the themes and sub-themes of their adventure role-plays. The background screens and characters, without exception, are painted gorgeously. As you journey the lands and meet people, you must test out your theories and try to solve the crisis, whatever it is: Who is double-dealing, or not telling the truth? Who is friend or foe? How may I convince others to join my side? What act of friendship can earn important trust, to be redeemed later when I'm in a fix?

Think carefully and build useful alliances. In these games, little good fortune happens by accident or chance. Prove your mettle and earn your supper. You'll need it. In **Quest for Glory 1**, a sleepy thirteenth or fourteenth century burg has been beset by marauders who destroy and pillage. Their methods and timing seem to speak of inside collusion…someone in the town is helping them. The shopkeepers and guildsmen are distraught, beaten, and at a loss about what to do, and, not surprisingly, you must save the day.

In **Quest for Glory 3**, you are summoned to a kingdom of Liontaurs by their leader, who is a close friend from a previous adventure. You arrive and find that a conflict between the Liontaurs and a nearby kingdom is quickly escalating into war. You quickly come to the conclusion that a third force is egging the conflict along, hoping to profit as the two kingdoms collide. You must make sure cool heads prevail as you unravel the mystery.

**Quest for Glory 4** is so meticulously painted that the screen-shots themselves are genuine works of art. Noteworthy features of the **Quest for Glory** series are the extensive dialogue options available to you when you meet someone. Click the cursor, and lots of conversational paths appear right on the screen, and branch out logically, as your interview or conversation progresses. You may always go backward a branch or two and continue previous angle of questioning. Another feature is that you may play any **Quest for Glory** game as a fighter, magician, or thief. Slightly different story options unfold depending which character you are, so it's rewarding to go back and play again as a different character.

**Chapter 6** tells you how to set up your computer so your kids can safely start up all their own programs without bothering yours.

Kids learn a lot about rational sequencing of events by playing these kinds of games, not based on some sort of machine-like logic cube, but based on how a human being might react in a given situation. Another fun feature is a bar graph that shows your character increasing in various abilities and skills as the game progresses. You start the game by allotting yourself a certain amount of points in various skill categories, such as intelligence, stamina, climbing, or, well, the ability to pick locks. Good reading skills.

War scenes

Violent scenes

## STRATEGY GAMES AS A LEARNING TOOL

*First, let's compare them to video arcade games. Video arcade games demand lightning-fast thinking along one single plane, one "neural groove." As soon as the eye sees a target, the hand shoots it, faster and faster, more reliably and exactly, over and over. This hypertrophied sense of "alertness" almost mimics a long-distance runner's feelings of euphoria, at the peak of high exercise, when the endorphins begin to circulate. Except with video arcade games, there is no real exercise, only the euphoria of intense, all-involving concentration on "the chase," the task at hand that allows for no intervening thoughts.*

*Strategy games teach the skill of making methodical decisions on multiple levels. In a strategy game, today's advantage can bring on tomorrow's curse, if care is not taken. Strategy games encourage judicious use of limited resources, and give rewards to the thoughtful and prudent investor. Squanderers lose quickly. A good strategy game sets up several interdependent chores that must be undertaken in gradual steps, each step taken while considering the others that must follow. Strategy games encourage careful planning.*

*It's interesting to watch a child play a strategy game. You can almost see those wheels turn upstairs, mulling over some problem until a solution is in sight. That is a skill I would cultivate, and hope to encourage such enthusiastic problem-solving aptitudes in real life (real life? oh that!).*

## SAM AND MAX

The cartoon saga of two detectives—a rabbit and a bear—sent to track down two missing (and fully alive) amusement park attractions: a bigfoot, now unfrozen and presumably rampaging the populace, and his lovely, long-necked girlfriend Trixy. Sam (Spade?) and Max crisscross the U.S. in an old car in search of their quarry. Filled with largely absurd humor, **Sam and Max** appeals to a sophisticated funnybone while simultaneously sending young children into fits of unstoppable giggles. Not droll enough to beg comparisons to Monty Python or Ren & Stimpy, much more original than the usual get-smashed-in-the-face-and-get-back-up Saturday morning cartoons we've all had to bear, **Sam and Max's** silliness works well because the characters are interesting and truly exotic. Rocky and Bullwinkle come to mind. The gag lines seem to be split 50/50 between reaching for the kids who are interested in the cartoon characters and the parents who just might find themselves volunteering to do the mouse on this one. Growing readers.

## KING'S QUEST 5

Books use the power of words to make you imagine what a story might look like. **King's Quest 5** has drawn and painted a world straight out of every child's imagination, and eggs you on to discover the story yourself. It's there, all right, hidden beneath conversations with dozens of curious and bizarre characters. Everyone you talk to serves a purpose, to be revealed only after you've circled the world a couple of times. You're the King of Daventry, and you must save your family from the clutches of black magic. You cross oceans and deserts with the rather spotty companionship of…well…an owl named Cedric, and save the day before your family becomes toast. Playing this game is like re-living a thousand of your favorite bedtime stories. Good reading skills.

Very good story

## BLUE FORCE

Disregarding all the macho bluster on the box, **Blue Force** is a rather touching police role-play adventure in which you play the part of a rookie cop following in his father's footsteps. Ten years ago your father left the force to become a private detective. He stumbled on a piece of evidence, and somebody out there murdered him  to prevent it from coming to light. A decade later, you team up with your father's old private eye partner, determined to solve the case of your parent's murder, a case long left on the docks by official agencies. **Blue Force** has a smooth interface and better than average graphics, but is surprisingly skimpy on dialogue. The characters are interesting enough that my kids and I had hoped to get to know them a little better. Near the end of the game, there's one "shoot-out," although there is no graphic violence. Scenes from the hero's past are reenacted with the violence off-screen; most often, **Blue Force** reminded me of Perry Mason, not Dirty Harry. Good reading skills.

## GABRIEL KNIGHT

Interactive role-play adventures fall somewhere in between a computerized novel, perhaps offering a few possible endings or plot branches with a point and click interface, and just a glorified shooting match, a series of puzzles and challenges connected by a thin plot line. **Gabriel Knight** swings way into the computerized novel territory. There are some things for you to "do," clues to uncover, conversations to initiate, dangers to avoid, but really and truly, you are being told a story. **Gabriel Knight** is the first computerized Gothic novel, complete with an ancient family curse, illicit brotherhoods with untold influence, untimely deaths, mistaken identity, unrequited love, and a man coming to grips with his own destiny. Sierra's done rather well with all this neo-Gothic funnery. There's not much to shoot at, but if you've ever wanted to hear actor Tim Curry whisper "What do you know about the voodoo murders?" then this game's for you. The introduction is like watching the frames of an old Marvel Comic book go by in 256 colors. The initial setting is a dark night in colonial Virginia, its subjects terrorized by

Violent scenes

Requires fast computer

superstition and bound by fear of the unknown. What follows is undeniably spooky, but, as usual with Sierra, the humor works best. Advanced readers. Fair replay value.

## POLICE QUEST

Is there a benefit to children learning the work-a-day routine of police work, where you punch a time card and attend boring briefings and seldom, if ever, fire a gun? Kids who play this game hoping to blow away criminals will be disappointed, as they cruise freeways, write someone a speeding ticket, only to have it dismissed because the time of day was filled out incorrectly, or they forgot to bring the calibration record to court. The player must log clues carefully, or nothing makes sense and your character gets nowhere. At difficult moments, you must check your emotions and follow procedure, or lose your most important case. No room for Rambo here. You must call for backup or die. At the end of **Police Quest 1** through **3**, you are saved by gunfire, but not your own. In both cases, you'd better have foreseen events and called for backup beforehand. I stress this point because **Police Quest**'s box artwork certainly aims to appeal to the "Terminator 2" mentality

**Role-play Adventures:**

## *Pretend you're there!*

(Yep, that's you, standing in front of the monkey head.)

You play the part of Guybrush Threepwood. Currently, you must decide whether to enter the monkey head itself, or make off with one of the idols at your feet. You combine objects and situations on the main screen with the list of verbs, and watch your character perform those actions.

Your actions must make sense with the story. You may "talk to" the monkey head, for example. It might or might not talk back. Or it may do something rather rude. You'll have to find out.

These objects are what you are carrying around with you. You may combine them with the verbs and the objects on the screen to form an action. For example: "Use skull with wimpy little idol." Will that do anything? Who knows?

lurking in every young boy. Wait'll they get home. Ha! Ha! **Police Quest 1** through **3** were written largely by a retired policeman who has not lost his compassion nor his sense of humor. **Police Quest 4** was written by Los Angeles' ex-police chief Daryl Gates. I was expecting Gates to use this game as a forum to take to task the many groups who opposed him during his years at the helm. Instead, **Police Quest 4** has a spirit largely in keeping with the other three. Good reading skills.

Very good story

Violent scenes

# Children's Artwork and Desktop Publishing

## FINE ARTIST

Microsoft's **Fine Artist** is especially strong because there is a strong tutorial built in to the program. Good thing too. **Fine Artist** has so many features that a youngster could easily get lost without the little tutor "Maggie" on screen to lead the way. When you first load the program, kids are given a quick teach-in on defining and using an object's "positive and negative space" when drawing. This is followed by a fast run-through on how to design a picture using perspective, and defining the picture's "vanishing point" and using it to help set up your objects. That being done, you are whisked into an "art studio," given the choice to either design a sticker, a cartoon strip, or make a multimedia slide show. Pains are taken to demonstrate the procedural aspects of setting up cartoon frames and text bubbles, how to add sounds to your slide show, and so on. Beyond any of these extras, the regular old "drawing program" aspect of **Fine Artist** is nothing to sneeze at. There's plenty of strange and wacky "brushes," special painting effects and interesting textures that kids can quickly add to their drawing. **Fine Artist** includes a healthy selection of clip art, making it easy to add predesigned pictures to drawings. These little black-and-white line drawings (which may be painted or simply filled with color) are more spirited and humorous than the usual frogs and sunflower paste-ups that get thrown into kid's art programs. You get more than 30 colors to choose from and dozens of "fill patterns" to choose from. Editing

Requires fast computer

A very, very good game

features include being able to resize objects and move them around freely. **Fine Artist** is a worthwhile, friendly creation from Bill the Conqueror and his ambitious friends. Good reading skills required to take advantage of "Maggie the tutor."

## DABBLER

Fractal Design's **Dabbler** is a real art program that prepares kids to work with the real thing. In **Dabbler**, children identify and select artist's brushes and pens and pencils, and the program tries to mimic, as closely as possible, the genuine look and "feel" of those chosen tools. A child's version of Fractal Design's legendary **Painter 2.0**, **Dabbler** is the least "toyish" of any of the child's-level art software sold today and requires the willingness to learn to…well…be a painter. Growing readers.

Highest learning value

## STORYBOOK WEAVER

With this program, your child may actually assemble an illustrated story. Beginning with the title page, you may select border art and font style. The following pages are divided into text and picture segments. Your child may compose four or five sentences of text per illustrated page, and then may get to work choosing from pre-set selections of scenery, creating the mood for the story to come. Kids can pepper their stories with objects found in nature, both mythical and real people, forms of shelter, such as castles or log cabins, and other bric-a-brac. These features make composing short stories especially rewarding for children. There is no "free-draw" mode available. You must make do with the items and situations the makers have provided for you, and although there is provision to resize and flip objects to face the other direction, objects can begin to look a little funny if you tweak them beyond their intended proportion. Your child may also assign little snatches of music to open and close the story. The program is compatible with a hefty list of popular printers. Children often daydream about pasting up their stories into books, and with **Storybook Weaver**, they can do it easily. No reading required to enjoy this game, but you can write stories as complex as you choose.

## KIDPIX

Two years after purchasing **Kidpix**, our children are still discovering new features in it. This is the most entertaining drawing program for young children. You only get sixteen colors and there is no color blending or shading. You cannot "edit" curves or line, to reshape them to your liking. **Kidpix** will never teach anyone about the subtle side of art, but, jeese, is it fun. Children can draw fairly simple shapes and forms and recognizable objects and then, by applying a couple of the many widgets and doodads that **Kidpix** comes packed with, they may transform their pictures into the most bizarre abstract landscapes. Saving and loading pictures is easy and quick. Your kids can pull out a picture they worked on a year ago and play with it some more, and save the new and the old version, which is standard procedure around our house. Text may be added to the drawing. **Kidpix** comes with "stamps," little predrawn figures that you may paste throughout your drawing at will. You may alter and redraw your own stamps. You may also "cut" a portion of your picture, and "paste" it somewhere else…even in a different picture. In this case, the old advertising claim, "For children 3 to 103" really does apply. Beyond words like "save" and "load" on the menu bar, no reading is required to play **Kidpix**. You may also type words into your stories.

## CREATIVE WRITER

This is a word processing program for kids to use, full of splashy features like a button that makes the title of your story automatically take on a zany shape. You may punctuate your story with sound effects (not relevent to the printed version of your story, obviously), and you can even put your story "in code" so only a chosen friend may read it. You have access to all the fonts stored on your Windows system, and the program comes with cute, full-color clip art. Accordingly, you may import any Windows-compatible picture into the story, and the text will wrap neatly around it. (You may resize the artwork, just like big-people art programs.) Unlike other children's word processing programs, Microsoft's **Creative Writer** provides drawing tools so you can hand-illustrate your story, as well as import clip art pictures. Perhaps the most fun and unique feature is a little juke-box machine: It spits out a story idea (one of 3,000) for your child to expound upon and illustrate for a few paragraphs. These little teasers are clever enough to stir up the embers of a little creative thought. For the down side, you know that any program of this nature will run slow, simply because it's in Windows, and all the little doodads will slow things down. Kids will put multiple fonts in their stories, put in lots of pictures, cool sound effects just for fun, and not surprisingly, the computer will grind to a halt, inevitably before Junior has saved the final version of his story he's been working on all afternoon. Consider this an 8MB-of-RAM program on a fast computer, unless you want to subject your children to much frustration. Printing out the stories has not proved entirely glitch-free either. One suggestion: Encourage the kids *not* to use the sound effects very often. The program's other functions will run smoother without being dragged down by your computer frequently having to access your sound card.

Requires fast
computer

## CREATIVE PUBLISHING WORKSHOP

The Learning Company's **Creative Publishing Workshop** is the least intimidating desktop publishing program for kids. It's not overloaded with features, and what's available is helpful, not overwhelming. There's an easily accessible spell checker, a thesaurus, even online punctuation advice. You may apply pictures wherever you like in the text, and the text automatically "wraps around" the picture. **Creative**

**Publishing Workshop** also helps kids design a bibliography. I'd recommend it for ages 9 through 14. Kids will quickly exhaust the "clip art" that comes with the program, but **Creative Publishing Workshop** permits the importing of any Windows-supported graphic file, such as PCX or BMP.

Good desktop publishing programs have a lot in common. Take a peek at **Chapter 12** to learn about a few of them.

## VISTAPRO

**VistaPro** is great for teaching children about Cartesian coordinates, the X-Y-Z axis used for mapmaking and architecture and drafting. **VistaPro** re-creates well-known landscapes, such as Half Dome and Morro Bay and the Matterhorn, and allows you to view them from any angle or height. You may also alter the water line and tree line, raise or lower mountains, and change vegetation type. **VistaPro** provides such lavish flexibility through a process known as fractal geometry, the notion that geometrical patterns found in nature, such as the shapes found in a leaf or a rock, differ only in scale. Examine closely the geometry of a rock, and you'll see its smallest patterns rendered larger and larger as you look at larger sections of the rock. Look at a whole leaf, and you'll see a pattern that repeats itself as you look closer and closer. **VistaPro** seeks to recreate this method of rendering shapes, hoping to give objects a more natural look, rather the boxy, pixilated look found in many paint programs or photo styling programs. Very little reading required.

Works OK on an older computer

# Software Grab Bag

### FUN SCHOOL'S LEARNING ADVENTURES WITH SAMMY SPY

This is an inexpensive, compelling little piece of software that teaches a surprisingly broad palette of skills. The box artwork is cluttered, and there is no shapely gladiator princess on the cover to arouse your curiosity as to what might be inside. **Fun School** has five activities and by pressing the F10 key, you increase the difficulty level of whatever activity your working on at the moment. There is a map recognition game, ranging from "What continent is this?" up to "Where is the Pyrenees mountain range?" There's a proportion game, "Out of 30 people on the screen, six have blonde hair." This game can be programmed to accept answers in percentages, decimals, or fractions, and switching back and forth helps kids quickly see the relationships between those three number systems. To help a little spy character climb up a wall, you must answer a number of questions correctly. The questions range from simple chemistry to historical events, to trick spelling words and word math problems, thrown out randomly to keep you hopping. Finally, there's a currency conversion exercise, where you are left at customs until you complete your math correctly, and pass through with the correct amount of lira or pounds or marks or pesos. As in real life, the rates change from time to time. As for the cost, well, it was a choice between scoops of ice cream for the four of us, or purchasing this game. I think we chose well. I haven't seen it in the stores recently, so you may have to contact the company directly. Beginning readers okay (short passages).

### TRIVIA MACHINE

Morgan's **Trivia Machine** sports interesting information in the form of brief videos and narration, and kids score points for correct answers in three different game formats. The correct answer is automatically given after a wrong guess, so next time the question comes around, your child will be familiar with it. Also, since the main action on the screen is cartoon-based, it will not tax your system's resources, so your computer will have enough firepower left to keep the videos and questions moving along at a brisk pace. The game formats are Science, Geography, and Grab Bag, and may be played in one- or two-player mode. The characters are happy-faced cartoons that might not be appreciated by anyone over 12, although the information covered would challenge some early teens. Growing readers.

## AUTOWORKS

**Autoworks** examines an automobile in its entirety, from headlights to exhaust pipe, from a superficial overhead view down to the most detailed close-up of a brake drum or timing dwell. At the opening screen, you are presented with a car. You simply click on the portion of the car you wish to study more closely, and the view zooms in. Click again and you zoom in again. Click the right mouse button and a text bubble flashes on the screen describing in depth of the car part you have zoomed in on. As you zoom in, the right portion of the screen becomes two rows of "tags." These tags correspond to the currently visible automobile parts available on the screen. These tags will change as you zoom around or change your viewing angle. When you click on a car part, a line is automatically drawn from the tag to the part, so you'll know the name of what you're looking at. Along the bottom of the screen is a row of icons that represent various options available to you, such as the ability to print the screen content at the moment, either as a picture, or as a text document. There are animations that show particular automotive systems in motion. **Autoworks** is a thoughtfully designed tool for learning about how cars work. **Autoworks** is fun for any age, and no reading skills are necessary to enjoy this program, although the text descriptions are helpful and intelligently laid out.

Highest learning
value

## INDIANA JONES AND THE SEARCH FOR ATLANTIS

In this role-playing adventure, you are Indiana Jones. It's 1939 and the Nazis are racing to locate the lost city of Atlantis and discover the ultimate weapon. (If your children are learning twentieth century history, here's a good tie-in to discuss the race to build the A-bomb.) Indy must intercept the Nazis, and he (you) are led by a series of clues to Central America, Greece, and finally, underground to a rather dramatic showdown. The interface is easy to use. The people and their environments are shown in the upper screen, and the lower screen has written verbs you click on with your mouse—open, close, talk to, pick up—followed by a click on the object on the upper screen you wish to affect. The effect is quite smooth. This role-play comes in a disk version that has written text you must read, and the CD-ROM version has actors speaking instead. The fun of this game is in the various modes of transportation Indy must use, from a broken-down truck in Istanbul, to an air balloon in Algeria, and finally, a submarine ride underground. Good reading skills.

## RETURN TO ZORK

One of the new breed of adventure role-plays that features videos of an entire cast of live actors and actresses that walk and talk and interact in a beautifully drawn imaginary world. Some of the backgrounds are photographs, and some are animated, but all are digitally rendered to look like they fit together. The story is this: You are the winner of a contest and travel to investigate a time-share vacation arrangement and are quickly sucked into an ancient magic world, facing the usual battles between good and evil. It is a big, colorful, ambitious production, and in creating a vast, magical underworld, they have largely succeeded. The characters you chat with along the way provide clues to propel you into the next world within a world. As the main character, you are allowed to choose in what manner you wish to listen to the person talking to you: with suspicion, with interest, with sympathy, etc. Your facial features evidently bring on different responses, and thus, new plot branches, all depending on your temperament. The CD-ROM version fully talks. The videos are smooth and pretty clear. Good reading skills (long passages).

## BETRAYAL AT KRONDOR

It's big, medieval, and roto-scoped. The story is half sci-fi and half old English legend. Civilizations clash, spurred on not only by racial and cultural differences, but by big "rifts" in time that appear and reappear, allowing armies to cross through and settle ancient differences. The story centers on the well-mapped journeys of three men. You cast spells, fight, and wander through an amazing world. **Betrayal at Krondor** boasts enough plot branches and multiple solutions that each person pretty much designs his or her own game. Dynamix has pulled off quite a feat here. Good reading skills (long passages). Assumes familiarity with standard science fiction concepts like "time rifts."

## MONKEY ISLAND 2

**Monkey Island 2** is embarrassingly silly. Even when accompanied by a child, any adult caught playing this ridiculous game should be disciplined. That being said, let me point out that I've seldom had more fun. You're a wanna-be pirate who must explore the Caribbean Islands. Most people you meet are as seriously deranged as thou art. The humor is

Screen from LucasArts' Monkey Island 2.

not profane, or "obvious" like TV sitcoms. You're just left to wonder, "What planet did the writers of **Monkey Island 2** come from?" What kids must figure out (on their own) in **Monkey Island 2** are situations like, "How is a library card going to get me off this island?" "How can I convince this forlorn sailor to take to the seas again?" "If I put these two objects together, can I get enough leverage to lift myself out of this pit in the ground?" Kids end up remembering an impressively long sequence of events, or objects and people that interact with each other. **Monkey Island 2** is creative, disgusting, and rather smart. Good reading skills.

## ADVENTURES OF WILLY BEAMISH

While most role-play adventures are set in another time and another place, the **Adventures of Willy Beamish** is painfully contemporary, featuring a suburban family whose values run as deep as a rain puddle. Dad gets fired, and mom worries about where the money for her nail wraps will come from. Tiffany, the teenage daughter, talks of traveling to France with her beau's family, who are in the lingerie business. You are Willy, a nine-year-old boy who must save his city from…well…sludge. You have a pet frog, two loyal friends, a school bully who requires strategic appeasement, and even a genuine "baby-sitter from hell." Unlike most TV sitcoms in which parents exist only to be maligned, Willy Beamish's dad finally ends up showing some backbone and behaving quite admirably. Good reading skills (long passages). Familiar "sit-com" level dialogue.

Very exceptional music

Very good story

## LOST IN TIME

This game offers a more sophisticated and "adult interest" story than most interactive role-plays. The picture on the box of the girl in the low-cut blouse reminds you of a Caribbean travel poster, which turns out to be half the case. There's some clever time-travel twists going on here. The lead character (a girl, for a change, with much more smarts than the blowsy photo on the cover would indicate) inadvertently foils a simple plot to steal something invaluable, store it in a ship, arrange for a shipwreck, zip ahead 500 years into the future, emerge, and regain the goods. The game's interface involves lots of using objects with other objects to obtain unexpected results, all occurring in gorgeously painted, digitally retouched environs. The story is a fresh twist on a favorite sci-fi theme of what happens when you mess with history. My seven-year-old is able to follow it quite nicely,

Many common computer problems do not require an expert. With a little sleuthing, you can fix it yourself. See **Chapter 10.**

owing to Coktell Vision's intuitive icon system, which helps you forget you're only using a mouse in front of a computer. Good reading skills (long passages).

Good use of video

A female heroine

Very good story

## THE JOURNEYMEN PROJECT

**The Journeymen Project** is a lavish time-travel role-play adventure of the type that strikes a pleasant balance between movie and arcade game. The plot is sophisticated, if predictable, but, in contrast to most sci-fi adventure games that take their violent little selves so dang seriously, **The Journeymen Project** at least throws in a dollop of gentle self-mockery. There is one big problem here, though. Due to the fact that the program places virtually no files on your hard drive, the game must reach onto the CD-ROM itself for all information at every turn. Consequently, it runs terribly, terribly slowly, even on the fastest machine. When quadruple-speed CD-ROM players get cheap, we're looking forward to playing **The Journeyman Project**.

Requires
CD-ROM

## CORELDRAW

For years, **CorelDRAW** has been the industry standard for drawing programs on the IBM computer, with programs like Harvard graphics and Aldus Photoshop filling the related niches of designing business presentations and altering photographs and digital images. **CorelDRAW** has stayed on top as an all-around drawing program. Buying it off the shelf can be expensive, except during the times of year that they are interested in pushing everybody to by their newest version. At those times, you can find an older version (still very, very adequate for normal humans to use) for a quarter of what you'd normally pay. **CorelDRAW** sets up a Corel Graphics group in Windows, and in the group are several programs. First is **CorelDRAW** itself, which allows you to draw unlimited numbers and styles of lines and curves and shapes, color them as you wish, move and stretch and skew them, add perspective and "extrude" functions, which makes the shapes look like they are going forward and backward from the screen.

A complete look at the best software for creating fine art and graphics can be found in **Chapter 13.**

You may add hundreds of different kinds of text, and all the functions you may perform on the shapes and lines, you may also perform on the text blocks. You may import drawings from other programs, or clip art of just about any kind. The next program included in **CorelDRAW** is CorelCHART, which allows you to make various sorts of charts or graphs. CorelCHART is designed so that you merely enter the data you wish to chart (something as simple as how much money I spend on gas in a week relative to my total budget, or complex data involved in running a business), and CorelCHART does the rest, creating the chart components, sizing and shaping everything correctly. You may alter the size and style of font that appears in your chart, or change the label titles or graph titles at any time. You may easily change the color or groups of colors found in your graph or chart. **CorelDRAW** also comes with PhotoPaint, with which you may edit and paint and add special effects to all kinds of picture files. To learn more about computer artwork and design, see Chapter 13.

## LOOM

Having certainly mentioned enough role-play adventures for you to get the idea, I'm gonna tell you about LucasArt's **Loom**, because it's so curious and not what one would expect. First of all, **Loom** is based, as so many role-play adventures are, at the end of some golden age of magic, and a few kind-hearted spell-casting folk find that the world is poised upon an age in which the powers of the supernatural have fallen into less caring hands. **Loom** follows the journeys of a young textile weaver named Bobbin Threadbare. The characters of the story are divided into members of various guilds, and bring to mind the struggling artisans and metallurgists, farmers and weavers of old. As a member of the Weaver's Guild, Bobbin Threadbare possesses the skill of magic. The elders of his guild desert him, warning him of a dark age to come. Bobbin understands only that he must leave his private world to try to save the larger one. Bobbin must learn to use certain spells before he can make his way, and the spells are based on musical notes. To use these spells and save the day, your child must memorize these notes, either visually on a musical staff or by ear. Each time your child advances in skills, a new note becomes available on his or her musical staff.

The other curious thing about the game **Loom**, with its bright music and lavish color-work, is that the day doesn't get saved. **Loom** doesn't have a happy ending, and it leaves the kids with a rather difficult lesson about the human cost of "progress," or as the Bobbin's elders keep reminding him: "The fabric has been rent." **Loom's** accompanying literature says that in this game, nobody will "kill" you, as opposed to most adventure role-plays whose programmers seem to derive great joy from sending you to Meet Thy Maker in as many unpleasant ways as possible.

Yet **Loom** has the most troubling and unnerving story line of any role-play I've seen. During one sequence, you, as Bobbin, befriend a young boy, who, later in the game, gets eaten by a dragon. It was your fault, and the boy returns as a ghost to tell you so. **Loom** is a dark gem, and is compelling enough to run the story a few times with your kids, but don't do it right before bedtime. Good reading skills (long passages).

## THE MULTIMEDIA GUINNESS BOOK OF WORLD RECORDS

This is the CD-ROM version of the tallest, smallest, fastest, richest, and so forth, with lots of videos and pictures of firsts and foremost. The program is efficiently laid out, and you can get right to the heart of what you are looking up quite quickly, or take a random browse through some of the general weirdness of the human race. You can copy the text and pictures to your word processing program and impress your friends and teachers with your knowledge of the bizarre. Includes the book version. Good reading skills.

Requires
CD-ROM

## CONSPIRACY

It's Moscow, mid-1991: the days preceding the downfall of the Communist government and the end of Gorbachev and the Politburo. You're a career soldier in the Soviet army, but now you're kicked upstairs to the KGB. You're supposed to help clean it up, something to do with skimming profits off of products exported to the United States. It gets worse, it gets ugly, and then suddenly, it's the end of an era. It's a bit like role-playing a Robert Ludlum novel. You are an angel in a den of vipers, and the truth is always uglier than it seems. What makes this highly technical and sometimes humorous romp through the streets of the empire "different than the rest" is the inclusion of actor Donald Sutherland as your father, also a career soldier. Donald, dressed up in soldier's garb and sporting a thick Russian accent, sits in the corner of your screen as a little icon, waiting for you to click on him. When you do, he expands to a full-screen video and movingly explains to you your next step in solving the mystery. Think of it as an online hint book in movie form. It's quite a nice touch. "You have earned your vodka today, Max." Advanced readers.

## AUCTION

In **Auction**, you are an art connoisseur, sent to outbid your peers and possess the world's most precious art treasures. The trick is this: The game is set in the future, so not only

To learn how to upgrade your computer without spending money unnecessarily, see **Chapter 10.**

do you bid for vintage works by Van Gogh or Da Vinci, but also for somebody's rather hilarious take on the kind of artwork people will produce after the year 2000. This is mainly a game of financial strategy, in which you snoop around and predict which pieces will grow in value, then zero in your bidding on those. The interface is clever and sophisticated, state-of-the-art and quite funny. Advanced readers.

Requires
CD-ROM

Requires fast
computer

## QUANTUM GATE

**Quantum Gate** is largely a free-running movie in which you participate in some of the decisions, and you're supposed to shoot something, I gather. **Quantum Gate** is futuristic: You are set up on some sort of colonial outpost, à la Dune, mining some important material. You are stuck with an incorrigible and outspoken partner who claims that your superiors are not to be trusted. Not surprisingly, your main gaming choices lie therein: Who to believe? The video sequences are dazzling and interwoven rather masterfully. I was surprised at how smoothly they ran. The script has high intentions, and aims to be thoughtful and even tender when appropriate, and is not merely a Rambo-in-the-Skies shootout. (The ending packs more of an emotional jolt, more Orson Wells than Larry Nevin.) Although at times there is little to do, **Quantum Gate's** story line puts you at the helm at important moments. But most often, you just watch.

Good use of
video

Requires fast
computer

Requires
CD-ROM

## THE SEVENTH GUEST

I saw the Vincent Price movie *The Pit and The Pendulum* when I was about 4 years old—too young for such scary stuff. I insisted, I begged, I pleaded, and finally, I peeked through the bedroom door and saw the TV image of that poor lady being locked away in some frightful dark hole. The picture stuck in my head, and I was still very much awake when the sun rose seven hours later. Virgin Game's **The Seventh Guest** is like that. The story begins with children dying in their sleep after receiving cursed dolls as gifts. I'm sorry if I ruined somebody's surprise, but from one parent to another, I feel I should give give away that much. Everything about this game, its music, the lavish painting and 3D rendering, and especially the creepy characters, are all designed to scare you to death. Good music, though. **The Seventh Guest** took years to make, and it was nice to see someone take advantage of CD-ROM technology and produce a soundtrack worthy of listening to even after the game is gone. Advanced readers.

# CLASH OF THE TITANS:
## EXPLORING AND RATING THE MULTIMEDIA ENCYCLOPEDIAS

Now that Microsoft's **Encarta** has become a staple on late-night infomercial TV, most people have some idea what a multimedia encyclopedia is. You may quickly research any idea, pointing and clicking rather than flipping pages. When you find the information you want, copy it to the Windows clipboard and use it in your document, book report, research paper, what have you. But this just scratches the surface. Multimedia encyclopedias are packed with video clips and narrated slide shows on just about any subject. You may trace the history of women's suffrage in the United States, or humankind's trek from across the Bering strait. Listen to Poe's "The Raven" read aloud or watch a "dove in flight" while a scientist comments on the animal's perfect aerodynamics. There are three top-selling multimedia encyclopedias that you are likely to run into at the local software store. There's Microsoft

**Encarta**, which, by far, has more razzle dazzle than the other two. Then there's Compton's **Interactive Encyclopedia** and Grolier's **Multimedia Encyclopedia**.

### ENCARTA

**Encarta** is laid out for the distinct purpose of taking your breath away. They really want that $89 and they want you to spread the gospel of multimedia to all your friends with missionary's zeal. To achieve that gleam in your eye, you are hit with a layout that puts **Encarta**'s best foot forward: The audio and video clips. There are hundreds and hundreds of 'em. The narrated American Literature clips alone could provide a couple evenings of enjoyment. **Encarta** provides enough general science study resources to keep some bright sixth-graders busy for half a semester. They acquaint you with a decent selection classical composers and manage not to entirely ignore ethnic music. They have photos of Pakistani street merchants, and creative photos of important but overlooked people and places. (There is one of Indian sitarist Ravi Shankar who looks like he could be thinking, "What do you mean, play 'Within You, Without You'?")

## INTERACTIVE ENCYCLOPEDIA

But there are times when I turn to **Encarta** to look something up and I can't find it. **Encarta's** actual knowledge base, the amount of retrievable information that your child can cut and paste and use in school reports, is not as large as you'd think. In particular, Compton's **Interactive Encyclopedia** (the 1994 and '95 versions, not the 1993) seems to include more information on many topics. Compton's layout is designed to help you hone in and find what you need. Compton's selection of photographs is not as impressive as Encarta's. However, Compton's includes a "search-the-encyclopedia" feature called "Idea Search" which frees you from the usual "I typed in the word *factories* and got 3,476 responses" problem. What Compton's has tried to design with their Idea Search function is the ability for you to type a question, for example: "Why is the sky blue?" and get an answer, rather than 32,334 references to the word "sky" and the word "blue." They've succeeded in achieving this, somewhat.

HERE'S THE INFO PILOT FROM COMPTON'S **INTERACTIVE ENCYCLOPEDIA**. CLICK ON ANY SUBJECT, AND IT BECOMES THE MAIN TOPIC. NEW SUBTOPICS BRANCH OUT EVERY TIME YOU SELECT A NEW CENTRAL RESEARCH THEME.

Another excellent feature of Compton's is their "Info Pilot": Select the name of a subject and your subject appears in the center of a visual layout of squares. Subjects deemed closely related to your subject make up the

Scroll down, enlarge, and read the whole article.

CD-ROM multimedia encyclopedias like Compton's are superb educational tools.

surrounding squares. Typing **Patagonia** results in "Argentina" occupying the next square, and "South American Literature" pops up one square to the right or left. Moving "South American Literature" to the center square would result in "English Literature" suddenly occupying a square nearby, and "Patagonia" being removed altogether. This research aid can be very helpful for students fishing to bring more substance to a research topic, or just make knowledge exploring more fun.

Compton's Virtual Workspace turns your computer into nine "desktops," wherein you may move information "to the back" if you don't need it for a moment, and keep two or three articles handy and at your fingertips. Compton's accomplishes this by placing a tiny "mini-

The "Virtual Workspace" screen.

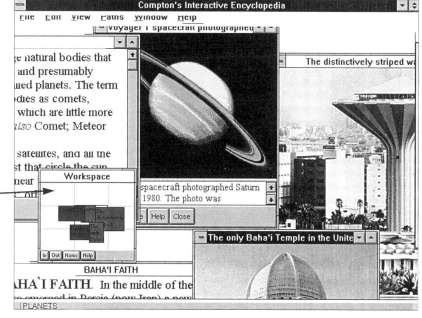

Screen showing Compton's Virtual Workspace. With it you can move an article or picture "to the back," using the small "Workspace" box to drag an article to another screen for later use.

The small box "Workspace" in the lower right shows how your computer has been transformed in many "desktops." I overlapped the pictures and articles so you could see how the same pattern is represented in the "Workspace" box. Of course, the point is for you to spread everything across several screens, and only click on something when you want it front and center.

screen" representation of the articles and word processing programs you might have open at once. This mini-screen is divided into nine squares, and when you click on one square in the mini-screen, your main screen also changes to a new screen. The document, article, photograph, or whatever you had previously set aside in that main screen is now front and center. It's now become "the thing" you are working on at the moment. Whatever was up in front before is not "closed" or gone, but just moved aside while you work elsewhere. Pretty neat, huh?

While Compton's video selection and slide show selection is not nearly as complete as **Encarta's**, the selections they do include are arranged more usefully. The video sequences that they do include are well-rounded and apt to end up as part of someone's serious lesson plan for a school day. By comparison, **Encarta's** videos are like gazillions of little "McNuggets" for you to scroll through fairly quickly. Of the big three multimedia encyclopedias, Compton's has the most impressive dictionary. Click on any word in any article, and you'll be whisked away to the dictionary and given a rather detailed definition of the word. **Encarta's** dictionary has quicker, less developed entries. **Encarta** has the best thesaurus, though.

## MULTIMEDIA ENCYCLOPEDIA

I've barely mentioned Grolier's **Multimedia Encyclopedia**, because Grolier's is quite outshined by the other two. Grolier's has one nice inclusion, called Knowledge Explorer, a loose series of a dozen or so videos that covers subjects like ancient and modern architecture, artwork through the ages, various animal classifications and other science topics, and even the history of women's suffrage in the U.S. Considering their brevity, these little videos include quite a bit of information. A child's attention span fades just around where a computer's video capacity ends. Even with 640MB to throw around, no one has time to get very windy.

## MY VOTE

Well, because of its sheer expansiveness, I must say **Encarta** is still the big favorite around our house. We use it more than the others, and it continues to amaze us. We use Compton's **Interactive** as more of an organizational workspace and research guide.

## EXPLOROPEDIA

This is Microsoft's encyclopedia of the natural world for the very young. **Exploropedia** is well-rounded, quite thorough, and inviting. The CD includes songs, movies, and games that exploit the vast reference capabilities of the encyclopedia itself. Fact tidbits regarding all subjects from starts and galaxies to forests and mammal groups are presented in appropriate doses for kindergarten through third or fourth graders. Your average fifth grader would find it condescending. One of Exploropedia's best features is a game called Wise Crackers that sends your child searching the entire information base for clues to a mystery. Hints are provided along the way and will gently steer your child toward the correct answer before frustration sets in. Currently, Exploropedia is the best natural science program for the target age group. Growing readers.

## RANDOM HOUSE/KNOWLEDGE ADVENTURE'S INTERACTIVE ENCYCLOPEDIA

This program is two CD-ROMs long. One CD contains 2,000 encyclopedia entries, all fully narrated. Very well organized and laid out, each article includes reference tips for further reading, and tools for your child to assemble his or her own notebook of personal favorites, including pictures. CD number two is a series of colorful, lively fact-based games that include about 100 brief videos.

# MUSIC PROGRAMS

Lots of new software aims to bring the world of music to your PC. You are encouraged to sample little snippets of operas or symphonies or songs, then read an accompanying article about the musical selection, then click and watch a video with that particular performer, either "in concert" or perhaps a sit-down interview. After this, you may click somewhere on the screen to journey a related musical era or a similar performer's work. Microsoft has put together CD-ROMs that explore the work of Mozart, Beethoven, Shubert, Stravinski, Billy Holliday, and Duke Ellington. These CDs are rich with related photographic and video material, as well as providing a lots of recorded music, all "CD quality." You may get bogged down in minutiae if you like, and if you are the type of person who comes to blows over the exact number of measures in Beethoven's Third Symphony, these informative CDs set all the records straight.

## MUSICAL INSTRUMENTS

Microsoft produces a CD-ROM called **Musical Instruments** which provides you with a selection of 150 instruments you may sample briefly from your computer keyboard, or listen to recorded pieces. Some are quite exotic, like the Dijjori, a tube-like instrument used by Aborigine tribesmen. You may read articles about an instrument's background and history and see close-up pictures. This analytical approach to an art as intuitive as music might seem a bit sterile. I doubt if all this "point and click" dabbling ever increases anybody's "soul connection" to music. A love of music comes from relaxed and repeated exposure to entire songs, not by wading through an archive of musical "McNuggets." Nonetheless, spending an afternoon with this CD-ROM will leave you with a renewed appreciation for the sheer diversity of the music in our world.

Windows programs will let you import music as a .wav file.

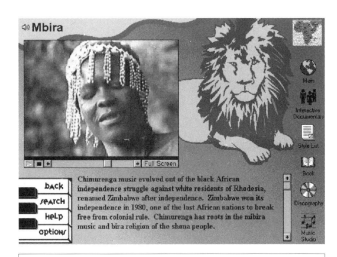

**Screens from Medio's World Beat music CD-ROM, which is one of the best CD-ROM music anthologies to date. The performances are lively, and you really do get a little bit of everything.**

# WORLD BEAT

One CD that strives to be more than a cursory exploratory tool is Medio's **World Beat**. **World Beat** music is a multicultural hybrid. Its whirlwind diversity is what makes it fun, and all that globe-trotting looks good on a computer. **World Beat** also provides little tutorials that teach you how to recognize and experiment with different melodies and rhythms. The performance videos are very colorful and lively, as is the music itself. Very few software anthologies are compiled with such obvious enthusiasm as this CD-ROM. The reason why **World Beat** is such an important CD-ROM is that the people who put it together love music. You can tell they dug doing this project. The editors took the time to inject a good deal of heart and soul into this project. And not surprisingly, one link all the musicians involved have in common is that they seem to be having quite a fun time.

# MULTIMEDIA ROCK STARS

Several pop-rock artists have ventured into the world of multimedia, with majestic results. Peter Gabriel, Prince, Todd Rungren, and Heart all have taken a stab at PC multimedia. Peter Gabriel's and Todd Rungren's, especially, are creative, very interactive, and actually contribute to your musical experience, rather than merely add more heft to the bill from your visit to the mall. On Peter Gabriel's CD-ROM, you can actually "remix" one of his songs to your own liking.

## MAKING MUSIC WITH YOUR COMPUTER

If you decide to delve into the music making possibilities of your PC, perhaps eventually buying synthesizers and making electronic music and such, here are some things you should know: Most PCs manufactured since 1993 have MIDI capability. MIDI stands for *musical instrument digital interface* and it's a language that permits all modern keyboards to talk to each other, meaning that the notes you play on one synthesizer can be instantly applied to another. These notes you've recorded via computer can also be stored on a disk and played back on another synthesizer at a later date. Not only are the notes you played saved on your computer disk, but so are the song's tempo, the metronome signature, and other arcane information like "pitch bend" and "after touch."

So if you intend to use your computer to program some serious music, the sky is the limit. You may compose pieces and edit them endlessly, adding layer upon layer of instruments, so long as you own enough synthesizers to "play back" all the parts you have written. There are some "entry level" MIDI music packages that divide your computer screen into two parts: On the top is a score sheet, and you use your mouse or keyboard to create the music you will eventually hear coming out of your computer's speakers. Most MIDI software for beginners allows you to score up to eight instruments to be played back simultaneously. What really determines how many instruments you can program and how good or cheesy they sound is your sound card. You may alter the time signature, note duration, number of measures, and tempo of your song. You can also "cut" and "paste" bars of music just as you would do to written text. The bottom of your screen is a "mixer," that allows you to edit the sound of each instrument you wrote music for. You can make any instrument louder or softer, send it to the right speaker or left, or add special effects to any of the instruments you composed music for in this particular piece of music.

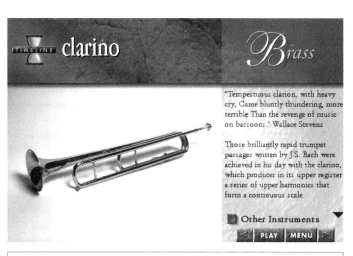

Midisoft's full color **Music Mentor** provides a guided tour of musical instruments, classical composers, some basic music instruction, and even allows you to "improvise" along on with music selections from your computer keyboard.

To program other synthesizers from your PC, you'll need dedicated music composition software, like **Performer** or **Cakewalk. Music Time** by Passport is a fairly simple, user-friendly program that introduces many aspects of MIDI composing for the beginner. Writing music with your computer is not very intuitive. The technical aspects can drain your inspiration, and leave you wondering why in the world you thought this would be fun. The fun begins when you've composed something that sounds good to you, which can then be edited and blended with other parts. It's a little bit like painting a picture in which you can go back and choose your colors and composition over again, as many times as you wish. Remember to start with a simple MIDI package. The higher-end music software brings incredible capabilities to those musicians with incredible IQs, but just drives the rest of us crazy.

# PRODUCTS AND MANUFACTURERS MENTIONED IN THIS BOOK

Adobe Systems Incorporated
(Adobe Photoshop)
1585 Charleston Road
P.O. Box 7900
Mountain View, CA 94039-7900
(415) 961-4400

Binary Zoo
(Mystery at the Museum)
P.O. Box 3210
Champlain, NY 12919-3210

Broderbund Software
(Carmen SanDiego; Treehouse)
P.O. Box 6125
Novato, CA 94948
or
Broderbund Software
500 Redwood Blvd.
Novato, CA 94948-6121
(415) 382-7818

Central Point
(PC Tools Diagnostic Software)
15220 N.W. Greenbrier Parkway, Suite 150
Beaverton, OR 97006-5798
(503) 690-8090

Claris Corporation
(From Alice to Oceans)
Box 58168
Santa Clara, CA 95052-8168
(408) 727-8227

Cliff Notes, Inc.
(U.F.O.)
P.O. Box 80728
Lincoln, NE 68501

Compton's NewMedia, Inc.
(Compton's Encyclopedia)
2320 Camino Vida Roble
Carlsbad, CA 92009
(619) 929-2500

Corel Corporation
(CorelDRAW)
1600 Carling Avenue, Ottawa
Ontario, Canada  K1Z 8R7
(613) 728-8200

Creative Labs, Inc.
(Sound Blaster)
2050 Duane Avenue
Santa Clara, CA  95054
(405) 742-6622
or
1901 McCarthy Blvd.
Milpitas, CA  95035
(800) 998-LABS

Davidson & Associates, Inc.
(Math Blaster; Zookeeper)
P.O. Box  2961
Torrance, CA  90509
(800) 545-7677

D.C. True
(Shadow President)
1840 Oak Avenue
Evanston, IL  60201

Dorling Kindersley Multimedia & Houghton
& Mifflin
(The Way Things Work; Encyclopedia of
Science; Incredible Cross-Section
Stowaway)
95 Madison Avenue
New York, NY  10016

Edmark
(KidDesk)
P.O. Box 3218
Redmond, WA  98073-3218

Electronic Arts
(Eagle Eye Mysteries)
P.O. Box 7530
San Mateo, CA  94403
(415) 571-7171

Europress Software
(Fun School-Sammy Spy)
P.O. Box 2961
Torrance, CA  90509
(310) 793-0620

Fauve Software
(Fauve Matisse)
975 Walnut Street, Suite 242
Cary, NC  27511
(919) 380-9933

Fractal Design
(Painter; Dabbler; Sketcher)
335 Spreckels Drive
Aptos, CA  95003
(408) 688-8800

Grolier Electronic Publishing
(Multimedia Encyclopedia; Guinness Book
of World Records)
Sherman Turnpike
Danbury, CT  06816
(203) 797-3530

Impressions Software
(Detroit)
222 Third Street, Suite 0234
Cambridge, MA  02142
(617) 225-2042

Infocom
(Return to Zork)
P.O. Box 67713
Los Angeles, CA  90067
(310) 207-4500

Interplay Productions
(Mario Teaches Typing)
3710 S. Susan, Suite 100
Santa Ana, CA 92704
(714) 549-2411

Knowledge Adventure, Inc.
4502 Dyer Street
La Crescenta, CA 91214
(800) 542-4240

Landmark
(WinProbe Diagnostic Software)
703 Grand Central Street
Clearwater, FL 34616
(800) 683-6696

Laser Tools
(Print Cache)
1250 45th Street
Emeryville, CA 94608
(510) 843-2234

The Learning Company
(Treasure Mountain; Spellbound)
6493 Kaiser Drive
Fremont, CA 94555
(800) 852-2255

Logitech, Inc.
(Logitech Mouse)
6505 Kaiser Drive
Fremont, CA 94555
(510) 795-8500

Lotus
(Ami Pro)
5600 Glenridge Drive
Atlanta, GA 30342

LucasArts Entertainment
(Loom; Monkey Island)
P.O. Box 10307
San Rafael, CA 94912
(415) 721-3300

Magic Quest
(Word City; MathAce)
125 University Avenue
Palo Alto, CA 94301
(415) 321-5838

MAXIS
(SimCity; SimFarm; etc.)
2 Theatre Square
Orinda, CA 94563-3346
(510) 254-9700

MECC
(StoryBook Weaver; Amazon Trail)
6160 Summit Drive North
Minneapolis, MN 55430-4003
(612) 569-1500

Media Vision
(Quantum Gate)
47300 Bayside Parkway
Fremont, CA 94538-9713
(510) 770-8600

Medio Multimedia Inc.
(World Beat)
2703 152nd Avenue, NE
Redmond, WA 98052
or
P.O. Box 2949
Redmond, WA 98073-9964
(800) 788-3866

Merit Studios
(Merchant Colony)
13707 Gamma Road
Dallas, TX 75244
(800) 238-4277

MicroHelp
(Uninstaller for Windows)
4359 Shallowford Industrial Parkway
Marietta, GA  30066
(800) 922-3383

Microprose Entertainment Software
(Civilization)
180 Lakefront Drive
Hunt Valley, MD  21030-2245

Microsoft Corporation
One Microsoft Way
Redmond, WA  98052-6399
(206) 637-7098

Midisoft Corporation
(Music Software)
P.O. Box 1000
Bellvue, WA  98009
(206) 881-7176

Mindscape
(World Atlas; U.S. Atlas)
P.O. Box 54984
Santa Clara, CA  95056-0984

The National Geographic Society
(The Presidents; Mammals)
Washington, DC  20036

NIAD Corporation
(Puddles to Pondwater)
85 River Rock Drive, Suite 200
Buffalo, NY  14207

Novell Applications Group
(WordPerfect)
1555 N. Technology Way
Orem, UT  84057-2399
(800) 451-5151

Optimum Resource, Inc.
(StickyBear)
10 Station Place
Norwalk, CT  06058
(800) 327-1473

Passport Designs, Inc.
(Music Time)
100 Stone Pine Road
Half Moon Bay, CA  94019
(415) 726-0280

PCGlobe, Inc.
(Bushbuck)
4700 South McClintock
Tempe, AZ  85282
(602) 730-9000

Pigworks
(Capitalist Pig)
1116 E. Greenway, No. 101
Mesa, AZ  85203
(602) 969-9441

Pixar
(Typestry)
1001 West Cutting Boulevard
Richmond, CA  94804
(510) 236-4000

Quadra Interactive
(The Journeyman Project)
P.O. Box 188033
Carlsbad, CA  92009-9793
(619) 931-4755

Qualitas Corporation
(386Max)
7101 Wisconsin Avenue, Suite 1386
Bethesda, MD  20814
(301) 907-6700

Quarterdeck Office Systems
(QEMM)
150 Pico Boulevard
Santa Monica, CA  90405
(310) 392-9851

Serif, Inc.
(Page Plus)
P.O. Box 803
Nashua, NH  03061
(603) 889-8650

Sierra On-Line
(King's Quest; Space Quest)
P.O. Box 978
Oakhurst, CA  93644-0978
or
Sierra On-Line
P.O. Box 85007
Bellevue, WA  98015-8507
1-800-SIERRA-5

Softkey
(KeyDraw)
4800 North Federal Highway
3rd Floor, Building D
Boca Raton, FL  33431
(407) 367-1415

Software Marketing Corporation
(Bodyworks Voyager)
9830 South 51st Street
Building A-131
Phoenix, AZ  85044
(602) 893-3377

STAC
(Stacker Disk Compression)
5993 Avenida Encinas
Carlsbad, CA  92008
(619) 431-7474

Strategic Simulations, Inc.
(Serf City)
675 Almanor Avenue, Suite 201
Sunnyvale, CA  94086-2901
(408) 737-6800

Tanager Software Productions
(Cipher)
1933 Davis Street, Suite 208
San Leandro, CA  94577
(510) 430-0900

T/Maker
(Clickart)
1390 Villa Street
Mountain View, CA  94041
(415) 962-0195

Tsunami Media
(Blue Force)
P.O. Box 790
Coarsegold, CA  93614
(209) 683-8266

View Software
(Long File Names)
916 Commercial Street
Palo Alto, CA  94303
(415) 856-VIEW

Virgin Games, Inc.
(Risk)
18061 Fitch Avenue
Irvine, CA  92714
(800) Vrgin07

Virtual Reality Studios
2341 Ganador Court
San Luis Obispo, CA  93401
(805) 545-8515

Westwood Studios
(Legend of Kyrandia)
3450 W. Sahara Avenue, No. 323
Las Vegas, NV  89102
(800) 874-4607
or
18061 Fitch Avenue
Irvine, CA  92714
(800) Vrgin07

## DISCOUNT AND OUT OF DATE SOFTWARE

(In the software biz, "out of date" can mean six months old.)

AMPLICOM
7710 Arjons Drive, Suite B
San Diego, CA  92126
(619) 693-3366

Computer Discount Warehouse
(800) 886-4CDW

Computers At Large
18728 Cabernet Drive
Saratoga, CA  95070-3561
(408) 255-1081

Einstein Technology
2812 1/2 S. Roberton
Los Angeles, CA  90034
(310) 836-4441

MicroWarehouse
(800) 367-7080

Most Significant Bits, Inc.
15508 Madison Avenue
Lakewood, OH  44107
(800) 755 4619

NEWWARE
3511 Glover Road
Easton, PA  18042
(800) 2NEWARE

PC Connection
6 Mill Street
Marlow, NH  03456
(800) 800-5555

The PC Zone
15815 37th Street
Bellevue, WA  98006-1800
(800) 258-2088

PKWARE
9025 N. Deerwood Drive
Brown Deer, WI  53223-2437
(414) 354-8699

Raceway CD
44443-B Phoenix
Sterling Heights, MI  48314
(800) 240-0055

Software Support
2700 NE Andresen Road, Suite A-10
Vancouver, WA  98661
(800) 356-1179

Surplus Software
489 North 8th Street
Hood River, OR  97031
(800) 753-7877

Walnut Creek CD-ROM
4041 Pike Lane, Suite D-452
Concord, CA  94520
(800) 786-9907

# Index

# Ziff-Davis Press Survey of Readers

Please help us in our effort to produce the best books on personal computing.
For your assistance, we would be pleased to send you a FREE catalog
featuring the complete line of Ziff-Davis Press books.

## 1. How did you first learn about this book?

Recommended by a friend . . . . . . . . . . . . . . . ☐ -1 (5)

Recommended by store personnel . . . . . . . . ☐ -2

Saw in Ziff-Davis Press catalog . . . . . . . . . . . ☐ -3

Received advertisement in the mail . . . . . . . ☐ -4

Saw the book on bookshelf at store . . . . . . . ☐ -5

Read book review in: _____ ☐ -6

Saw an advertisement in: _____ ☐ -7

Other (Please specify): _____ ☐ -8

## 2. Which THREE of the following factors most influenced your decision to purchase this book? (Please check up to THREE.)

Front or back cover information on book . . . ☐ -1 (6)

Logo of magazine affiliated with book . . . . . . ☐ -2

Special approach to the content . . . . . . . . . . ☐ -3

Completeness of content . . . . . . . . . . . . . . . . ☐ -4

Author's reputation. . . . . . . . . . . . . . . . . . . . ☐ -5

Publisher's reputation . . . . . . . . . . . . . . . . . . ☐ -6

Book cover design or layout . . . . . . . . . . . . . ☐ -7

Index or table of contents of book . . . . . . . . ☐ -8

Price of book . . . . . . . . . . . . . . . . . . . . . . . . . ☐ -9

Special effects, graphics, illustrations . . . . . . . ☐ -0

Other (Please specify): _____ ☐ -x

## 3. How many computer books have you purchased in the last six months? _____ (7-10)

## 4. On a scale of 1 to 5, where 5 is excellent, 4 is above average, 3 is average, 2 is below average, and 1 is poor, please rate each of the following aspects of this book below. (Please circle your answer.)

Depth/completeness of coverage    5   4   3   2   1   (11)

Organization of material    5   4   3   2   1   (12)

Ease of finding topic    5   4   3   2   1   (13)

Special features/time saving tips    5   4   3   2   1   (14)

Appropriate level of writing    5   4   3   2   1   (15)

Usefulness of table of contents    5   4   3   2   1   (16)

Usefulness of index    5   4   3   2   1   (17)

Usefulness of accompanying disk    5   4   3   2   1   (18)

Usefulness of illustrations/graphics    5   4   3   2   1   (19)

Cover design and attractiveness    5   4   3   2   1   (20)

Overall design and layout of book    5   4   3   2   1   (21)

Overall satisfaction with book    5   4   3   2   1   (22)

## 5. Which of the following computer publications do you read regularly; that is, 3 out of 4 issues?

Byte . . . . . . . . . . . . . . . . . . . . . . . . . . . . . . . . . ☐ -1 (23)

Computer Shopper . . . . . . . . . . . . . . . . . . . . . ☐ -2

Home Office Computing . . . . . . . . . . . . . . . . ☐ -3

Dr. Dobb's Journal . . . . . . . . . . . . . . . . . . . . . ☐ -4

LAN Magazine . . . . . . . . . . . . . . . . . . . . . . . . . ☐ -5

MacWEEK . . . . . . . . . . . . . . . . . . . . . . . . . . . . ☐ -6

MacUser . . . . . . . . . . . . . . . . . . . . . . . . . . . . . . ☐ -7

PC Computing . . . . . . . . . . . . . . . . . . . . . . . . . ☐ -8

PC Magazine . . . . . . . . . . . . . . . . . . . . . . . . . . ☐ -9

PC WEEK . . . . . . . . . . . . . . . . . . . . . . . . . . . . . ☐ -0

Windows Sources . . . . . . . . . . . . . . . . . . . . . . ☐ -x

Other (Please specify): _____ ☐ -y

**Please turn pag**

6. What is your level of experience with personal computers? With the subject of this book?

|  | With PCs | With subject of book |
|---|---|---|
| Beginner | ☐ -1 (24) | ☐ -1 (25) |
| Intermediate | ☐ -2 | ☐ -2 |
| Advanced | ☐ -3 | ☐ -3 |

7. Which of the following best describes your job title?

Officer (CEO/President/VP/owner)........ ☐ -1 (26)
Director/head............................ ☐ -2
Manager/supervisor...................... ☐ -3
Administration/staff..................... ☐ -4
Teacher/educator/trainer................ ☐ -5
Lawyer/doctor/medical professional....... ☐ -6
Engineer/technician..................... ☐ -7
Consultant............................. ☐ -8
Not employed/student/retired............ ☐ -9
Other (Please specify): _____ ☐ -0

8. What is your age?

Under 20............................. ☐ -1 (27)
21-29............................... ☐ -2
30-39............................... ☐ -3
40-49............................... ☐ -4
50-59............................... ☐ -5
60 or over.......................... ☐ -6

9. Are you:

Male................................ ☐ -1 (28)
Female.............................. ☐ -2

Thank you for your assistance with this important information! Please write your address below to receive our free catalog.

Name: _____

Address: _____

City/State/Zip: _____

**Fold here to mail.**

3334-16-19